The Geometry of Normal Faults

Geological Society Special Publications

Series Editor J. BROOKS

GEOLOGICAL SOCIETY SPECIAL PUBLICATION NO 56

The Geometry of Normal Faults

EDITED BY

A.M. ROBERTS, G. YIELDING & B. FREEMAN

Badley Ashton & Associates
Winceby, Lincolnshire
UK

1991

Published by

The Geological Society

London

THE GEOLOGICAL SOCIETY

The Geological Society of London was founded in 1807 for the purposes of 'investigating the mineral structures of the earth'. It received its Royal Charter in 1825. The Society promotes all aspects of geological science by means of meetings, special lectures and courses, discussions, specialist groups, publications and library services.

It is expected that candidates for Fellowship will be graduates in geology or another earth science, or have equivalent qualifications or experience. All Fellows are entitled to receive for their subscription one of the Society's three journals: *The Quarterly Journal of Engineering Geology*, the *Journal of the Geological Society* or *Marine and Petroleum Geology*. On payment of an additional sum on the annual subscription, members may obtain copies of another journal.

Membership of the specialist groups is open to all Fellows without additional charge. Enquiries concerning Fellowship of the Society and membership of the specialist groups should be directed to the Executive Secretary, The Geological Society, Burlington House, Piccadilly, London W1V 0JU.

Published by the Geological Society from:
The Geological Society Publishing House
Unit 7
Brassmill Enterprise Centre
Brassmill Lane
Bath
Avon BA1 3JN
UK
(*Orders:* Tel. 0225 445046)

First published 1991

Distributors
USA
  AAPG Bookstore
  PO Box 979
  Tulsa
  Oklahoma 74101–0979
  USA
(*Orders*: Tel: (918)584–2555)

Australia
  Australian Mineral Foundation
  63 Conyngham St
  Glenside
  South Australia 5065
  Australia
(*Orders*: Tel: (08)379–0444)

British Library Cataloguing in Publication Data
The geometry of normal faults.
  1. Strata. Faults
  I. Roberts, A.M. (Alan Michael) *1959–* II.
  Yielding, G. (Graham) *1957–* III. Freeman, B.
  (Brett) *1958–* IV. Series 551.87

ISBN 0–903317–59–1

Printed in Great Britain at the Alden Press, Oxford

Contents

ROBERTS, A. M., YIELDING, G. & FREEMAN, B. Preface   vii

HARDMAN, R. F. P. & BOOTH, J. E. The significance of normal faults in the exploration and production of North Sea hydrocarbons   1

Seismic and subsurface studies

BARR, D. Subsidence and sedimentation in semi-starved half-graben: a model based on North Sea data   17

CARTWRIGHT, J. The kinematic evolution of the Coffee Soil Fault   29

KUSZNIR, N. J., MARSDEN, G. & EGAN, S. S. A flexural-cantilever simple-shear/pure-shear model of continental lithosphere extension: applications to the Jeanne d' Arc Basin, Grand Banks and Viking Graben, North Sea   41

ROBERTS, A. M. & YIELDING, G. Deformation around basin-margin faults in the North Sea/mid-Norway rift   61

YIELDING, G., BADLEY, M. E. & FREEMAN, B. Seismic reflections from normal faults in the northern North Sea   79

Field-based studies

COWARD, M. P., GILLCRIST, R. & TRUDGILL, B. Extensional structures and their tectonic inversion in the Western Alps   93

KOESTLER, A. G. & EHRMANN, W. U. Description of brittle extensional features in chalk on the crest of a salt ridge (NW Germany)   113

ROBERTS, S. & JACKSON, J. A. Active normal faulting in central Greece: an overview   125

WESTAWAY, R. Continental extension on sets of parallel faults: observational evidence and theoretical models   143

Fault-displacement studies

BEACH, A. & P. TRAYNER, The geometry of normal faults in a sector of the offshore Nile Delta, Egypt   173

CHAPMAN, T. J. & MENEILLY, A. W. The displacement patterns associated with a reverse-reactivated, normal growth fault   183

WALSH, J. J. & WATTERSON, J. Geometric and kinematic coherence and scale effects in normal fault systems   193

Analogue-modelling and section-balancing

DRESEN, G., GWILDIS, U. & KLUEGEL, Th. Numerical and analogue modelling of normal fault geometry   207

KRANTZ, R. W. Normal fault geometry and fault reactivation in tectonic inversion experiments   219

McCLAY, K. R., WALTHAM, D. A., SCOTT, A. D. & ABOUSETTA, A. Physical and seismic modelling of listric normal fault geometries   231

VENDEVILLE, B. Mechanisms generating normal fault curvature: a review illustrated by physical models   241

WHITE, N. J. & YIELDING, G. Calculating normal fault geometries at depth: theory and examples   251

Index   261

Preface

During the 1980s a resurgent interest in extensional tectonics resulted, to a large extent, from the ever-increasing, non-proprietary availability of seismic-reflection data. This interest has generated two previous Geological Society publications: *The Journal of the Geological Society*, **141**, part 4 (1984), and *Continental Extensional Tectonics* (1987). This third publication includes papers presented at the Geometry of Normal Faults Meeting, June 1989 (for a full report, see *Journal of the Geological Society*, **147**, 185−187).

In the early-to-mid 1980s much (although not all) work on extensional fault-systems focussed on the innovative application of thrust-belt-type models to extensional basins. In particular the concepts of section-balancing were introduced to those investigating normal faults.

By the late 1980s it was becoming apparent, however, that the universal application of such models was fraught with difficulty. In particular the evidence of both earthquake seismology and detailed field studies began to indicate that faults involved in crustal extension may be, on all scales, essentially planar structures, not linked in a 'listric', thrust-type array.

It is now clear from the geological record that both planar and listric normal faults exist. The Geometry of Normal Faults Meeting was therefore convened as a forum at which the geological setting and interpretation of these structures could be discussed. An emphasis was placed on the presentation of observational data, from which some ground-rules could be established, rather than simply the discussion of synthetic models. The meeting was jointly sponsored by both the Petroleum Group and Tectonic Studies Group of the Geological Society, in recognition of the fact that both industry and academia have contributed to the advance in knowledge throughout the 1980s.

Recognizing the importance of normal fault geometry to those involved in hydrocarbon exploration, R. Hardman (Chairman of the Petroleum Group) was invited to introduce the meeting and this volume (in collaboration with J. Booth) by reviewing the significance of normal faults in the success of the North Sea hydrocarbon province. Following this introduction the volume is divided into four sections.

Section One, *Seismic and subsurface studies*, deals with the geometry and kinematics of large-scale, crustal-stretching faults. It is faults such as these which typically delimit major hydrocarbon accumulations.

Section Two, *Field-based studies*, presents four separate case studies from disparate geographical areas. These range from the study of small-scale fractures associated with the movement of salt, to the large-scale, intra-plate kinematics of whole fault-arrays.

Section Three, *Fault-displacement studies*, covers a relatively new, but increasingly important discipline, namely the study of detailed displacement-patterns shown by individual faults and small fault-arrays, and the information this can give us about the way in which fault systems evolve.

Section Four, *Analogue-modelling and Section balancing*, presents five different modelling studies of normal fault geometry, and compares the results of these studies with observational data. In this way the geological circumstances in which each model might be applicable can be gauged.

As a volume drawing from largely European participants this Special Publication does not aim to cover all of the aspects and all of the problems of normal fault geometry. In particular we have avoided the still-contentious issue of normal fault geometry in the Basin and Range Province. We believe, however, that the papers within the volume will help to clarify the circumstances in which the diverse models of normal fault geometry might be applicable, and thus provide a useful source of reference for both the industry interpreter and academic research worker interested in problems of extensional tectonics.

A. M. Roberts, G. Yielding & B. Freeman
Badley Ashton & Associates Limited, Winceby House, Winceby, Horncastle, Lincoln-shire, LN9 6PB, UK   May 1990

The significance of normal faults in the exploration and production of North Sea hydrocarbons

R. F. P. HARDMAN & J. E. BOOTH

Amerada Hess Limited, 2 Stephen Street, London W1P 1PL, UK

Abstract: The Mesozoic geological history of the northern North Sea was dominated by extensional faulting. In addition to forming the most important hydrocarbon traps, such faults can be shown to exert a significant degree of control over the distribution of mature source rocks, and the deposition and erosion of reservoir rocks. As exploration and production have progressed the importance of small normal faults has been increasingly recognized. Although they do not totally offset reservoir formations, such small faults may provide lateral seals, thus disrupting hydrocarbon migration routes, forming subtle traps and causing technical problems during production by unanticipated compartmentalization of fields. Consequently, as the commercial size of fields is reduced by improving production technology and the North Sea matures as a hydrocarbon province, a thorough understanding of the origins and characteristics of normal faults as well as a command of the increasingly sophisticated techniques for analysing the behaviour of these faults will be vital to successful exploration programmes.

The Collins English Dictionary (Hanks 1986) variously defines a fault as: "1. an imperfection, failing of flaw; 2. a mistake or error; 3. an offence or misdeed".

These definitions, particularly the last, seem very appropriate when considering the interpretation of seismic sections. It is often very difficult to correlate seismic reflections across a fault and when the result of an expensive exploration well is an unpleasant surprise there is a tendency to believe that the interpreter has made a mistake. In many cases this finger-pointing is unfair as the original interpretation was an honest one, widely accepted at the time and only improved by hindsight. The simple fact is that our knowledge about the geometry of faults is still modest and interpreters do not have a set of foolproof 'analytical' tools at their disposal. For this reason the hydrocarbon exploration industry continues to dedicate considerable resources to efforts aimed at improving the quality of both interpreters and interpretation techniques in the knowledge that this will lead to greater success in the hunt for our diminishing oil and gas resources.

This paper is intended to show how important an understanding of normal faults has been and continues to be in the exploration of the North Sea, stemming from the fact that the Mesozoic geological history of this area, especially in northern waters, was dominated by extensional tectonics. The spatial configuration, timing of motion and geometry of the major normal faults largely control the distribution of mature source rocks, often result in the erosion or preservation of reservoir rocks and are usually the main element defining the largest and economically most important hydrocarbon traps. Increasingly the significance of smaller faults, sometimes below the limits of seismic resolution, is being recognized; particularly their ability to form effective lateral seals, beneficial when they create traps but a liability when they fragment an accumulation into several independent compartments.

What is a normal fault?

The graben system that dominates the structural framework of the northern North Sea was recognized and mapped early in the exploration effort. The confluence of the South Viking, Central and Witch Ground graben was explained as a triple junction, an hypothesis apparently supported by the recognition from the geological record of a domal uplift centred on the confluence (Enyon 1981).

With this model in place the major faults in the Moray Firth basins were regarded as being normal (Chesher & Bacon 1975). Recently the matter has been reconsidered and, among others, Roberts *et al.* (1990) have suggested that the extension within the Moray Firth was accommodated by major lateral motion along the Great Glen fault system and that many of the faults previously regarded as being purely normal probably have a considerable strike-slip component (Fig. 1).

Today we are convinced that the motion histories of the major 'normal' faults in the

From ROBERTS A. M., YIELDING, G. & FREEMAN, B. (eds), 1991, *The Geometry of Normal Faults*, Geological Society Special Publication No 56, pp 1–13

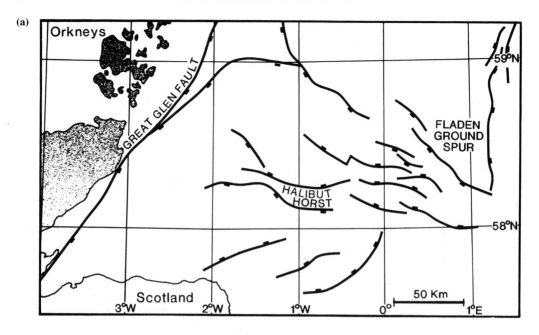

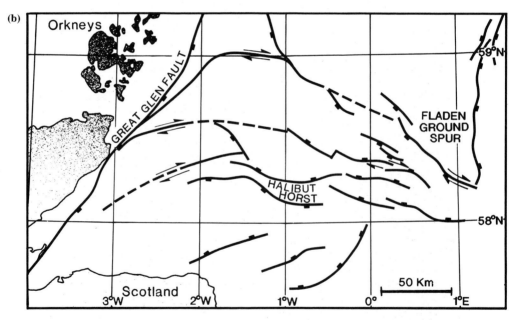

Fig. 1. A comparison of two views of the development of the Moray Firth basin complex: **(a)** extension accommodated by normal faulting; **(b)** extension accommodated by major lateral motion along the Great Glen fault system.

North Sea have been complex, with several periods of reactivation and changes in the direction of throw. Take for example the fault (system) bounding the western side of the Lindesnes ridge (Fig. 2), in the Norwegian sector of the Central graben. As early as 1978 a major normal fault was recognized as offsetting the Top Permian from 4.0 to 4.5 seconds. However, as shown by Norbury (1987), at shallower levels this fault displays a reverse sense of offset.

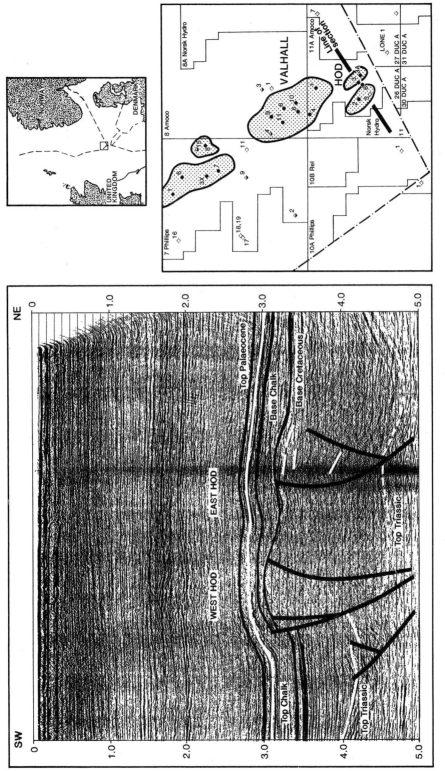

Fig. 2. A seismic line across the Lindesnes ridge (after Norbury 1987) showing the compound nature of the major faults. Note that fault marked A is normal at Top Triassic level but reverse in the Cretaceous section.

Whilst the details of this interpretation could be disputed it cannot be denied that the motion history of this fault is far from simple.

It is important at this stage to establish a definition of a normal fault, at least in the context of this paper. The definition in Whitten & Brooks (1972) is 'a fault with a major dip-slip component in which the hangingwall is on the downthrown side'. We find this definition is usually adequate and clearly according to it the fault systems in the Moray Firth and along the Lindesnes Ridge are normal. It is, nevertheless, important to recognize those faults which have only a dip-slip history and those with a complex, but dominantly dip-slip history, as there may be important differences in the physical properties of the two groups. We refer to the former as pure normal faults and the latter as compound normal faults.

Normal faults and source rock distribution

It has been established clearly by Cornford (1984) among others, that the main source of oil and probably most of the gas in the northern North Sea is the Humber Group, especially the Kimmeridge Clay Formation. These organic rich rocks were lain down, under conditions of restricted circulation, in normal fault bounded basins that developed in response to renewed crustal extension in the Late Jurassic. Figure 3, which is a combination of the ideas expressed by Cornford (1984) and Parsley (1984), sets out the role normal faulting played in the origin of these very prolific source rocks.

In the southern North Sea, Leeder & Hardman (1990) have shown that the gas-prone Namurian source rocks were deposited in topographic depressions, which were the expression of semi-starved basins created by normal faulting in the Visean. Anoxic, deep water conditions existed in parts of these basins, some of which were fully marine, allowing the accumulation of organic-rich sediments.

Normal faults and hydrocarbon migration

Some of the important ways in which normal faults influence the migration of hydrocarbons, and hence the distribution of fields, can be illustrated by examples from the East Shetland basin.

Successful exploration of the Lower Jurassic Statfjord−Upper Triassic Cormorant sandstone play has been restricted to the northern and eastern margins of this basin, in the vicinity of the End-of-the-World fault and the Alwyn−Statfjord fault (Fig. 4). These reservoirs are

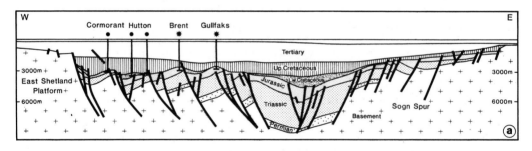

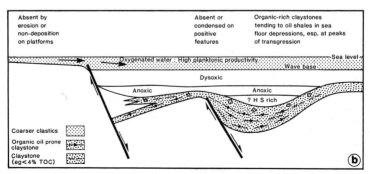

Fig. 3. (a) East−west geological cross section through the North Viking Graben (after Parsley 1984). (b) A simplified model of the deposition of the Kimmeridge Clay Formation (after Cornford 1984).

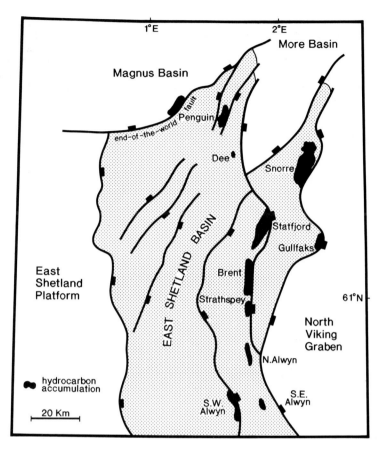

Fig. 4. Distribution of known hydrocarbon accumulations within the East Shetland basin contained in Statfjord (Lower Jurassic) and/or Cormorant (Upper Triassic) reservoirs. Note that the accumulations are restricted to the northern and eastern flanks of the basin where large normal faults have locally juxtaposed these reservoirs with mature Upper Jurassic source rocks.

stratigraphically much deeper than the Humber Group source rocks and so it is only along these two major normal fault systems that they are juxtaposed with a mature source. This, combined with the alluvial origins of these sands, with laterally impersistent sand bodies of low permeability preventing long distance migration, is the reason for the areal restriction of this play. The only exception we are aware of is a small accumulation within the Cormorant field, where complex faulting has fortuitously juxtaposed the Triassic reservoir with a Brent section through which oil migrated.

Most of the hydrocarbons discovered in this basin are trapped in sandstones of the Middle Jurassic Brent Group. This prolific play has proved successful across the entire basin; which is attributable to the near omnipresence of reservoir quality Brent sands, a superb top seal that is rarely breached by faults and a massive

hydrocarbon charge which has migrated long distances through the Brent sands themselves. The main risk of a dry prospect appears to be whether or not there is a viable migration route into the structure. Although it is possible to determine the catchment area of any particular prospect by using a structure map of the Top Brent surface and assuming that oil migrates directly updip (reasonably valid in the East Shetlands Basin where no areas of appreciable over/under pressure have been encountered), it is increasingly obvious from post-mortems on dry holes that apparently valid migration routes are often 'disrupted'.

The most likely cause of this 'disruption' is that faults which are not large enough to totally offset the Brent sands nevertheless provide lateral seals (the actual sealing mechanism is discussed later). The vicinity of the Don field is a good example of this phenomenon (Fig. 5). Oil

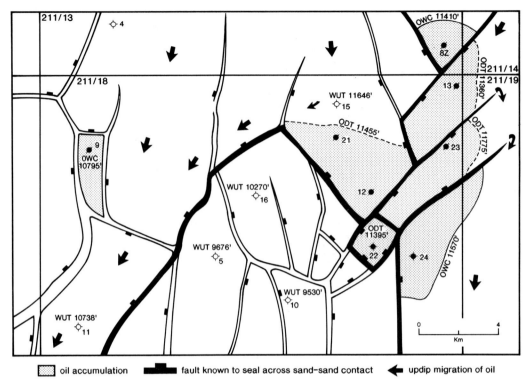

Fig. 5. The Don Field. Note that the main trapping mechanism is sand–sand contact fault seal. Internally the field is compartmentalized by sealing faults with several separate pressure regimes and oil–water contacts. Sealing faults deflect oil that has (is) migrated into the area, from the kitchen in 211/13, to the east and west of the structures tested by the dry holes 211/18–5, 10 and 16.

has (and still is) migrated into this area from the north and northeast. The sealing faults that form the trap for the main part of Don itself have deflected this migrating oil away from superficial more attractive structures immediately to the south, several of which were drilled before the discovery of Don by well 211/18–12. This explains a string of dry holes, 211/18–5, 10, 14 and 16, along the southern flank of Don. As yet nobody has been able to predict whether or not a particular fault will provide seal or even to show any statistical bias towards faults of a particular orientation having a greater propensity to seal.

Normal faults and reservoir distribution

Perhaps the most celebrated example of a reservoir whose presence is closely linked to normal faulting is the Upper Jurassic sandstones of the Brae fields (Fig. 6). The existence of syn-tectonic sands and boulder beds of Jurassic age around Helmsdale in the Inner Moray Firth was well known long before the northern North Sea

was opened for exploration (Bailey & Weir 1932). Consequently most companies were aware of the possibility of finding wedges of coarse clastic sediments on the downthrown sides of the faults that bound the East Shetland platform. The eventual validation of this play with the discovery of Brae is well documented by Harms et al. (1980) and Turner et al. (1987).

The erosion of reservoir from the crests of tilted fault blocks as a result of footwall uplift is fairly common in the northern North Sea. The Snorre field (Fig. 7) provides an extreme example of this phenomenon (Hollander 1987). The normal faults that bound the Snorre structure were certainly active in the Late Jurassic and may well have been so in the Late Triassic. Crestal erosion cut deep into the Triassic, removing several thick layers of Upper Triassic sandstones of poor reservoir quality and exposing better quality Triassic sandstones, which are capped by Lower Cretaceous marls (Cromer Knoll Gp). During the Late Jurassic the Snorre fault block was not only tilted but also rotated so that the erosional bevelling exposed several

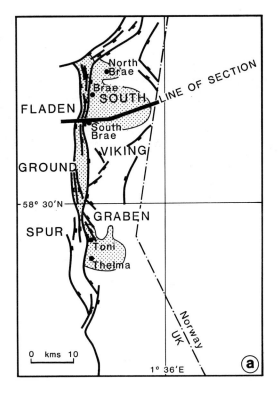

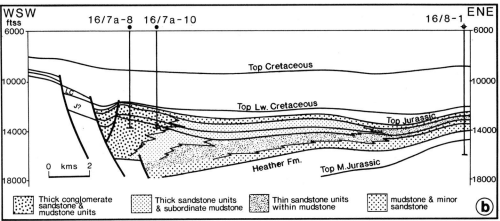

Fig. 6. (a) The South Viking graben in the UK sector showing the major faults and the distribution of Upper Jurassic clastic sediment fans (after Stoker & Brown 1986). (b) Geological cross section through the South Brae field showing approximate distribution of Upper Jurassic sedimentary facies (after Turner *et al.* 1987).

Triassic formations; as a consequence the oil column occupies the longest stratigraphic column of any North Sea field we are aware of.

Spencer & Larsen (1990) in a comprehensive review of North Sea fields have drawn attention to the fact that Snorre has experienced more crestal erosion that any other field, attributed by Yielding (1990) to the exceptional width of this particular tilted fault block.

Exploration in the vicinity of the Marnock fields shows how useful predictive modelling of the effects of faulting reservoir deposition are becoming, albeit in a negative sense in this case. Fig. 8 shows a comparison between an east–

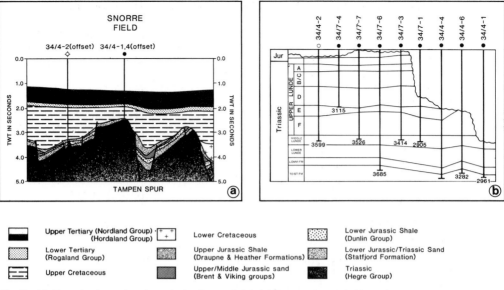

Fig. 7. (a) Geoseismic section through the Snorre field. (b) Reservoir subdivision of the Snorre field showing the deep erosion across the field at the Base Cretaceous Unconformity.

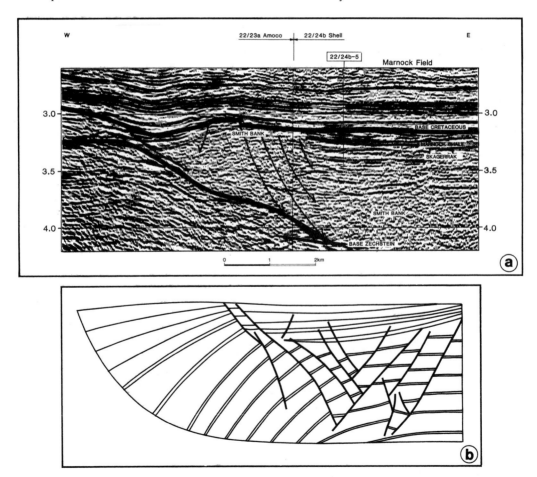

Fig. 8. (a) Seismic section through the Marnock field, Central graben. (b) Sand-box model of Ellis & McClay (1988) showing that with certain syn-sedimentary fault geometries strata can thin on the downthrown side. Compare this with the pre-Cretaceous section on the seismic section.

west seismic section across the Marnock field and one of the sandbox models of Ellis & McClay (1988). The model indicated that with certain fault geometries syn-sedimentary listric faulting can cause thinning rather than thickening of strata on the downthrown side. An interpretation of the seismic line, reproduced in Fig. 8, using this particular model as an analogue suggested that in the vicinity of the lease line between blocks 22/23a and 22/24a, the reservoir could be expected to thin westwards. This was proved to be the case by subsequent drilling.

Aspects of hydrocarbon traps associated with normal faults

Within the pre-Tertiary of the North Sea normal faulting is almost invariably an essential ingredient of trap formation, albeit indirectly as in the case of reservoir pinch-out towards the crest of tilted fault blocks.

Footwall traps

Such classic traps on the upthrown side of normal faults as the tilted fault-blocks of the Brent, Statfjord, Cormorant and Thistle fields are very familiar to all explorationists (Illing & Hobson 1981; Brooks & Glennie 1987). A slightly different example is provided by the Hudson field (Fig. 9). This is one of the new generation of

medium to small sized fields that will form the bulk of the new developments in the next decade. Its exploration history is a reminder that, as production technology improves and cuts the commercial threshold, perseverance and an open, optimistic mind are essential attributes in a successful exploration programme.

Block 210/24 was awarded in the 4th UKCS Licensing Round (1973) to a partnership comprising Amoco, Gas Council (Enterprise), Mobil, Amerada Hess and Texas Eastern. The block was applied for because a small four-way dip closure had been mapped close to the East Shetland platform.

The first well in the block was drilled on this prospect in 1974 but penetrated an entirely water-wet Middle Jurassic Brent Group sandstone sequence, albeit with excellent reservoir properties. At the time it was thought that this failure was due either to a poor top seal, which was unlikely because the reservoir is capped by a thick succession of Humber Group shales unbreached by faulting, or some problem with the migration route from the nearest source kitchen, some 15 km to the east. A second well, 210/24−2, was drilled in 1977 in preparation for the compulsory 50% relinquishment at the end of the initial term of the licence. It found a short oil leg in the Ness Formation of the Brent Group, but this was thought to be a local stratigraphic trap and of little importance.

It was only with the advent of much better

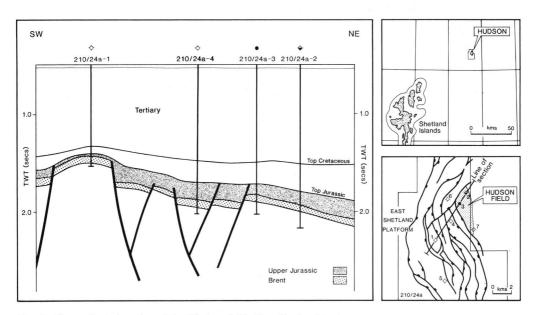

Fig. 9. The geological setting of the Hudson field, East Shetland basin.

quality seismic data in the 1980s that the significance of this oil leg was appreciated. A hitherto unsuspected normal fault, dipping to the west and thus antithetic to the basin bounding fault, was mapped to the west of this well, separating it from the 210/24−1 dry hole. As a result, in 1987 a well (210/24−3) was drilling towards the crest of this small tilted fault block and proved successful, flowing at a rate of some 4000 barrels of oil per day.

Hangingwall traps

In the early days of North Sea exploration one of the most contentious issues was whether or not traps on the downthrown side of faults could be viable if they depended on seal against the fault plane. Rollover anticlines in such positions were of course a well established play but often the additional reserves needed to exceed the economic threshold relied on extra volume provided by a downthrown fault closure. The only documented example of such a downthrown trap in the early 1970s was the Cantagallo Field in Colombia (Morales *et al.* 1956). Unfortunately the published reserves of this field, 3.5 million barrels, were so small that to sceptical exploration managers it was not an attractive analogue. Today the situation is quite different; indeed, although hangingwall fault plays are generally regarded as having less chance of success than their footwall counter-

parts, Hindle (1990) has shown that in the Witch Ground graben the hangingwall traps have a higher success rate than their footwall counterparts. The Scott field (Fig. 10) is an example where both hangingwall and footwall traps make up one of the biggest oil fields to be discovered in the North Sea in recent years.

Sealing fault traps

As exploration of the North Sea has progressed, evidence has mounted concerning the ability of even quite small faults to provide lateral seals and thus trap hydrocarbons. Here we are specifically referring to faults that juxtapose sand against sand, either because they are too small to totally offset the reservoir or by stratigraphic coincidence in the case of larger faults.

Little is known about the nature of the sealing mechanism as very few cores have been taken that include the plane of a known sealing fault; in any case such data is of obvious economic importance and is not published. Consequently we are left to speculate, based on field observations of exposed fault planes. The two most popular hypotheses are that an impermeable fault gouge is created by the smearing along the fault plane of shales interbedded with the sands or (possibly in combination) that there has been unusually heavy cementation around the fault plane by such minerals as calcite, silica and barites. An example of such excessive, fault

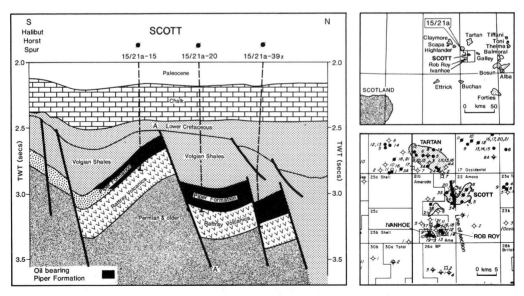

Fig. 10. The geological setting of the Scott field, Outer Moray Firth. Note that oil sealed in the downfaulted block by fault A−A is at a higher pressure than that in the upthrown block to the south.

related cementation within the Alwyn Field was described by Johnson & Eyssautier (1987). Although probably of little importance in the Brent province, it is possible that an effective seal can be formed by a fault that juxtaposes good quality reservoir sands with low permeability sands. The large differences in the capillary pressures between the two pore systems might retain an oil column of some tens of feet, but not the hundreds of feet as documented in the Don and Osprey fields (Figs 5 & 11).

In the Witch Ground graben, Hindle (1990) has found that as a rule of thumb only those faults with throws in excess of 2000 feet are likely to provide seals. In contrast, within the East Shetland basin every field with a Brent reservoir has experienced problems with sealing faults during its development or production. Often these problems were not anticipated as the faults can be small enough to be below seismic resolution (Hallett 1981). Such sealing faults need not be detrimental, indeed in the case of the Don field (Fig. 5) they are the primary element of the trap. It is clear from the results of its extensive appraisal that this field is divided into several mutually sealed compartments by faulting. This is evident from the considerable differences between wells in oil−water contacts, pressures and oil composition. It appears that although these faults juxtapose

reservoir quality Brent sands they are capable of retaining oil columns in excess of 400 feet.

The Osprey field (Fig. 11) is another example from the Brent province where internal faulting has separated the accumulation into at least two compartments, with a difference in oil−water contacts of 141 feet. As yet there is insufficient data to indicate if any particular fault trend in the East Shetlands basin has a greater propensity to seal, yet alone estimate the probability that any individual fault might seal or the length of the hydrocarbon column it is strong enough to retain.

The effect of fault geometry on reserve calculations

A detailed knowledge of the geometry of normal faults is essential if the reserves of most fields are to be calculated accurately. The volume of reservoir is affected by the 'cut-effect' of faults; in the case of normal faults the shallower the dip of the fault the greater the reduction in reservoir volume. This can be particularly important in equity determinations, as the early studies of the Leman gas field by Shell and Amoco showed (Fig. 12). It was calculated that the effect of changing the interpreted dip of the normal faults from 60° to 45° would, in addition to the obvious overall reduction in reserves, have resulted in increasing the proportion of the equity split in one licence block by 1.5% at the expense of the other.

The effects of faults on hydrocarbon recovery

It is obvious that where fields are segmented to an undue degree there are problems with recovering the hydrocarbons efficiently and economically. An example of this is provided by the Hild gas field (Ronning et al. 1986) which, despite reserves reputed to be of the order of 1 trillion cubic feet, is not economic at the present time because of excessive faulting (Fig. 13).

As improving production technology reduces the economic size of fields one of the prime concerns of development teams will be to maintain high production rates from a minimum number of wells yet recover as much hydrocarbon as possible. An awareness and knowledge of the behaviour of sealing faults within the accumulation will become increasingly important in the modelling of reservoir dynamics. It may, for example, be possible to breach the seal on a semi-permeable fault during pro-

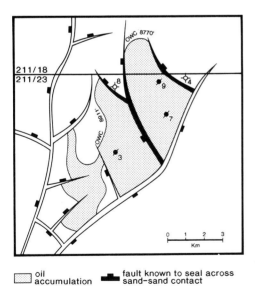

oil accumulation
fault known to seal across sand–sand contact

Fig. 11. The Osprey Field. Note that faults which seal across sand-sand contacts form part of the trap and divide the field into two compartments with different oil-water contacts.

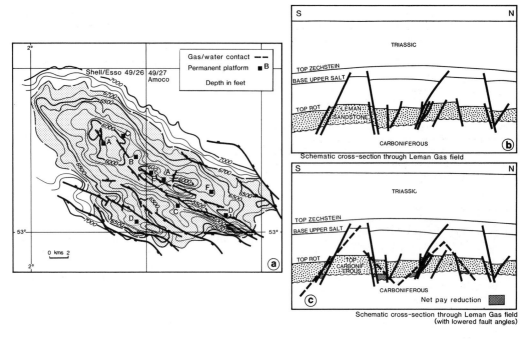

Fig. 12. Showing how a decrease in the interpreted dip of normal faults in the Leman gas field would lead to a significant reduction in the volume of net pay.

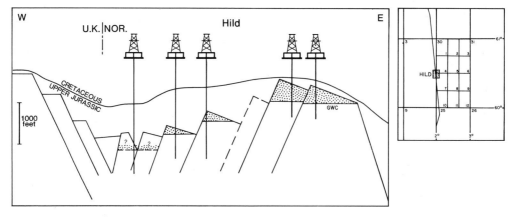

Fig. 13. Cross section through the Hild gas field, Viking graben, showing the excessive fault compartmentalization that makes this field currently uncommercial despite reserves of 1 TCF. After Ronning *et al.* (1986).

duction drawdown or excessive water injection, causing unswept oil to be left in the ground. Alternatively it may be that some faults which are permeable on a geological time scale allow oil to migrate across them so slowly that when production starts they act as effective seals.

Conclusions

From the foregoing discussion it can be said that normal faults are directly or indirectly responsible for the majority of the pre-Tertiary oil and gas accumulations in the North Sea. As the economic size of fields is reduced the modern geologist will need a better understanding of the origins, geometry and sealing capabilities of normal faults.

The authors thank: the Amoco Group (Amoco, Enterprise, Mobil, Amerada Hess and Texas Eastern) for granting permission to publish cross sections through the Hudson and Marnock Fields; and Amerada Hess, Deminex, Kerr-McGee and Pict for permission to publish the section through the Scott Field. Thanks are also given to Steve Hedley for drawing the figures and to Julie Stevens and Carol Tait for typing the text.

References

BAILEY, E. B. & WEIR, J. 1932. Submarine Faulting in Kimmeridgian Times: East Sutherland. *Transactions of the Royal Society of Edinburgh*, **47**, 431–467.

BROOKS, J. & GLENNIE, K. W. 1987. *Petroleum Geology of North West Europe*, Graham & Trotman, London.

CHESHER, J. A. & BACON, M. 1975. A deep seismic survey in the Moray Firth. Institute of Geological Sciences, Report No. 75/11.

CORNFORD, C. 1984. Source rocks and hydrocarbons of the North Sea. *In*: GLENNIE, K. W. (ed), *Introduction to the Petroleum Geology of the North Sea*. Blackwell, Oxford, 171–204.

ELLIS, P. G. & McCLAY, K. R. 1988. Listric extensional fault systems — results of analogue model experiments, *Basin Research*, **1**, 55–70.

EYNON, G. 1981. Basin development and sedimentation in the Middle Jurassic of the northern North Sea. *In*: ILLING, L. V. & HOBSON, G. C. (eds), *Petroleum Geology of the Continental Shelf of North-west Europe*, Institute of Petroleum, Heyden, London, 196–204.

HALLETT, D. 1981. Refinement of the geological model of the Thistle Field. *In*: ILLING, L. V. & HOBSON, G. C. (eds), *Petroleum Geology of the Continental Shelf of North-west Europe*, Institute of Petroleum, Heyden, London, 315–325.

HANKS, P. (ed.) 1986. *Collins Dictionary of the English Language*, 2nd Edn, Collins, Glasgow.

HARMS, J. C., TACKENBERG, P., PICKLES, P. & POLLOCK, R. E. 1981. The Brae oilfield area. *In*: ILLING, L. V. & HOBSON, G. D. (eds), *Petroleum Geology of the Continental Shelf of North-west Europe*. Heyden, London, 352–357.

HINDLE, A. 1989 Downthrown traps of the NW Witch Ground Graben, UK North Sea, *Journal of Petroleum Geology*, **12**, 405–418.

HOLLANDER, N. B. 1987. Snorre. *In*: SPENCER, A. M. (ed.) *Geology of the Norwegian Oil and Gas Fields* Graham & Trotman, London, 307–318.

ILLING, L. V. & HOBSON, G. C. 1981. *Petroleum*

Geology of the Continental Shelf of North-West Europe, Institute of Petroleum, Heyden, London.

JOHNSON, A. & EYSSAUTIER, M. 1987. Alwyn North Field and its regional geological context. *In*: BROOKS, J. & GLENNIE, K. W. (eds), *Petroleum Geology of North West Europe*, Graham & Trotman, London, 963–978.

LEEDER, M. & HARDMAN, M. 1990. Palaeozoic Controls on North Sea prospectivity. *In*: HARDMAN, R. F. P. & BROOKS, J. (eds), *Tectonic Events Responsible for Britain's Oil and Gas Reserves*, Geological Society, London, Special Publication, **55**, 87–105.

MORALES, L. G. & The Columbian Petroleum Industry, 1956. General Geology and Oil Occurrences of the Middle Magdalena Valley of Colombia. *In*: WEEKS L. G. (ed), *Habitat of Oil — a symposium*, AAPG Special Publication.

NORBURY, I. 1987. Hod. *In*: SPENCER, A. M. (ed), *Geology of the Norwegian Oil and Gas Fields*. Graham & Trotman, London, 107–116.

PARSLEY, A. J. 1984. North Sea hydrocarbon plays. *In*: GLENNIE, K. W. (ed), *Introduction to the Petroleum Geology of the North Sea*. Blackwell, Oxford, 205–230.

ROBERTS, A., BADLEY, M., PRICE, J. & HUCK, I. 1990. The Structural History of a Transtensional Basin — Inner Moray Firth, NE Scotland, *Journal of the Geological Society, London*, **147**, 87–103.

RØNNING, K., JOHNSTON, C. D., JOHNSTAD, S. E. & SONGSTAD, P. 1986. Geology of the Hild Field. *In*: SPENCER, A. M. *et al.*, *Habitat of Hydrocarbons on the Norwegian Continental Shelf*, Graham & Trotman, London, 199–206.

STOKER, S. J. & BROWN, S. 1986. *Coarse clastic sediments of the Brae field and adjacent areas, North Sea: a core workshop*. British Geological Survey, Edinburgh.

SPENCER, A. M. & LARSEN, V. B. 1990. Factors controlling the development of fault block traps in the Northern North Sea. *In*: HARDMAN, R. F. P. & BROOKS, J. (eds), *Tectonic Events Responsible for Britain's Oil and Gas Reserves*. Geological Society, London, Special Publication **55**, 281–298.

TURNER, C. C., COHEN, J. M., CONNELL, E. R. & COOPER, D. M. 1987. A depositional model for the South Brae Oilfield. *In*: BROOKS, J. & GLENNIE, K. W. (eds), *Petroleum Geology of North West Europe*, Graham & Trotman, London, 853–864.

WHITTEN, D. G. & BROOKS, J. R. V. 1972. *The Penguin Dictionary of Geology*, Penguin Books, London.

YIELDING, G. 1990. Footwall uplift associated with Late Jurassic normal faulting in the Northern North Sea, *Journal of the Geological Society of London*, **147**, 219–222.

Seismic and subsurface studies

Subsidence and sedimentation in semi-starved half-graben: a model based on North Sea data

DAVID BARR

BP Exploration, Britannic House, Moor Lane, London EC2Y 9BU, UK

Abstract: By combining simple extensional fault-block geometries with overall tectonic subsidence curves generated by geodynamic mechanisms such as uniform lithospheric stretching, it is possible to generate forward tectono-stratigraphic models of basin evolution. Previous studies have used simplistic assumptions about sedimentation, e.g. that half-graben were filled to sea level or to the crests of their constituent fault blocks. A better appreciation of the range of possible natural geometries can be obtained by inputting subsidence and sedimentation histories derived by observation of a real sedimentary basin.

The central North Sea is a well studied basin which in general terms can be explained by a simple model of uniform lithospheric stretching in the Late Jurassic, followed by thermal subsidence to the present day. Long-period departures from this model principally reflect the waning thermal effect of Permo-Triassic rifting, but short-period complications are shown to result primarily from variations in the externally controlled sediment input rate. Periods of sediment starvation permitted a substantial increase in water depth, and subsequent rapid sediment input resulted in episodes of load-driven subsidence.

Three typical central North Sea subsidence histories have been combined with a simple model of domino faulting with a 10 km initial fault spacing. Contrasting depositional geometries, with or without the emergence of footwall islands, result from relatively subtle variations in sediment input rate within a small area which can reasonably be inferred to have had a consistent tectonic history.

Forward models for the stratigraphic evolution of extensional basins whose sediment fill builds up to or beyond the crests of the tilted fault blocks are relatively well established (e.g. Surlyk 1978; Barr 1987a; Vendeville *et al.* 1987; Jackson *et al.* 1988; Vendeville this volume). Such models are appropriate to near-shore, shallow-marine basins where sediment supply exceeded subsidence rate, or to certain non-marine settings where maximum surface dips were effectively limited to the slope of an alluvial floodplain. Leeder & Gawthorpe (1987) have provided qualitative sedimentological models for extensional basins with more general characteristics. The present paper attempts to explain the gross stratigraphic evolution of a partially starved marine basin where the syn-rift 'sediment' load consisted largely of sea water, and explores the impact of such a depositional history on model half-graben geometries.

There are many published examples of basins in which substantial water depths and irregular sea-bed topography can be observed directly or inferred from seismic stratigraphy or the distribution of contemporary deep- and shallow-marine sediments (e.g. the Aegean Sea (McKenzie 1978), the Galicia continental margin (Montadert *et al.* 1979; Chenet *et al.* 1983) and the Gulf of Lyons (Bessis 1986). The typical pattern is of a rapid syn-rift increase in both water depth and sea-bed relief, followed by progressive sea-floor shallowing as post-rift subsidence rates decline exponentially and topography is infilled by fans or deltas with a gentle depositional profile.

Failure to appreciate the effects of sea-floor topography can lead to unrealistic geodynamic models and, perhaps more seriously, to a misinterpretation of the tectono-sedimentary history of an observed basin. Typically, isopach maps of time-bounded stratigraphic units are used to infer relative subsidence; where thickness changes take place across faults, tectonic activity, extensional or otherwise, is inferred during the specified interval. Often, lip service is paid to the influence of varying water depth but the problem is dismissed as intractable and ignored, with serious impact on the interpreted basin history. Bertram & Milton (1989) give a number of recent examples of this error in the North Sea and elsewhere.

The wealth of well and seismic data available in the North Sea basin provides an excellent opportunity to combine theoretical models

From ROBERTS A. M., YIELDING, G. & FREEMAN, B. (eds), 1991, *The Geometry of Normal Faults*, Geological Society Special Publication No 56, pp 17–28

of fault-block geometry (Wernicke & Burchfiel 1982) with an actualistic subsidence/ sedimentation history which takes realistic account of syn-depositional water depths.

The North Sea basin

A complete analysis of the formation of the North Sea basin is beyond the scope of this paper — see Ziegler (1981, 1982) and Glennie (1984) for general summaries and Sclater & Christie (1980), Barton & Wood (1984) and Hellinger et al. (1989) for geodynamic models.

The key tectonic elements of the central North Sea are shown in Fig. 1. A generalized lithostratigraphic column is presented in Fig. 2 (based primarily on Deegan & Scull 1977).

Few central North Sea wells penetrate beneath the Middle Jurassic, but those that do typically encounter Triassic and Lower Permian red sandstones and mudstones, often separated by Upper Permian (Zechstein) evaporites. The Lower Jurassic is usually thin or absent. The Middle Jurassic typically comprises non-marine coastal plain deposits. Thick coals provide a

prominent seismic marker and tuffs are common in the lower part of the section. A major pile of extrusive basalts was deposited in the Forties area, west of Location D.

The Humber Group is dominated by marine mudstones of the Heather Formation and anoxic Kimmeridge Clay Formation, deposited during and after a major basin-deepening event. Graben-margin locations record several episodes of delta and open-marine shelf progradation during the Callovian to Kimmeridgian. Coarse, deep-water clastic deposition was fault-controlled and gave rise to major submarine fans and aprons such as Brae (Turner et al. 1987).

The Cromer Knoll Group is dominated by grey, often calcareous mudstones and thin limestones. Turbidite sand bodies are locally developed. Chalk, in part re-sedimented, dominates the Upper Cretaceous and lowermost Palaeocene (Danian).

The later Palaeocene marked a return to clastic deposition with abundant sandy turbidites representing the deposits of a major basin-floor submarine fan system (Stewart

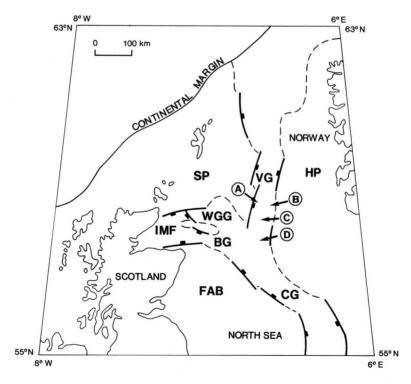

Fig. 1. Central North Sea location map. BG, Buchan Graben; CG, Central Graben; FAB, Forth Approaches Basin; HP, Horda Platform; IMF, Inner Moray Firth Basin; SP, Shetland Platform; VG, Viking Graben; WGG, Witch Ground Graben. Locations A to D are referred to in the text.

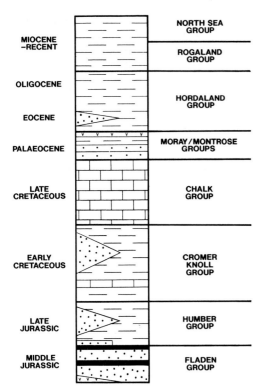

Fig. 2. Simplified mid-Jurassic to Recent stratigraphic column for the central North Sea (after Deegan & Scull 1977). The lithostratigraphic units closely, but not precisely, correspond to the chronostratigraphic intervals listed on the left.

1987). The Balder Tuff forms a widespread marker near the Palaeocene/Eocene boundary. Eocene-to-Oligocene sediments are represented by prograding slope and basinal muds with local deep-water sands (although deltas existed further west throughout the Palaeogene — see Milton *et al.* 1990). Later deposits are also mud-dominated but in the area under discussion have an onlapping rather than a progradational geometry.

For a rigorous discussion of the use and abuse of sediment thickness data in the central and northern North Sea the reader is referred to Bertram & Milton (1989) and Milton *et al.* (1990). Their conclusions, supported by the present author, are that the Viking, Central and Witch Ground graben (Fig. 1) owe their gross structure to a short-lived (<25 Ma) late Jurassic rifting event representing about 40% extension (β = 1.4), followed by exponential thermal subsidence which continues to the present day. Superimposed on this general pattern is a minor

component of thermal subsidence derived from an earlier, Permo-Triassic rifting event whose syn-rift deposits can only locally be recognised beneath the Jurassic overprint (e.g. Badley *et al.* 1984, 1988). Subsidence was briefly interrupted by an episode of Palaeogene uplift related to the opening of the North Atlantic. This event can only be recognised with certainty where delta-top coals provide palaeo-sea-level markers, but sufficient data are available to demonstrate that its magnitude declined eastwards within the basin (Milton *et al.* 1990). This uplift probably represents a thermal 'shoulder' to the permanent uplift suffered by the Scottish-Shetland and greater North Atlantic margin at the same time. The permanent nature of this more westerly uplift suggests a non-thermal contribution — perhaps crustal underplating by basic magmas produced by unusually voluminous decompression melting in the palaeo-vicinity of the Iceland hot-spot (cf. White's (1988) model for the Greenland and Rockall/Norway margins).

Evidence previously advanced for significant post-Jurassic rifting was rejected by Bertram & Milton (1989) because it fell into one of two spurious classes: compaction-driven faulting at the edge of a basement ridge or incorrect interpretation of isopach data (i.e. failure to recognize that a submarine fan entering a static basin will preferentially deposit thick section in the pre-existing lows).

Central North Sea subsidence curves

Methods

Four locations in the central North Sea were chosen to typify Mesozoic-to-Tertiary subsidence (Fig. 1). They are superficially different and exhibit phenomena which have previously been interpreted as evidence for post-Jurassic rifting, but can all be explained by a single, self-consistent mechanism. In each case mean sediment thicknesses were derived from a combination of well and seismic data and represent the average over an area corresponding to about half a UK Licence Block (*c.* 10 km × 10 km) — large enough to be unaffected by local structure but small enough to ignore lithospheric flexure.

Location A (West Viking Graben) lies in the general vicinity of the Miller oilfield (U.K. Licence Block 16/7b) but excludes the conglomeratic Brae fans (Turner *et al.* 1987). It represents a locus of high Late Jurassic clastic input.

Location B (East Viking Graben — vicinity

of Block 16/13) is distal to Location 1 and
contains a thick, shale-prone Upper Jurassic
section.

Location C (South Viking Graben — vicinity
of Block 16/18) has a modest Upper Jurassic
section.

Location D (East Forties Basin — vicinity of
Block 22/3) lies at the northern end of the
Central Graben in an area of Late Jurassic
sediment starvation but tapped a major Early
Cretaceous basin-floor fan system.

Backstripping of the observed sediment-fill
followed the established procedures of Steckler
& Watts (1978) and Sclater & Christie (1980).
The 'typical North Sea' exponential compaction
curves of Sclater & Christie (1980) were used a
reference, modified on a well-by-well basis so
that they tied observed log-derived porosity and
density values. Interbedded units were treated
as the weighted mean of their components. Two
significant zones of over-pressuring or under-
compaction were observed: the Eocene to
Oligo-Miocene and the Upper Jurassic. Density
and velocity logs in the former interval have
near-constant values from about 1500 metres
(sub-sea) downwards, so no decompaction was
applied until that depth and the interval was
then decompacted along a normally-pressured
curve. The Upper Jurassic displays a slight
downwards increase in velocity and density, so
a gentle decompaction gradient was applied
until the sediments intersected the appropriate
normal compaction curve.

Results

Location C will be discussed first as it has the
thinnest Upper Jurassic section and so shows
the maximum contrast between interpretations
which make different assumptions about water
depth. Figure 3 shows a family of subsidence
curves for Location C. Backstripped curve (1)
maintains the present-day water depth (any
other constant water depth simply displaces this
curve vertically). Curve (1) generates an equivalent water-loaded subsidence curve (2), using
the density correction method of Steckler &
Watts (1978) but balancing loads against
asthenospheric rather than lithospheric mantle
following the arguments of Barr (1987b). Two
episodes of rapid subsidence are apparently
followed by two episodes of declining subsidence rate. Dewey (1982) and Beach et al. (1987)
interpreted similar curves from the Central and
Viking Graben as the result of two post-mid
Jurassic rifting episodes (Late Jurassic and Late
Cretaceous to Palaeocene). In fact there is no
reflection seismic evidence for such a history —

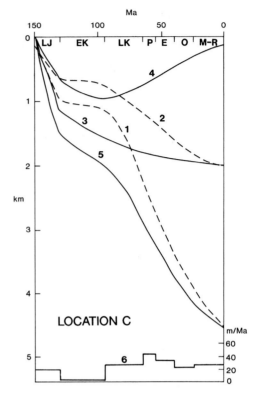

Fig. 3. Subsidence curves, Location C. (1)
backstripped 'basement' subsidence curve, constant
water depth; (2) water-loaded subsidence curve,
constant water depth; (3) theoretical water-loaded
subsidence curve, $\beta = 1.407$; (4) calculated water
depth profile; (5) backstripped 'basement' subsidence
curve, water depth as in curve (4); (6) net
sedimentation rate. LJ, Late Jurassic; EK, Early
Cretaceous; LK, Late Cretaceous; P, Palaeocene; E,
Eocene O, Oligocene; M—R, Miocene—Recent. See
text for further explanation.

no significant intrabasinal faults penetrate Base
Cretaceous and all sediment packages from the
Lower Cretaceous through the Tertiary are sub-
horizontal, i.e. unrotated (Bertram & Milton
1989).

A more plausible subsidence history, consistent with reflection seismic observations, can
be modelled by assuming a single rate Jurassic
rifting event. A stretching factor β can be derived by equating the total present-day subsidence with the expected syn- and post-rift
subsidence after homogeneous lithospheric
stretching (McKenzie 1978). Taking the parameters compiled by Barr (1987b) for a water-
loaded basin:

S_i (initial subsidence) $= 3.3(1 - 1/\beta)$ (1)

$S_{t(\infty)}$ (thermal subsidence at infinite time)
$$= 4.2(1 - 1/\beta) (2)$$

$S_{(\infty)}$ (total subsidence at infinite time)
$$= 7.5(1 - 1/\beta) (3)$$

(all depths are expressed in kilometres sub-sea).

After the first 20 Ma, thermal subsidence decays exponentially with a 62.8 Ma time constant (Parsons & Sclater 1977). Following Le Pichon & Sibuet (1981), a simple exponential relationship has been assumed of the form:

$$S_{t(a)} = 4.2(1 - e^{-a/62.8}) (1 - 1/\beta) (4)$$

where a is the age of the last rifting event in Ma. The total subsidence at time a is given by

$$S_{(a)} = (7.5 - 4.2e^{-a/62.8}) (1 - 1/\beta). (5)$$

The more rigorous treatment of McKenzie (1978) generates more rapid subsidence in the first 20 Ma and a flatter exponential curve, but the difference in the case under analysis reaches a maximum of 100 m at 10 Ma and declines rapidly thereafter. It can safely be ignored, given the magnitude of other possible errors. The rifting event is assumed to have lasted from 150 Ma to 130 Ma (mid-Oxfordian to mid-Ryazanian). The principal effect of slow rifting is to aggregate some of the post-rift subsidence into the syn-rift (Jarvis & McKenzie 1980; Cochran 1983). The remainder of the thermal subsidence curve approximates to that of an instantaneous event which took place halfway through the rifting episode (e.g. see the sample curves in Hellinger et al. 1989, fig. 5).

At location C, the total subsidence of 4.6 km at 140 Ma is equivalent to a water-loaded subsidence of 2.035 km and so from equation (5), $\beta = 1.407$. The appropriate water-loaded basement subsidence curve (3) is shown in Fig. 3. For simplicity, linear subsidence is assumed during rifting (cf. Hellinger et al. 1989, fig. 5). Assuming that this simple rifting model is correct, the water depth at any time equates to the difference between the water-loaded tectonic subsidence curve (3) and the water-equivalent sediment load (curve 2) minus the present-day water depth) and is shown as curve (4). The actual basement subsidence curve (5) equals the sum of the water depth (4) and the backstripped sediment thickness (curve (1) minus the present-day water depth). At the bottom of Fig. 3, the dry-sediment input rate (net sedimentation, matrix grains expressed as an equivalent zero-porosity column) is displayed for each major time interval.

Initial basin deepening implies that sediment input was unable to keep pace with syn-rift subsidence. This is corroborated by a widely observed transition at or about this time (Late Callovian to Late Oxfordian) from marginal or shallow-marine sediments of the Fladen group or shelfal or deep-marine sediments of the Humber Group (e.g. Turner et al. 1984; Badley et al. 1988). The precise timing of the major marine transgression varies within the basin (youngest at the margins) and is modified by short-term flooding and progradational events presumably related to changes in sea level, sediment supply or rate of fault movement.

Lower Cretaceous sediments of the Cromer Knoll Group are represented by hemipelagic shales and marls and were unable to keep pace with the rapid initial stages of thermal subsidence. Note that the low sedimentation rate reflects deposition in a starved, 1 km-deep basin rather than sediment bypass on a shallow shelf or submarine high (cf. Bertram & Milton 1989 and Barton & Wood 1984). Sea-floor shallowing in the Late Cretaceous, during deposition of the Chalk Group, resulted from a substantial increase in biogenic sediment input (coccoliths) although the basin remained starved of siliciclastics. Basinal locations may also have received resedimented chalk derived from the highly productive shelf-slope transition (cf. Hancock 1984; Johnson 1987).

The Palaeocene Moray and Montrose groups record renewed siliciclastic input, reflecting the uplift of a westerly hinterland (Milton et al. 1990). The basin was then gradually filled in by sediments derived from the European and uplifted Atlantic-margin land-masses. High net sedimentation rates in the Eocene (lower Hordaland Group) reflect the fact that this location lay in the progradational part of a major shelf-slope-basin system. Note that the actual basement subsidence curve (5) shows inflexions at times of increased sediment input — these are real events but are driven by sediment loading rather than underlying tectonic processes.

This analysis has ignored a number of additional factors which are either contentious, or impossible to quantify from the available data: eustatic sea-level changes, thermal subsidence due to Permo-Triassic rifting, compaction of pre-Upper Jurassic sediments and the magnitude of any Palaeogene uplift east of the control provided by delta-top coals. Specimen calculations indicate that these effects would be relatively minor (up to about 200 m impact on water depth) and that for most of the Late

Jurassic through Tertiary, eustatic sea-level changes had the largest magnitude and acted in opposition to the other three factors.

Data from the remaining three locations are presented in Figs 4–6. In each case the water-loaded curve (2) assuming present-day water depths is included to demonstrate the spurious effects which can arise from a failure to account for variations in water depth. Locations A and B are broadly similar to Location C: two pulses of subsidence are generated which could be misinterpreted as two episodes of rifting. However their timing is subtly different and Location A has a tightly curved Jurassic–Cretaceous segment which could not be made to fit exponential cooling with any reasonable (30–100 Ma) time constant. Location D exhibits linear subsidence, which would be difficult to explain by any rifting model.

An alternative approach is to generate single-stage rifting models using the method described for Location C. All four locations yield very similar stretching factors ($\beta = 1.4$–1.46) and

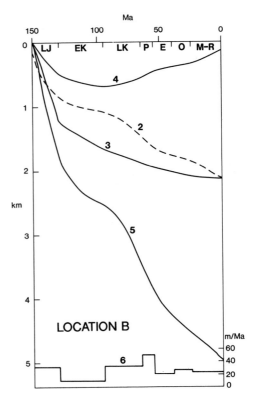

Fig. 5. Subsidence curves, Location B. Labels as in Fig. 3 but $\beta = 1.436$ and curve (1) is omitted for clarity.

similar overall subsidence histories. Water depth was primarily controlled by sediment input. Location A received major sand input in the Late Jurassic, but this created a subtle topographic high which was bypassed in the Early Cretaceous. Location B received rather more Lower Cretaceous sediments while Location D was starved in the Late Jurassic but formed a depocentre for Lower Cretaceous turbidites. All three locations record major basin-filling events in the Late Cretaceous and Palaeocene.

Contrasts in the Eocene-to-Oligocene curves result from the specific location of each site on the prograding shelf/slope system. Maximum net sedimentation takes place on the slope, with sediment bypass in shelfal locations and sediment starvation on the distal basin floor. The slope prograded across Locations A and C in the Eocene and Locations B and D in the Oligocene. All four locations subsequently recorded a change in style of sedimentation to passive backfilling (marine onlap).

In conclusion, the gross depositional record

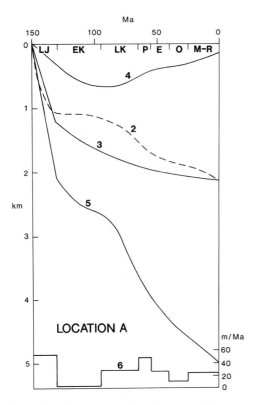

Fig. 4. Subsidence curves, Location A. Labels as in Fig. 3 but $\beta = 1.436$ and curve (1) is omitted for clarity.

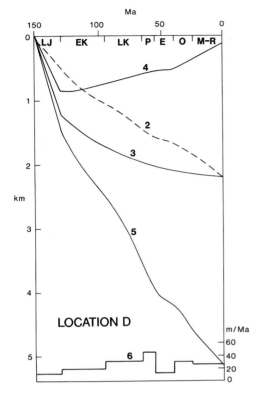

Fig. 6. Subsidence curves, Location D. Labels as in Fig. 3 but $\beta = 1.464$ and curve (1) is omitted for clarity.

at all four locations can be explained by a single Late Jurassic rifting phase whose thermal subsidence stage was strongly influenced by externally controlled sedimentation rates.

Model half-graben

Introduction

It is instructive to consider the effect of varying sediment input rate on the type of half-graben modelled by Barr (1987a), Jackson et al. (1988) and Vendeville & Cobbold (1988). In these models the 'basement' (i.e. pre-rift) fault-block geometry is assumed to conform to that generated by the rotated planar-fault or domino mechanism (Morton & Black 1975; Wernicke & Burchfiel 1982) while the total subsidence, averaged over the width of a fault-block, is driven by some other mechanism such as uniform lithospheric stretching (McKenzie 1978). By varying the initial fault-plane dip and spacing it is possible to model emergent footwall blocks

which may or may not be eroded, or submerged basement faults which propagate up into the sediment cover as listric growth faults. Note that the models do not strictly depend on the domino mechanism, only on the sawtooth 'top basement' geometry. Similar geometries can be produced by more physically realistic models, such as flexural isostasy (Kusznir et al. this volume).

Results

Locations A, C and D were modelled by the method described above and compared with a previous model (Barr 1987a) which allowed the sediment fill to build up to sea level. (Location B has been omitted as its results were not qualitatively different from Location A.) Overall 'basement' subsidence was defined by curves (5) of Figs 4, 2 and 6, and the 'top basement' geometry modelled using the method of Barr (1987a), with initial fault-plane dip of 60° and spacing of 10 km. Note that the purpose of this exercise was not to emulate specific cross section geometries at these locations, but merely to use a convenient subsidence history to explore the impact of water-depth variations on the earlier model.

Figure 7 is based on fig. 8c of Barr (1987a) and represents a basin which was filled to sea level with sediments which followed the North Sea 'shaly sand' compaction law of Sclater & Christie (1980). Early footwall erosion resulted from the low density which the Sclater & Christie model generates for uncompacted sediments and will not be duplicated in the observation-based central North Sea models. The main points to note are the significant cover of syn-rift sediments across the crests of the fault blocks and the basement-rooted growth faults which are beginning to propagate into the sediment column.

A set of model half-graben for Location A is shown in Fig. 8. Upper-crustal geometry is modelled by domino faults with 10 km initial fault spacing, 60° initial fault-plane dip and 40% extension. Figure 8a is directly comparable with Fig. 7 and represents the situation at the end of rifting. Upper Jurassic sediments were dominantly deposited by gravity flows and so have been allowed to fill the triangular basins up to a horizontal sea bed determined by the total decompacted area of the sediments (i.e. the area of Upper Jurassic sediments in one half-graben, divided by the 14 km fault-spacing, equals the average decompacted thickness of the Upper Jurassic sediment column). The crests of the fault blocks are submerged but interrupt the

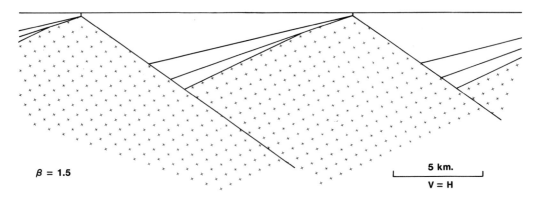

$\beta = 1.5$

5 km.

V = H

Fig. 7. Model half-graben filled to sea level with syn-rift sediments, prior to thermal subsidence (Fig. 8c of Barr 1987a).

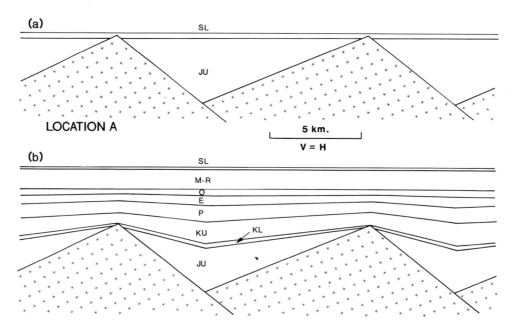

(a)

SL

JU

LOCATION A

5 km.

V = H

(b)

SL

M-R
O
E
P
KU   KL

JU

Fig. 8. Model half-graben for Location A, generated using subsidence curves (4) and (5) of Fig. 4. **(a)** at end-Jurassic; **(b)** at present-day. JU, Upper Jurassic; KL, Lower Cretaceous; UK, Upper Cretaceous; P, Palaeocene, E, Eocene; O, Oligocene; M−R, Miocene−Recent; SL, sea level.

distribution of syn-rift sediments (in practice, there will probably be a very thin pelagic cover). There are no growth faults.

Figure 8b represents the same basin after 130 Ma of thermal subsidence. Condensed Lower Cretaceous pelagic sediments are widely distributed on North Sea highs and so they were added as a uniform layer. Later units were given a flat upper profile and allowed to fill in the basin as far as possible. The development of

a hangingwall compaction syncline in noteworthy (cf. White *et al.* 1986 and Frost 1989). This basin would readily be recognized as having undergone only a single stage of rifting. The only contentious point might be whether extension continued during the Lower Cretaceous. In fact, this might be impossible to determine if the sediments were genuinely pelagic and insensitive to pre-existing topography.

The next model is of Location C (Fig. 9). In

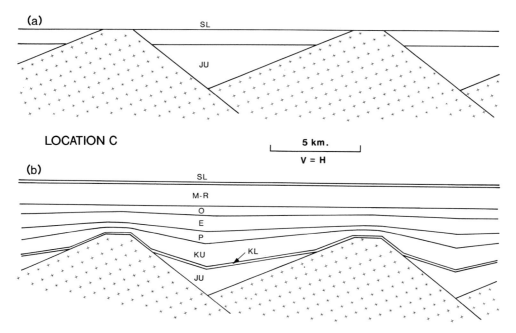

Fig. 9. Model half-graben for Location C, generated using subsidence curves (4) and (5) of Fig. 3. (**a**) at end-Jurassic; (**b**) at present-day. Abbreviations as in Fig. 8.

this case the reduced syn-rift sediment load caused less overall subsidence and footwall blocks emerged above sea level. It is assumed here that they were eroded down to sea level (plausible for the North Sea, where pre-rift sediments form the upper parts of the fault blocks, but not for the Suez example studied by Jackson *et al*. (1988), where crystalline basement was exposed at surface during rifting). The post-rift stage was modelled as before. Thin Lower Cretaceous sediments drape the fault blocks, but the Upper Cretaceous shows marked thickness variations and substantial compaction-induced dips into the basin centre. Thickness variations greater than 2:1 persist into the Palaeocene, despite the fact that the fault blocks had been submerged for 70 Ma. In practice, compaction-induced differential subsidence of this magnitude would probably give rise to faulting within the post-rift fill (the 'drape-slip' faulting of Bertram & Milton (1989)) and gravitational redistribution of sediments towards the basin centre. Uncritical examination of isopach maps, footwall/hangingwall sediment thickness ratios and even dipmeter data could lead to the erroneous conclusion that renewed rifting took place in the Late Cretaceous and Early Tertiary, perhaps following a pause during the Early Cretaceous.

Location D (Fig. 10) presents yet another contrast. The syn-rift stage is very similar to that of Location C, but the Lower Cretaceous sediments in this area are turbidites which preferentially deposit in pre-existing lows and display enormous thickness variations between crestal and basinal locations. The total Upper Jurassic plus Lower Cretaceous sediment load is similar to that at Location A, so the succeeding stages are comparable to those in Fig. 8. The fault-block profiles are very different because the low Jurassic sediment input left the crests emergent and vulnerable to erosion. It would require careful examination of reflector geometries *within* the sequences depicted there to distinguish this model from a basin which had extended continuously throughout the Late Jurassic and Early Cretaceous. Even with careful examination it would be difficult.

Conclusions

Sediment-input rate plays a major role in the stratigraphic development of extensional basins which develop by an isostatically compensated mechanism, such as that proposed by McKenzie (1978). Overall subsidence is strongly dependent on the mean density of the basin fill and hence on the sediment/sea-water ratio, whereas

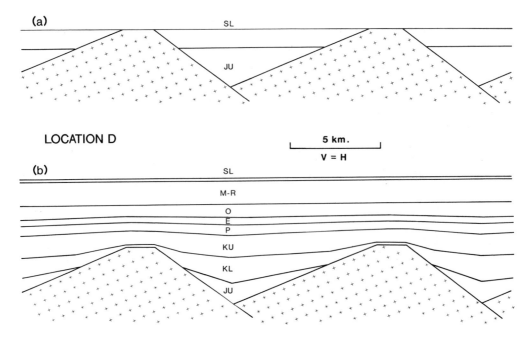

Fig. 10. Model half-graben for Location D, generated using subsidence curves (4) and (5) of Fig. 6. (**a**) at end-Jurassic; (**b**) at present-day. Abbreviations as in Fig. 8.

tilted fault-block geometry depends mainly on the upper crustal deformation mechanism and the absolute stretching factor.

Central North Sea subsidence curves, of a type which has sometimes been interpreted in terms of two-stage rifting, are considered to result from the inability of sedimentation to keep pace with rapid syn-rift and early post-rift subsidence. Water depths approaching 1 km were not uncommon in the Late Jurassic and Early Cretaceous.

Semi-starved half-graben whose overall subsidence history conforms to the model discussed above can display a wide range of depositional geometries despite similar stretching factors and underlying fault-block geometries: fault-block crests may or may not be emergent and successive sediment packages may or may not show substantial thickness and dip variations from crest to basin. Careful seismic-stratigraphic and well or outcrop study of sub-sequence geometries and depositional facies is essential to a correct interpretation: thickness data alone are not enough.

I thank my colleagues in BP and elsewhere for many fruitful discussions on basin geometry. This contribution is published with the permission of BP Exploration, but the views expressed are entirely my own.

References

BADLEY, M. E., EGEBERG, T. & NIPEN, O. 1984. Development of rift basins illustrated by the structural evolution of the Oseberg feature, Block 30/6, offshore Norway. *Journal of the Geological Society, London,* **141**, 639–649.

——, PRICE, J. D., RAMBECH DAHL, C. & AGDESTEIN, T. 1988. The structural evolution of the northern Viking Graben and its bearing on extensional modes of basin formation. *Journal of the Geological Society, London,* **145**, 455–472.

BARR, D. 1987a. Structural/stratigraphic models for extensional basins of half-graben type. *Journal of Structural Geology,* **9**, 491–500.

—— 1987b. Lithospheric stretching, detached normal faulting and footwall uplift. *In*: COWARD, M. P., DEWEY, J. F. & HANCOCK, P. L. (eds) *Continental Extensional Tectonics.* Geological Society, London, Special Publication, **28**, 75–94.

BARTON, P. & WOOD, R. 1984. Tectonic evolution of the North Sea basin: crustal stretching and subsidence. *Geophysical Journal of the Royal Astronomical Society,* **79**, 987–1022.

BEACH, A., BIRD, T. & GIBBS, A. 1987. Extensional tectonics and crustal structure: deep seismic reflection data from the North Sea Viking graben. *In*: COWARD, M. P., DEWEY, J. F. & HANCOCK, P. L. (eds) *Continental Extensional Tectonics.* Geological Society, London, Special Publication, **28**, 467–476.

BESSIS, F. 1986. Some remarks on the study of subsidence in sedimentary basins. Application to the Gulf of Lyons margin (western Mediterranean). *Marine and Petroleum Geology*, **3**, 37−63.

BERTRAM, G. T. & MILTON, N. J. 1989. Reconstructing basin evolution from sedimentary thickness; the importance of palaeobathymetric control, with reference to the North Sea. *Basin Research*, **1**, 247−257.

BROWN, S. 1984. Jurassic. *In*: GLENNIE, K. (ed) *Introduction to the Petroleum Geology of the North Sea*. Blackwell, Oxford, 127−132.

CHENET, P., MONTADERT, L., GAIRAUD, H. & ROBERTS, D. G. 1983. Extension ratio measurements on the Galicia, Portugal and northern Biscay continental margins: implications for evolutionary models of passive continental margins. *In*: WATKINS, J. S. & DRAKE, C. L. *Studies in continental margin geology*. American Association of Petroleum Geologists Memoir, **34**, 703−715.

COCHRAN, J. R. 1983. Effects of finite rifting times on the development of sedimentary basins. *Earth and Planetary Science Letters*, **66**, 289−302.

DEEGAN, C. E. & SCULL, B. J. 1977. A standard lithostratigraphic nomenclature for the North Sea. *Report of the Institute of Geological Sciences*, 77/25.

DEWEY, J. F. 1982. Plate tectonics and the evolution of the British Isles. *Journal of the Geological Society, London*, **139**, 371−412.

FROST, R. E. 1989. Discussion on the structural evolution of the northern Viking Graben and its bearing on extensional modes of basin formation; reply by M. E. Badley, J. D. Price, C. Rambech Dahl, & T. Agdestein. *Journal of the Geological Society, London*, **146**, 1035−1040.

GLENNIE, K. (ed.) 1984 *Introduction to the Petroleum Geology of the North Sea*. Blackwell, Oxford.

HANCOCK, J. M. 1984. Cretaceous. *In*: GLENNIE, K. (ed.) *Introduction to the Petroleum Geology of the North Sea*. Blackwell, Oxford, 133−150.

HELLINGER, S. J., SCLATER, J. G. & GILTNER, J. 1989. Mid-Jurassic through mid-Cretaceous extension in the Central Graben of the North Sea — part 1: estimates from subsidence. *Basin Research*, **1**, 191−200.

JACKSON, J. A., WHITE, N. J., GARFUNKEL, Z. & ANDERSON, H. 1988. Relations between normal-fault geometry, tilting and vertical motions in extensional terrains: an example from the southern Gulf of Suez. *Journal of Structural Geology*, **10**, 155−170.

JARVIS, G. T. & MCKENZIE, D. 1980. Sedimentary basin formation with finite extension rates. *Earth and Planetary Science Letters*, **48**, 42−52.

JOHNSON, H. 1987. Seismic expression of major chalk reworking episodes in the Palaeocene of the Central North Sea. *In*: BROOKS, J. & GLENNIE, K. (eds) *Petroleum Geology of North-west Europe*. Graham & Trotman, London, 591−598.

KUSZNIR, N. J., MARSDEN, G. & EGAN, S. S. (This volume) A flexural cantilever simple shear/pure shear model of continental extension: application to the Jeanne d'Arc Basin, Grand Banks and Viking Graben, North Sea.

LE PICHON, X. & SIBUET, J.-C. 1981. Passive margins: a model of formation. *Journal of Geophysical Research*, **86**, 3708−3720.

LEEDER, M. R. & GAWTHORPE, R. L. 1987. Sedimentary models for extensional tilt-block/half-graben basins. *In*: COWARD, M. P., DEWEY, J. F. & HANCOCK, P. L. (eds) *Continental Extensional Tectonics. Geological Society, London, Special Publication*, **28**, 139−152.

MCKENZIE, D. 1978. Some remarks on the development of sedimentary basins. *Earth and Planetary Science Letters*, **40**, 25−32.

MILTON, N. J., BERTRAM, G. T. & VANN, I. R. 1990. Early Palaeogene tectonics and sedimentation in the North Sea. *In*: HARDMAN, R. F. P. & BROOKS, J. (eds) *Tectonic Events Responsible for Britain's Oil and Gas Reserves*. Geological Society, London, Special Publication, **55**, 339−352.

MONTADERT, L., ROBERTS, D. G., DE CHARPAL, O. & GUENNOC, P. 1979. Rifting and subsidence of the northern continental margin of the Bay of Biscay. *In*: MONTADERT, L. & ROBERTS, D. G. (eds) *Initial Reports of the Deep Sea Drilling Project*, **48**, 1025−1060.

MORTON, W. H. & BLACK, R. 1975. Crustal attenuation in Afar. *In*: PILGER, A. & ROSLER, A. (eds) *Afar depression of Ethiopia. Inter-Union Commission for Geodynamics Scientific Report*, **14**, 55−56.

PARSONS, B. & SCLATER, J. C. 1977. An analysis of the variation of ocean floor bathymetry and heat flow with age. *Journal of Geophysical Research*, **82**, 803−827.

SCLATER, J. G. & CHRISTIE, P. A. F. 1980. Continental stretching: an explanation of the post-mid Cretaceous subsidence of the Central North Sea. *Journal of Geophysical Research*, **85**, 3711−3739.

STECKLER, M. S. & WATTS, A.B. 1978. Subsidence of the Atlantic-type continental margin off New York. *Earth and Planetary Science Letters*, **41**, 1−13.

STEWART, I. J. 1987. A revised stratigraphic interpretation of the Early Palaeogene of the Central North Sea. *In*: BROOKS, J. & GLENNIE, K. (eds) *Petroleum Geology of North West Europe*. Graham & Trotman, London, 557−576.

SURLYK, F. 1978. Submarine fan sedimentation along fault scarps on tilted fault blocks (Jurassic-Cretaceous boundary, E. Greenland). *Bulletin Gronlands Geologiske Undersokels*, **128**.

TURNER, C. C., COHEN, J. M., CONNELL, E. R. & COOPER, D. M. 1987. A depositional model for the South Brae oilfield. *In*: BROOKS, J. & GLENNIE, K. (eds) *Petroleum Geology of North West Europe*. Graham & Trotman, London, 853−864.

——, RICHARDS, P. C., SWALLOW, J. L. & GRIMSHAW, S. P. 1984. Upper Jurassic stratigraphy and sedimentary facies in the central Outer Moray Firth basin, North Sea. *Marine and Petroleum Geology*, **1**, 105−117.

VENDEVILLE, B. (This volume) Mechanisms generating normal fault curvature: a review illustrated by physical models.

—— & COBBOLD, P. R. 1988. How normal faulting and sedimentation interact to produce listric fault profiles and stratigraphic wedges. *Journal of Structural Geology*, **10**, 649–659.

——, ——, DAVY, P., BRUN, J. P. & CHOUKROUNE, P. 1987. Physical models of extensional tectonics at various scales. *In*: COWARD, M. P., DEWEY, J. F. & HANCOCK, P. L. (eds) *Continental Extensional Tectonics*. Geological Society, London, Special Publication, **28**, 95–107.

WERNICKE, B. & BURCHFIEL, B. C. 1982. Modes of extensional tectonics. *Journal of Structural Geology*, **4**, 105–115.

WHITE, N., JACKSON, J. A. & MCKENZIE, D. 1986. The relationship between the geometry of normal faults and that of the sedimentary layers in their hanging walls. *Journal of Structural Geology*, **8**.

897–909.

WHITE, R. S. 1988. A hot-spot model for Early Tertiary volcanism in the North Atlantic. *In*: MORTON, A. C. & PARSON, L. M. (eds) *Early Tertiary Volcanism and the Opening of the North Atlantic*. Geological Society, London, Special Publication, **39**, 3–13.

ZIEGLER, P. A. 1981. Evolution of sedimentary basins in North-west Europe. *In*: ILLING, L. V. & HOBSON, G. D. (eds) *The Petroleum Geology of the Continental Shelf of North-West Europe*. Heyden, London, 3–39.

—— 1982. Faulting and graben formation in western and central Europe. *Philosophical transactions of the Royal Society of London Series A*, **305**, 113–143.

The kinematic evolution of the Coffee Soil Fault

JOSEPH CARTWRIGHT

Department of Geology, Royal School of Mines, Imperial College, Prince Consort Rd, London SW7 2BP, UK

Abstract: This paper addresses the problem of the dating of motion on large, extensional faults, from the seismic expression of the sedimentary sequences deposited during and after the extensional deformation. A general discussion of the interpretational methods and pitfalls involved in a seismically based, kinematic analysis is made by reference to a case study of the Coffee Soil Fault. The Coffee Soil Fault forms the eastern boundary of the Central Graben of the North Sea Rift, and is located in the Danish Sector. From a comparison of the stratigraphy of the hanging wall and footwall blocks, it is suggested that rifting commenced in the Late Permian/Early Triassic. The rifting proceeded in two distinct phases, a non-rotational Triassic phase, resulting in parallel reflection configurations, and a rotational Mid−Late Jurassic phase, resulting in divergent reflection configurations. Basin-floor and fault-scarp relief that resulted from a Late Jurassic acceleration of motion across the fault was infilled in a parallel-onlap configuration by the post-rift Lower Cretaceous sequence. The case study is used to demonstrate that onlap of remnant fault scarps can easily be mistaken for syn-rift deposition, and that this can lead to considerable errors in the timing of the end of rifting.

One of the most important parameters in the study of extensional basins is the timing of the active crustal-extension. Early models of extensional-basin formation assumed for simplicity that rifting was instantaneous, and any thermal perturbation of the lithosphere associated with the rifting began to decay after the rifting terminated (McKenzie 1978). Refinements of this model have emphasized the more realistic case of a finite duration for the rifting and the impact that this has on the decay of any associated thermal anomaly (Jarvis & McKenzie 1980). Attempts to estimate lithospheric extension based on the analysis of post-rift thermal subsidence patterns require that the timing of active basement extension is tightly constrained. The exponential form of most theoretical curves for thermal subsidence following lithospheric extension means that any errors in the timing of the rifting will significantly impair the analysis of the post-rift subsidence.

Modern, multichannel, reflection-seismic data have been used extensively in the study of extensional tectonics and extensional-basin formation (e.g. Montadert *et al.* 1978; Bally 1983; Gibbs 1984; Harding 1984). The emphasis of most of the research on extensional tectonics using seismic data has been geometrical. There are few published case studies that concentrate specifically on the kinematic aspects of extensional faulting as determined from seismic data. The aim of this paper is to present a qualitative, kinematic analysis of a major extensional fault, that is based largely on an interpretation of the reflection configurations in the fault blocks adjacent to the fault. The emphasis of the paper is on the interpretational methodology, and the pitfalls and difficulties that may be encountered in attempting such an analysis. The subject of this analysis is the Coffee Soil Fault, the principal boundary structure to the Central Graben in the Danish Sector of the North Sea.

The study is based on a dense grid of high-resolution seismic data acquired over the Danish Sector by Merlin Profilers Ltd in 1982. The seismic data were calibrated by correlation with twenty released wells. Detailed accounts of the stratigraphy of the study area have been presented by Michelsen (1982), Gowers & Saeboe (1985), Frandsen *et al.* (1987), and Cartwright (1987).

Structural setting of the Coffee Soil Fault

The Coffee Soil Fault is the main boundary structure of the Central Graben in the Danish Sector of the North Sea (Fig. 1). It marks the eastern boundary to the Tail End Graben, a major, Late-Palaeozoic-to-Late-Mesozoic depocentre that runs in a NNW−SSE trend through the Danish Sector and separates the prominent E−W-trending Mid North Sea and Ringkobing−Fyn Highs. The Tail End Graben is asymmetric in cross sectional form, exhibiting a pronounced rotational thickening to the east, towards the Coffee Soil Fault.

From Roberts A. M., Yielding, G. & Freeman, B. (eds), 1991, *The Geometry of Normal Faults*, Geological Society Special Publication No 56, pp 29−40

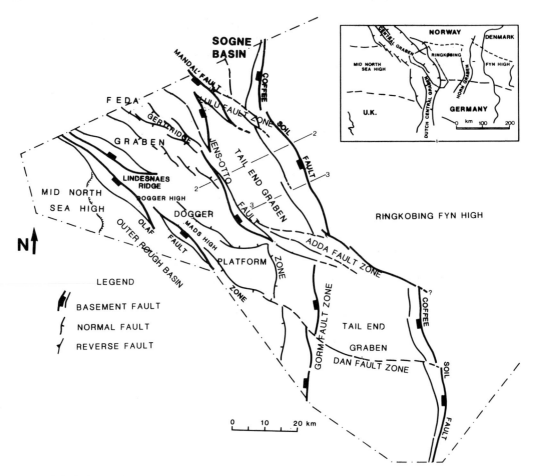

Fig. 1. Principal tectonic elements of the Danish Sector of the Central Graben. The inset figure gives the regional location and shows the curvilinear form of the Coffee Soil Fault as depicted on early maps of the area.

The Coffee Soil Fault was mapped initially from a coarse grid of seismic data as a single, curvilinear fault-trace (Michelsen 1982), but recent mapping based on a much closer spaced seismic grid shows that it is composed of at least five major, linear segments (Fig. 1). The segmented fault pattern is also reflected in the detailed structure of the western hinge margin of the Tail End Graben, and in the internal structure and stratigraphic expression of the graben-fill sequences (Cartwright 1987). The stratigraphic segmentation of the Tail End Graben points directly to a partitioning in the motion history of the Coffee Soil Fault according to the segmented fault-pattern. Stratigraphic evidence also suggests that individual segments of the Coffee Soil Fault moved at different rates and at different times from their adjacent

segments, over certain intervals in the evolution of the Tail End Graben (Cartwright 1987). The kinematic analysis presented here focusses on the segment of the Coffee Soil Fault immediately north of the major, sinistral dog-leg in the Tail End Graben (Fig. 1). This is the deepest part of the Tail End Graben, where the maximum displacement on the fault of over eleven kilometres is recorded.

Geometrical interpretation

The segment of the Coffee Soil Fault bordering the Northern Tail End Graben (Fig. 1) strikes in a NNW−SSE direction. The seismic grid is oriented NNW−SSE and ENE−WSW. The dip lines in the grid are thus ideally oriented for an optimum seismic migration. The quality of the seismic data is excellent for this type of rift setting, and bedding reflections are imaged to two-way-travel-times in excess of six seconds. Fault-plane reflections are imaged only rarely, however, and the structural interpretation of the fault is based mainly on identifying stratal terminations against the fault.

Two main problems were encountered in making the fault interpretation. In the shallow part of the graben-fill sequence, the bedding dips away from the fault plane. The seismic facies is highly discontinuous along a zone parallel to the fault, for distances of up to five kilometres away from the approximate position of the fault (Fig. 2). Since the crystalline basement lithologies of the footwall block of the Ringkobing—Fyn High also have a characteristic, discontinuous seismic-expression, there is often no clear demarcation between the discontinuous strata of the hangingwall and footwall blocks. By picking out the gross stratification in the hangingwall sequence, however, it is usually possible to establish an approximate position for the fault plane. Deeper in the section, the graben-fill is usually more continuous, and the contrast with the discontinuity of the footwall block is easier to recognize. Problems arise, however, from interference patterns produced by the overmigration of long period sea-bottom multiples of the Top and Base Chalk reflections, and from the decreasing accuracy of the migration with increasing depth. These problems are clearly apparent on a second representative seismic line across the Coffee Soil Fault illustrated in Fig. 3. The position of the upper tip of the fault is constrained by the presence of a pronounced monocline in the Upper Cretaceous sequence (cf. Fig. 2). This monocline is interpreted to have developed as a result of differential compaction of the hangingwall and footwall blocks during burial under the load of the Early Tertiary sequences. The upper tip of the fault is located on the seismic data at the point of maximum break of slope of this monocline.

The structural interpretation presented in Fig. 3 can be compared with the uninterpreted data presented in Fig. 4, to give an impression of the degree of interpretative error involved in identifying the position of the fault. The position of the fault can be interpreted with a fair degree of certainty in the upper part of the section using the shallow compactional monocline as a guide to the upper tip location, and then tracing the fault downwards using the hangingwall bedding cut-offs. The fault clearly extends to the base of the section, but its position is obscured by the interference of multiples and

migration smiles with the genuine bedding plane reflections. On Fig. 2, the deepest-recognizable stratal-reflections can be seen from the western flank of the half-graben dipping down towards the fault, and a projection of their intersection is close to the base of the section. The effective acoustic basement in this deepest part of the Tail End Graben is the Base Zechstein.

The fault appears to be slightly listric on the seismic data (e.g. Fig. 2). Depth conversion of several lines across this segment of the Coffee Soil Fault shows the geometry to be planar with a slight, upward-steepening curvature in the upper kilometre. The fault dips on average between 30 and 35 degrees. This fairly modest inclination has been attributed to the presence of low-angle shear zones in the basement, of probable Caledonian affinity, which were later reactivated in a brittle mode to give the current half-graben structure (Cartwright 1990).

Stratal geometries of the hangingwall block

The strong asymmetry of the Tail End Graben is evident on Fig. 2. This is most-markedly expressed in the divergent reflection configurations of the Middle and Upper Jurassic sequences. Within the Upper Jurassic sequence several minor onlap surfaces can be observed. These surfaces are most easily recognizable in the highly convergent zone, immediately downflank from the hinge zone forming the western limit to the half-graben. Similar onlap surfaces are also observed in neighbouring graben segments, but they do not correlate across the various segments to form single, contiguous surfaces of onlap. This suggests that the development of the onlap surfaces is more probably related to phases of localized acceleration of fault motion within individual segments along the Coffee Soil Fault rather than to any eustatic effect.

Deeper in the graben-fill succession there is a transition from the strongly-divergent reflection configurations of the Middle and Upper Jurassic, to a more parallel form as exhibited by a basal sequence of Late-Permian-to-Triassic-age. Well correlations suggest that this transition occurs at or close to the base of the Middle Jurassic. The upper part of the Triassic is truncated at a prominent high-amplitude event representing the base of the Middle Jurassic. This truncation is most apparent on the western convergent flank of the half-graben (Fig. 2). The truncation surface is recognized along the western flank throughout the Tail End Graben (Michelsen 1982).

Figure 3 is a portion of a dip seismic section

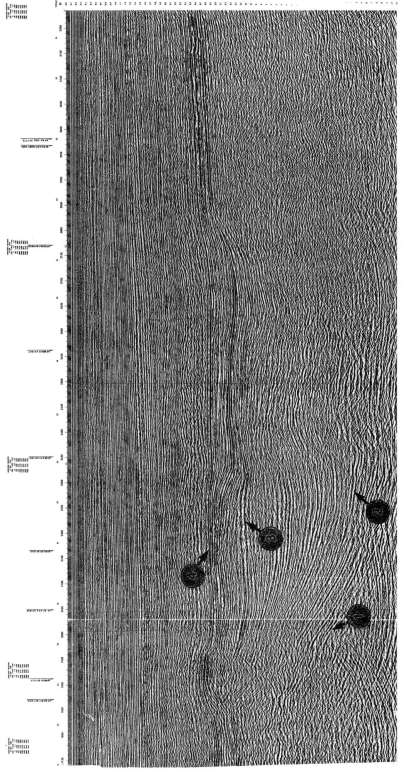

Fig. 2. Seismic section from the northern Tail End Graben. Location on Fig. 1. Key to stratigraphy: 1, Base Zechstein; 2, Base Middle Jurassic; 3, Base Cretaceous; 4, Base Tertiary.

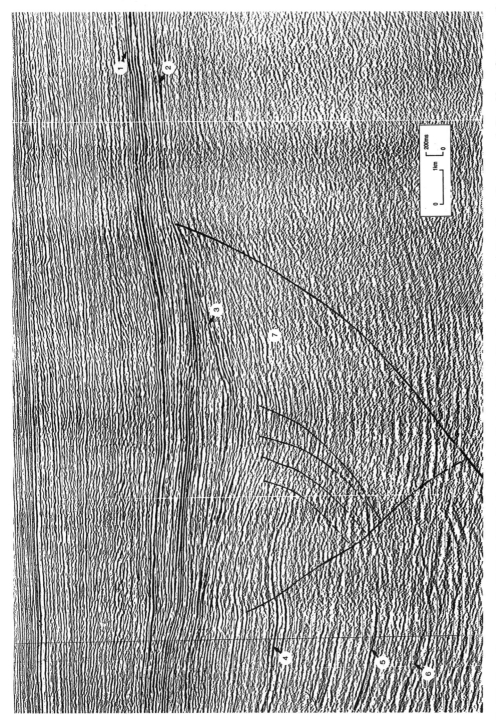

Fig. 3. Seismic section across the Coffee Soil Fault. Location is indicated on Fig. 1. Key to stratigraphy: 1, Top Upper Cretaceous; 2, Base Upper Cretaceous; 3, Base Lower Cretaceous; 4, Base Volgian; 5, Base Upper Jurassic; 6, Base Middle Jurassic. Note the discontinuous seismic facies and wedge-progradational configurations of the Upper Jurassic adjacent to the Coffee Soil Fault (7).

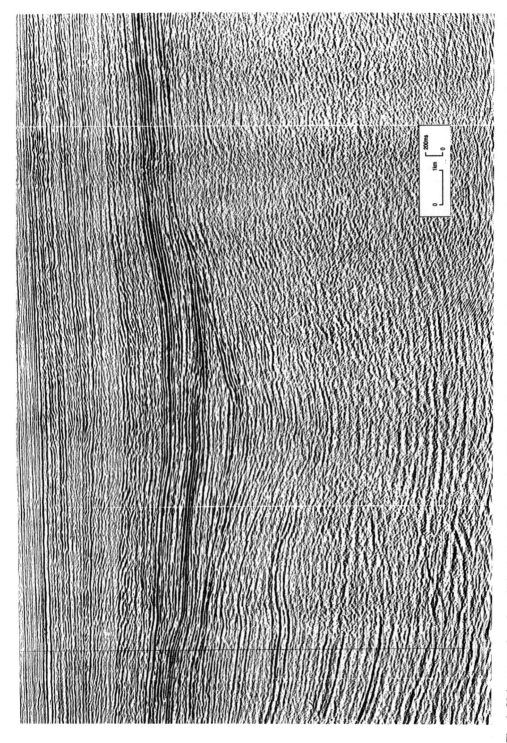

Fig. 4. Uninterpreted version of Fig. 3. Note the increasing difficulty in disciminating multiples and migration artefacts from genuine stratal reflections with increasing depth in the section.

crossing the Coffee Soil Fault, some 15 kilometres south of the traverse illustrated in Fig. 2. This section illustrates the general stratigraphic relationships observed for the Lower and Upper Cretaceous sequences. The Lower Cretaceous is developed in a parallel form on the western sector of Fig. 3, but then thickens rapidly into a synclinal structure located immediately adjacent to the Coffee Soil Fault. The Lower Cretaceous thins to a pinch-out located immediately down-flank from the upper tip of the Coffee Soil Fault. This abrupt thinning is in the form of a parallel onlap, since the stratal reflections of the Lower Cretaceous sequence are concordant with the top of the sequence. This geometrical relationship indicates that the west-dipping slope of the Base Cretaceous onlap surface must, therefore, represent a surface of depositional or structural relief established prior to the initial onlap of the Lower Cretaceous. The dips of the underlying Upper Jurassic sequence are approximately concordant with the Base Cretaceous event. The seismic facies of the Upper Jurassic adjacent to the fault plane is markedly discontinuous, and numerous local surfaces of erosion and downlap are observed. Equivalent units on the western side of the synclinal axis are more laterally continuous, and display onlap relationships towards the western margin of the graben.

The Upper Cretaceous sequence forms a monoclinal structure over the upper tip of the Coffee Soil Fault. The basal units of this sequence onlap the dipping flank of the monocline, and overstep the onlapping units of the Lower Cretaceous. Upper units of the Upper Cretaceous are seen to pass across the monocline without any appreciable thickness variation (cf. Figs 2 & 3). The structural relief across the monocline is present in the sequences up to and including the Middle Miocene (Fig. 2). The magnitude of the relief decreases progressively up section. This indicates that differential compaction across the Coffee Soil Fault occurred throughout the Early Tertiary.

Kinematic analysis

Dating the onset of rifting

The ideal method for determining the onset of active faulting in extensional basins is to examine the stratigraphy of the footwall and hangingwall blocks adjacent to the major border-faults to the basin, and establish the earliest time at which stratigraphic expansion occurred across the faults. This may give a good approximation

to the time at which the faults ruptured through to the surface, but it is only reasonably precise if sedimentary preservation in the hangingwall was coeval with the initial fault displacement. In rift environments which are prone to sediment starvation, such as deep marine rifts or terrestrial rifts, the earliest sedimentary infill of the basin floor relief created by the early fault activity may lag considerably behind the fault-controlled subsidence, and the stratigraphic expansion will then only give a minimum age for the onset of rifting.

Uplift and erosion of the footwall block during rifting commonly results in an attenuated or incomplete stratigraphic record (Roberts & Yielding, this volume). This presents immediate problems for the definition of stratigraphic expansion across the fault. This problem is particularly acute for the major boundary structures to large grabens where the magnitude of the cumulative footwall uplift is often so large as to lead to complete bevelling of pre- and syn-rift sequences deposited on the footwall block. If this is the case, then the dating of the onset of the rifting can only be constrained by reference to the stratigraphy of the hangingwall block.

In extensional basins with a half-graben geometry, such as the Tail End Graben, it is often assumed that since the graben is asymmetric, then syn-rift sequences must be divergent in form. From this assumption it follows that sequences that exhibit parallel stratal-configurations, observed stratigraphically beneath a divergent sequence, must be designated as pre-rift. In this analysis, the boundary between parallel and divergent sequences would be taken as the surface representing the onset of rifting (Fig. 5). Applying this analysis to the Tail End Graben, it would be logical to place the onset of rifting at the Base Middle Jurassic event. It could additionally be argued that the truncation of the uppermost Triassic observed on the western flank of the graben was produced by an initial, rotational uplift of the apical region of the hangingwall block, immediately prior to the more widespread subsidence as the rifting proceeded. Stratigraphic evidence from the footwall block to the Coffee Soil Fault, from the region beyond that affected by pronounced footwall uplift associated with the graben formation, indicates that the rifting commenced much earlier than would be suggested by the classification of pre- and syn-rift sequences as illustrated in Fig. 5.

The footwall of the Coffee Soil Fault is the Ringkobing–Fyn High. This is a large E–W-trending region of positive structural relief separating the Northern and Southern Permian

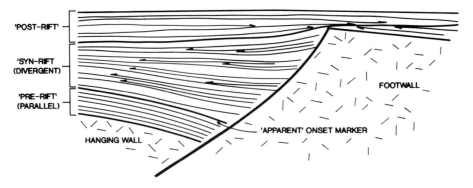

Fig. 5. Schematic representation of a classification of pre-, syn-, and post-rift sequences, based on gross configurations and relationship to the fault surface. The 'apparent' rift-onset marker is often placed at the boundary between parallel and divergent sequences in the hangingwall block, based on the assumption that syn-rift sequences in a half-graben must have a divergent configuration. This assumption is invalid in the case of the Coffee Soil Fault.

Basins (Bertelsen 1980; Michelsen 1982; Cartwright 1988, 1990). It is difficult to estimate the total amount of footwall uplift associated with the extension on the Coffee Soil Fault, since there are no reliable structural markers preserved beneath the post-rift cover of the Upper Cretaceous. The Upper Cretaceous overlies crystalline basement over much of the Ringkobing–Fyn High, and it is evident that the footwall uplift adjacent to the Coffee Soil Fault was superimposed on a more regional uplift, or resistance to subsidence, that affected large parts of the high. Mesozoic sequences thin without onlap or erosional truncation onto the high, from the thick depocentres to the north and south, across a series of step-faults that form the margins of the high. This observation, taken together with isopach and well data, implies that the central axis of the Ringkobing–Fyn High was an area of non-deposition for most of the Late Permian, Triassic and Jurassic (Bertelsen 1980; Cartwright 1988). Several wells drilled on the crestal region encountered condensed sequences representing most of the stages of the Early Cretaceous (Cartwright 1988), indicating that by this time deposition was restored under fairly deep-water conditions.

The stratigraphic data from the Ringkobing–Fyn High demonstrates that during the Late Permian and the Triassic, whilst considerable thicknesses of sediments were accumulating in the Tail End Graben, over the greater part of the crestal region of the high deposition was limited or non-existent. It seems unrealistic to presume that this contrast between a region of non-deposition and deposition could have resulted from any process other than active faulting along the Coffee Soil Fault. The basement

faulting is therefore interpreted to have commenced at least as early as the beginning of the Triassic, and although poorly resolved on the seismic data it could conceivably have been as early as the Late Permian. This example demonstrates that the contrast between parallel and divergent reflection configurations should not be used in isolation as evidence for classifying sequences as pre- or syn-rift.

Motion styles and reflection configurations

The change from the parallel configurations of the Triassic sequence to the divergent configurations of the Middle and Upper Jurassic sequences observed in the Tail End Graben clearly represents a significant change in the style of the fault-controlled subsidence. In both the parallel and the divergent sequences there is a high degree of lateral reflection continuity. There is no evidence for any significant progradation in the form of sigmoidal reflection configurations, such as would be expected if there had been an imbalance between sediment supply and subsidence. The continuity and concordance of the stratal reflections indicates that sediment supply and fault-controlled subsidence were closely matched for most of the period of active development of the graben. Given this equilibrium between sediment supply and fault-controlled subsidence, it is then possible to relate the reflection configurations directly to the motion of the hangingwall block in a qualitative way.

The gross reflection-configurations observed in the Tail End graben are schematically illustrated in Fig. 6. The parallelism of the Triassic sequence can only be explained if the depo-

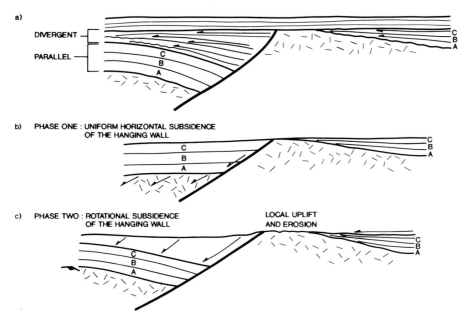

Fig. 6. Two phase rifting in the Tail End graben. The parallel and divergent configurations of the Tail End Graben are interpreted as having resulted from an initial non-rotational motion of the hangingwall block, followed by a rotational motion. Relationships depicted on the footwall block are schematic, and are extrapolated from the margins of the Ringkobing–Fyn High.

sitional surface subsided in a uniform horizontal manner throughout this interval. This in turn implies that the hangingwall motion was non-rotational during this interval, and slip vectors within the hangingwall block were parallel and of equal magnitude with the slip vector on the fault surface (Fig. 6b). Lithostratigraphic data from boreholes that penetrate the Triassic further south along the Tail End Graben confirm this pattern of lateral continuity and uniformity of palaeoenvironments, lithofacies and thickness suggested by the seismic facies (Michelsen 1982). It is not known how such a horizontal, fault-controlled subsidence was achieved, but it is probable that the graben was more symmetric, and the motion on the Coffee Soil Fault was matched by motion on a series of step faults throwing down to the east. Erosionally attenuated remnants of these faults are known from the platform area west of the graben (Cartwright 1988).

The divergence of the Jurassic sequence implies that the hangingwall motion was rotational during this interval, and slip vectors of the hangingwall block progressively decrease in magnitude away from the Coffee Soil Fault (Fig. 6c). Lithostratigraphic data are inconclusive as to whether or not there was any deepening of the marine environments across the graben, but as noted above, for most of the interval the uniformity of seismic expression argues against any radical basin-deepening towards the Coffee Soil Fault. It is evident therefore, that the unconformity at the base of the Middle Jurassic represents a change in the motion of the hangingwall block from non-rotational to rotational. An attempt at backstripping the observed thicknesses of the parallel and divergent sequences suggested that the change in motion style was accompanied by a significant acceleration in motion rate from average values of c. 100 m/ma in the Triassic to 300 m/ma in the Jurassic (Cartwright 1988).

An exception to the general equilibrium between sediment supply and subsidence occurred in the latest Jurassic. The discontinuous units observed immediately adjacent to the Coffee Soil Fault exhibit a weakly progradational form (Fig. 3), and the erosion surfaces and lensoid forms are suggestive of a complex stacking of thin progradational units whose upper surfaces dip away from the fault plane. This juxtaposition of progradational units against the fault plane suggests that, in the Late Jurassic, the sediment supply rates were unable to match the creation of accommodation by the faulting, and that progradation of fault-scarp-derived material into deeper water was initiated by this imbalance.

Dating the end of basement faulting

The precise timing of the end of active basement extension is in general difficult to establish. A simplistic approach would be to identify a marker horizon that forms the base of the earliest sequence to pass across the upper tip of the fault without any appreciable thickness variation (Fig. 5). In this approach, the assumption is made that all the sequences contained within the hangingwall block, deposited immediately prior to this overstepping marker, were effectively 'syn-rift.' This is a reasonable assumption only if the sediment supply was in equilibrium with the fault motion right up to the end of the active basement-faulting, such that there was no relief developed at the fault scarp.

Complexities in the dating of the end of fault motion arise when there is an imbalance in the sediment supply and fault-controlled sub-sidence. If the sediment supply is insufficient to infill the accommodation produced by the fault-controlled subsidence, then basin-floor relief will be accentuated and the fault will be expressed at surface as a fault scarp. In marine settings, it may be common to observe the development of a slope dipping away from the fault scarp, built up from relatively high energy progradational units, possibly including material derived directly from the erosion of the fault scarp (Fig. 7).

If the faulting ceases before the sediment supply has caught up with the excess accommo-dation produced by the earlier imbalance, then there will be a measure of basin-floor relief left over from the phase of fault-controlled subsid-ence. Depending on the organisation of the depositional systems and the shape and magni-tude of the depositional relief, this 'left-over accommodation' will then be infilled by se-quences which may look identical to the earlier syn-rift sequences, particularly if they onlap abruptly against the inactive fault scarp. Under these circumstances, sequences which are post-

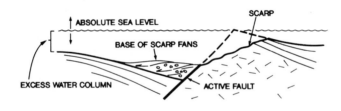

a)   **RAPID DISPLACEMENT OUTPACING SEDIMENT SUPPLY**

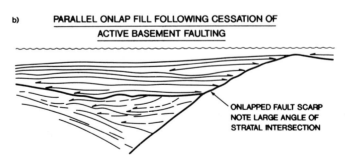

b)   **PARALLEL ONLAP FILL FOLLOWING CESSATION OF ACTIVE BASEMENT FAULTING**

Fig. 7. Stratigraphic relationships developed in the hangingwall block immediately prior to and following the end of active, basement faulting. Towards the end of rifting the fault-controlled subsidence exceeds the sediment supply, and basin-deepening and fault-scarp exposure result (Fig. 7a). Material derived from the retreating fault-scarp may form progradational wedges at the base of the fault-scarp. The 'left-over' relief at the end of rifting is then infilled in a more passive, parallel-onlap-fill geometry by post-rift sequences (Fig. 7b). The abrupt onlap of the remnant inactive fault scarp may easily be mistaken as a structural contact, particularly if the scarp has a similar dip to the underlying fault surface. This may lead to the post-rift sequence being designated as syn-rift, and to an error in the dating of the end of rifting.

rift may be misinterpreted as syn-rift, and the duration of the fault motion may be overesti- mated. This possible source of error in the interpretation of the stratigraphic relationships relating to the termination of major, exten- sional, fault activity has been discussed for several examples in the North Sea by Bertram & Milton (1989).

In certain cases, the confusion between genuine and apparent syn-rift sequences can be resolved by looking in detail at the internal reflection configurations of the sequences above and below the postulated syn-rift to post-rift boundary. If the post-rift infill takes the form of parallel onlap fill (Fig. 7b), then it can be safely assumed that the basin-floor relief was not being modified by any active deformational process during the deposition of the onlapping units, and the parallel-onlap fill can be interpreted as a post-rift sequence. In the case of the Coffee Soil Fault, the Lower Cretaceous onlaps a pro- nounced slope that dips away from the upper tip of the fault and the internal configurations of the sequence are of parallel onlap fill (cf. Figs 3 & 7b). It is apparent, therefore that 'left-over' relief was being infilled by the beginning of the Cretaceous, and that basement faulting had ceased by this time.

The configuration of the latest Jurassic units immediately beneath the prominent, basal onlap-surface (Fig. 3) are gently divergent towards the Coffee Soil Fault. This might in- itially suggest that there was active rotation of the hangingwall block throughout this interval. As noted earlier, however, the seismic facies of the units dipping away from the fault are suggestive of a stacked series of progradational bodies. The weak divergence may in part reflect the stacking geometry of the prograding wedges (Bertram & Milton 1989), and the relief ob- served at the Base Cretaceous therefore prob- ably represents the topography of the upper surface of the latest progradational cycle (Fig. 7). The gross, divergent configuration may not be fully representative, therefore, of active extension and rotation of the hangingwall block, and it is possible that fault activity ceased at some time during the deposition of the Late Jurassic prograding wedges. The vertical stack- ing and limited progradational extent of the wedges does, however, suggest that basin floor relief was being periodically rejuvenated and infilled by a combination of faulting and base of scarp progradation (Fig. 7a).

In summary, the faulting probably continued throughout much of the Late Jurassic, but the precise marker for the end of the fault activity could be at any of the upper surfaces of the individual progradational units. This example clearly demonstrates the difficulties encoun- tered in looking for unequivocal stratigraphic evidence for the termination of active basement faulting, and the circumstantial nature of many of the arguments involved in the analysis. Most importantly, this example reinforces the con- clusions drawn by Bertram & Milton (1989), regarding the mis-identification of syn- and post- rift sequences, and the significance of depo- sitional thickening related to progradation as opposed to thickening related to increments of fault displacement.

Summary of the kinematic evolution

The analysis of the reflection configurations and stratigraphy of the hangingwall and footwall blocks adjacent to the Coffee Soil Fault, in the northern part of the Tail End Graben, leads to the following kinematic evolution.

(1) The onset of rifting can only be estimated as early as the seismically resolved stratigraphy allows. Acoustic basement is at the Base Zechstein, and stratigraphic expansion across the Coffee Soil Fault is inferred to date from the Late Permian or the Early Triassic. Rifting may have been initiated much earlier in the Late Palaeozoic, but there is no seismic evidence for this in this segment of the graben.

(2) Mesozoic rifting occurred in two distinct phases, a broadly Triassic phase, which may include part or all of the Late Permian, and part of the Early Jurassic; and a broadly Mid−Late Jurassic phase. The style and magnitude of these two phases are markedly contrasting. The Triassic phase was essentially non-rotational and produced parallel reflection-configurations. The Mid−Late Jurassic phase was strongly rotational, and produced divergent reflection configurations and led to the development of the highly asymmetric, half-graben form.

(3) Towards the end of the second phase of rifting, the sediment supply was unable to keep pace with the extremely rapid fault-controlled subsidence of the hangingwall block, and the style of sedimentation adjacent to the fault plane changed from a uniform, continuous type, to a discontinuous type with repeated and vertically stacked pulses of progradation. The high rates of displacement of the hangingwall block would have been accompanied by a complimentary amplification in the rate of footwall uplift, and exposure of the fault as a scarp on the depo- sitional surface would have resulted.

(4) Close to the end of the Late Jurassic, active extension ceased. The basin floor de- pression created by the imbalance between

sediment supply and subsidence during the latest stages of the rifting was gradually infilled, initially by the final products of any remnant fault scarp degradation, and then later, during the Early Cretaceous, by less locally derived material which onlapped the upper surface of the last slope-wedge to prograde away from the trace of the inactive fault scarp.

(5) Compaction during the Early Cretaceous maintained or accentuated minor, depositional relief across the upper tip of the fault, and lowermost Chalks onlapped the crest of the progressively developing differential compaction monocline. Differential compaction continued to influence sediment accumulation adjacent to the underlying trace of the fault until the Middle Miocene.

Concluding remarks

The analysis of the reflection configurations of the hangingwall and footwall blocks to a major extensional fault can provide a considerable amount of supportive evidence for a kinematic analysis of the fault. In this study of the Coffee Soil Fault the analysis has been fairly simplistic and qualitative. The main aim has been to demonstrate some of the common problems encountered in defining the duration of extensional deformation in rift settings. Even with the uncertainties discussed for this case study, however, it has nevertheless been possible to place reasonable limits on the motion history of the Coffee Soil Fault and to identify an important contrast in style between the two main phases of motion.

The next stage in a kinematic analysis based on seismic data would ideally be to proceed to a rigorous attempt at quantifying the slip vector of the fault through its period of activity, over a series of time increments which were as small as possible. This kind of analysis would only be possible if the seismic data were fully calibrated by wells for which a high-resolution chronostratigraphy was available, and if the fluid pressures for the syn- and post-rift sequences were adequately constrained. This type of quantitative analysis could provide important data on the rates of displacement and the periodicity of the growth of displacement on longer time-scales than is possible with seismological or geomorphological studies.

This paper was written partly during the tenure of a post-doctoral fellowship funded by Sun Oil Britain Ltd., and their funding is gratefully acknowledged. The manuscript was revised under the guidance of several reviewers, and my thanks go to Harold Reading, Bruce Levell, Mark Helman, David James, George Bertram, Dick Pegrum and Alan Roberts. The seismic data was generously provided by Merlin Profilers Ltd. (now GECO Ltd.).

References

BALLY, A. W. 1983. *Seismic Expression of Structural Styles*. American Association of Petroleum Geologists, Studies in Geology **15**.

BERTELSEN, F. 1980. Lithostratigraphy and depositional history of the Danish Triassic. *Danmarks Geologiske Undersogelse*, Series B,4, 1–59.

BERTRAM, G. T. & MILTON, N. J. 1989. Reconstructing basin evolution from sedimentary thickness; the importance of palaeobathymetric control, with reference to the North Sea. *Basin Research*, **1**, 247–257.

CARTWRIGHT, J. A. 1987. Transverse structural zones in continental rifts-an example from the Danish Sector of the North Sea. *In*: BROOKS, J. & GLENNIE, K. W. (eds), *Petroleum Geology of North West Europe*. Graham & Trotman, London, 441–452.

—— 1988. *A seismic interpretation of the Danish North Sea*. D.Phil Thesis, University of 'Oxford.

—— 1990. The structural evolution of the Ringkobing-Fyn High. *In*: BLUNDELL, D. J. & GIBBS, A. D. (eds). *The tectonic evolution of the North Sea Rifts*. Oxford University Press.

FRANDSEN, N., VEJBAEK, O., MOLLER, J. J. & MICHELSEN, O. 1987. A dynamic geological model of the Danish Central Trough during the Jurassic- Early Cretaceous. *In*: BROOKS, J, & GLENNIE, K. W. (eds). *Petroleum Geology of North West Europe*. Graham & Trotman, London, 453–468.

GIBBS, A. D. 1984. Structural evolution of extensional basin margins. *Journal of the Geological Society, London*, **141**, 609–620.

GOWERS, M. B. & SAEBOE, A. 1985. On the structural evolution of the Central Trough in the Norwegian and Danish Sectors of the North Sea. *Marine and Petroleum Geology*, **2**, 298–318.

HARDING, T. P. 1984. Graben hydrocarbon occurrences and structural style. *Bulletin of the American Association of Petroleum Geologists*, **68**, 333–362.

JARVIS, G. T. & McKENZIE, D. P. 1980. Sedimentary basin formation with finite extension rates. *Earth and Planetary Science Letters*, **48**, 42–52.

McKENZIE, D. P. 1978. Some remarks on the development of sedimentary basins. *Earth and Planetary Science Letters*, **40**, 25–32.

MICHELSEN, O. 1982. The Geology of the Danish Central Graben. *Danmarks Geologiske Undersogelse*, Series B, 8.

MONTADERT, L., ROBERTS, D. G. & CHARPAL, O. 1979. Rifting, crustal attenuation and subsidence in the Bay of Biscay. *Nature*, **275**, 706–711.

ROBERTS, A. M. & YIELDING, G. (This volume) Deformation around basin-margin faults in the North Sea/mid-Norway Rift.

A flexural-cantilever simple-shear/pure-shear model of continental lithosphere extension: applications to the Jeanne d'Arc Basin, Grand Banks and Viking Graben, North Sea

N. J. KUSZNIR[1], G. MARSDEN[1] & S. S. EGAN[2]

[1]*Department of Earth Sciences, University of Liverpool, Liverpool, L69 3BX, UK*
[2]*Department of Geology, University of Keele, Keele, Staffs, ST5 5BG, UK*

Abstract: Mathematical models have been constructed of the geometric, thermal and flexural-isostatic response of the lithosphere to extension by faulting (simple-shear) in the upper crust and plastic, distributed deformation (pure-shear) in the lower crust and mantle. Models involving upper-crustal extension by both listric and planar faults have been developed. These coupled simple-shear/pure-shear models have been used to calculate extensional sedimentary basin geometry, subsidence history and crustal structure. Basin geometry and subsidence history are controlled by fault geometry (planar or listric), the amount of fault extension, fault dip, the depth of the transition from simple-shear to pure-shear, and the flexural rigidity of the lithosphere during both syn-rift and post-rift stages of basin formation.

For the planar fault model, footwall and hangingwall blocks are considered to behave as two interacting flexural cantilevers; the response of these cantilevers to the isostatic forces produced by extension generating footwall uplift and hangingwall collapse. For a set of adjacent planar faults the lateral superposition of flexural footwall uplift and hangingwall collapse generates the familiar 'domino'-style block-rotation of such multiple block fault systems. The listric fault model assumes that the hangingwall collapses onto a rigid footwall by vertical shear, and that the tectonic denudation of the upper crust by faulting generates isostatic uplift producing limited footwall uplift. Deep seismic reflection data and earthquake seismology suggest that the fundamental basement faults controlling lithosphere extension are planar. It is argued that the vertical shear construction of hangingwall collapse onto a rigid footwall is inappropriate for basement response.

The coupled simple-shear/pure-shear models of extensional basin formation, using both listric and planar fault geometries, have been applied to the formation of the Jeanne d'Arc basin, Grand Banks, and the Viking Graben of the northern North Sea. The numerical modelling shows that the crustal thinning, thermal and sediment-fill loads generated during and after lithosphere extension need to be distributed flexurally in order to generate the observed basin depth and geometry. The flexural-cantilever, planar-fault model provides closer agreement to observed basin depth and subsidence than the listric-fault model. The planar fault model also produces more footwall uplift than a listric fault model. Erosion of this footwall uplift generates substantial isostatic uplift through unloading, leading to a large underestimate of the horizontal displacement on basin-bounding faults.

The low values of effective elastic thickness obtained by extensional basin modelling are substantially less than the thickness of the cool, brittle upper crust. It is suggested that flexural bending stresses associated with lithosphere extension on planar faults are sufficiently large to generate brittle failure within the upper crust, so producing the low values of effective elastic thickness. This is consistent with the predictions of the flexural-cantilever model.

Deep seismic reflection data show the fundamental importance of major basement faults in controlling continental lithosphere extension and the formation of major extensional sedimentary basins (Fig. 1). These major basement faults extend down into the lower crust where faulting gives way to distributed, plastic deformation. To date no unequivocal example of a major dip-slip fault or shear zone passing continuously from the surface down into the upper mantle, as suggested by the model proposed by Wernicke (1985), has been observed on any deep seismic section (Kusznir & Matthews 1988).

From ROBERTS A. M., YIELDING, G. & FREEMAN, B. (eds), 1991, *The Geometry of Normal Faults*, Geological Society Special Publication No 56, pp 41−60

W   E

184 km

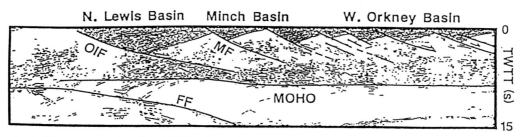

Fig. 1. Line interpretation of the DRUM deep seismic reflection profile, acquired by BIRPS to the north of Scotland, showing the control of major basement faults on lithosphere extension and sedimentary basin formation.

The major basement faults imaged on deep seismic data appear to be restricted to the cool, brittle, topmost part of the lithosphere corresponding to the seismogenic layer. Beneath the seismogenic layer, which typically has a thickness between 10 and 15 km, deformation takes place by a plastic rather than by a brittle mechanism (Jackson & McKenzie 1983; Kusznir & Park 1987). Within this region of plastic deformation in the lower crust and mantle, lithosphere extension is probably achieved by pure-shear (i.e. distributed stretching e.g. McKenzie 1978), rather than by the simple-shear (i.e. faulting) of the upper lithosphere.

Considerable debate has taken place as to whether the basement faults controlling extensional deformation within the upper and middle crust are listric or planar. Earthquake seismology (Jackson 1987) and deep seismic reflection data (e.g. Fig. 1) suggest that these fundamental basement faults are planar. However, listric faults are used by many workers in examining continental extension, probably due

to the ease with with which hangingwall collapse may be computed using the vertical shear construction (Verrall 1981) or one of its many derivatives.

Lithosphere extension causes crustal thinning and perturbations of the lithosphere temperature field. Crustal thinning and lithosphere temperature field modification lead to changes in the lithosphere density field which in turn, through isostasy, generate the subsidence responsible for extensional sedimentary basin formation (McKenzie 1978 and derivatives). Both simple-shear extensional deformation in the upper crust and pure-shear deformation in the lower-crust and mantle contribute to crustal thinning and geotherm perturbation.

A quantitative model of continental extension and sedimentary basin formation should include both simple shear and pure-shear lithosphere deformation processes and their geometric, thermal and flexural-isostatic responses. Such a quantitative model would need to compute:
(i) crustal thinning during lithosphere exten-

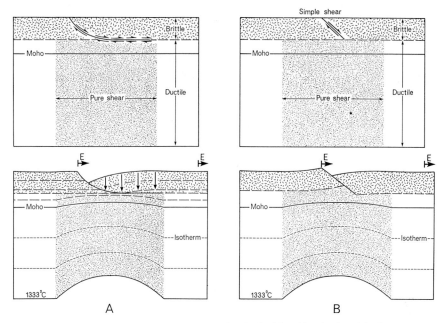

Fig. 2. A schematic representation of lithosphere extension by faulting (simple-shear) in the upper crust and pure-shear in the lower crust and mantle, showing crustal thinning and temperature field perturbation by both simple and pure-shear. (**a**) listric fault, (**b**) planar fault.

sion due to simple-shear by basement faulting in the upper crust and pure-shear (distributed plastic deformation) in the lower crust and mantle;

(ii) perturbation of the lithosphere temperature field by both simple- and pure-shear during extension;

(iii) thermal re-equilibration of the lithosphere temperature field after extension;

(iv) flexural-isostatic response of the lithosphere to crustal thinning and thermal loads; both syn-rift and post-rift.

A schematic representation of lithosphere extension by simple-shear in the upper crust and pure-shear in the lower crust and mantle for both listric and planar basement fault geometries is shown in Fig. 2. A fundamental assumption of a coupled simple-shear/pure-shear model of lithosphere deformation is that upper crustal extension by faulting is balanced at depth by pure-shear stretching within the lower crust and mantle.

In the following sections of this paper, quantitative, coupled simple-shear/pure-shear models of continental lithosphere extension and basin formation, using both planar and listric faults, are presented, their fundamental properties examined, and their predictions tested.

Lithosphere extension and sedimentary basin formation on listric faults

Introduction to the model

The formulation of the model for listric faults has been described in detail elsewhere (Kusznir & Egan 1990). The listric faults are given an exponential geometry and hangingwall deformation prior to isostatic readjustment is assumed to be accomplished by vertical-shear collapse onto the footwall (Verrall 1981; Gibbs 1984). Crustal structure and basin geometry are shown in Fig. 3a at 100 Ma following lithosphere extension by 30 km on a single fault, for a listric fault detaching at 20 km depth within the lower crust. The region of pure-shear has been given a sinusoidal distribution over a width of 100 km and is situated under the listric fault. The flexural rigidity used to distribute isostatically the lithosphere loads arising from extension corresponds to an effective elastic plate thickness of 5 km. The sedimentary basin consists of a syn-rift component locally controlled by the hangingwall collapse on the listric fault, overlain by a flexurally-distributed, post-rift, thermal-subsidence component. The footwall, proximal

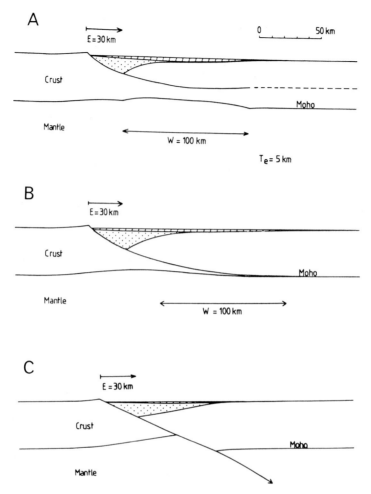

Fig. 3. Sedimentary basin geometry and crustal structure predicted by the listric fault coupled simple-shear/pure-shear model at 100 Ma after 30 km extension. Flexural rigidity corresponds to $T_e = 5$ km. W denotes the width of the pure-shear deformation. Syn-rift basin fill — dotted ornament, post-rift fill — diagonal ornament. (**a**) intracrustal detachment, (**b**) base crustal detachment, (**c**) base lithosphere detachment (Wernicke model).

to the footwall basement cutoff, shows uplift. This uplift is generated by the isostatic rebound of the basin region as faulting tectonically denudes the footwall, and basement material in the hanging wall of the fault is replaced by lighter sediment.

The mathematical model allows the detachment depth, the transition from brittle to ductile deformation, to be placed at any depth within the lithosphere. The McKenzie (1978) stretching model (detachment at the surface) and the Wernicke (1985) model (detachment at the base of the lithosphere) represent end members of the coupled simple-shear/pure-shear model.

Other notional variants on the model have been described by Weissel & Karner (1989). In Fig. 3b & 3c crustal structure and basin geometry are shown for a listric fault detaching at the base of the crust and the base of the lithosphere respectively. Fig. 3c represents a mathematical equivalent to the Wernicke model; however as discussed earlier no unequivocal evidence from deep seismic data exists showing faults extending continuously from the surface down to the base of the lithosphere or displacing the Moho. Application of the listric fault model to extension on multiple faults has been described in Kusznir & Egan (1990).

Application of the listric fault model to the Jeanne d'Arc Basin

The coupled simple-shear/pure-shear model of extensional sedimentary basin formation has been applied to the formation of the Jeanne d'Arc basin, Grand Banks, offshore eastern Canada (Fig. 4a). The Jeanne d'Arc basin formed by rifting beginning in the Triassic and continuing through into the early Cretaceous. The basin has been imaged by deep seismic reflection profiles (Fig. 4b) and contains a maximum sediment thickness of the order of 20 km (Keen et al. 1987). Tankard et al. (1990) on the basis of industry seismic, deep seismic and well data have constructed four regional cross sections across the Jeanne d'Arc basin, of which the two most northerly are shown in Fig. 5. The cross sections show a maximum thickness of Mesozoic basin fill of 17 km on the most northern line.

Fault positions and fault heaves for the major faults controlling the formation of the basin have been taken from the cross section shown in Fig. 5 and used to define a listric-fault, coupled simple-shear/pure-shear model of the Jeanne d'Arc basin. A simple model of the most northerly line of Fig. 5 uses two eastward-dipping faults, with fault heaves of 5.5 and 6.5 km respectively. The faults within the model are given surface dips of 60°, and the crust an initial thickness of 35 km. An average basin sediment-fill density of 2.6 g cm^{-3} has been used and is appropriate to the observed depth of the basin allowing for compaction.

Crustal structure and basin geometry using these faults positions and heaves and a detachment depth of 26 km (Tankard et al. 1990) are shown in Fig. 6a, predicted by the listric fault model using Airy isostasy ($T_e = 0$). The maximum depth of the basin 150 Ma after the end of rifting is 8.5 km, compared with the observed thickness of c. 17 km. Both fault geometry and Moho are highly distorted as a consequence of the local (Airy) isostasy.

The effect of using a finite flexural strength for the lithosphere ($T_e = 5$ km) is shown in Fig. 6b. The effect of flexurally distributing the isostatic forces is to deepen the basin to c. 11.5 km maximum depth. The finite flexural rigidity also leaves the Moho and fault geometries smoother and less deformed. The calculated basin depth is still substantially less than the observed 17 km. The effect of deepening the detachment depth to the base of the crust (Fig. 6c) changes the crustal structure and basin geometry and increases the footwall uplift. Deepening the detachment level does not,

however, perceptibly increase the depth of the basin.

The listric fault model does not seem able to generate the profile of Tankard et al. across the Jeanne d'Arc basin.

Listric versus planar faults and the inapplicability of the vertical-shear construction to basement deformation

The listric fault model does not seem able to simulate the formation of the Jeanne d'Arc basin. One possible reason may be that the major basement faults are not in reality listric. Even on time sections the major basement reflections seen on deep seismic sections (Figs 1 & 7a) appear to be straight rather than listric as they descend from the surface down into the lower crust, where they are lost in the sub-horizontal reflections of the lower crust. When depth-converted these faults are shown to be planar (Fig. 7b). This planar geometry revealed by seismic reflection data for basement extensional faults is also supported by the evidence of earthquake seismology (Jackson 1987; Stein & Barrientos 1985). Peddy (pers. comm) has shown that the major basin-bounding fault of the Jeanne d'Arc basin (Fig. 4b) is also planar when depth converted. The fundamental architecture of continental lithosphere extension, consisting of planar faults cutting the seismogenic brittle upper crust with distributed plastic deformation in the lower crust and mantle, is summarized in Fig. 2b.

If a planar basement-fault geometry is used with the hangingwall vertical-shear construction (Verrall 1981) then the crustal structure and basin geometry shown in Fig. 8 result. The basin so produced is unrealistic with a flat bottom, and inclined straight sides, and does not resemble real extensional sedimentary basins. The explanation for this unrealistic basin geometry rests with the vertical-shear construction. The vertical-shear construction assumes that the weak hangingwall collapses onto a rigid footwall, i.e. it assumes that the hangingwall is infinitely weak while the footwall is infinitely strong. This fundamental assumption of the vertical shear construction is clearly invalid for basement response, where rocks of similar rheology are juxtaposed by faulting. The vertical-shear construction is equally invalid for basement response irrespective of whether the basement faulting is planar or listric. A superior model for footwall and hangingwall lithosphere behaviour during extension would give both footwall and hangingwall blocks similar mechanical properties.

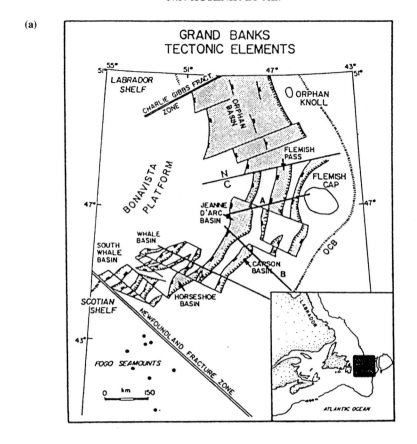

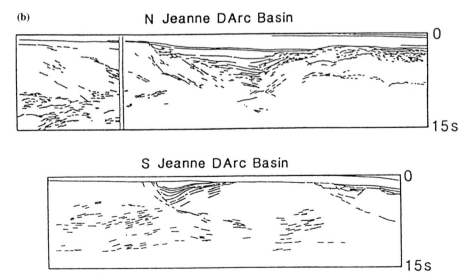

Fig. 4. (**a**) Location map showing the Mesozoic Jeanne d'Arc basin on the Grand Banks east of Newfoundland (Tankard *et al.* 1990). (**b**) Deep seismic reflection profiles (Keen *et al.* 1987) across the northern and southern Jeanne d'Arc basin.

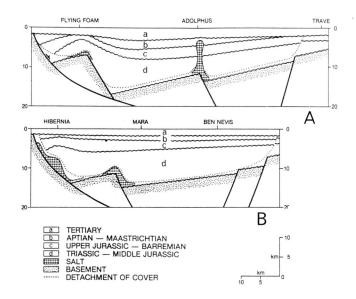

Fig. 5. Cross sections across the northern Jeanne d'Arc basin (Tankard *et al.* 1990). (a) Flying Foam — Trave profile. (b) Hibernia — Ben Nevis profile.

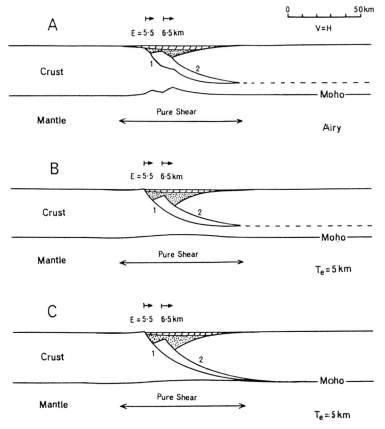

Fig. 6. Application of the listric simple-shear/pure-shear model to the Flying Foam — Trave profile across the northern Jeanne d'Arc basin (Fig. 5). Extension on fault 1 is 5.5 km and fault 2 is 6.5 km. Initial fault dip = 60°. Crustal thickness = 35 km. (**a**) Airy isostasy ($T_e = 0$) and detachment depth = 26 km. (**b**) Flexural isostasy ($T_e = 5$ km) and detachment depth = 26 km. (**c**) Flexural isostasy ($T_e = 5$ km) and detachment depth = 35 km.

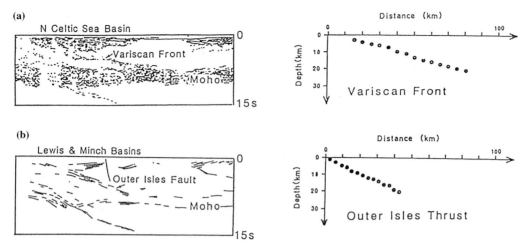

Fig. 7. (**a**) Deep seismic reflection profiles acquired by BIRPS across the North Celtic Sea and Lewis/Minch basin showing major extensional basement faults controlling basin formation extending down from surface to the top of the reflective lower crust at approximately 6 sec two-way traveltime. These faults look planar rather than listric even on the time sections. (**b**) Depth converted fault geometries of (a) using stacking velocities, showing the planar basement faults of (a) extending down to 20 km depth.

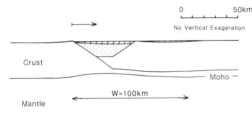

Fig. 8. An unrealistic, symmetric and flat-bottomed basin produced by extension on a planar fault using the vertical-shear hangingwall-collapse construction.

Lithosphere extension and sedimentary basin formation on planar faults

The flexural cantilever model

To overcome the problem of the vertical-shear construction when used with planar faults, a mathematical model has been developed which assumes that during extensional faulting the footwall and hangingwall blocks behave as two interacting flexural cantilevers, the response of these cantilevers to the isostatic forces produced by extension generating footwall uplift and hangingwall collapse. The hangingwall collapse so produced is generated by flexural isostatic bending of the lithosphere, as is the footwall uplift (Fig. 2b). In reality such bending may be accomplished by the summation of co-seismic displacement during individual earthquakes and isostatic post-seismic uplift (King *et al.* 1988; Stein *et al.* 1988). This new model has been named the flexural cantilever model (Kusznir & Egan 1990).

The flexural cantilever model considers the long-term, post-seismic isostatic balance of the lithosphere following extension and is applicable over timescales $> 0.1-1.0$ Ma. It is not a dynamic, fault-growth model (cf. Walsh & Wattesson 1987) to be used over the co-seismic timescale. Co-seismic footwall and hangingwall vertical displacements during active faulting have been shown to be consistent with an elastic-dislocation process within a self-gravitating lithosphere (King *et al.* 1988). Co-seismically the flexural-isostatic process experiences a large effective elastic thickness comparable with the thickness of the lithosphere. However, as creep within the lower crust and mantle progresses with time and the initial elastic dislocation and lower lithosphere bending stresses are relieved, the effective elastic thickness of the lithosphere is greatly reduced, such that the flexural strength of the lithosphere arises solely from the brittle/elastic upper crust. Rheological modelling suggests that this post-seismic flexural-isostatic relaxation takes of the order of $0.1-1.0$ Ma to reach equilibrium (Kusznir & Park 1984; Kusznir & Karner 1985). During post-seismic relaxation, footwall and hangingwall blocks are assumed to be welded together, with the lithosphere behaving as a single plate. In this respect the flexural cantilever model differs from earlier analyses of the mechanics of footwall/hangingwall interaction during crustal extension on a planar fault by Heiskanen & Vening-Meinesz (1958) and Jackson & McKenzie (1983), who assumed that the fault is not welded as long-term isostatic balance is achieved. The flexural cantilever model is more similar to the model described by Buck (1988).

The flexural cantilever model is also a coupled simple-shear/pure-shear model of continental extension and assumes that the brittle (seismogenic) upper crust deforms by faulting on planar faults, while the ductile lower crust and mantle deform by distributed pure-shear. As with the listric fault model, the flexural cantilever model incorporates the isostatic consequences of syn-rift lithosphere temperature field perturbation and post-rift re-equilibration on sedimentary basin formation. Sediment loading effects are also included. The assumptions and behaviour of the model are summarized in Fig. 2b. The model and its mathematical formulation are described briefly in Appendix 1, and will be described in greater detail in a subsequent paper.

The calculated predictions of the flexural cantilever model are shown in Fig. 9 for lithosphere extension by 10 km on a planar fault. Crustal structure and basin geometry are shown at the end of rifting but before geotherm re-equilibration and thermal subsidence. The isostatic-loading consequences of filling the rift to a regional datum (sea level) with sediment are included. The hangingwall shows the familiar rollover geometry. The pure-shear within the lower crust and mantle is distributed symmetrically beneath the fault.

The effect of extending the lithosphere on a set of planar faults is shown in Fig. 10. For a set of adjacent planar faults the lateral superposition of flexural footwall uplift and hangingwall

collapse produces the familiar 'domino'-style block rotation of such multiple fault systems. For each internal block, the block is flexed upward by its hangingwall fault and downward by its footwall fault, such that it is first bent one way and then unbent the other, thereby suffering a net rotation. The fault itself is also rotated, becoming shallower in dip. The region of 'domino'-style extension terminates by footwall uplift and hangingwall collapse on its bounding faults. The flexural cantilever model also allows for multiple fault extension on unequally spaced faults with differing fault heaves and dips.

The effect of thermal subsidence on the multiple planar-fault model is shown in Fig. 10b. At the time of rifting footwall uplift can elevate fault block crests above sea level where they may be eroded. If this erosion takes place at the time of rifting, thermal re-equilibration and cooling generates a basin consisting of discrete rift sub-basins with a continuous cover of post-rift, thermal-subsidence sediment (Fig. 10c).

Application of the planar fault model to the Jeanne d'Arc Basin

Application of the flexural cantilever (planar fault) model to the Jeanne d'Arc basin is shown in Fig 11. Similar fault position, fault heave, effective elastic thickness and other lithosphere parameters are used as in the listric model of Fig. 8. The effect of using the flexural cantilever model rather than the listric model is to deepen the basin to 14.5 km.

The planar fault model also produces more footwall uplift, approximately 2.5 km adjacent to the western basin-bounding fault given the fault heaves of Fig. 11. Today no footwall uplift is observed in this region (the Bonavista platform) and presumably any footwall uplift that had existed has now been eroded. Since the extension that gave rise to the Jeanne d'Arc basin spanned the Triassic through to Early Cretaceous, the erosion may have kept pace with footwall uplift such that the erosion may have been complete before the start of thermal subsidence in the mid Cretaceous. If erosion of the footwall uplift adjacent to the western basin-bounding fault has occurred, as it almost certainly has, then the fault heave of the basin-bounding fault seen on the section of Tankard *et al.* (1990; and Fig. 5 of this paper) and used in the models of Figs 6 and 11 must be an underestimate. Roberts & Yielding (this volume) reached similar deductions about eroded basin margins in the North Sea.

The preferred model for the northern line of

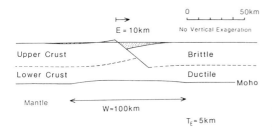

Fig. 9. Syn-rift basin geometry and crustal structure predicted by the flexural cantilever model following lithosphere extension by 10 km on a planar fault. $T_e = 5$ km. Thermal uplift and sediment loading is included in the model.

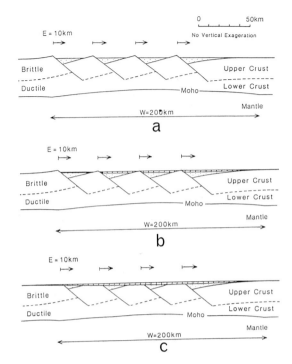

Fig. 10. Sedimentary basin geometry and crustal structure following lithosphere extension by 10 km each on 4 planar faults. (**a**) Syn-rift. (**b**) Post-rift at 100 Ma after extension. (**c**) Post-rift at 100 Ma after syn-rift erosion of uplifted fault block crests. Syn-rift basin-fill represented by dotted ornament and post-rift fill by diagonal ornament.

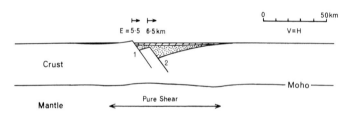

Fig. 11. Application of the flexural cantilever, planar fault model to the Flying Foam-Trave Jeanne d'Arc basin profile (Fig. 5). Extension on fault 1 is 5.5 km and fault 2 is 6.5 km. Initial fault dip = 60°. Crustal thickness = 35 km. T_e = 5 km. The planar fault model produces a deeper, broader basin than the listric model, with more footwall uplift (Fig. 6).

Tankard *et al.* across the Jeanne d'Arc is shown in Fig. 12 and has a total pre-erosion fault heave of 12 km on the basin-bounding fault. Two smaller faults (one synthetic and one antithetic) have been included in the planar fault model. The effective elastic thickness of the preferred model is 10 km. The syn-rift stage of the model is shown in Fig. 12a and shows a basin-bounding footwall uplift of *c.* 3 km. Erosion of this footwall uplift and the subsequent isostatic rebound, which in turn results in further erosion and

rebound, has been computed and is shown in Fig. 12b. The post-erosion heave is 5.5 km and is consistent with that observed today (Fig. 5). Some 5 km of footwall must have been eroded off the Bonavista platform basin-bounding footwall. If this erosion was distributed through the 80 Ma or so during which extension took place (Triassic to Early Cretaceous), the erosion rates of 0.07 mm a^{-1} are not unreasonable.

If the model is allowed to cool and thermally subside to a time equivalent to the present day,

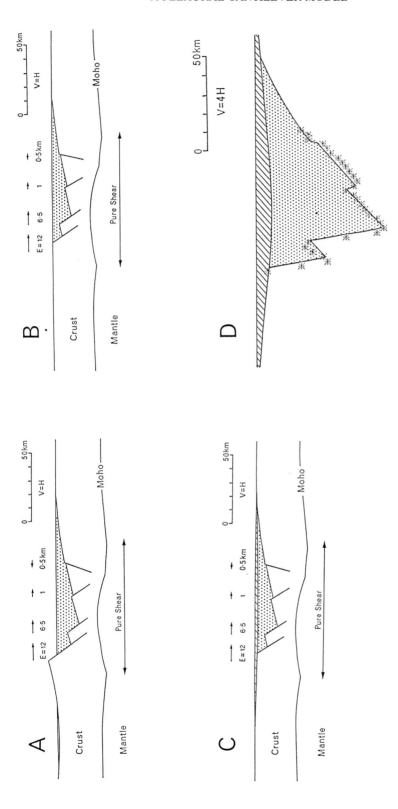

Fig. 12. The preferred flexural cantilever model of the Flying Foam — Trave profile across the Jeanne d'Arc basin. The basin-bounding fault has an extension of 12 km. The other large fault has a heave of 6.5 km. Two smaller faults have been included with fault heaves of 1 and 0.5 km — one of the faults being antithetic. Crustal thickness = 35 km, T_e = 10 km, and initial fault dip = 60°. (**a**) Basin geometry and crustal structure at syn-rift stage. (**b**) End syn-rift removal of footwall uplift by erosion, which has induced further flexural-isostatic rebound. (**c**) Present-day post-rift geometry and crustal structure. The modelled basin depth of 17 km is comparable with that observed. (**d**) Comparison of basin depth predicted by the flexural cantilever model (solid lines) with observed basin depth (*ornament). Vertical exaggeration = 4.

then the crustal structure and basin geometry shown in Fig. 12c results. The maximum basin depth of 17 km agrees with that observed. In Fig. 12d the observed and modelled basin depths are compared. The agreement is generally good both within the basin and on the basin flanks.

The results of modelling the second more southerly cross section of Tankard et al. (1990, Fig. 5) are shown in Fig. 13 for syn-rift, post-erosion, and post-rift thermal subsidence (present day) stages. The agreement between observed and model predictions are good. The flexural cantilever model gives a reasonable prediction of the observed thicknesses of syn- and post-rift sequence within the Jeanne d'Arc basin (Fig. 5).

Both the flexural cantilever and listric fault models described above are instantaneous stretching models. As discussed earlier the formation of the Jeanne d'Arc basin started in the Triassic and continued through into the Early Cretaceous, spanning a period of 80 Ma, a significantly long time compared with the thermal time-constant of the lithosphere. Compared with the instantaneous rifting model, the cooling during extension of a protracted rift model would generate more syn-rift subsidence and a higher ratio of syn- to post-rift sediments. The duration of rifting should not, however, have a major effect on the total basin depth at large times after the cessation of rifting.

The above models of the formation of the Jeanne d'Arc basin are also a simplification in that the extension direction for the Jeanne d'Arc basin changed by 90° from NW−SE during the Triassic to SW−NE during the Cretaceous (Hubbard 1988). Only extension within the plane of the sections of Tankard et al. (Fig. 5) has been modelled.

Discussion and conclusions

Coupled simple-shear/pure-shear models incorporating the geometric, thermal and flexural-isostatic consequences of lithosphere extension have been developed and applied to the formation of extensional sedimentary basins. The numerical modelling of the Jeanne d'Arc basin shows that the crustal thinning, thermal perturbation and sediment-fill loads generated during and after lithosphere extension need to be distributed flexurally in order to generate the observed basin depths, subsidence history and Moho topography of the Jeanne d'Arc basin.

Deep seismic reflection profiling and earthquake seismology suggest that the major faults controlling lithosphere extension are planar rather than listric. Lithosphere extension is achieved by extension on these planar faults within the brittle upper crust and by distributed plastic stretching (pure-shear) within the lower crust and mantle. The vertical shear construction is inappropriate for modelling lithosphere extension on planar faults. Instead a model in which both footwall and hangingwall basement blocks are regarded as acting as two mutually-self-supporting flexural cantilevers is preferred. This model, the flexural cantilever model, may be applied to lithosphere extension on multiple faults and predicts the familiar 'domino-style' block rotations of extensional tectonics. In contrast to earlier multiple-fault-block rotation models (Jackson & McKenzie 1983; Barr 1987) the flexural cantilever model may be applied to faults of arbitrary spacing, horizontal displacement and throw direction, and does not require the structure to be repeated laterally to infinity.

The flexural cantilever planar fault model, when applied to the Jeanne d'Arc basin, provides closer agreement to observed basin depth and subsidence than does the listric fault model using vertical shear. The application of the flexural cantilever model to the Jeanne d'Arc basin suggests that lithosphere extension on planar basement faults generates substantial footwall uplift, leading to significant footwall erosion.

The flexural-cantilever coupled simple-shear/pure-shear model shows that the fundamental building-block of extensional sedimentary basin formation is a localized rift sub-basin overlain by a broader and thinner post-rift thermal-subsidence sub-basin (Figs 12 & 13). Extensional sedimentary basins, formed by lithosphere extension on many major faults, are generated by the superposition of the above fundamental building blocks forming a series of discrete rift sub-basins overlain by a continuous post-rift thermal subsidence basin (Fig. 10c). Because of this superposition effect multiple fault basins have a relatively thicker post-rift thermal subsidence sequence than single fault basins.

The Viking Graben, North Sea

This effect can be illustrated by the application of the flexural cantilever model to the formation of the Viking Graben, northern North Sea (Marsden et al. 1990). Both Triassic and Jurassic stages of rifting have been modelled, and compaction is included. Jurassic fault extensions and positions, for input to the mathematical model, have been determined using industry seismic reflection data (Figure 2 of Marsden et al. 1990). Crustal structure, basin geometry and the thicknesses of syn- and post-rift se-

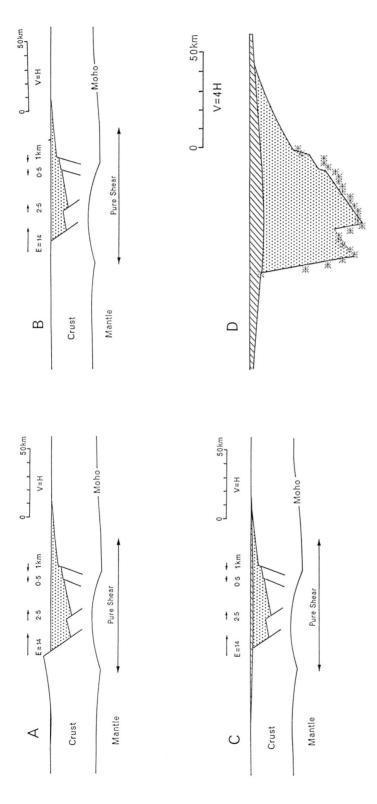

Fig. 13. The preferred flexural cantilever model of the Hibernia − Ben Nevis profile across the Jeanne d'Arc basin. The basin-bounding fault has an extension of 14 km. Three smaller faults have fault heaves of 2.5, 0.5 and 0.5 km — two of these smaller faults being antithetic. Crustal thickness = 35 km, T_e = 10 km, and initial fault dip = 60°. (**a**) Basin geometry and crustal structure at syn-rift stage. (**b**) End syn-rift removal of footwall uplift by erosion, which has induced further flexural-isostatic rebound. (**c**) Present day post-rift geometry and crustal structure. The modelled basin depth is comparable with that observed. (**d**) Comparison of basin depth predicted by the flexural cantilever model (solid lines) with observed basin depth (* ornament). Vertical exaggeration = 4.

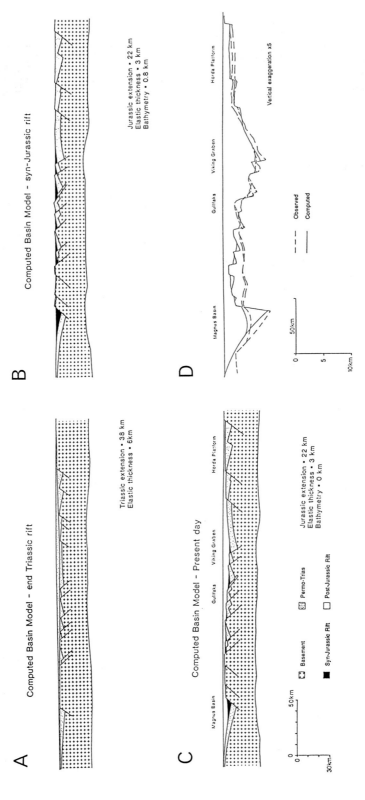

Fig. 14. Application the flexural cantilever model to a northern North Sea profile, running across the Viking Graben from the Magnus Basin (NW) to the Horda Platform (SE) (from Marsden *et al.* 1990). Predicted crustal structure and basin geometry: (**a**) at the end of the Middle Jurassic after initial Triassic rifting, (**b**) at the end of the Jurassic after Late Jurassic rifting, (**c**) at the present day after Cretaceous – Tertiary post-rift thermal subsidence. (**d**) comparison of modelled and observed thicknesses of Jurassic syn-rift and Cretaceous-Tertiary post-rift basin fill. Vertical exaggeration = 4.

quences predicted by the flexural cantilever model are shown at the end of the Middle Jurassic after Triassic rifting and thermal subsidence (Fig. 14a), at the end of Jurassic rifting (Fig. 14b), and at the present day after Cretaceous and Tertiary thermal subsidence (Fig. 14c). A comparison of observed and modelled Jurassic syn-rift and Cretaceous–Tertiary post-rift thicknesses are shown in Figure 14d. The agreement is generally good. The model predicts the uplift and erosion of the rotated fault block crests over the Shetland Terrace (e.g. Gullfaks) and the large thickness of Cretaceous–Tertiary within the Viking Graben.

Bending stresses and the effective elastic thickness

A best fit of observed and calculated basin geometry for the Viking Graben is achieved using an effective elastic thickness (T_e) of 6 km for the initial Triassic extension and 3 km for the subsequent Jurassic rifting. The best fit T_e for the Jeanne d'Arc basin is slightly greater at 10 km. Application of the flexural cantilever model to the formation of the Lake Tanganyika rift in East Africa (Kusznir & Morley 1990) gives a value of T_e of 3 km. Flexural backstripping of the same Viking Graben profile described above gives a Cretaceous–Tertiary T_e of 3 km or less (Kusznir, unpublished results).

These values of T_e are substantially less than the 15–20 km or so thickness of the brittle seismogenic layer which contains the planar faults. The T_e is by definition the thickness of an unbroken, perfectly elastic lithosphere plate that would have the same effective flexural rigidity as the lithosphere. What then is the physical relationship between the T_e and the thickness of the brittle seismogenic layer?

The flexural bending of the lithosphere associ-

(a)

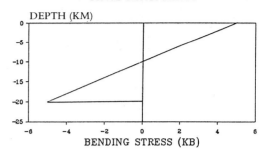

(b)

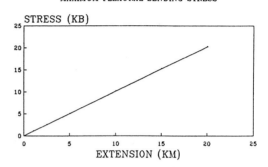

(c)

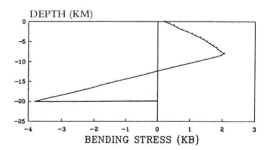

(d)

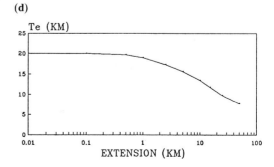

Fig. 15. (**a**) Elastic bending stresses versus depth for a perfectly elastic plate 20 km thick. Maximum bending stress = ± 5 kbars. (**b**) Relationship between maximum elastic bending stress and fault extension predicted by the flexural cantilever model. Fault dip = 60°. T_e = 20 km. (**c**) Bending stresses versus depth after brittle failure within a plate 20 km thick. Initial elastic bending stress = ± 5 kb. Brittle failure envelopes have been computed by Griffiths theory using a coefficient of friction of 0.5, a uniaxial tensile strength of 0.2 kbars and an overburden density of 3.0 g cm^{-3}. (**d**) The predicted decrease in T_e with increase in fault extension, due to brittle failure generated by bending stresses.

ated with the flexural 'collapse' of the hanging-wall and uplift of the footwall generates bending stresses within the lithosphere (also see Buck 1988). For a perfectly elastic plate the bending stresses are greatest at the top and bottom of the plate (but of opposite sign), and zero at the mid-depth of the plate (the neutral fibre), as illustrated in Fig. 15a. Using the flexural cantilever model, for an unbroken elastic plate of thickness 20 km, 7.5 km extension on a single planar fault, gives maximum flexural bending stresses of the order of many kbars (Fig. 16a). For the flexural cantilever model the maximum bending stress is directly proportional to the fault extension (Fig. 15b).

Bending stresses of several kilobars would exceed the brittle strength of the upper lithosphere and cause extensive fracturing of the brittle upper crust. The bending stresses would still be distributed over a thickness of 20 km but would be limited to lie within the brittle-failure envelope (Fig. 15c). This brittle failure would greatly reduce the flexural rigidity of the lithosphere generating a T_e much less than the original value of 20 km. Since bending stresses increase with fault extension, as extension is increased the degree of fracturing would be expected to increase, leading to a decrease in T_e. The computed relationship between extension and T_e is shown in Fig. 15d.

The corresponding maximum bending stresses to those shown in Fig. 16a, for T_e of 3 km (still distributing the stresses over a depth of 20 km) are shown in Fig. 16b and are of the order of 1 kbar or less. The mathematical theory relating to the calculation of bending stresses will be described in detail in a subsequent paper. The maximum-bending-stress profile for the Jurassic Viking graben profile is shown in Fig. 17.

While the values of effective elastic thickness,

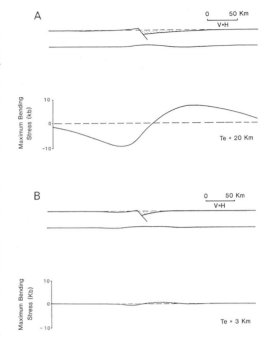

Fig. 16. Maximum bending stresses predicted by the flexural cantilever model arising from 7.5 km extension on a planar fault initially dipping at 60°. (**a**) No brittle failure. $T_e = 20$ km with flexural bending stresses distributed over 20 km depth. (**b**) With brittle failure. $T_e = 3$ km with flexural bending stresses distributed over 20 km depth, corresponding to the brittle-elastic upper crust.

T_e, operative during continental rifting may be small and of the order of only a few kilometres, it should be noted that the difference between $T_e = 0$ and $T_e = 3$ km, for example, is substantial in terms of the geological consequences. For small but finite values of T_e, of the

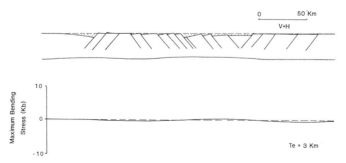

Fig. 17. Maximum bending stresses, after brittle failure, predicted by the flexural cantilever model for the Viking Graben profile, arising from Late Jurassic rifting. $T_e = 3$ km. Bending stresses are distributed over a depth of 20 km corresponding to the approximate thickness of the brittle seismogenic layer.

order of a few kilometres, footwall uplift and the familiar 'domino-style' block rotations of extensional tectonics can occur. However if the elastic thickness T_e were zero, corresponding to perfect Airy isostasy, these processes would not occur and their associated structural and sedimentological consequences would be absent.

We are indebted to our colleagues within the Department of Earth Sciences at the University of Liverpool and elsewhere for their valuable inspiration, discussion, help and encouragement. In particular we would like to thank (in alphabetical order!): Mike Badley, Derek Blundell, Garry Karner, Mark Newall, Alan Roberts, Tony Tankard, John Walsh, Juan Watterson, Rob Westaway, Graham Yielding and Peter Ziegler. Dave Barr and Joe Cartwright provided very useful critical reviews of this paper.

Appendix A: a description of the flexural cantilever model

1. The flexural cantilever model assumes that continental lithosphere extension occurs by planar faulting in the upper crust and plastic deformation in the lower crust and mantle (Fig. A1).

2. Let us first consider the effects of the extension of the upper crust by the planar fault. Consider a hypothetical lithosphere in which there is no mantle, only crust, and as a consequence no Moho with its associated density contrast (Fig. A2a). The planar fault is assumed to terminate at some depth within a fluid of similar density to the upper crust. If the planar fault is given a horizontal displacement E and the footwall and hangingwalls blocks are kept in contact, in the absence of gravity, the geometry shown in Fig. A2b results. The upper crustal surface $u(x)$ is given by

$$
\begin{array}{ll}
u(x) = 0 & x < 0 \\
u(x) = x \tan(\theta) & 0 < x < E \\
u(x) = E \tan(\theta) & E < x
\end{array}
$$

where $x = 0$ corresponds to the horizontal coordinate of the footwall cutoff and θ is the dip of the planar fault.

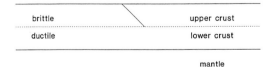

Fig. A1. Lithosphere extension is assumed to take place by planar faulting in the brittle upper crust and distributed (pure-shear) deformation within the lower crust and mantle.

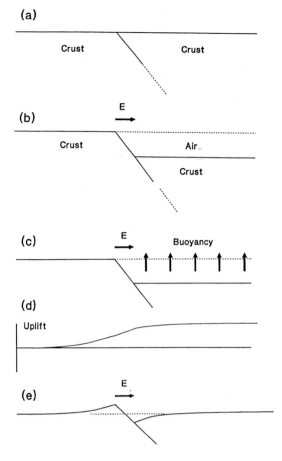

Fig. A2. Diagram summarizing the flexural isostatic interaction of foot-and hangingwall blocks during extension on a planar fault, neglecting the density contrast across the Moho between crust and mantle. See text for further explanation.

For the geometry shown in Fig. A2b, crust has been replaced by air in the hangingwall region. If gravity is 'switched on' this will result in a buoyancy force acting in the hangingwall (Fig. A2c). The buoyancy force, $l_b(x)$ is given by

$$
l_b(x) = -u(x)\,\rho_c\,g
$$

where ρ_c is crustal density and g is gravitational acceleration.

Assuming that this buoyancy force is distributed flexurally, i.e. the lithosphere has finite flexural strength, then the flexural-isostatic uplift shown in Fig. A2d results. The flexural-isostatic uplift $w_b(x)$ can be computed in the wavenumber domain by

$$
W_b(k) = R(k)\,L_b(x)
$$

where $R(k)$ is the isostatic response function such that

$$R(k) = 1/((\rho_c - \rho_a) g + Dk^4)$$

and D is flexural rigidity, k is wavenumber = $2\pi/\lambda$, and ρ_a is the density of air. $W_b(k)$ and $L_b(k)$ are the Fourier transforms of $w_b(x)$ and $l_b(x)$ respectively.

If this uplift is applied to the post-extensional geometry shown in Fig. A2b, then the foot- and hangingwall geometry shown in Fig. A2e results. The resultant upper crustal surface $s(x)$ is given by

$$s(x) = u(x) + w_b(x).$$

3. Let us consider the conservation of brittle upper crust, thickness t, during the extension process (Fig. A3a). During the extension process an area $E\ t$ of upper brittle crust is laterally taken out of the section. Four regions are identified in Fig. A3a (areas A, B, C and D). By conservation of area

$$E\ t + A - B - C + D = 0$$

where a gain in area is positive and a loss negative. Since $A = B$ this becomes

$$E\ t - C + D = 0.$$

Clearly the upper crustal layer around the fault loses an area equivalent to $(C - D)$ at its base. This loss of area at the base of the brittle upper crust will be compensated by an upward flow of the fluid lower crust. This inward flow of the fluid lower crust will in turn be compensated by an upward flow of fluid mantle material. The resultant perturbation of the Moho assuming vertical flow is shown in Fig. A3b and results in abrupt Moho topography. It is perhaps more reasonable to assume that the ductile flow within the lower crust and mantle, arising from area conservation, would become more distributed with increasing depth as shown in Fig. A3c. Whatever the geometry of the flow, an area $(C - D)$ of lower crust will be replaced by mantle. No density contrast is yet assumed to exist across the Moho between crust and mantle.

4. The ductile lower crust is also assumed to be thinned by pure-shear during extension. A fundamental assumption of the coupled simple-shear/pure-shear model is that extension in the upper lithosphere on planar faults is balanced at depth by pure-shear extension.

Let us assume that the pure-shear beneath the brittle-ductile transition is localized and can be represented by a sinusoidal pure-shear stretching factor (cf. McKenzie 1978) β such that

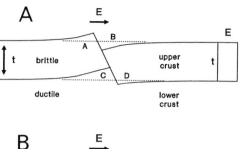

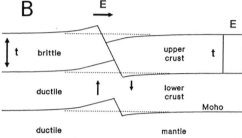

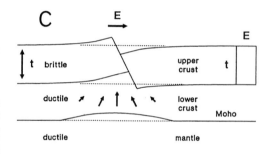

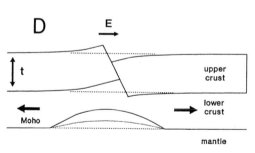

Fig. A3. Diagram summarizing mass conservation requirements following brittle, upper-crustal extension and the associated ductile flow in the lower crust and mantle and consequent perturbation of the Moho. See text for further explanation.

$$\beta = 1 + C \sin (\pi x/W)$$

where $1 + C$ is the maximum stretching β factor (N.B. $\beta = 1$ represents no extension), and W is the width of the pure-shear region.

Upper lithosphere extension E by faulting (simple-shear) must be exactly balanced by deep lithosphere extension by pure-shear.

Hence

$$E = \int_0^{W'} (\beta(x) - 1)\, dx$$

$$= \int_0^{W'} C \sin(\pi x/W)\, dx$$

where W' is the pre-extension width of the pure-shear region.

Provided $W \gg E$ integration of the above equation yields

$$E = 2\, C\, W'/\pi$$

or

$$C = (\pi E)/(2\,(W - E))$$

where W is post-extension pure-shear width.

5. The thinning of the lower crust by pure-shear extension will also cause an elevation of the Moho. If $r_{lc}(x)$ is this Moho elevation due to lower crustal pure-shear

$$r_{lc}(x) = -(d - t)(1 - 1/\beta_{lc}(x))$$

where d is crustal thickness, $\beta_{lc}(x)$ is the stretching factor in the lower crust and mantle, and depth is measured positive down.

The elevation of the Moho due to the thinning of the upper brittle crust, $r_{uc}(x)$, may also be represented by a pure-shear stretching factor $\beta_{uc}(x)$ such that

$$r_{uc}(x) = -t\,(1 - 1/\beta_{uc}(x)).$$

The total elevation of the Moho, $r(x)$ due to 'real' pure-shear in the lower crust and 'pseudo' pure-shear in the upper crust is given by

$$r(x) = -(d - t)(1 - 1/\beta_{lc}(x)) \\ - t\,(1 - 1/\beta_{uc}(x)).$$

If the 'real' and 'pseudo' pure-shear are given the same shape such that $\beta_{lc}(x) = \beta_{uc}(x) = \beta(x)$ then

$$r(x) = -(d - t)(1 - 1/\beta(x)) - t\,(1 - 1/\beta(x)) \\ = -d\,(1 - 1/\beta(x)).$$

The resultant upward perturbation of the Moho is represented in Fig. A3d.

6. Any vertical displacement which disturbs the Moho will invoke an isostatic restoring force by virtue of the density constrast between crust and mantle. If the Moho is elevated by $r(x)$, a load $l_m(x)$ will be generated such that

$$l_m(x) = r(x)\,(\rho_c - \rho_m)\,g$$

where ρ_m is mantle density.

The flexural-isostatic response $w_m(x)$ arising from this load is given by

$$W_m(k) = R(k)\, L_m(k)$$

where $R(k) = 1/((\rho_m - \rho_a)\,g + D\,k^4)$.

7. The resultant surface topography, Moho and fault geometries are given by

Surface topography

$$s(x) = u(x) + w_b(x) + w_m(x)$$

Moho topography

$$m(x) = d + r(x) + w_m(x)$$

Fault geometry

$$f(x) = x\,\tan(\theta) + w_b(x) + w_m(x).$$

8. Other isostatic loads are generated during both syn- and post-rift stages of basin formation and must be included in the model. These are as follows.

Syn-rift

Thermal uplift (computed using pure-shear approximation); sediment fill (computed iteratively); erosion (computed iteratively).

Post-rift

Thermal subsidence (computed using pure-shear approximation); sediment fill (computed iteratively); compaction.

Flexure for all loads is calculated in the wave-number domain using

$$W(k) = R(k)\, L(k).$$

References

BARR, D. 1987. Lithospheric stretching, detached normal faulting and footwall uplift. *In*: COWARD, M. P., DEWEY, J. F. & HANCOCK, P. L. (eds). *Continental Extensional Tectonics.* Geological Society, London, Special Publication **28**, 75−94.

BUCK, R.W. 1988. Flexural Rotation of Normal Faults. *Tectonics*, **7**, 959−973.

GIBBS, A. D. 1984. Structural evolution of extensional basin margins. *Journal of the Geological Society, London*, **141**, 609−620.

HUBBARD, R. J. 1988. Age and significance of Sequence Boundaries on Jurassic and Early Cretaceous Rifted Continental Margin. *American Association of Petroleum Geologists Bulletin*, **72**, 49−72.

HEISKANEN, W. A. & VENING-MEINESZ, F. A. 1958. *The Earth and its gravity field.* McGraw-Hill, New York.

JACKSON, J. A. 1987. Active normal faulting and crustal extension. *In*: COWARD, M. P., DEWEY, J. F. & HANCOCK, P. L. (eds). *Continental Exten-*

sional Tectonics. Geological Society, London, Special Publication **28**, 3–17.

—— & McKenzie, D. P. 1983. The geometrical evolution of normal fault systems. *Journal of Structural Geology*, **5**, 471–482.

Keen, C. E., Boutilier, R., de Voogd, B., Mudford, B. & Enachescu, M. E. 1987. Crustal geometry and extensional models for the Grand Banks, eastern Canada: constraints from deep seismic reflection data. *In*: Beaumont, C. & Tankard, A. J. (eds). *Sedimentary basins and basin forming mechanisms.* Canadian Society of Petroleum Geologists, Memoir **12**, 101–115.

King, G. C. P., Stein, R. S. & Rundle, J. B. 1988. The Growth of Geological Structures by Repeated Earthquakes, 1, Conceptual Framework. *Journal of Geophysical Research*, **93**, 13307–19.

Kusznir, N. J. & Egan, S. S. 1990. Simple-shear and Pure-shear models of extensional sedimentary basin formation: application to the Jeanne d'Arc Basin, Grand Banks of Newfoundland. *In*: Tankard, A. J. & Balkwill, H. R. (eds) *Extensional Tectonics of the North Atlantic Margins.* American Association of Petroleum Geologists Memoir **46**, 305–322.

—— & Karner, G. D. 1985. Dependence of the flexural rigidity of the continental lithosphere on rheology and temperature. *Nature*, **316**, 138–142.

—— & Matthews, D. H. 1988. Deep seismic reflections and the deformational mechanisms of the continental lithosphere. *Journal of Petrology*, Special Lithosphere Issue, 66–87.

—— & Morley, C. 1990. The Lake Tanganyika Rift, East Africa: Application of the Flexural Cantilever Model of Continental Extension. *Geophysical Journal International*, **101**, 275.

—— & Park, R. G. 1984. Intraplate lithosphere deformation and the strength of the lithosphere. *Geophysical Journal of the Royal Astronomical Society*, **70**, 513–538.

—— & —— 1987. The extensional strength of the continental lithosphere: its dependence on geothermal gradient, crustal composition and thickness. *In*: Coward, M. P., Dewey, J. F. & Hancock, P. L. (eds). *Continental Extensional Tectonics.* Geological Society, London, Special

Publication **28**, 35–52.

Marsden, G., Yielding, G., Roberts, A. M. & Kusznir, N. J. 1990. Application of a flexural cantilever simple-shear/pure-shear model of continental lithosphere to the formation of the northern North Sea Basin. *In*: Blundell, D. J. & Gibbs, A. D. (eds). *Tectonic Evolution of the North Sea Rifts*, Oxford University Press, 236–257.

McKenzie, D. 1978. Some remarks on the development of sedimentary basins. *Earth and Planetary Science Letters*, **40**, 25–32.

Roberts, A. M. & Yielding, G. (This volume). Deformation around basin-margin faults in the North Sea/mid-Norway Rift.

Stein, R. S. & Barrientos, S. E. 1985. Planar High-Angle Faulting in the Basin and Range: Geodetic Analysis of the 1983 Borah Peak, Idaho, Earthquake. *Journal of Geophysical Research*, **90**, 11355–66.

——, King, G. C. P. & Rundle, J.B. 1988. The Growth of Geological Structures by Repeated Earthquakes, 2, Field Examples of Continental Dip-Slip Faults, *Journal of Geophysical Research*, **9**, 13319–31.

Tankard, A. J., Welsink, H. J. & Jenkins, W. A. M. 1990. Structure and stratigraphy of the Jeanne D'Arc Basin offshore Newfoundland: Analysis of Basin Subsidence, *In*: Tankard, A. J. & Balkwill, H. R. (eds) *Extensional Tectonics of the North Atlantic Margins.* American Association of Petroleum Geologists Memoir **46**.

Verrall, P. 1981. *Structural Interpretation with Applications to North Sea Problems.* Joint Association for Petroleum Exploration Courses Course Notes *No. 3.*

Walsh, J. J. & Watterson, J. 1987. Distribution of cumulative displacement and seismic slip on a single normal fault surface. *Journal of Structural Geology*, **9**, 1039–1046.

Weissel, J. K. & Karner, G. D. 1989. Flexural uplift of rift flanks due to mechanical unloading of the lithosphere during extension. *Journal of Geophysical Research*, **94**, 13919–50.

Wernicke, B. 1985. Uniform-sense normal simple-shear of the continental lithosphere. *Canadian Journal of Earth Sciences*, **22**, 108–125.

Deformation around basin-margin faults in the North Sea/mid-Norway rift

ALAN M. ROBERTS & GRAHAM YIELDING

Badley Ashton & Associates Limited, Winceby House, Winceby,
Horncastle, Lincolnshire LN9 6PB, UK

Abstract: It has been demonstrated previously that the rigid-domino model of extensional faulting can account well for the uplift/subsidence patterns observed within particular areas of the North Sea rift. This model, however, provides an unsatisfactory solution to deformation occurring at the basin margins.

It is suggested here that the domino model is an elegant, geometric simplification of the more complete flexural-isostatic solution to fault displacements. Application of a flexural model allows a unified treatment of the basin and its margins.

The basin-margins to the North Sea/Mid-Norway rift are all shown to have responded to extensional faulting by experiencing isostatic uplift in the footwalls to the marginal faults. Uplift magnitude varies from a few hundred metres adjacent to small faults to perhaps 5 km adjacent to the largest faults. Uplift patterns can be modelled or predicted by use of the flexural-cantilever basin model.

Recognition of marginal uplift throughout the rift means that geometric section balancing techniques, all of which require the footwall to be rigid during extension, are inapplicable as a method for analysis of large, basement faults within the North Sea.

Marginal, fault-related uplift is considered to have been a primary source of syn-rift clastic detritus. The precise locus of deposition for material eroded from emergent basin margins will depend on local drainage patterns, but deposition in the hangingwall basin and on the footwall platform may both be anticipated.

Domino fault blocks and basin margins

The internal structure of extended sedimentary basins is typically characterized by a rotated fault-block/half-graben morphology. Two end-member, geometric models exist to account for the development of such an array of half-graben. The linked-fault model (e.g. Gibbs 1983, 1984) assumes that the fault blocks are bounded by listric faults, which ride on a physical detachment surface and form sequentially by propagation of the fault system into rigid, undeformed footwall. The domino model (e.g. Ransome *et al.* 1910; Morton & Black 1975; Barr 1987a; Davison 1989) assumes that the internal faults are planar structures, all of which are active together, with the ensuing 'space problem' at the base of each domino block accommodated by an unspecified form of plastic deformation. Rapid thermal re-equilibration at the base of the dominoes (Jackson *et al.* 1988) may in fact largely negate such 'space' problems.

The geometric properties of a domino-fault system in extending and subsiding basins have been quantified by Barr (1987a, b, this volume). An important property of this type of fault system is that, except when fault block width is small, (perhaps <10 km, depending on sediment load), the footwall crests of the individual fault blocks initially rise above their pre-faulting elevation, commonly taken to be sea level. Such footwall uplift cannot be predicted by the linked-fault model unless the physical sole-fault rises upwards in the direction of tectonic transport. The geometric, stratigraphic and erosional effects of footwall uplift are widespread throughout the North Sea Basin (Jackson & McKenzie 1983; Badley *et al.* 1984, 1988; Barr 1987a, this volume; Roberts *et al.* 1990b; Yielding 1990; Yielding & Roberts in press), suggesting that a domino-type fault-block model may be appropriate for this basin. In addition, in any transect across the basin, the internal, syn-rift fill of individual half-graben is always of the same age range (Callovian−Ryazanian) (e.g. Bertram & Milton 1989; Barr this volume; Roberts *et al.* 1990a), suggesting that the fault blocks concerned developed synchronously and not by progressive footwall collapse. We therefore believe that a quantitative application of the domino model (e.g. Barr 1987a, b) provides a good first-order approximation to the internal geometry of the North Sea Basin (e.g. Yielding 1990).

There has always remained a conceptual problem, however, in relating the domino-style

From ROBERTS A. M., YIELDING, G. & FREEMAN, B. (eds), 1991, *The Geometry of Normal Faults*,
Geological Society Special Publication No 56, pp 61−78

fault-blocks of the basin interior to the style of faulting at the basin margin (Barr 1987a; Sclater & Celerier 1989; Jackson & White 1989). The domino model assumes that each individual fault-block has infinite rigidity and that block rotation is achieved by a rigid-body rotation against the adjacent fault. The basin-margin fault is the last fault in an array, and thus, in a rigid-domino model its footwall must remain static during extension. Barr (1987a, fig. 8) has shown how such an argument requires the boundary fault to a domino array to be listric in form and quite distinct from the internal faults of the basin.

This is an unsatisfactory solution to the problem of what happens at the ends of domino-block arrays, as it assumes that slip on the basin-margin fault is accommodated in a different manner to slip on the internal faults. Both surface and sub-surface mapping have shown that major basin-margin faults are commonly discontinuous along-strike and may pass with diminishing displacement into intra-basinal or intra-platform faults (e.g. Jackson & White 1989; Roberts et al. 1990a; Roberts & Jackson this volume). Thus we should perhaps look to a unified model of fault-related deformation, which does not distinguish between intra-basinal and basin-margin faults, if we are to model satisfactorily the domino-style of fault-block rotation and fault slip at the marginal fault to this array. This we attempt in this paper by examining the structural and stratigraphic relationships, seen on reflection seismic data, of the basin margins in the North Sea/mid-Norway area.

'Flexural' fault-block models

Before examining data from the North Sea we first draw attention to a model of fault-related deformation which achieves similar geometric results to the domino model, but incorporates the rheological properties of the deforming fault blocks and their long-term response to gravity (isostasy). Such models are generally referred to as flexural-isostatic models and owe their origin to the work in the East African Rift of Vening Meinesz (1950) and Heiskanen & Vening Meinesz (1958). Jackson & McKenzie (1983) showed that the isostatic response adjacent to an isolated normal fault can produce both subsidence of the hangingwall and uplift of the footwall. Patterns of uplift and subsidence predicted by flexural models are similar to those observed adjacent to large normal faults (King et al. 1988; Stein et al. 1988; Weissel & Karner 1989). Flexural models have recently been taken

further by Kusznir et al. (1988, this volume), Kusznir & Egan (1989) and Marsden et al. (1990), who have combined the isostatic response to an array of normal faults with a generalized model of lithospheric extension. They term their model the flexural-cantilever model of basin formation. It addresses the same problems as Barr's (1987a) domino model, but has the additional advantage of incorporating internal deformation of the fault blocks. A geometrically similar fault-model has also been introduced by Walsh & Watterson (this volume). This model, however, does not include isostatic effects, which at the scale of basin-margin faults must play an important role in determining long-term uplift/subsidence patterns.

Figure 1 summarizes the flexural-cantilever model. Figure 1a shows the modelled response of the lithosphere to an isolated normal fault, producing both hangingwall subsidence and footwall uplift. Figures 1b and c show the modelled response of the lithosphere to an array of faults, each of which is similar to the isolated fault in Fig. 1a. The two most important aspects of this multi-fault model are the predicted footwall-uplift adjacent to the basin-margin fault, and the way in which the flexural profiles of the individual faults combine to produce a domino-style fault block morphology within the basin. This is a model of basin formation which allows the basin margin and basin interior to deform in the same manner, avoiding the listric fault solution to the compatibility problem (Barr 1987a, fig. 8). The clear geometric difference between the flexural-cantilever and listric-fault solutions to the basin-margin geometry is the prediction of footwall uplift in the former and assumption of footwall stability in the latter. This geometric response at basin margins should be testable with observational evidence from seismic data.

A note of caution should be added here that flexural models are most appropriate for analysis of the deformed volume around large faults, which cut the entire seismogenic layer (King et al. 1988; Jackson & White 1989; Yielding & Roberts in press). A simplifying assumption of these models is that deformation within the footwall and hangingwall of a fault is accommodated purely by elastic strain. In reality such an assumption may be unrealistic as the bending stresses imposed by such elastic strain will be partially relieved by faulting on a scale smaller than that of the main fault. Thus an observed 'flexural' profile around a large fault may be accommodated by both small-scale faulting and a permanent distributed strain (e.g. Walsh &

a) Single fault model

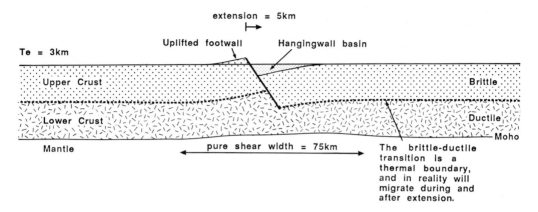

b) Multiple fault model

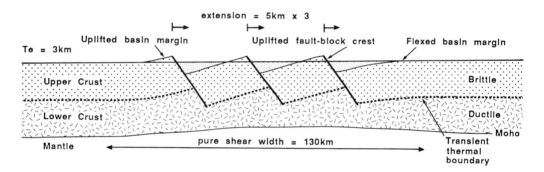

c) Multiple fault model, includes erosion and thermal subsidence

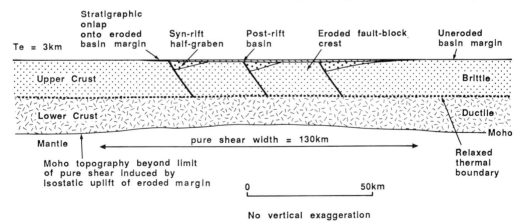

No vertical exaggeration

Fig. 1. Examples of the flexural-cantilever basin model. (**a**) Single normal fault, producing hangingwall subsidence and footwall uplift, (**b**) Multi-faulted model (no erosion), producing domino-style fault blocks within the basin, while the basin margin and fault-block crests are uplifted above sea level, (**c**) Multi-faulted model, incorporating erosion of the basin margin and fault-blocks crests, followed by post-rift thermal relaxation.

Watterson this volume). On a large-enough scale, however, this composite deformation is well modelled by a flexural solution. We use flexure as a filter to describe the response of the earth to isostatic loads, given that the long-term strength of the continental lithosphere is small but not zero (Barton & Wood 1984; Watts 1988; Fowler & McKenzie 1989).

The low strength of the continental lithosphere confines fault-related deformation around any individual fault to a radius of c. 20–30 km. Thus by explicitly investigating fault-related deformation at basin margins we are, in this paper, addressing the problem of uplift on a scale smaller than that treated by whole-basin stretching models. Such models may also produce marginal uplift, but over a much wider area than the deformation radius around individual faults (e.g. White & McKenzie 1988).

Basin margins in the North Sea/Norwegian rift

The basin margins to the North Sea rift can be crudely divided into two categories: those which preserve a recognizable stratigraphic sequence (pre-thermal-subsidence) in the footwall to the marginal fault and those on which no seismically resolvable sequence (pre-thermal subsidence) can be recognized. Three examples of each are described here.

Basin margins devoid of pre-rift sequence

Basin margins such as these juxtapose pre-rift (in places metamorphic) basement in the footwall of the marginal fault, against the sedimentary fill of the basin in the hangingwall. They are closest perhaps to the classic perception of a basin margin, defined by a single large fault zone. We describe here briefly three such examples from the North Sea Rift.

Shetland Platform. The Shetland Platform lies in the UK sector of the North Sea and forms the western margin of the Viking Graben (Fig. 2). It extends south from c. 61°N for about 250 km and is everywhere a near-flat-topped platform, on which pre-rift basement is capped by Cretaceous or Tertiary post-rift sediments. A number of cross sections illustrating the featureless nature of the platform have been published, e.g. Turner et al. (1987, fig. 2), Harris & Fowler (1987, fig. 4), Wheatley et al. (1987, fig. 2). We illustrate the Shetland Platform/Viking Graben relationship here with a seismic line at 60°N (Fig. 3). This line illustrates very clearly the

flat-topped and uniform nature of the platform, contrasted against the rotated fault blocks of the graben. It appears on first inspection very similar in geometry to Barr's (1987, fig. 8) listric-fault solution to the basin-margin problem. From the seismic data alone, however, we cannot tell whether the Shetland Platform remained static and rigid during extension, as the listric-fault solution requires. The flat top to the platform could alternatively be interpreted as an erosional unconformity, but with no pre-rift sequence preserved to show truncation. This too cannot be demonstrated from the seismic data alone. We know, however, that major submarine fans occur along much of the basin margin (e.g. Harris & Fowler 1987, fig. 13), fed into the basin perhaps via transfer zones in the bounding fault-system (Jackson & White 1989). The occurrence of these volumetrically significant fans, capable of trapping hydrocarbons, suggests to us that major erosion of the platform has indeed occurred, and that if erosion was initiated by uplift in the footwall of the bounding fault system then the assumption of a rigid basin margin during extension may be invalid.

Ringkøbing–Fyn High. The Ringkøbing–Fyn High forms the footwall to the Central Graben in the Danish sector of the North Sea (Fig. 2; Cartwright this volume). It marks the eastern margin of the Late Jurassic rift in this area. It has a similar appearance to the Shetland Platform, being a flat-topped structural high, with Upper Cretaceous chalk resting on pre-rift basement (e.g. Møller 1986, Frandsen et al. 1987). Internally it shows more evidence of pre-rift deformation than the Shetland Platform (Cartwright 1990). Figure 4 illustrates a depth-converted cross section across the Ringkøbing–Fyn High/Central Graben. It shows how, if we assume that the basin margin remained as a static regional-marker during extension, section-balancing will automatically predict a detachment fault below the graben (a Chevron construction has been used to predict fault geometry). Again the geometrical similarity with the listric-fault solution is clear, but is it correct? Was the Ringkøbing–Fyn High static during extension? These questions are returned to later.

Frøya High. The Frøya High forms the footwall to the northeastern part of the Møre Basin, offshore Mid-Norway (Fig. 2). It is separated from the Møre Basin by a large-displacement segment of the Kristiansund–Bodø Fault Complex (Gabrielsen et al. 1984). Seismic data

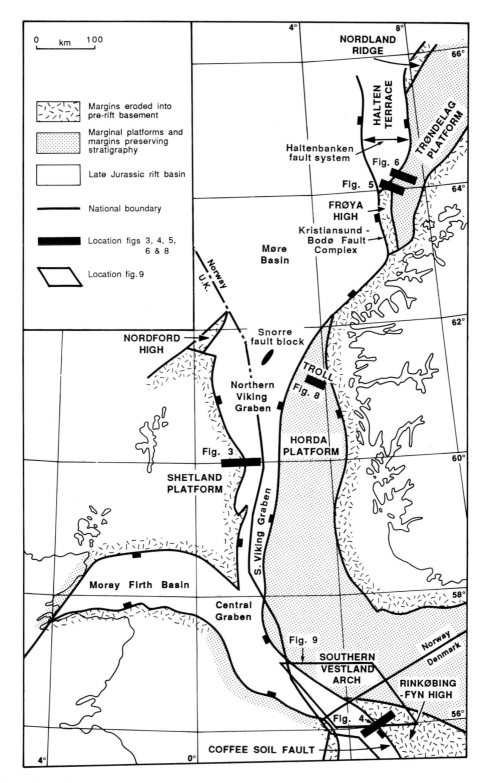

Fig. 2. The main basins and marginal platforms to the North Sea/Mid Norway rift. Note location of Figs 3, 4, 5, 6, 8 & 9.

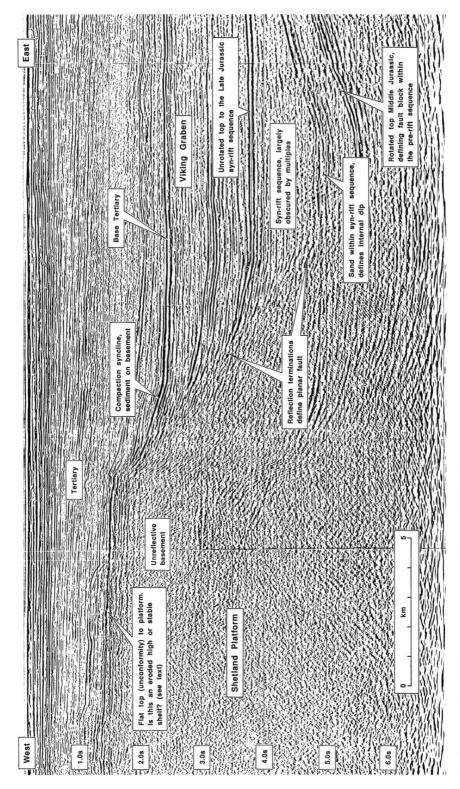

Fig. 3. Seismic line (60°N) across the Shetland Platform/Viking Graben basin margin (UK sector). Note the contrast between the dipping tilted-block within the graben and the flat-topped basin margin. (Location Fig. 2).

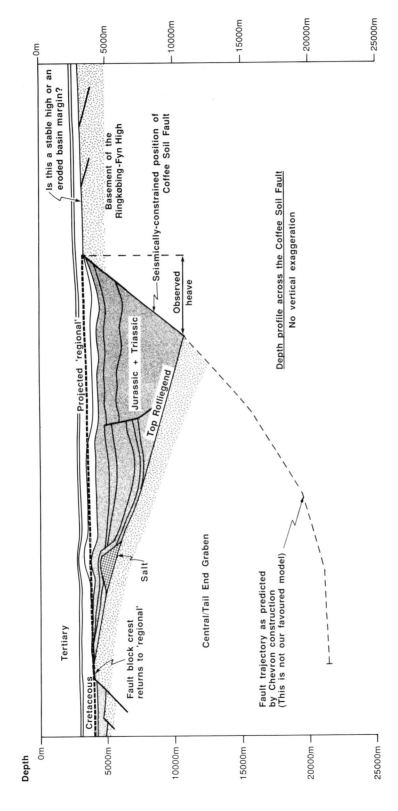

Fig. 4. Depth-section across the Central Graben/Rinkøbing–Fyn High (Danish sector). A constant-heave section-balance (Chevron construction) has been used to illustrate the detachment predicted by application of a stable-margin, listric-fault model. This solution to the geometry of the Coffee Soil Fault is considered incorrect (see text). (Location Fig. 2).

show that, like the Shetland Platform and Ringkøbing–Fyn High, the Frøya High is a flat-topped structure with Upper Cretaceous sediments resting on pre-rift basement (Fig. 5, see also Brekke & Riis 1987, fig. 10; Caselli 1987, fig 12; Gabrielsen & Robinson 1984, fig. 3). It might thus be interpreted as the rigid footwall to a rotational fault-system developed in its hangingwall.

The Frøya High is different, however, in one important respect from the two previously described margins. At the western margin of the high, adjacent to the main fault zone, the seismic response is that of typically featureless basement (Fig. 5). About 10 km east of the fault zone, however, a vestige of pre-rift sequence is preserved. This sequence ties to the basal part of the Triassic/Permian? succession recognizable throughout much of the Mid-Norway area. Reflections within this remanent pre-rift sequence are truncated at the flat top to the Frøya High, defining this surface as an erosional unconformity (Fig. 5). This relationship is very clearly illustrated in fig. 10 of Brekke & Riis (1987). Erosion associated with this unconformity cuts down-section to the west, suggesting that differential uplift was responsible for the development of the unconformity, and that such uplift increased in magnitude westwards towards the marginal fault zone. It seems unlikely that the Frøya High was a stable, rigid block during extension on the fault zone.

Basin margins preserving pre-rift sequence

The three marginal platforms described above are each separated from the interior of the rift by faults with as much as c. 10 km of observable displacement on them. Offset of the top Middle Jurassic at each of these margins confirms the

displacement as largely Late Jurassic in age. These faults, however, probably also accommodated some earlier Triassic movement (e.g. Cartwright this volume). In other parts of the rift the displacement seen on these large faults is partitioned into a number of smaller faults, forming a more gradational margin to the basin. Adjacent to such faults, platform areas may preserve a clearly identifiable sedimentary sequence, pre-dating the Late Jurassic period of extension.

The Haltenbanken Margin. North of the Frøya High the Kristiansund–Bodø fault complex shares its displacement into a distributed network of faults, which we refer to here informally as the Haltenbanken fault system (Fig. 2). The most eastern fault zone of this fault system separates the Halten Terrace from the Trøndelag Platform. A clear pre-Cretaceous sequence is preserved on the Trøndelag Platform, with seismic events tied to wells in the Draugen Field (Ellenor & Mozetic 1986) and the stratigraphically deep well 6507/12–2.

Figure 6 is an interpreted depth section across the western margin of the Trøndelag Platform and the major fault zone separating it from the Halten Terrace. The platform at base Cretaceous and top Lower Cretaceous levels has a gentle tilt to the west imposed by post-Pleistocene uplift of the Norwegian mainland, and the sea bed is a marked, erosional unconformity on seismic data. Allowing for this tilt, however, there is still a demonstrable asymmetry to the structure of the platform. At a distance of 15–20 km east of the boundary fault, the Triassic–Middle Jurassic (c. 2000 m above upper salt) is overlain by a thin syn-rift Upper Jurassic sequence (100 m) and thin (early post-rift) Lower Cretaceous (100 m). The Lower

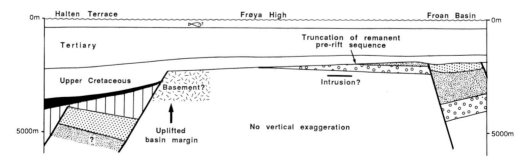

Fig. 5. Depth-section across the Frøya High (Norwegian sector). Note that although basement may be exposed at the western margin of the high, remanent pre-rift sequence is present in the east. The full footwall sequence seen on Fig. 6 indicates that c. 3000 m of uplift occurred at the western margin. Key to ornament as in Fig. 6. (Location Fig. 2).

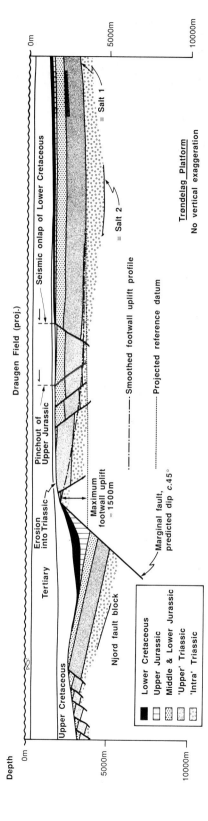

Fig. 6. Depth-section across the Trøndelag Platform/Halten Terrace basin margin (Norwegian sector). Note the *c.* 1500 m of erosion into the pre-rift sequence adjacent to the marginal fault, interpreted as the result of footwall uplift. The reservoir in the Draugen Field on the footwall block may comprise the erosion products of this uplift. (Location Fig. 2).

Cretaceous onlapped a pre-existing structural high and is seismically unresolvable within 15 km of the marginal fault, although well data show it to be thinly developed in the Draugen Field, west of the seismic onlap point. The Upper Jurassic also thins westwards, terminating c. 10 km back from the fault (see also Ellenor & Mozetic 1986, fig. 2) and appears also to have onlapped a contemporary high. Within 10 km of the marginal fault, erosion of the Triassic−Middle Jurassic occurs, cutting down-section to the west. At the marginal fault itself erosion has almost reached to the upper Triassic salt. The uplift causing this erosion has been accommodated by a series of normal faults, antithetic to the main structure.

Using the regional dip of the upper salt in the 'undeformed' eastern part of the section, a 'smoothed' uplift profile can be drawn through the small fault blocks. Maximum uplift at the fault, when measured against a projection of the regional dip, is c. 1500 m. The age of the uplift is constrained as post-Middle Jurassic and likely syn-Late Jurassic, causing the Upper Jurassic to onlap an emergent/emerging high. The Upper Jurassic in the Draugen Field comprises mainly sandstones (Frøya Formation) which were probably the erosion products of the emergent footwall immediately to the west, shed eastwards down the dip-slope of this structure. The main period of extensional faulting in this area was also of Late Jurassic age, and thus we infer that the footwall to the basin-margin fault zone became uplifted and emergent during extension.

There are obvious geometric similarities between Fig. 6 and the emergent basin margin of the model flexural-cantilever system (Fig. 1). We have forward-modelled the Trøndelag Platform margin using the flexural-cantilever model (Kusznir et al. 1988, this volume; Kusznir & Egan 1989; Marsden et al. 1990), and find that the observed 1500 m of footwall-uplift is consistent with models invoking flexural isostasy of low-strength lithosphere, in the footwall of the marginal fault (Fig. 7). The models have been run assuming both a 40° and 50° initial dip to the marginal (planar) fault, and also for two sections across the fault. The first section is the simpler case and models the situation 8 km north of Fig. 6, where the Trøndelag Platform and Halten Terrace are separated by a single major fault. The second section is more complex and models the situation along the line of Fig. 6, where platform and terrace are separated by an intervening tilted fault block (the Njord structure). In both cases, a 50° initial dip gives an extension on the main, marginal fault of 3 km;

lowering the dip to 40° increases the extension to 4 km. The models were run with and without syn-rift erosion of the footwall, but the Trøndelag Platform is itself observed to be eroded. A sediment/water load of 2.0 g cm^{-3} was used in all cases in order to simulate partial sediment starvation in the evolving hangingwall basin (Bertram & Milton 1989; Yielding 1990; Barr this volume).

Uplift of the platform in the single-fault model (incorporating erosion) is c. 1500 m for a 50° fault and c. 1250 m for a 40° fault. In the more complex second case, the western fault zone contributes some extra uplift to the platform, and thus the total uplift, in the footwall of the eastern fault, is c. 1850 m for the 50° case and c. 2050 m for the 40° case. The observed wave-length of deformation around the fault (i.e. a reverse-drag radius of c. 15 km), indicates that the continental lithosphere has a low flexural rigidity. Forward-modelling of the profiles (Fig. 7) suggests that an effective elastic thickness (T_e) of c. 3 km is most appropriate. The same value of T_e has been used in modelling of the Viking Graben (Marsden et al. 1990), while gravity modelling studies also suggest that the long-term strength of the continental lithosphere corresponds with a value of T_e <5 km (Barton & Wood 1984; Watts 1988; Fowler & McKenzie 1989).

The single fault model predicts the observed uplift (within acceptable deviation) for both 40° and 50° cases. The multi-faulted models predict somewhat more uplift than that observed. The models were run assuming instantaneous stretching of thermally-equilibrated lithosphere during the Late Jurassic. Incorporation of finite-rate stretching (Jarvis & McKenzie 1980) would act to reduce the overestimate. The main point is that uplift of the Trøndelag Platform by c. 1500 m is readily predictable by application of the flexural cantilever, planar-fault model to the structure. Maximum footwall-uplift calculated by applying flexural-isostasy to a listric system, with a deep detachment at 25 km, and the same upper crustal geometry as the depth-model, is only one-third of the observed uplift (see also Kusznir & Egan 1989; Kusznir et al. this volume). Such a model is therefore incompatible with the data. We have also achieved a good fit applying the flexural cantilever model to the Nordland Ridge/Halten Terrace fault zone in the north Haltenbanken area (Fig. 2), suggesting that it too can be considered as an extensional, isostatically compensated fault system (cf. Gabrielsen & Robinson 1984), similar in most respects to the Trøndelag Platform margin.

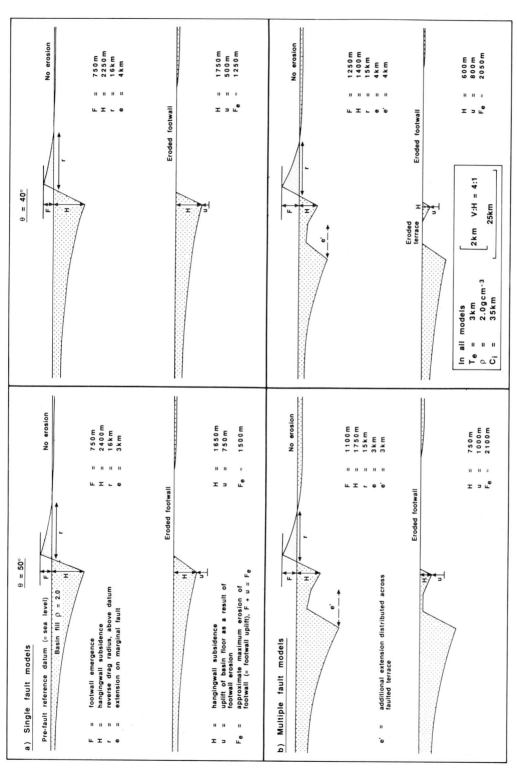

Fig. 7. Flexural-cantilever models of two sections, (**a**) single fault, (**b**) multiple fault, across the Trøndelag Platform/Halten Terrace margin. Models have been run with and, without erosion and for initial fault-dips of 40° and 50°. T_e = effective elastic thickness of the lithosphere, ρ = density of basin fill, C_i = initial crustal thickness.

Horda Platform. The Horda Platform forms the western margin of the Viking Graben in the Norwegian sector of the North Sea (Fig. 2). It was the site of considerable Triassic extension and subsidence, but experienced little subsequent extension during the Late Jurassic (Giltner 1987; Badley *et al.* 1988; Marsden *et al.* 1990). The Troll field, however, which lies on the Horda Platform, sits in the footwall of two large Triassic faults reactivated with a few hundred metres displacement during the Late Jurassic (Hellem *et al.* 1986; Marsden *et al.* 1990; Yielding *et al.* this volume). On reflection seismic data the Troll hydrocarbon/water contact forms a prominent flatspot (flat in depth, slightly tilted in TWT) (Birtles 1986), against which the structural relief of other reflections can be measured.

A seismic line across Troll East (Fig. 8), shows the hydrocarbon-bearing closure confined within the uplifted footwall to one of the Triassic/Jurassic faults. The flatspot is coincident with the regional elevation of the top reservoir *c.* 8 km remote from the fault. Footwall uplift at the fault was of approximately 200 m magnitude, accounting for *c.* 40% of the Late Jurassic fault-slip. The 'exponential' shape of the uplift profile is once again similar to the uplift profile predicted by flexural-isostatic models (cf. Fig. 1). At Troll East only minor erosion has occurred as a result of footwall uplift; there is, however, a crestal condensing of the syn-rift sequence above the top reservoir (Fig. 8).

Southern Vestland Arch. The Southern Vestland Arch is the northwards, down-plunge continuation of the Ringkøbing–Fyn High (Fig. 2). Like the Ringkøbing–Fyn High it sits in the footwall of the Coffee Soil Fault (Gowers & Sæbøe 1985, fig. 2). In the Danish sector the observable throw on the Coffee Soil Fault, at top Rotliegend level, is *c.* 7 km (Figs 4 & 9), but this decreases gradually to (near-)zero in the southernmost part of the Norwegian sector. No pre-rift sequence is preserved in the footwall of the Danish sector (Figs 4 & 9). However, as throw decreases northwards, the transition from Ringkøbing–Fyn High to Vestland Arch is marked by a reduction in the amount of footwall erosion and a consequent increase in the preservation of pre-rift sequence in the footwall (Fig. 9; Skjerven *et al.* 1983, figs 5d and e). Thus, using a grid of regional seismic data, it is possible to map the relationship between throw on the Coffee Soil Fault and preserved/absent pre-rift sequence in the footwall (Fig. 9). The principal observation is that increased fault

throw, which in the case of the Coffee Soil Fault is of composite Triassic–Late Jurassic age (Cartwright this volume), produced increased footwall-uplift. From this we conclude that neither the Southern Vestland Arch nor the Ringkøbing–Fyn High behaved as rigid footwalls during Late Jurassic extension of the Central Graben, but instead were uplifted in proportion with slip on the Coffee Soil Fault. These observations are in accordance with the predictions of flexural models and a very clear comparison can be made between the observed erosion profiles (Figs 9b and 9c) and the modelled basin margin erosion profile (Fig. 1c).

Erosional unconformities within the North Sea rift

We have so far investigated the possible cause of uplift and erosion of the margins to the North Sea rift. Similar flat-topped unconformities to those seen at the margins also occur at the crests of intra-basinal highs, perhaps the most notable of which are the Nordfjord High and Snorre structures in the northern Viking Graben (Fig. 2, Roberts *et al.* 1990b). These unconformities mark pronounced erosion surfaces at the crests of tilted fault blocks (Nelson & Lamy 1987, figs 6–8; Hollander 1987). The magnitude of crestal erosion seen on the Viking Graben fault blocks has recently been shown to be consistent both with the domino model of block rotation (Barr 1987a; White 1990; Yielding 1990) and with the more sophisticated flexural-cantilever model for basin formation (Marsden *et al.* 1990).

The reason that both the domino and flexural-cantilever models can accurately predict the magnitude of uplift of block crests in the Viking Graben is because all of the fault blocks here approximate a uniform internal dip (i.e. are geometrically similar to a rigid domino model). In detail, however, internal deformation (bending) of the fault blocks can be observed (e.g. Fig. 8; Bowen 1975, fig. 7; Kirk 1980, fig. 8). We have successfully modelled the internal deformation of the Brent and Snorre fault blocks (Bowen 1975; Hollander 1987) by applying a flexural-isostatic model to the observed fault displacements adjacent to these structures (not illustrated). In the case of the Snorre structure the simplifying assumption was made that a flexural curve could be 'smoothed' through the small internal fault blocks (cf. Fig. 6). Marsden *et al.* (1990) have gone further and modelled a section across the whole basin with the flexural-cantilever model.

There therefore appears to be no conflict

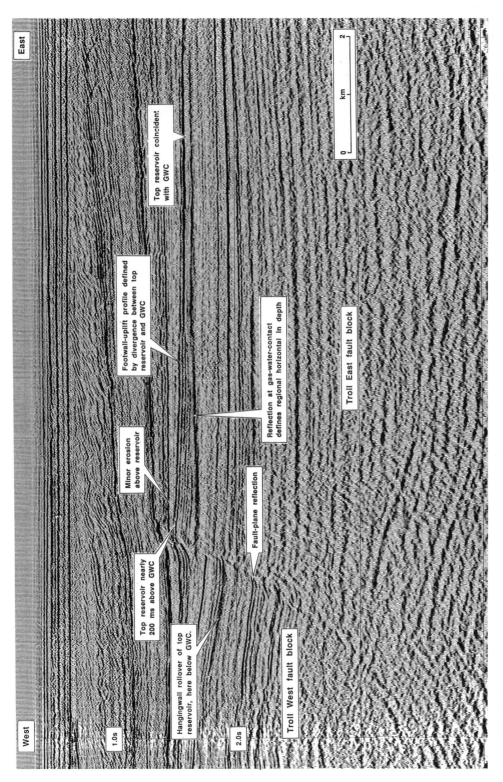

West

East

1.0s

2.0s

Top reservoir coincident with GWC

Footwall-uplift profile defined by divergence between top reservoir and GWC

Minor erosion above reservoir

Reflection at gas-water-contact defines regional horizontal in depth

Top reservoir nearly 200 ms above GWC.

Fault-plane reflection

Hanglingwall rollover of top reservoir, here below GWC.

Troll East fault block

Troll West fault block

0   1   2
km

Fig. 8. Seismic line across the Troll East structure (Norwegian sector). Footwall uplift is highlighted by the divergence between the hydrocarbon-water flat-spot and the top reservoir reflection, and is c. 200 m in magnitude. (Location Fig. 2).

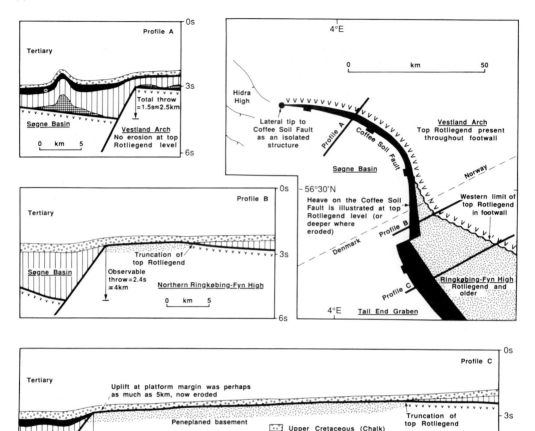

Fig. 9. Three geoseismic sections (vertical scale in two-way-time, seconds) across the Coffee Soil Fault, together with a simplified map of the northern part of the fault zone. The sections (A−C) illustrate how progressively-increasing fault slip has resulted in deeper and wider erosion of the footwall (cf. Fig. 1). The top Rotliegend is present everywhere on the Vestland Arch, but is absent at the western margin of the Ringkøbing−Fyn High. The map indicates the westwards truncation of the top Rotliegend. Footwall uplift on the Coffee Soil Fault varies from zero at the lateral tip, to perhaps c. 5000 m in the Danish sector. (Location Fig. 2, see also Cartwright this volume).

between models which can be successfully applied to the basin margins of the rift and those which can be applied internally. A flexural-isostatic model can account for the observed deformation in all circumstances, whereas a listric-fault model or geometric Chevron-type construction is incapable of predicting the observed and ubiquitous uplift, within and marginal to the rift.

Maximum likely uplift of the basin margins

Where a pre-rift sequence is preserved on the basin margins (e.g. Horda Platform, Trøndelag Platform) a ready estimate can be made of uplift magnitude. This is more difficult in the case of margins devoid of such a sequence (e.g. Shetland Platform, Ringkøbing−Fyn High). The observed relationship between throw on the Coffee Soil Fault and presence/absence of pre-rift sequence in its footwall suggests strongly that the Ringkøbing—Fyn High was uplifted during extension, and truncated by erosion into the pre-rift basement. The Shetland Platform is very much an analogous structure and contains numerous syn-extension outwash fans in its hangingwall. The weight of evidence suggests that it too was uplifted and eroded in the footwall to the Viking Graben.

An attempt can be made to predict how much erosion may have occurred on these truncated margins, using similar iterative forward-models to those of Kusznir & Egan (1989) and Kusznir *et al.* (this volume). The forward models attempt to match the observed hangingwall basin depth, and from this predict likely magnitudes of footwall uplift and erosion.

The Viking Graben on Fig. 3 is *c.* 6 km deep, as measured from the platform margin to the deepest top Middle Jurassic (see also depth profiles in Marsden *et al.* in press). The currently observable heave on the marginal fault of this profile (platform-top Middle Jurassic) is 10 km. This provides a minimum estimate of extension on this fault, and such an estimate requires there to have been no footwall erosion. We have forward-modelled a basin controlled by a fault inclined initially at 45°, accommodating 10 km of extension (within continental lithosphere of T_e 3 km), and loaded by a basin fill of 2.5 g cm^{-3} (i.e. full sediment loading). Such a model produces a resulting basin 6 km in depth, flanked by an emergent footwall with 1700 m topography. This model assumes that no footwall erosion occurred, and provides a minimum estimate of uplift at the Shetland Platform. In reality some erosion almost certainly occurred, as illustrated by the basin margins in Figs 5, 6 & 9. Erosion would affect the modelling in two ways. Firstly it requires a greater extension on the fault than that currently 'observable'. Secondly, erosion of the footwall would initiate further isostatic uplift of the eroded area. Both of these factors would act to increase the magnitude of footwall uplift at the Shetland Platform. In addition, assuming the syn-rift fill to be of density 2.5 g cm^{-3} is probably an overestimate. Considerable, syn-rift bathymetry almost certainly existed in the Viking Graben (Bertram & Milton 1989; Barr this volume) and indeed such bathymetry is indicated in Fig. 3 by onlap of the top Late Jurassic onto the marginal fault (see also Cartwright this volume). Considerable bathymetry would act to lower the average density of the graben fill, and as in the case of our modelling of the Haltenbanken margin, we believe a syn-rift fill of 2.0 g cm^{-3} might be more appropriate. Reducing the weight of the hangingwall load below that in the above model

would act to enhance the magnitude of footwall uplift.

Alteration of the model parameters in order to simulate erosion, greater extension and lower density basin-load indicate that footwall uplift and erosion of the Shetland Platform may have been as much as *c.* 5 km. This is similar to the estimate by Kusznir & Egan (1989) of *c.* 4 km of footwall erosion adjacent to the structurally-deep Jeanne d'Arc Basin, offshore Canada.

It is interesting to note that the site of this postulated significant uplift adjacent to the Viking Graben is also the site of a postulated high-level granitic intrusion into the platform basement (Donato & Tully 1982; Zervos 1987). If the basement has in fact been elevated by *c.* 5 km at this location, it is not surprising to find pre-rift granitic rocks sub-cropping post-rift Tertiary sediments. The Ringkøbing—Fyn High shares many of the features of the Shetland Platform margin (cf. Figs 3, 4 & 9; Cartwright this volume). In addition it has demonstrably been subject to footwall erosion. Uplift of the Ringkøbing—Fyn High by a magnitude of 2—5 km (depending on model assumptions) therefore also seems a reasonable estimate. Note, however, that in extreme cases of perhaps 5 km uplift, a footwall 'island' of this height would never have existed, because uplift of this magnitude requires erosion to accompany emergence above sea level.

Conclusions

The main conclusions derived from this study are considered as follows.

1. All the examples of basin margins within the North Sea/Mid-Norway rift that we have studied responded to extensional faulting by isostatic uplift. The basin margins were not rigid and static.

2. Flexural modelling suggests that both basin margin and the main intra-basinal faults can be modelled, within the basement, as planar structures.

3. Adjacent to large faults, the pre-rift footwall sequence is completely eroded, as a result of uplift by perhaps as much as *c.* 500 m in extreme cases. Adjacent to smaller faults, the pre-rift footwall sequence may be preserved, providing a direct means of quantifying fault-displacement and associated uplift. Observed or calculated magnitudes of uplift for each of our examples are summarized in Table 1.

4. Basin-margin unconformities define erosion surfaces, which were probably close to contemporary sea level (wave-base?). They are

Table 1. *Values of observed and modelled footwall uplift for each of the examples described in the text*

Location	'Observed' uplift	Uplift predicted by modelling
Horda Platform, Troll East	c. 200 m	—
Trøndelag Platform	c. 1500 m	1500 m
Southern Vestland Arch	Zero at fault tip, increasing progressively southwards onto Ringkøbing–Fyn High	—
Frøya High	c. 3000 m	—
Shetland Platform	—	1700 m minimum, perhaps c. 5000 m
Ringkøbing–Fyn High	—	2000–5000 m

not necessarily diagnostic of stable basement highs.

5. Uplift in the footwalls of extensional faults provides a mechanism for deriving volumetrically significant erosional detritus, which, depending on local drainage patterns, may be redeposited either in hangingwall (Viking Graben fans) or footwall (Draugen field) lows.

6. Basin-margin unconformities cannot be used to define pre-faulting, regional markers for the purpose of geometric section balancing.

We are greatly indebted to Nick Kusznir, Gary Marsden and Mark Newall, of the Liverpool basin modelling group, for many discussions about the flexural-cantilever model and footwall-uplift. We are also grateful to Nick for allowing us the unrestricted use of the basin modelling programme STRETCH. Our understanding of footwall uplift has, in addition, slowly evolved as a result of many discussions with Mike Badley, Dave Barr, John Price, Brett Freeman, Juan Watterson, John Walsh, James Jackson, Terkel Olsen and Charles Jourdan. The initial manuscript was much improved by constructive reviews from Nicky White and Roy Gabrielsen.

References

BADLEY, M. E., EGEBERG, T. & NIPEN, O. 1984. Development of rift basins illustrated by the structural evolution of the Oseberg feature, Block 30/6, offshore Norway. *Journal of the Geological Society, London,* **141**, 639–649.
——, PRICE, J. D., RAMBECH DAHL, C. & AGDESTEIN, T. 1988. The structural evolution of the northern Viking Graben and its bearing upon extensional modes of basin formation. *Journal of the Geological Society, London,* **145**, 455–472.
BARR, D. 1987a. Lithospheric stretching, detached normal faulting and footwall uplift. *In:* COWARD, M. P., DEWEY, J. F. & HANCOCK, P. L. (eds). *Continental Extensional Tectonics,* Geological Society, London, Special Publication **28**, 75–94.
—— 1987b. Structural/stratigraphic models for ex-

tensional basins of half-graben type. *Journal of Structural Geology,* **9**, 491–500.
—— (This volume). Subsidence and sedimentation in semi-starved half-graben: a model based on North Sea data.
BARTON, P. & WOOD, R. 1984. Tectonic evolution of the North Sea basin: crustal stretching and subsidence. *Geophysical Journal of the Royal Astronomical Society,* **79**, 987–1022.
BERTRAM, G. T. & MILTON, N. 1989. Reconstructing basin evolution from sedimentary thickness; the importance of palaeobathymetric control, with reference to the North Sea. *Basin Research,* **1**, 247–257.
BIRTLES, R. 1986. The seismic flatspot and the discovery and delineation of the Troll Field. *In:* SPENCER, A. M. *et al.* (eds). *Habitat of Hydrocarbons on the Norwegian Continental Shelf,* Graham & Trotman, 207–216.
BOWEN, J. M. 1975. The Brent Oil-field. *In:* WOODLAND, A. W. (ed.) *Petroleum and the Continental Shelf of Northwest Europe,* 353–360.
BREKKE, H. & RIIS, F. 1987. Tectonics and basin evolution of the Norwegian shelf between 62°N and 72°N. *Norsk Geologisk Tidsskrift,* **67**, 295–322.
CARTWRIGHT, J. A. (This volume). The kinematic evolution of the Coffee Soil Fault.
—— 1990. The structural evolution of the Ringøbing–Fyn High. *In:* BLUNDELL, D. J. & GIBBS, A. D. (eds). *Tectonic evolution of the North Sea rifts,* Oxford University Press.
CASELLI, F. 1987. Oblique-slip tectonics, Mid-Norway shelf. *In:* BROOKS, J. & GLENNIE, K. W. (eds). *Petroleum Geology of North West Europe,* Graham & Trotman, 1049–1064.
DAVISON, I. 1989. Extensional domino fault tectonics: Kinematics and geometrical constraints. *Annales Tectonicae,* III, 12–24.
DONATO, J. & TULLY, M. C. 1982. A proposed granite batholith along the western flank of the North Sea Viking Graben. *Geophysical Journal of the Royal Astronomical Society,* **69**, 187–196.
ELLENOR, D. W. & MOZETIC, A. 1986. The Draugen oil discovery. *In:* SPENCER, A. M. *et al.* (eds). *Habitat of Hydrocarbons on the Norwegian Conti-

nental Shelf, Graham & Trotman, 313–318.

FOWLER, S. & MCKENZIE, D. P. 1989. Gravity studies of the Rockall and Exmonth Platlaux using SEASAT altimetry. *Bosin Research*, **2**, 27–34.

FRANDSEN, N., VEJBÆK, O. V., MØLLER, J. J. & MICHELSON, O. 1987. A dynamic geological model of the Danish Central Trough during the Jurassic-Early Cretaceous. *In*: BROOKS, J. & GLENNIE, K. W. (eds). *Petroleum Geology of North West Europe*, Graham & Trotman, 453–468.

GABRIELSEN, R. H., FÆRSETH, R., HAMAR, G. & RØNNEVIK, H. 1984. Nomenclature of the Main Structural Features on the Norwegian Continental Shelf North of the 62nd Parallel. *In*: SPENCER, A. M. *et al.* (eds). *Petroleum Geology of the North European Margin*, Graham & Trotman, 41–60.

—— & ROBINSON, C. 1984. Tectonic inhomogencities of the Kristiansund-Bodø Fault Complex, Offshore Mid-Norway, *In*: SPENCER, A. M. *et al.* (eds). *Petroleum Geology of the North European margin*, Graham & Trotman, 397–406.

GIBBS, A. D. 1983. Balanced cross-section construction from seismic lines in areas of extensional tectonics. *Journal of Structural Geology*, **5**, 153–160.

—— 1984. Structural evolution of extensional basin margins. *Journal of the Geological Society, London*, **141**, 609–620.

GIBSON, J. R., WALSH, J. J. & WATTERSON, J. 1989. Modelling of bed contours and cross-sections adjacent to planar normal faults. *Journal of Structural Geology*, **11**, 317–328.

GILTNER, J. P. 1987. Application of extensional models to the Northern Viking Graben. *Norsk Geologisk Tidsskrift*, **67**, 339–352.

GOWERS, M. B. & SÆBØE, A. 1985. On the structural evolution of the Central Trough in the Norwegian and Danish sectors of the North Sea. *Marine and Petroleum Geology*, **2**, 298–318.

HARRIS, J. P. & FOWLER, R. M. 1987. Enhanced prospectivity of the Mid-Late Jurassic sediments of the South Viking Graben. *In*: BROOKS, J. & GLENNIE, K. W. (eds). *Petroleum Geology of North West Europe*, Graham & Trotman, 879–898.

HEISKANEN, W. A. & VENING MEINESZ, F. A. 1958. *The Earth and its Gravity Field*. McGraw-Hill, New York.

HELLEM, T., KJEMPERUD, A. & ØVREBØ, O. K. 1986. The Troll Field: a geological/geophysical model established by the PLO85 Group. *In*: SPENCER, A. M. *et al.* (eds). *Habitat of Hydrocarbons on the Norwegian Continental Shelf*, Graham & Trotman, 217–240.

HOLLANDER, N. B. 1987. Snorre. *In*: SPENCER, A. M. *et al.* (eds). *Geology of Norwegian Oil and Gas Fields*. Graham & Trotman, 307–318.

JACKSON, J. & MCKENZIE, D. 1983. The geometrical evolution of normal fault systems. *Journal of Structural Geology*, **5**, 471–482.

JACKSON, J. A. & WHITE, N. J. 1989. Normal faulting in the upper continental crust: observations from regions of active extension. *Journal of Structural Geology*, **11**, 15–36.

JARVIS, G. T. & MCKENZIE, D. P. 1980. Sedimentary Basin Formation With Finite Extension Rates. *Earth and Planetary Science Letters*, **48**, 42–52.

KING, G. C. P., STEIN, R. S. & RUNDLE, J. B. 1988. The growth of geological structures by repeated earth-quakes; 1, Conceptual Framework. *Journal of Geophysical Research*, **93**, 13307–13319.

KIRK, R. H. 1980. Statfjord field — a North Sea giant. *In*: HALBOUTY, M. T. (ed). Giant oil and gas fields of the decade: 1968–1978. *American Association of Petroleum Geologists Memoir*, **30**, 95–116.

KUSZNIR, N. J. & EGAN, S.S. 1989. Simple-shear and pure-shear models of extensional sedimentary basin formation: application to the Jeanne d'Arc Basin, Grand Banks of Newfoundland. *In*: TANKARD, A. J. & BALKWILL, H. R. (eds) *Extensional Tectonics and Stratigraphy of the North Atlantic Margins*. American Association of Petroleum Geologists Memoir **46**, 305–322.

——, MARSDEN, G. & EGAN, S. 1988. Fault block rotation during continental lithosphere extension: a flexural cantilever model. (Abstract). *Geophysical Journal*, **92**, 546.

——, —— & —— (This volume). A flexural cantilever simple-shear/pure-shear model of continental lithosphere extension: applications to the Jeanne d'Arc Basin, Grand Banks and Viking Graben, North Sea.

MARSDEN, G., YIELDING, G., ROBERTS, A. M. & KUSZNIR, N. J. 1990. Application of a flexural cantilever simple-shear/pure-shear model of continental lithosphere extension to the formation of the northern North Sea Basin. *In*: BLUNDELL, D. J. & GIBBS, A. D. (eds) *Tectonic evolution of the North Sea Rifts*. Oxford University Press.

MØLLER, J.J. 1986. Seismic structural mapping of the Middle and Upper Jurassic in the Danish Central Trough. *Danmarks Geologiske Undersøgelse*. Serie A Nr. 13.

MORTON, W.H. & BLACK, R. 1975. Crustal attenuation in Afar. *In*: PILGAR, A. & ROSLER, A. (eds). *Afar Depression of Ethiopia*, Inter-Union Commission on Geodynamics. Proceedings of International Symposium on the Afar Region and related rift problems. E. Schweizerbart'sche Verlagsbuchhandlung, Stuttgart, Germany. Scientific Report No. 14, 55–65.

NELSON, P. H. H. & LAMY, J. M. 1987. The Møre/West Shetland area: a review *In*: BROOKS, J. & GLENNIE, K. W. (eds). *Petroleum Geology of North West Europe*. 775–784. Graham & Trotman.

RANSOME, F. L., EMMONS, W. H. & GARREY, G. H. 1910. Geology and ore deposits of the Bullfrog District, Nevada. *United States Geological Survey Bulletin* **407**, 1–130.

ROBERTS, A. M., PRICE, J. D. & OLSEN, T. S. 1990a. Late Jurassic half-graben control on the siting and structure of hydrocarbon accumulations: UK/Norwegian Central Graben. *In*: HARDMAN, R. F. P. & BROOKS, J. (ed.) *Tectonic Events*

Responsible for Britain's Oil and Gas Reserves, Geological Society, London, Special Publication **55**, 229–257.

——, YIELDING, G. & BADLEY, M. E. 1990b A kinematic model for the orthogonal opening of the Late Jurassic North Sea Rift System, Denmark-Mid Norway. *In*: BLUNDELL, D. J. & GIBBS, A. D. (eds). *Tectonic Evolution of the North Sea Rifts*, Oxford University Press.

SCLATER, J. G. & CELERIER, B. 1989. Errors in extension measurements from planar faults observed on seismic reflection lines. *Basin Research*, **1**, 217–221.

STEIN, R. S., KING, G. C. P. & RUNDLE, J. B. 1988. The growth of geological structures by repeated earth-quakes; 2, field examples of continental dip-slip faults. *Journal of Geophysical Research*, **93**, 13319–13331.

ROBERTS, S. & JACKSON, J. A. (This volume). Active normal faulting in Central Greece: an overview.

SKJERVEN, J., RIJS, F. & KALHEIM, J. E. 1983. Late Palaeozoic to early Cenozoic structural development of the south-southeastern Norwegian North Sea. *Geologie en Mijbouw*, **62**, 35–46.

TURNER, C. C., COHEN, J. M., CONNELL, E. R. & COOPER, D. M. 1987. A depositional model for the South Brae oilfield. *In*: BROOKS, J. & GLENNIE, K. W. (eds). *Petroleum Geology of North West Europe*, Graham & Trotman, 853–864.

VENING MEINESZ, F. A. 1950. Les grabens africains, resultat de compression ou de tension dans le croute terrestre? *Inst. R. colonial Belge Bull.*, **21**, 539–552.

WALSH, J. J. & WATTERSON, J. (This volume). Geometric and kinematic coherence and scale effects in normal fault systems.

WATTS, A. B. 1988. Gravity anomalies, crustal structure and flexure of the lithosphere at the Baltimore Canyon Trough. *Earth and Planetary Science Letters*, **89**, 221–238.

WEISSEL, J. K. & KARNER, G. D. 1989. Flexural uplift of rift flanks due to mechanical unloading of the lithosphere during extension. *Journal of Geophysical Research*, **94**, 13919–13950.

WHEATLEY, T. J., BIGGINS, D., BUCKINGHAM, J. & HOLLOWAY, N. H. 1987. The geology and exploration of the Transitional Shelf, an area to the west of the Viking Graben. *In*: BROOKS, J. & GLENNIE, K. W. (eds). *Petroleum Geology of North West Europe*, Graham & Trotman, 979–990.

WHITE, N. J. 1990. Does the uniform stretching model work in the North Sea? *In*: BLUNDELL, D. J. & GIBBS, A. D. (eds). *Tectonic Evolution of the North Sea Rifts*. Oxford University Press.

—— & MACKENZIE, D. P. 1988. Formation of the 'steer's head' geometry of sedimentary basins by differential stretching of the crust and mantle. *Geology*, **16**, 250–253.

YIELDING, G. 1990. Footwall uplift associated with Late Jurassic normal faulting in the northern North Sea. *Journal of the Geological Society, London*, **147**, 219–222.

——, BADLEY, M. E. & FREEMAN, B. (This volume). Seismic reflections from normal faults in the northern North Sea.

—— & ROBERTS, A. M. (In press) Footwall uplift during normal faulting-implications for structural geometries in the North Sea. *In*: LARSEN, R. M. *et al.* (eds). Structural and tectonic modelling and its application to petroleum geology.

ZERVOS, F. 1987. A compilation and regional interpretation of the northern North Sea gravity map. *In*: COWARD, M. P., DEWEY, J. F. & HANCOCK, P. L. (eds). *Continental Extensional Tectonics*. Geological Society, London, Special Publication **28**, 477–493.

Seismic reflections from normal faults in the northern North Sea

G. YIELDING, M. E. BADLEY & B. FREEMAN

*Badley Ashton & Associates Limited, Winceby House, Winceby,
Horncastle, Lincolnshire LN9 6PB, UK*

Abstract: Fault-plane reflections from gravity-driven, listric faults in thick sedimentary sequences are well known. However, reflections from normal faults associated with crustal extension are much rarer and less well studied. We discuss a number of examples of such reflections, present on commercial seismic reflection data from the northern North Sea. Some of these examples have previously been described as reflected refractions, but we show that this requires unrealistic velocities within the sedimentary column. Instead, we consider it more likely that these events are true fault-plane reflections. Depth migration and image-ray migration are used to determine the probable geometry of the faults in both cross section and map view. Estimates of the true geological dip remain sensitive to the velocity structure used, particularly that applied to the Triassic half-graben fill. Despite this uncertainty, the depth-migrations show that these faults are composed of two near-linear segments in cross section. The upper parts (in the Jurassic and Upper Triassic section) dip at 40−50°, but the deeper parts (Triassic hangingwall against basement in the footwall) typically dip at 30−35°. Occasionally, reflections indicate that faults continue into the basement with a 30−35° dip. We interpret this fault geometry as originating from two phases of fault movement. Triassic extension caused rotation of sets of initially steep planar faults. Following Late-Triassic-to-Middle-Jurassic thermal subsidence, renewed extension in the Late Jurassic caused the faults to cut up through the overburden at a steeper angle. Without recognition of a two-phase extension history, such faults might be mistakenly interpreted as forming with a listric geometry.

In recent years, many papers have been published on the prediction of normal-fault geometry from the shape of deformed beds in the hangingwall (e.g. Gibbs 1983; White *et al.* 1986; Williams & Vann 1987; Wheeler 1987). Each of these studies assumes a rigid footwall, with hangingwall deformation being a direct consequence of curvature of the fault plane. Such a model of fault-related deformation appears to be appropriate for gravity-driven listric faults in thick sedimentary successions such as the Gulf Coast and Niger Delta. These listric faults are commonly observed directly on seismic reflection data (e.g. Wernicke & Burchfield 1982, fig. 15; Jackson & Galloway 1984; White & Yielding, this volume). However, studies of fault-related deformation in basement and compacted sediment indicate that hangingwall rollover can be produced by *planar* faults. The shape of the rollover is controlled by factors such as the extent of the fault plane, the slip distribution on the fault plane, and the mechanical properties of the upper lithosphere (e.g. Stein & Barrientos 1985; King *et al.* 1988; Kusznir *et al.* 1988; Gibson *et al.* 1989). Application of conventional 'section-balancing' to such hangingwall rollovers would erroneously predict a curved fault plane. With such a plethora of models available, for both curved and

planar faults, there is generally not a unique solution to the problem of deducing fault geometry from a limited number of deformed beds around a fault.

The purpose of this paper is to present some *observations* of basement-involved faulting, using commercial seismic reflection data. We therefore avoid using a structural model to tell us about fault geometry, but rather use the observations to indicate which of the many models may be the most appropriate for the faults we describe. The uncertainty in the fault geometry is then dependent on the ability of the seismic reflection method to produce a depth image, and this uncertainty can be constrained within limits.

The structures we discuss are fault-plane reflections in the northern North Sea, a Mesozoic extensional basin now covered by Cretaceous and Tertiary post-rift sediments. We have chosen examples that show clear, dipping seismic events associated with major normal faults with several kilometres of throw. These faults are basement-involved, though do not always produce a reflection from within the basement. Our strategy has been to obtain depth sections (using the Sattlegger Interpretive Seismic Processing package) for selected lines across the structures. We have chosen lines approximately normal to the fault traces, to avoid out-of-plane reflections that cannot be migrated.

For each line, we have performed depth migration on the stack section and image-ray migration on the time-migrated section. 'Depth migration' moves dipping subsurface reflectors into their true subsurface positions. Conventional industry migrated sections, however, are 'time-migrated', a process which is computationally cheaper than depth migration, but neglects refraction caused by dipping structure within the overburden. However, if the overburden is simple and flat-lying, time-migration should produce acceptable results (Yilmaz 1987). The resulting section is displayed in the time domain. 'Image-ray migration' attempts to move time-migrated events to their correct depth position. The 'image ray' is the notional ray that emerges vertically at the surface, and it can be used to account for the refraction that is neglected by time migration (Hubral 1977; Larner *et al*. 1981). Conventional 'vertical depth conversion' is conversion of time to depth along vertical rays, and is only strictly correct in the complete absence of dipping structure in the overburden. By performing both depth migration and image-ray migration on each line we can check on the extent to which standard time migration has adequately imaged the structure.

The first examples we discuss are both from the Horda Platform, in the Norwegian sector of the northern North Sea. We then examine a fault in the East Shetland Basin (UKCS). Finally, we summarize our observations and use them to show that although the fault geometries may superficially be interpreted as 'listric', they are in fact approximately planar in the basement.

Horda platform faults

Figure 1(a) shows an unmigrated (stack) section across the Øygarden Fault, offshore Norway. The east end of the line is close to the Norwegian coast, and Caledonian basement is at less than 1 s two-way-time (TWT) (horizon picks are shown in Fig. 1(b)). Basement is then downfaulted to >3 s TWT across the Øygarden Fault, forming the first of a series of tilted basement blocks which underlie the Horda Platform (Eynon 1981; Badley *et al*. 1984, 1988). This faulted basement surface has only been reached by one well 31/6−1, which found Early Triassic sediments resting on gneiss (Lervik *et al*. 1989). Much of the half-graben fill comprises poorly reflective Triassic clastics, passing upwards into more reflective Jurassic, Cre-

Table 1. *Velocities used for Horda Platform profiles*

Interval	Velocity (m s^{-1})
1. Water column	1500
2. Plio-Quaternary	1650
3. Post-Palaeocene	1850
4. Palaeocene	1900
5. Cretaceous	2540
6. Draupne Fm.	2340
7. Viking Gp clastics	3380
8a. Triassic−Middle Jurassic	3000/3800/4500
8b. Triassic−Middle Jurassic	2070 + 0.48z

taceous and Tertiary sequences. Most of the fault movement affecting the basement probably occurred in the latest Permian or early Triassic, followed by thermal subsidence which was interrupted by minor fault reactivation in the Late Jurassic and Early Cretaceous (Badley *et al*. 1988).

Of interest to us here is the prominent dipping event which appears to emanate from the fault zone. Day & Edwards (1983) interpreted this event as a reflected refraction, i.e. a refraction along one of the layers in the hangingwall which has been reflected at the fault surface (see Fig. 2). The two-way traveltime associated with such an event will increase linearly with distance from the fault, at a rate dependent on the velocities of the refractor and the over-burden. For a flat refractor, the slope of the event on an unmigrated time section is simply $2/V_R$ where V_R is the velocity of sound in the refractor. Day & Edwards (1983) showed that if the potential refractor dips away from the fault (as in Fig. 1), a higher refractor velocity is required to produce an event of the same slope. The event in Fig. 1 has a slope of *c*. 0.36 s km^{-1}. This would imply a refractor velocity of 5.5 km s^{-1} for a flat refractor, or an even higher velocity for a refractor dipping away from the fault, as in this case. Such a velocity is completely unrealistic for the succession present here (Jurassic sandstones and shales with velocities of 2.5−3.5 km s^{-1}). We therefore reject the interpretation of the dipping event as a reflected refraction. Instead, we consider it to be simply a reflection from the fault plane where it separates basement (to the east) from Triassic half-graben fill (to the west). As a reflection, the event can be migrated to give us the true dip of the fault surface.

Figure 1(c) shows a depth migration of the picks shown in Fig. 1(b), using the interval velocities listed in Table 1. These velocities are well-constrained by local wells, with the excep-

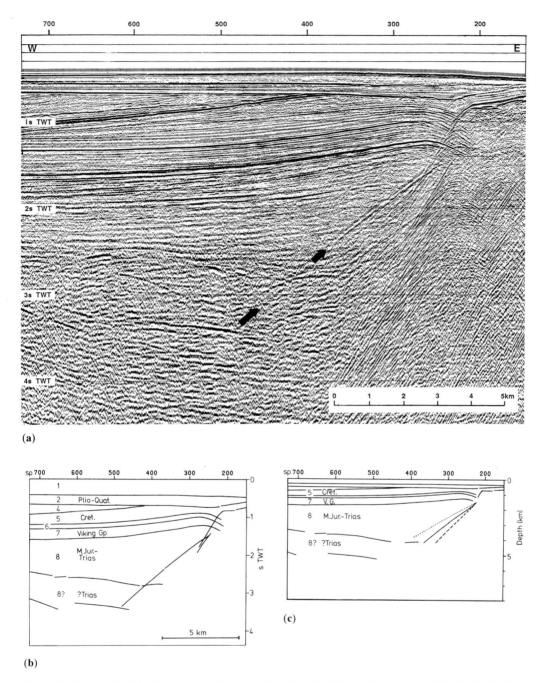

Fig. 1. (**a**) Unmigrated (stack) seismic section across the Øygarden Fault at the margin of the Horda Platform (Norwegian North Sea). Fault-plane reflection is arrowed (**b**) Horizon picks for the section in (a). Intervals are numbered as in Table 1. (**c**) Depth migration of the horizon picks in (b), using the velocities listed in Table 1. Dotted line (for fault-plane reflection) shows migration using lower velocity for half-graben fill, dashed line shows migration using a higher velocity.

Fig. 2. The generation of 'reflected refractions', by reflection (at a fault) of a ray refracted along a bed in the hangingwall.

tion of the lowermost interval (Triassic-Middle Jurassic). As stated earlier, only one well fully penetrates this interval, and gives a velocity of 3800 m s^{-1}. Because of the uncertainty in the velocity of this interval, which occupies about half of the sedimentary column, we have also performed the depth conversion for both higher (4500 m s^{-1}) and lower (3000 m s^{-1}) velocities. It is extremely unlikely that the real average velocity of the half-graben fill is outside these limits, and therefore the resulting depth structures will represent bounds on the real geometry of the fault plane. These bounds are also plotted on the depth section of Fig. 1(c). The main features of the fault plane in Fig. 1(c) are that it is approximately planar, and it has a true dip of *c*. 40° (>30° and <45°). There is some suggestion that the uppermost part may be rather steeper (*c*. 50°). The principal reflection segment arises from the contrast between basement in the footwall and Triassic sedimentary rock in the hangingwall. No reflection is seen from the fault within basement, presumably because of the lack of acoustic impedance contrast. However, this fault has a throw of over 4 km at top basement level, and is planar over this range. Thus before the fault moved, it was planar in the uppermost 4 km of basement (and more if footwall erosion is taken into account). There is no indication that the fault dip decreases at greater depths.

The next major fault to the west of the Øygarden Fault also gives rise to a fault-plane reflection, and this is shown in Fig. 3(a). The slope of the event on the stack section is only 0.17 s km^{-1}; if this were a reflected refraction, this slope would imply a refractor velocity of 11.5 km s^{-1}, which is clearly absurd. We are therefore confident that this event is also a true fault-plane reflection rather than a reflected refraction. Figs 3(b) & 3(c) show horizon picks and the depth-migrated section, respectively. Again, the principal uncertainty in the depth migration is the velocity of the half-graben fill. We have again used high and low velocities to constrain the range of possible fault dips. How-

ever, as the Triassic fill is even thicker in this half-graben, we also repeated the depth migration using a velocity gradient (see Table 1), to simulate the effect of compaction. This velocity function is based on a regional compilation of interval velocities (Marsden *et al.* 1990), and gives a good fit to local well data. The resulting depth profile is also shown on Fig. 3(c).

The fault in Fig. 3 has significantly lower dip than the Øygarden Fault (Fig. 1). The constant interval velocities give dips of 15−25°, whereas the velocity gradient gives a dip of 25−30°. The gradient effectively 'unbends' the slightly curved reflection on the time section. We consider the velocity gradient to be geologically more realistic and therefore favour the dip estimate of 25−30°. As with the Øygarden Fault, the lower part of the observed fault profile is approximately planar, between the footwall and hangingwall basement cut-offs. At least 5 km of displacement is accommodated at top basement level. The upper part of the fault, in the Jurassic and Cretaceous section, is well defined by the cut-off positions (though not by a fault-plane reflection), and has a dip of *c*. 50°. Displacement at this level is <1 km. Following Badley *et al.* (1988), we would interpret the basement offset as resulting mainly from early Triassic fault movement, with renewed but lesser movement in the latest Jurassic to early Cretaceous. The 'later', upper, part of the fault cuts up through the Jurassic−Cretaceous sequence at a higher angle than the 'older' pre-existing fault where it penetrates basement. We return to this point in the later discussion.

We have also performed image-ray migration and vertical depth conversion on the time-migrated versions of the lines shown in Figs 1 & 3. The results were almost indistinguishable from the full depth migrations of the stacks (shown in the figures). The reason for this is the extremely simple overburden structure. In such cases time migration works well, and only vertical velocity variations need to be considered in the time-to-depth conversion. However, we consider it prudent always to investigate the effect of the velocity structure rather than to assume its simplicity at the outset.

East Shetland Basin

Our principal example from the East Shetland Basin is the main boundary fault to the Hutton Field (see Fig. 4a). Many regional lines across this structure show a reflection dipping eastwards from the observed fault offsets at Jurassic levels. Often the reflection can be seen continuing at the bottom of the section (6−7 s TWT).

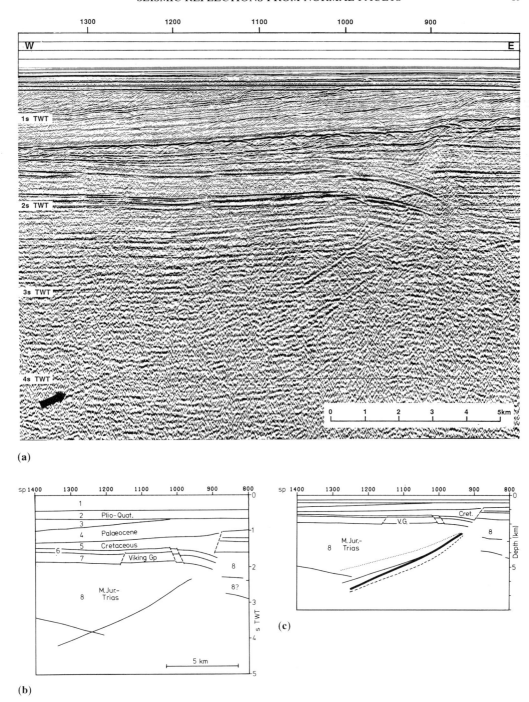

Fig. 3. (a) Unmigrated (stack) seismic section across a fault on the Horda Platform. This section is a westwards continuation of that shown in Fig. 1. Fault-plane reflection is arrowed. (b) Horizon picks for the section in (a). Intervals are numbered as in Table 1. (c) Depth migration of the horizon picks in (b), using the velocities listed in Table 1. Dotted line (for fault-plane reflection) shows migration using lower velocity for half-graben fill, dashed line shows migration using higher velocity, and bold line shows migration using a velocity gradient.

Table 2. *Velocities used for Hutton Fault*

Interval	Velocity (m s^{-1})
1. Water column	1500
2. Post-Palaeocene	$1855 + 0.215\,z$
3. Palaeocene	2460
4. Cretaceous	$1280 + 0.624\,z$
5. U. Jurassic	$2067 + 0.27\,z$
6a. Triassic–Middle Jurassic	3800/4500
6b. Triassic–Middle Jurassic	$2072 + 0.48\,z$
7. Basement	5500

Horizon picks from a representative (un-migrated) line are shown in Fig. 5a. On the Hutton–Ninian fault-block, top basement is known from released well data to be *c.* 0.8 s TWT below the crest of the field. On the Brent fault-block to the east, basement has not been reached. However, well over 2 km of Triassic–Middle Jurassic sequence has been penetrated, and from this we can make a conservative esti-

mate of the top basement position on the Brent block. (The intra-Triassic Lomvi Formation gives rise to the deepest reflection that can be positively identified, *c.* 1 s below the top of the Middle Jurassic (Brent Gp).) Despite this uncertainty in the depth to basement, the deeper parts of the fault-plane reflection (> 5 s TWT) must be from within basement, as it is extremely unlikely that the Triassic succession here would extend that deep.

Velocities used for depth migration (derived from local wells) are shown in Table 2. Again, we use a variety of velocity functions for the Triassic–Middle Jurassic interval, as it is the most poorly-constrained. A velocity of 5.5 km s^{-1} has been assumed for the basement of the Brent fault-block.

The depth-migrated picks are shown in Fig. 5b. We would again favour the gradient as the most realistic velocity model. However, regardless of the exact velocities used, the imaged fault plane is approximately planar rather than listric. Its average dip is about 30–35°. Its

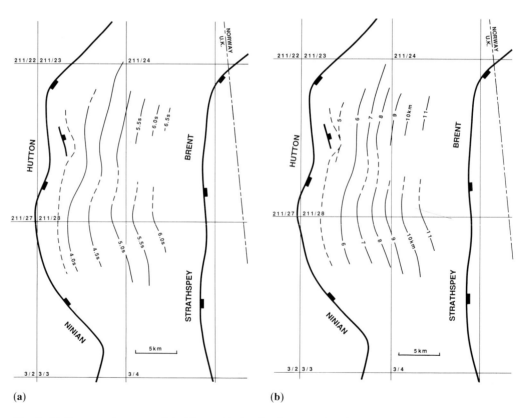

Fig. 4. (a) Two-way-time map of the Hutton Fault reflection, compiled from time-migrated regional seismic lines. **(b)** Depth map of Hutton Fault, based on depth migrations of the lines used to construct (a).

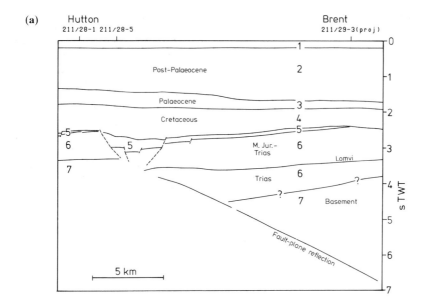

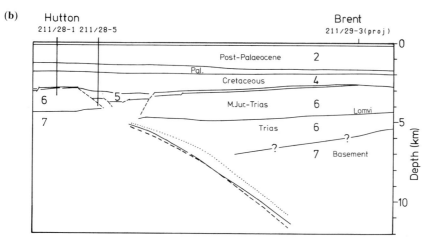

Fig. 5. (**a**) Horizon picks on a representative stack section across the Hutton Fault. Intervals are numbered as in Table 2. (**b**) Depth migration of the horizon picks in (a), using the velocities listed in Table 2. Dotted line (for fault-plane reflection) shows migration using 3800 m s^{-1} for velocity of half-graben fill, continuous line shows migration using a velocity gradient, and dashed line shows migration using a higher velocity.

down-dip extent from the basement footwall cutoff is c. 13 km. The displacement at top basement level is c. 6 km, compared to 1–2 km at Middle Jurassic levels. This again suggests significant Triassic movement followed by a smaller amount of later (mostly Late Jurassic) offset.

The upper part of the fault, cutting the Jurassic sedimentary section, does not give rise to a reflection, but the cut-off positions on our depth-migrated section imply a present dip of c.

40°. This is confirmed by data from released wells on the Hutton Field. In particular, well 211/28–5, targeted at a down-thrown terrace, penetrated the main fault-plane almost 1 km below the crest of the field, from which a fault-plane dip of 41° can be calculated. This upper part of the fault has a footwall composed of Triassic–Middle Jurassic sediments, and is now buried beneath c. 3 km of post-rift sediments. Decompacting the footwall sediments changes the fault dip to 50–55°. This is the dip that the fault would have had when active, i.e. prior to burial by the Cretaceous–Tertiary sediment pile. It is interesting to note that this is some 20° steeper than the estimated dip in the basement. We return to this point in the discussion.

As with the Horda Platform faults, we have produced depth sections by image-ray migration and vertical depth conversion. Again, the results are practically indistinguishable from the full depth migration, because the velocity structure of the overburden is so simple.

By depth migrating a number of lines, we are able to produce a depth map of the imaged fault plane, shown in Figure 4b. The regular spacing of the contours attests to the approximately planar nature of the fault, over its observed depth range of 5–11 km. However, it is worth noting that in map view the trace of the fault at Base Cretaceous level (shown in Fig. 4b) is broadly arcuate. Fault-plane reflections are absent to the north and south of the contoured area of Fig. 4, where the fault trace swings northeast and southeast, respectively. There is no obvious reason for this change of reflectivity along strike.

In our experience of seismic data from the East Shetland Basin, the Hutton Fault is unusual in generating a clear fault-plane reflection. It is plausible that most other faults are significantly steeper, and therefore less likely to be imaged. However, Nelson & Lamy (1987, their figs 4 & 5) show a fault-plane reflection from the Snorre Fault, very similar to those we observe from the Hutton Fault. Their depth conversion of the Snorre Fault shows a present dip in basement of 25–30°, broadly similar to that we observe for the Hutton and Horda Platform faults. Again, early Triassic movement appears to account for a significant proportion of the total fault offset.

Discussion

The principal observation we make from our depth-migrated sections is that the major normal faults are planar where they cut down into basement. In the case of the Horda Platform faults the fault-plane reflection is derived from the basement footwall juxtaposed against Triassic half-graben fill. In the case of the Hutton Fault the reflecting portion continues deep into probable basement with the same attitude. The present-day dips of these basement faults are typically 30–35°, though in some cases possibly as shallow as 25° or as steep as 45°.

The upper parts of the faults, where they cut through the sedimentary column overlying base-

ment, tend to be steeper than the basement portions, typically 40–50°. These upper parts do not give rise to reflections, probably because there is insufficient acoustic impedance contrast between footwall and hangingwall. In addition, they are too steep for conventional finite difference migration algorithms. However, their present dips are constrained by horizon cut-offs and well information. Original fault dips through Jurassic sediment were probably 50–55° before compaction beneath the Cretaceous–Tertiary sediment pile.

Thus the upper parts of the faults show a downward decrease in dip as they pass from sedimentary column to basement. However, it is important to stress that the dip does not continue to decrease downwards; the basement portions are planar. The faults are not listric in the sense of passing downwards into a horizontal detachment surface, at least over the depth range visible on industry seismic data.

Within each fault-block, top basement and Mesozoic sequences are tilted towards the underlying fault. Thus the overall structure comprises tilted fault-blocks bounded by planar faults. The most appropriate description of the gross structure is some form of 'domino' model, either of 'rigid' dominoes (Barr 1987; Jackson *et al.* 1988; Yielding, 1990) or 'soft' dominoes (Kusznir & Egan 1989; Gibson *et al.* 1989; Walsh & Watterson, this volume).

A common feature of all the faults we have examined is that offsets at top basement are much larger than at top Middle Jurassic (*c.* 5 km and *c.* 1 km, respectively). We interpret this to indicate major fault movement in the early Triassic, followed by reactivation in the late Jurassic (see also Badley *et al.* 1988; Marsden *et al.* 1990). Our interpretation is summarized in cartoon form in Fig. 6. Fault-block rotation in the early Triassic produced a tilted-block relief at top basement level. Major planar faults originally dipping at perhaps 45–50° were rotated by up to 10°, along with the intervening blocks. In terms of a rigid-domino model, this would correspond to an extension of $\beta = 1.2$. Late Triassic and Lower–Middle Jurassic sediments represent a thermal subsidence phase after this initial extension. Documented thickening of the Brent and Dunlin Groups over the sites of major faults (Brown 1986; Badley *et al.* 1988) may be partly related to compaction of the underlying Triassic half-graben fill (see Fig. 6a). However, renewed fault movement in the Late Jurassic caused a further 5–10° of fault-block rotation. Reactivation of the basement faults led to them cutting up through the overlying sediment, at an angle of perhaps 50–55°.

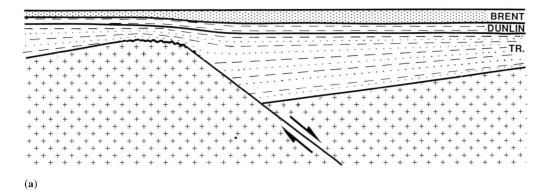

(a)

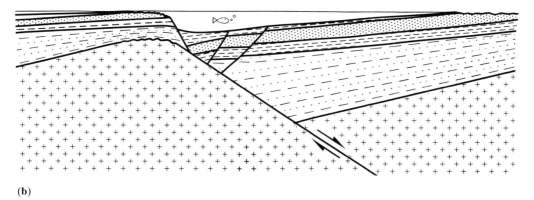

(b)

Fig. 6. Cartoon interpretation of the observations detailed in this paper. (**a**) shows the fault-block geometry at the end of the Middle Jurassic. Following early Triassic extension on planar basement faults, late Triassic–Middle Jurassic thermal subsidence has covered the basement topography. (**b**) Further fault movement and fault-block rotation in the Late Jurassic causes new fault segments to cut up through the sedimentary cover, at a steeper angle than the now-rotated basement faults.

Treating the basement as rigid dominoes, β for the Late Jurassic extension on the basement faults was again about 1.2, giving a total Mesozoic extension factor of about 1.45. This is in good agreement with crustal thickness observations for the terrace areas flanking the graben centre (Klemperer 1988; Marsden *et al.* 1990).

Upward steepening of active faults has been predicted in theoretical models by Barr (1987) and in analogue models by Vendeville & Cobbold (1988). Both these studies adopted the premise that although domino-style faults will rotate to shallower angles, any new fault development in overlying sediment will occur at a fixed angle, say 60°. In this way, the interaction of fault rotation and sedimentation can produce concave-upwards faults. This is the case in the examples we have shown, though two discrete periods of fault movement are separated by a period of sedimentation. The abrupt bend in the fault above the footwall basement cut-off

appears to have produced an accentuated roll-over in the hangingwall (cf Fig. 6b with Figs 1, 3 & 5).

Conclusions

Dipping events on seismic sections across basement faults are (in the cases we have studied) real fault-plane reflections, rather than refractions. The probable geometry of the fault plane can be obtained by depth migration of the fault-plane reflection. Velocity structure has a significant effect on the estimated fault geometry.

The examples we have studied (Horda Platform faults, and the Hutton Fault) comprise two near-linear segments in cross section. The upper parts of the faults (cutting through the sedimentary column), now dip at 40–50°; prior to compaction during Cretaceous and Tertiary burial this dip would have been 50–55°. The lower parts of the faults (involving pre-Triassic basement) now dip at 30—35°, though they probably formed in the early Triassic with an initial dip of 40—50°. The observed geometry is consistent with Triassic rotation of near-planar faults, followed by reactivation of these faults in the Late Jurassic, cutting up through overlying sediment.

We are grateful to Alan Roberts and Oz Yilmaz for helpful discussions during the course of this work. The permission of Statoil to publish the seismic data is gratefully acknowledged.

References

BADLEY, M. E., EGEBERG, T. & NIPEN, O. 1984. Development of rift basins illustrated by the structural evolution of the Oseberg feature, Block 30/6, offshore Norway. *Journal of the Geological Society, London*, **141**, 639—649.

——, PRICE, J. D., RAMBECH DAHL, C. & AGDESTEIN, T. 1988. The structural evolution of the northern Viking Graben and its bearing upon extensional modes of basin formation. *Journal of the Geological Society, London*, **145**, 455—472.

BARR, D. 1987. Structural/stratigraphic models for extensional basins of half-graben type. *Journal of Structural Geology*, **9**, 491—500.

BROWN, S. 1986. Jurassic. *In*: GLENNIE, K. W. (ed.) *Introduction to the Petroleum Geology of the North Sea*, Blackwell, Oxford, 133—159.

DAY, G. A., & EDWARDS, J. W. F. 1983. Reflected refracted events on seismic sections. *First Break*, 14—17.

EYNON, G. 1981. Basin development and sedimentation in the Middle Jurassic of the northern North Sea. *In*: ILLING, L. V. & HOBSON, G. D. (eds). *Petroleum Geology of the Continental Shelf of North West Europe*, Heyden, London, 196—204.

GIBBS, A. D. 1983. Balanced cross-section construction from seismic lines in areas of extensional tectonics. *Journal of Structural Geology*, **5**, 153—160.

GIBSON, J. R., WALSH, J. J. & WATTERSON, J. 1989. Modelling of bed contours and cross-sections adjacent to planar normal faults. *Journal of Structural Geology*, **11**, 317—328.

HUBRAL, P. 1977. Time migration — some ray theoretical aspects. *Geophysical Prospecting*, **25**, 738—745.

JACKSON, M. P. A., & GALLOWAY, W. E. 1984. *Structural and Depositional Styles of Gulf Coast Tertiary Continental Margins: Application to Hydrocarbon Exploration*. AAPG Continuing Education Course Note Series **25**, AAPG, Tulsa, 1—226.

JACKSON, J. A., WHITE, N. J., GARFUNKEL, Z. & ANDERSON, H. 1988. Relations between normal-fault geometry, tilting and vertical motions in extensional terrains: an example from the southern Gulf of Suez. *Journal of Structural Geo-*

logy, **10**, 155—170.

KING, G. C. P., STEIN, R. S. & RUNDLE, J. B. 1988. The Growth of Geological Structures by Repeated Earthquakes, 1, Conceptual Framework. *Journal of Geophysical Research*, **93**, 13307—19.

KLEMPERER, S. 1988. Crustal Thinning and Nature of Extension in the Northern North Sea From Deep Seismic Reflection Profiling. *Tectonics*, **7**, 803—822.

KUSZNIR, N. J. & EGAN, S. 1989. Simple-shear and pure-shear models of extensional sedimentary basin formation: application to the Jeanne d'Arc Basin, Grand Banks of Newfoundland. *In*: TANKARD, A. J. & BALKWILL, H. R. (eds) *Extensional Tectonics and Stratigraphy of the North Atlantic Margins*. American Association of Petroleum Geologists Memoir **46**, 305—322.

LARNER, K. L., HATTON, L., GIBSON, B. S. & HSU, I. C. 1981. Depth migration of imaged time sections. *Geophysics*, **46**, 734—750.

LERVIK, K. S., SPENCER, A. M. & WARRINGTON, G. 1989. Outline of Triassic Stratigraphy and Structure in the central and northern North Sea. *In*: COLLINSON, J. D. (ed.) *Correlation in Hydrocarbon Exploration*, Graham & Trotman London, 173—189.

MARSDEN, G., YIELDING, G., ROBERTS, A. M. & KUSZNIR, N. J. 1990. Application of a flexural cantilever simple-shear/pure-shear model of continental lithosphere extension to the formation of the northern North Sea Basin. *In*: BLUNDELL, D. J. & GIBBS, A. D. (eds), *Tectonic evolution of the North Sea Rifts*, Oxford University Press.

NELSON, P. H. H. & LAMY, J. M. 1987. The Møre/West Shetland area: a review. *In*: BROOKS, J. & GLENNIE, K. W. (eds). *Petroleum Geology of North West Europe*. Graham & Trotman, London, 775—784.

STEIN, R. S. & BARRIENTOS, S. E. 1985. Planar High-Angle Faulting in the Basin and Range: Geodetic Analysis of the 1983 Borah Peak, Idaho, Earthquake. *Journal of Geophysical Research*, **90**, 11355—11366.

VENDEVILLE, B. & COBBOLD, P. R. 1988. How normal faulting and sedimentation interact to produce listric fault profiles and stratigraphic wedges. *Journal of Structural Geology*, **10**, 649—659.

WALSH, J. J. & WATTERSON, J. (This volume). Geometric and kinematic coherence and scale effects in normal fault systems.

WERNICKE, B. & BURCHFIELD, B. C. 1982. Modes of extensional tectonics. *Journal of Structural Geology*, **4**, 105—115.

WHEELER, J. 1987. Variable-heave models of deformation above listric normal faults: the importance of area conservation. *Journal of Structural Geology*, **9**, 1047—1050.

WHITE, N. & YIELDING, G. (This volume). Calculating normal fault geometries at depth: theory and examples.

——, JACKSON, J. A. & MCKENZIE, D. P. 1986. The relationship between the geometry of normal faults and that of the sedimentary layers in their hangingwalls. *Journal of Structural Geology*, **8**, 897–909.

WILLIAMS, G. & VANN, I. 1987. The geometry of listric normal faults and deformation in their hangingwalls. *Journal of Structural Geology*, **9**, 789–795.

YIELDING, G. 1990. Footwall uplift associated with Late Jurassic normal faulting in the northern North Sea. *Journal of the Geological Society, London*, **147**, 219–222.

YILMAZ, Ö. 1987. *Seismic data processing. Investigations in Geophysics 2*, Society of Exploration Geophysicists, Tulsa.

Field-based studies

Extensional structures and their tectonic inversion in the Western Alps

M.P. COWARD, R. GILLCRIST[1] & B. TRUDGILL[2]

Department of Geology, Imperial College, Prince Consort Road,
London SW7 2BP, UK

Abstract: During Alpine collision the western margin of Tethys was uplifted on large-scale thrust zones, to preserve and give excellent 3D exposures of Mesozoic fault geometries. The faults are particularly well exposed along the margins of the Belledonne and Pelvoux basement massifs, east of Grenoble. Jurassic normal faults were in places reworked and the basins partially inverted during Cretaceous to Miocene compression. They were subsequently locally reworked by an important phase of late Alpine extension.

Both listric and straight (rotational) normal faults occur in Variscan granitic basement and Mesozoic cover. Several orders of synthetic and antithetic faults can be mapped, recording strains which are probably related to bends or kinks in the surfaces of the master faults. The extension directions vary, apparently related to variations in anisotropy of the Variscan basement, in particular to the trends of Variscan mylonites. In some regions there was apparently simultaneous extension on two orthogonal fault orientations. On the northern margin of the Pelvoux Massif, late Alpine extensional faults rework both Variscan fabrics in the basement and Alpine mylonites in the cover, producing a large extensional duplex whose roof is a low-angle fault zone in schistose Lias. The late Alpine extension may be caused by gravitational collapse of the thickened crust, or by regional continental extension as part of the opening of the Gulf of Lyon and the Rhone−Bresse Basins.

Pulses of compressional tectonics occurred in the Middle Cretaceous, latest Cretaceous−Early Palaeogene, Eocene−Oligocene and Miocene. During each pulse the deformation occurred principally on foreland-propagating fold and thrust sequences but there are important break-back thrusts, e.g. along the Frontal Pennine Zone, where the thrusts slice across already-sheared and back-tilted rocks to give apparent extensional cut-off relationships. The Alpine compression reactivated Mesozoic faults in basement and syn-rift sediments, deforming the syn-rift graben fill by tight upright folds and back-thrusts. NW-trending Mesozoic lateral ramps gave the basin margin a tooth-like geometry, which on compression did not fit back into the sockets of the opposite margin, causing material to be squeezed out laterally as well as vertically. Such variations in thrust displacement, a form of continental escape similar to large scale indentation tectonics, were partially responsible for the development of the Alpine arc.

In the western Alps the kinematics of Tethyan basin-boundary faults and their secondary structures are well preserved in the uplifted, but not extensively deformed, basement massifs in the Belledonne−Pelvoux region (Fig. 1). Half-grabens are well preserved and only partially inverted, (*sensu* Gillcrist *et al.* (1987), i.e. inversion means a change in the polarity of subsidence/uplift history). The evolution of the Alpine chain can be explained by the relative movements of the African and European Plates, caused by the episodic, northward propagation of the Atlantic rift. Reconstructions of plate movements (e.g. Smith 1971; Dercourt *et al.*

1986; Dewey *et al.* 1989) show that the break-up of Pangaea occurred during the Triassic and Liassic, forming a rift along the Central Atlantic, linked by transform faults to a Tethyan ocean between the European and African plates. The Alpine mountain belt formed during the Cretaceous and Tertiary from the closure of this Tethyan ocean and the continental collision between the African and western parts of the European plates. The mountain belt consists of fragments of European and African crust stacked as a series of thrust sheets (or nappes), thickening the crust to over 50 km. Several thrusts reworked earlier Mesozoic normal faults, uplifting the sedimentary basins which initially formed on the margins of Tethys (Gillcrist *et al.* 1987).

Several authors (e.g. Lemoine *et al.* 1981,

---

[1]Present address: Union Texas, London, UK
[2]Present address: Amerada Hess, London, UK

From ROBERTS A. M., YIELDING, G. & FREEMAN, B. (eds), 1991, *The Geometry of Normal Faults,*
Geological Society Special Publication No 56, pp 93−112

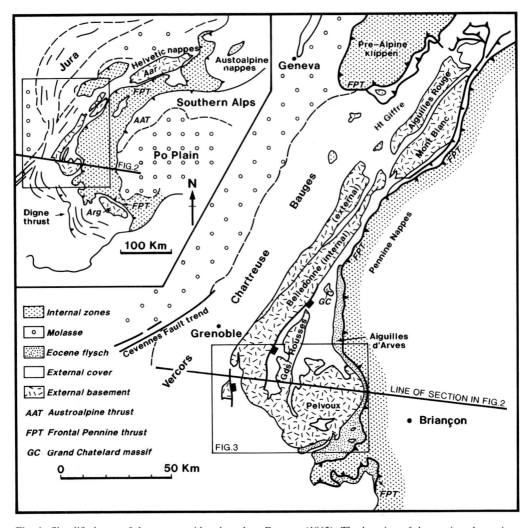

Fig. 1. Simplified map of the western Alps, based on Ramsay (1963). The location of the section shown in Fig. 2 is indicated, as is the area covered by the map in Fig. 3.

1986) have emphasized the importance of Mesozoic extensional tectonics prior to Alpine compression and have compared the fault blocks of the western Alps with the structures found at the Atlantic margin, the Bay of Biscay. Alpine compression masks the Mesozoic extension, as the region is one of high mountains and net crustal thickening. However, extensional faults are still clearly preserved in many parts of the western Alps and in some regions have been reactivated by later Alpine extension. This paper aims to discuss: (i) the age of the faults relative to Alpine tectonic history, including the evidence for locally large Alpine extension; (ii) the influence of the Mesozoic fault geometry on subsequent Alpine thrust geometries and (iii)

aspects of the fault geometry applicable to extensional fault tectonics in general. The region described will encompass the northern and western margins of the Pelvoux Massif, between Grenoble and Briancon (Fig. 1).

Summary of alpine geology

Regional synthesis

The main geological components of the western Alps are shown in Fig. 1, based on Ramsay (1963), Debelmas & Kerchove (1980) and Trumpy (1980). A simplified interpretive section is shown in Fig. 2, based on regional studies by

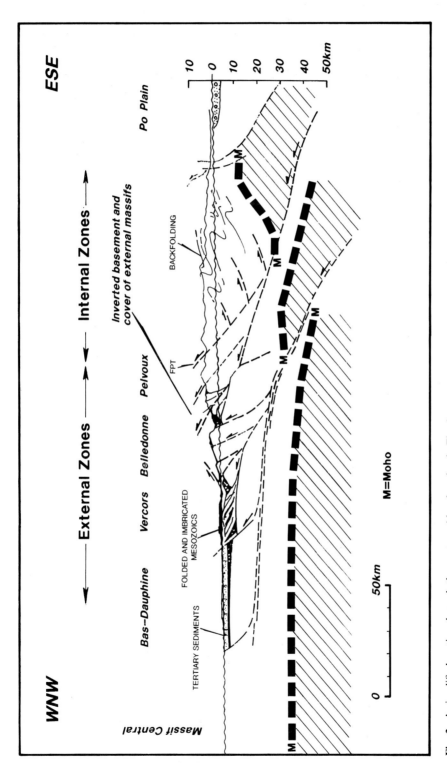

Fig. 2. A simplified section through the western Alps, location in Fig. 1.

the authors and the ECORS deep seismic line south of Mont Blanc (Bayer *et al.* 1987). The suture zone lies at the base of the Austro-Alpine nappes (Fig. 1) which have overthrust the European plate for a minimum of 200 km. The thrust sheets of the internal zone have been complexly folded and back-thrust. The west and northwest edge of the internal zone lies along the Frontal Pennine Thrust, along which there must have been a minimum of 50 km displacement, as Pennine rocks occur as large klippe in the Pre-Alps to the northwest. When the underlying, external-zone thrust-sheets are unravelled and restored, this distance becomes well over 100 km (Boyer & Elliot 1982; Butler 1983, 1986; Butler *et al.* 1986).

The external Alps, forming the Helvetic Alps in Switzerland and the Sub-Alpine Chains in France, consist of weakly metamorphosed sediments of the European Plate. On their internal margin are the basement massifs of the Aar

and Gotthard in Switzerland, the Aiguilles Rouges, Mont Blanc, Belledonne, Pelvoux and Argentera in France. Ramsay (1963) considered them to be uplifted autochthonous basement whilst Boyer & Elliot (1982), Butler (1983) and Butler *et al.* (1986) interpreted them as far-travelled, basement thrust-sheets. Recent publications (Lemoine *et al.* 1986; Gillcrist *et al.* 1987) have suggested that the basement massifs are Mesozoic fault blocks which were uplifted during Late-Cretaceous to Tertiary deformation. Figure 3 shows the distribution of the basement massifs in part of the French Alps, where some of the larger Mesozoic extensional faults are still well preserved. The faults are best preserved along the eastern edge of the Belledonne Massifs; in East Pelvoux and in the Mont Blanc region most of the Mesozoic normal faults have been obscured by subsequent thrusting.

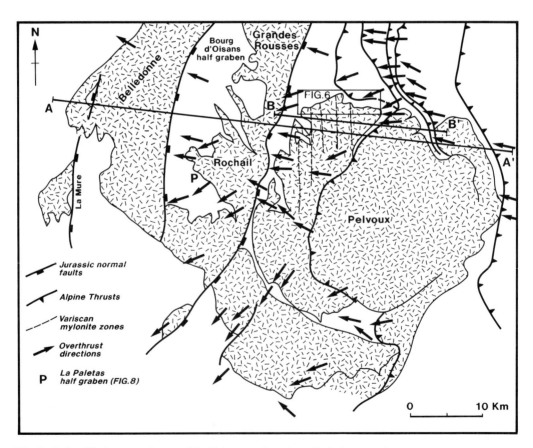

Fig. 3. A simplified structural map of the Pelvoux and southern Belledonne region, showing the main fault systems and over-thrust directions determined from field data (see Gilcrist 1988 for kinematic indicators). The locations of Fig. 4 (Section A–A) Fig. 5 (section B–B) and Fig. 6 (boxed area) are also indicated.

The Pelvoux—Belledonne massifs

Figure 3 shows a simplified map of the Pelvoux region of the French Alps and in particular the distribution of the major normal and thrust faults. A regional section from east of Grenoble to north of Briancon is given in Fig. 4, together with a more detailed section in Fig. 5. Figure 6 shows a detailed geological map of the Plateau d'Emparis at the northern margin of the Pelvoux Massif.

Two large normal faults bound the eastern margins of the Taillefer (southern end of the Belledonne) and Grandes Rousses—Rochail Massifs and form the master bounding faults to the Bourg d'Oisans and Deux Alpes half-grabens. The basement rocks which comprise the massifs consist of Variscan granites and gneisses. Their complex fold patterns, are cut by NW-to-NNW-trending steep zones of phyllonite and mylonite, which pre-date Mesozoic sediments and are associated with lower-amphibolite-to-greenschist-facies metamorphism and produce a local crustal-anistropy.

Permo-Carboniferous extension

The Variscan basement of the external Alpine massifs is unconformably overlain by Carboniferous conglomerates, sandstones and coals, bounded by NE—SW-trending faults. Thick, Carboniferous-to-Permian age sediments occur in the internal parts of the Alpine thrust belt, suggesting that an extensive late Carboniferous basin covered much of what subsequently became Tethyan margins during Mesozoic times. The shallow-water, conglomeratic sediments, interbedded with alluvial sands and coals imply that Carboniferous extension occurred across a region of prominant relief. This extension may reflect (i) regional crustal-spreading related to the tip of a proto-Tethyan ocean, or, (ii) gravitational spreading of the Variscan-thickened crust, similar to that suggested for the Devonian basins in the Scottish or Norwegian Caledonides (Enfield & Coward 1987, Seranne & Seguret 1987) and similar to Recent extensional tectonics in the Himalayas and Tibet (Dewey 1988; Dewey et al. 1988).

The Mesozoic extension

Extension was initiated in the Triassic in the internal zones of the western Alps and the northern margin of the African—Apulian plate, associated with the localized extrusion of alkali basalts. The Dauphinois shelf sequence was dismembered during the Jurassic leading to the development of large, fault-bounded graben and deposition of locally-thick Liassic sediments, without, however, any volcanism (Debelmas & Kerkhove 1980). The major faults dip east and the Liassic sediments thicken and dip towards these faults. Stratigraphic thickness variations, together with onlap relationships, tilting of the earlier syn-rift sequences and the development of olistoliths, reflect the position of the sediments on the tilted fault-blocks. Thus in the deeper parts of the Bourg d'Oisans half-graben (Fig. 3) there are over 4 km of Liassic shales, while on the top corners of the rotated fault blocks, this sequence may be condensed to only a few metres. Locally the basement was eroded to produce olistoliths in the hanging-walls of the normal faults during Liassic extension.

The early Liassic tilting of the fault blocks is recorded by bathymetric evidence from cyrto-crinoids and zoophycos from the La Mure half graben, in western Pelvoux (Roux et al. 1988). These data indicate that in the deeper parts of the half-graben the sediments were deposited at water depths of over 1 km, while close to the top corners of the blocks, the water depths were only 300—500 metres.

The large Jurassic syn-rift sequences on the Cevennes Fault, west of the Alps, (Fig. 1), the La Mure and the Ornon (Belledonne) and internal Grandes Rousses Faults (Fig. 3) appear to have developed on older coal-bearing basins (Debelmas & Lemoine 1970), suggesting a Carboniferous inheritance for the Mesozoic basins.

In the Dauphinois Zone of the French Alps, subsidence continued throughout the Jurassic and Cretaceous, producing a thick post-rift sequence of shales and carbonates. Well data from the Vercors indicate an increase in subsidence rate during the Oxfordian, suggesting renewed local extension (Gillcrist 1988). Much of this sequence has been removed from the Pelvoux region by Alpine thrusting or by erosion; the post-rift sequence is now best preserved west of Pelvoux, in the Sub-Alpine Chains where it is over 2 km thick.

Internal to the Dauphinois Zone, the Briançonnais Zone of the French Alps shows a different subsidence history, with a much thicker Triassic sequence of quartzites and carbonates overlying a thick Permo-Carboniferous basin. The Triassic sequence possibly reflects the waning phases of thermal subsidence following Carboniferous extension. In the southern Briançonnais zone, east of Pelvoux, there are no Jurassic syn-rift or post-rift sediments. The Triassic limestones show deep karstic weather-

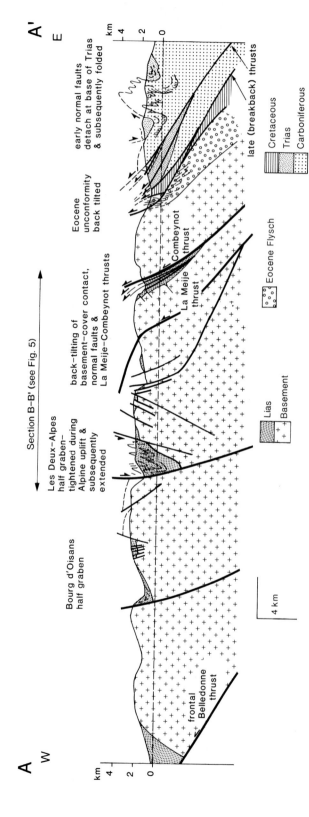

Fig. 4. A regional cross section across the major basement massifs of the external zones, illustrating the main fault geometries produced by a complex sequence of Mesozoic extension, Alpine inversion and a post-Alpine-thrusting phase of extension.

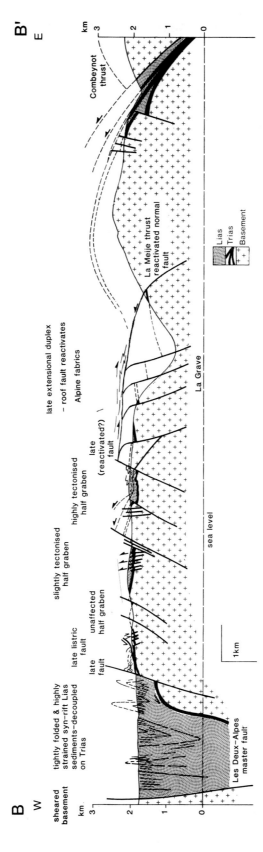

Fig. 5. A detailed cross section through the plateau d'Emparis and the La Meije basement massifs, illustrating the control of Mesozoic extensional faults on Alpine inversion, and the reactivation of Alpine structures during the post-thrusting phase of extension.

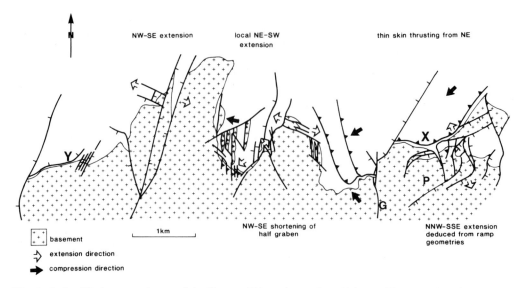

Fig. 6. A simplified structural map of the Plateau d'Emparis, northern Pelvous. X = post-thrusting normal shears; P = la Pisse Noir; G = Grand Clot.

ing, indicating uplift during Late Triassic or Jurassic times. The origin of this uplift is beyond the scope of this paper and will be discussed elsewhere.

Alpine compression

The main Alpine shortening in the Briançonnais Zone and many of the thrusts in the Dauphinois zone developed after the deposition of Eocene flysch (Gidon 1979, Chambers pers. comm). On the east side of the Pelvoux massif, the unconformity between basement and flysch is severely imbricated. Many of the thrusts follow easy-slip horizons in the Triassic or Jurassic, though in the Dauphinos zone the Mesozoic normal faults act as buttresses to this slip, causing steps in the thrusts or zones of folding. The folds are shown dramatically in the half-graben of Bourg D'Oisans and Deux Alpes where they are associated with an intense, axial-planar cleavage and steeply plunging stretching lineations (Gillcrist et al. 1987).

Schematic illustrations of the more common inversion geometries encountered in the French Alps are shown in Fig. 7, taken partly from Gillcrist et al. (1987). At the pre-rift and syn-rift stratigraphic level some faults still show net extension. Others, however, show net contraction and may form an imbricate thrust zone, which can only be differentiated from a thin-skinned imbricate thrust zone by the high cut-off angles between faults and bedding.

Examples of these high-angle imbricate zones, developed from the reworking of closely spaced extensional faults, can be seen near the summit of the Plateau d'Emparis (Figs 5 and 6). Locally there may be failure of the hangingwall back-thrust sequences where the back-thrusts slice through the previously-formed inversion anti-clines (Fig. 7.8). Floating blocks of basement may occur, bounded by the unconformity, the normal fault and the subsequent thrust (Fig. 7.1). Some extensional faults were re-activated to carry their pre-rift and syn-rift sequences along a footwall fault, parallel to bedding in the post-rift sediments (Fig. 7.6 and Fig. 8).

On a regional scale the thrusts generally developed in a foreland-propagating sequence (e.g. Butler et al. 1986), so that the earlier thrusts in eastern Pelvoux were back-steepened or back-folded by movements on the later thrusts at depth. There are some break-back fault systems, such as the Frontal Pennine Thrust at the eastern margin of Pelvoux (Fig. 4). Mapping shows the thrust to be a simple, planar structure, which cuts across the previously back-steepened strata and earlier thrusts, such that it appears locally as an extensional fault from cut-off relationships.

Thrust directions vary from NW-vergent, north and east of the Pelvoux Massif to SW vergent, south of the Massif. An anticlockwise rotation and change in thrust sense has been documented from other parts of the external

Alps. In the Helvetic Alps of Switzerland, Dietrich & Durney (1986) described a change from N-directed thrusting in the older, upper Helvetic nappes, to NW-to-W-verging shear in the youngest part of the nappe pile. Gourlay (1986) and Spencer (1989) described a similar deformation sequence from the Mont Blanc area. Vialon *et al.* (1989) discussed the changes in thrust direction around the Alpine arc in terms of a ring-shear model, involving radial compression directions in a vertical, dextral, simple-shear band between a stable, outer zone and a coaxially rotating inner cylinder. In plate tectonic terms this can be explained by the rotation of the Apulian plate relative to a fixed European plate (Fig. 9b) (Coward & Dietrich 1989).

In detail, however, the structures are difficult to relate to a simple model of a rotating, inner Alpine arc with compression along the ring shear; there are also small zones of body rotation and rotational strain. In western Pelvoux there are pronounced local variations in thrust direction, often within individual thrust sheets. Thus westward along the trace of the thrust sheet, the thrust directions may change from NW to W to SW (Fig. 3; Gillcrist *et al.* 1987, Gillcrist 1988). This suggests that there were local rotations, possibly near the lateral tips to thrusts, where lateral propagation has been hindered (Fig. 9a).

Gravitational collapse of the thickened thrust-pile could lead to variations in thrust direction. Dietrich & Casey (1989) interpret the Simplon normal fault in the Swiss Alps (e.g. Mancktelow 1985; Steck 1987) as such a collapse structure, inducing westward mass escape and hence allowing SW-directed thrusting in the southern French Alps (see also Fig. 9d).

Buttressing of thrust displacement by early basin-bounding faults or by earlier folds may lead to local pure shear strains and to lateral expulsion. The incremental strain work of Gourlay (1986) and Spencer (1989) shows a pronounced anticlockwise change in incremental extension direction with time. This could indicate either (i) rotation or (ii) thrust displacement and shortening initially in a *c.* WNW direction, with associated expulsion of material out to the SW. An increase in the amount of lateral expulsion would lead to an anticlockwise change in sense of the incremental extension direction. Such buttressing and lateral expulsion could occur several times during the growth of a thrust wedge and Tapponnier (1977) suggested that the whole Alpine arc formed by lateral expulsion of European crust away from the Apulian indentor. On a large scale, the

stretched crust of the Dauphinois and Valais basins was perhaps weaker than the more-rigid, unstretched European crust (Gillcrist *et al.* 1987), which therefore acted as a buttress, causing material to escape laterally to the SW in France and to the NE in the Eastern Alps and Carpathians. The buttressing effect of the Valais fault zone was discussed by Laubscher (1983), where compression between this basin boundary and the mobile thrust sheets to the south, caused important back-folds in the Central Alps.

On a smaller scale, however, lateral ramps offset zones of thinned crust developed during Mesozoic basin development (Fig. 10a), forming a tooth-like margin to the basin. If these lateral ramps were offset during early Alpine deformation, or if the compressional movements were oblique to the earlier extension, then the teeth of unstretched crust on one margin would not fit back into the sockets of stretched crust on the opposite margin, leading to localized lateral expulsion or escape of material (Fig. 10b). Alpine inversion could lead to strain complexities, where material did not just escape vertically, by crustal thickening, but also escaped laterally, so that 3D strains vary markedly over a small area. The various compression directions mapped out in the Plateau d'Emparis (Fig. 6), may reflect interference between NW−SE shortening of the Mesozoic half-graben and thin-skinned thrusting from the NE, related to lateral escape of material.

The amounts of Alpine thrust displacement are large. Using thrust balancing techniques, Butler (1983) estimated a shortening of over 100 km across the external French Alps south of Mont Blanc. However, these displacement figures must be considered as only approximate, as it is difficult to balance sections in 2D, where (i) the initial stratigraphic template is highly variable in thickness, due to Mesozoic basin development and (ii) the displacements are not confined to one section plane, that is, they are non-plane strain and involve rotations and lateral expulsion of material in and out of the plane of section.

Late alpine extensional movements

Many of the small structures at the base of the Pelvoux thrust sheets show evidence of extensional movement, where the hangingwall has moved down to the southeast. This is particularly visible on the Vallon Valsenestre and La Muzelle thrust sheets (Gillcrist *et al.* 1987) where the kinematic indicators include small-scale folds and shear bands. Similarly many of the normal faults in the La Grave region, at the

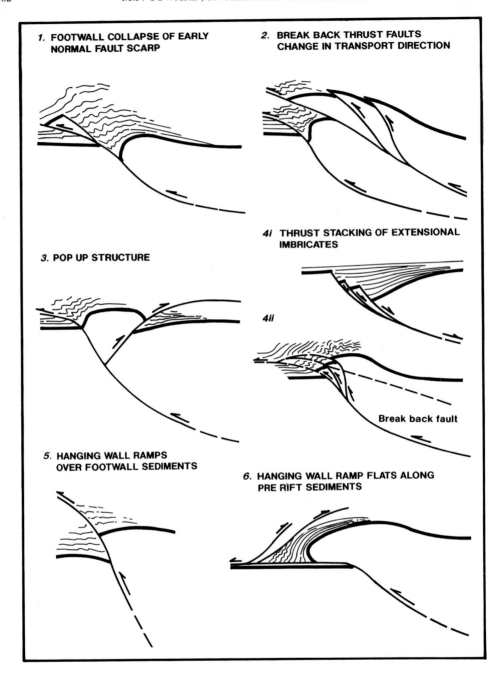

Fig. 7. Schematic illustrations of the more common inversion geometries encountered in the French Alps (based on Gillcrist *et al.* 1987 and Gillcrist 1988).

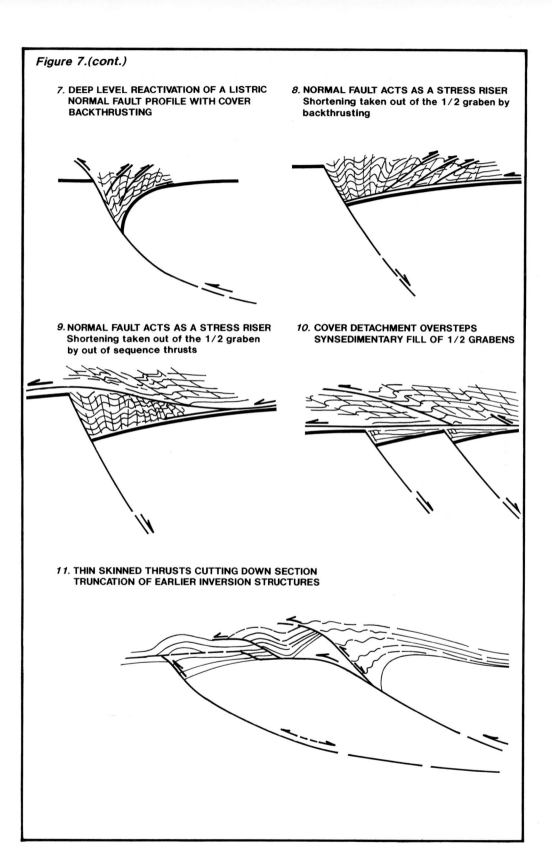

Figure 7.(cont.)

7. DEEP LEVEL REACTIVATION OF A LISTRIC
   NORMAL FAULT PROFILE WITH COVER
   BACKTHRUSTING

8. NORMAL FAULT ACTS AS A STRESS RISER
   Shortening taken out of the 1/2 graben by
   backthrusting

9. NORMAL FAULT ACTS AS A STRESS RISER
   Shortening taken out of the 1/2 graben
   by out of sequence thrusts

10. COVER DETACHMENT OVERSTEPS
    SYNSEDIMENTARY FILL OF 1/2 GRABENS

11. THIN SKINNED THRUSTS CUTTING DOWN SECTION
    TRUNCATION OF EARLIER INVERSION STRUCTURES

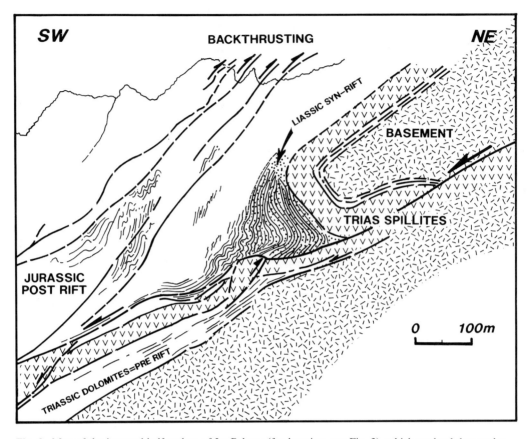

Fig. 8. Map of the inverted half-graben of La Paletas (for location, see Fig. 3), which evolved due to the reactivation of an Early Liassic extensional fault carrying pre-rift and syn-rift sequences along a footwall flat. The high cut-off angle between the syn-rift sediments and the reactivated fault plane is characteristic of an inverted half-graben.

eastern end of the Plateau d'Emparis, post-date the thrust movements, as they cut across sheared basement and cleaved Liassic rocks (Fig. 6). Most of these faults dip east and are associated with the westward tilting of the top of the basement. However, above Le Grand Clot (Fig. 6) there is a large, NW-dipping late-Alpine fault which offsets Liassic shales with two phases of NW-verging Alpine folds.

The Deux Alpes half-graben was again extended following Alpine compression, so that (i) there are late listric faults which affect bedding and Alpine cleavage at the top of the basement on the hangingwall of the fault and (ii) the main bounding-fault on the west side of the graben cuts across earlier thrusts.

The late-Alpine extension appears to be largely confined to the region east of the Deux Alpes–Aspres les Corps fault. In the Bourg d'Oisans half-graben to the NW, there is little

evidence of late-Alpine normal faulting and the faults and folds seem to be controlled by Mesozoic extension and early Alpine compression. Most of the normal faults carry syn-sedimentary breccias on their hangingwalls. However, even in this half-graben, in the Roches d'Armentier half-grabens on the east side of the main structure, there is evidence for some late extension as the Alpine cleavage is smeared into the normal faults.

The precise age of this Alpine extension is unknown as there is no syn-rift fill preserved. Extension occurred after considerable Alpine crustal shortening and thickening, presumably when the region was one of considerable positive relief. The Aspres les Corps fault, which is a southerly continuation of the Deux Alpes fault (Fig. 5), shows evidence of inversion in Miocene-or-later time.

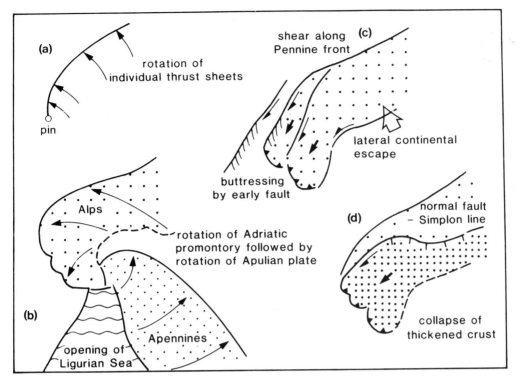

Fig. 9. Possible mechanisms for variations in directions of thrusting in the western Alps (see text for discussion).

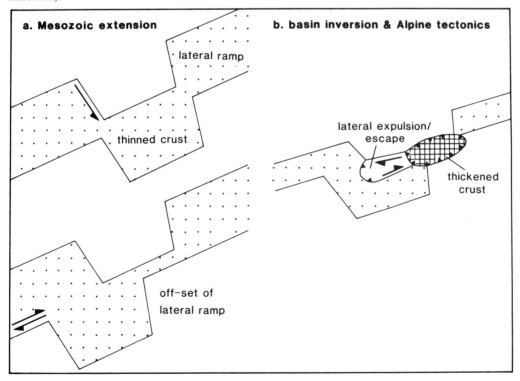

Fig. 10. Schematic illustration of the effects of offsetting Mesozoic lateral ramps during Alpine deformation, leading to a lateral expulsion of material as the margins do not 'fit' back together.

Geometry of normal faults

The geometries of normal faults will be described with particular reference to the region between Deux Alpes and La Grave (Figs 5 and 6).

Listric versus planar geometries

Large-scale crustal-extension has been presumed to occur on either (i) listric faults, which may be spoon-shaped in 3D, and hence curve in plan view and flatten in section (e.g. Gibbs 1984), or (ii) planar faults, bounding blocks, which rotate during extension, similar to a collapsing set of books or dominoes (e.g. Morton & Black 1975). Both listric and planar faults occur in northern Pelvoux, in both cover and basement rocks. On the east side of the Deux Alpes half-graben a late-Alpine listric fault can be seen to have detached at the base of the Lias, producing a pronounced roll-over fold in the Liassic sediments. This fold also affects Alpine cleavage. On the top of the Plateau d'Emparis, there are a series of faults which are apparently curved in map view, and seem to detach close to the base of the Mesozoic cover sequence. However, on la Pisse Noir (Fig. 6), there is a fault which affects basement and yet is curved in plan. All these faults affect rocks which were compacted and metamorphosed before faulting, i.e. they cannot be considered as growth structures.

The majority of extensional faults, however, appear to be approximately planar structures and much of the extension appears to have followed the rotated block model. In the area encompassed by Figs 5 & 6, there are three main orders of faulting.

(i) The master fault to the Deux Alpes half-graben dips to the east and has the most important displacement. It was active during Mesozoic and Alpine extension. On a large scale the master faults to the major half-graben are about 15 km apart.

(ii) There are west-dipping faults which appear antithetic to this structure, spaced at approximately 1 to 2 km.

(iii) There are smaller, east-dipping faults which are antithetic to the west-dipping faults; these are locally developed and are spaced at less than 100 metres.

These different orders of normal faults, involving dominantly antithetic systems, can be found in other half-graben in the Pelvoux massif. They may owe their origin to the strains developed on the local master fault. At some depth in the crust, presumably close to the brittle–ductile transition, faults in the upper crust will become ductile shears. These may form with dips lower than brittle faults, which presumably formed by typical Coulomb failure criteria (Ramsay & Huber 1987). Thus at depth, planar faults should decrease their dip as they change into ductile shear zones (see also Coward 1990). This change in dip would cause strain in the hangingwall of the master fault, observable as a system of antithetic structures. A step in the profile of a normal fault will also result in the generation of hangingwall strains. The cartoons in Fig. 11 are based on interpretation of seismic data. They illustrate how progressive extension and rotation of a master-fault with a stepped profile might lead to the generation of antithetic structures in the hangingwall, in order to accommodate the induced strain.

Interpretation of the ECORS deep-seismic data from the northern part of the Western Alps (Bayer et al. 1987), suggests that there is a zone of sub-horizontal seismic reflectors at approximately 20 km depth. This may represent sub-horizontal thrusts beneath the Mont Blanc and Belledonne massifs, or alternatively the region where brittle faults near the surface change to more penetrative ductile strain at depth. On the Deux Alpes–La Grave section (Fig. 5) assuming that the faults maintain reasonably constant dips with depth, the second-order antithetic faults must terminate near the master bounding-fault at depths of 10–18 km. This could suggest that the master bounding-fault of the Deux Alpes graben becomes a ductile structure at approximately 10 km depth and merges with a more ductile, basal detachment at approximately 18 km depth (see also Fig. 2). This is in broad agreement with cross sections through Pelvoux (Menard 1979), which were constructed from seismic and gravity data.

The Mesozoic and Alpine normal faults affected crust with a strong Variscan gneissic fabric. Prior to Alpine extension this fabric had been modified in intensity and orientation by Alpine compressional events. Assuming Coulomb failure criteria, earlier fabrics may fail in preference to the development of new faults, if the cohesion and friction along the early fabric planes are low. Thus the strike and dip of faults may vary, depending on the variation in orientation of the earlier fabric. Block-bounding faults could steepen or shallow with depth, similar to the geometry of stepped faults in a gravitational, growth-fault environment. Extension along a bent fault surface will lead to strains in the hangingwall and/or footwall and therefore to localized roll-over geometry and

a)

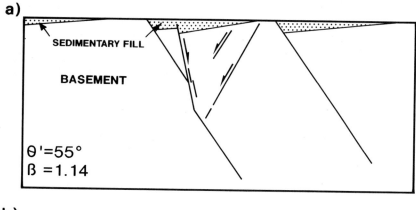

SEDIMENTARY FILL

BASEMENT

$\theta' = 55°$
$\beta = 1.14$

b)

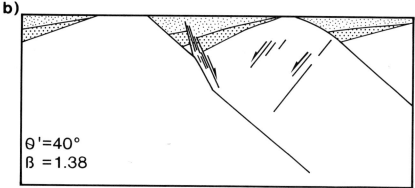

$\theta' = 40°$
$\beta = 1.38$

c)

ONLAP OF SEDIMENT   LISTRIC   REACTIVATED
TOWARDS BASEMENT HIGH   FAULT   ANTITHETICS

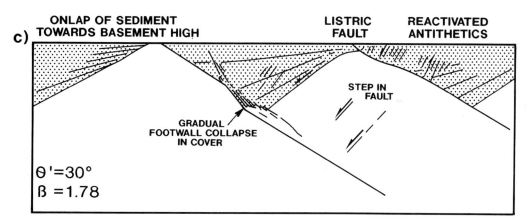

STEP IN
FAULT

GRADUAL
FOOTWALL COLLAPSE
IN COVER

$\theta' = 30°$
$\beta = 1.78$

Fig. 11. Cartoon cross sections, based on interpretation of seismic data, illustrating the sequential development of antithetic structures with increasing extension and rotation on a master fault possessing a stepped profile.

the development of synthetic and antithetic faults. Where the faults locally steepen with depth then the hangingwall is extended, perhaps producing systems of secondary normal faults above the bend (Fig. 11). Where the

rotational faults locally become shallower with depth, then second-order compressional structures could develop above the bend.

Continued movement could smooth out a small bend on a fault surface, as discussed by

Knipe (1985) for thrust-ramp geometries. Hence, systems of antithetic or synthetic faults should be only short lived, if they are related to irregularities in the surfaces of rotating fault planes. Such a pattern may be evident in the Bourg d'Oisans and Deux Alpes half-graben, where the second- and third-order faults were largely confined to movement during the Hettangian and Sinemurian, while the main basin-bounding faults were active till Bajocian times (e.g. Lemoine *et al.* 1987; Gillcrist *et al.* 1987). Note that if the graben-bounding fault was markedly listric, then antithetic and synthetic faults should form throughout its history, recording the cumulative strain in the hangingwall. This may be a method of distinguishing large-scale listric faults from essentially straight rotational faults.

Reworking of the Alpine structures: the large-scale duplex structure of the Plateau d'Emparis

According to Coulomb failure criteria, low-angle normal faults can form from the reworking of earlier fabrics or fracture surfaces, provided these surfaces have low cohesion and friction. Sliding on these pre-existing anisotropies is further facilitated by the presence of abnormally-high pore-fluid pressures, reducing the effective stress or (p-fluid) toward zero (Sibson 1985 for discussion). Examples of low-angle detachments which rework earlier thrust fabrics are documented from the Basin and Range of the USA (e.g. Wernicke 1985) and the Devonian basins of Scotland (Enfield & Coward 1987) and Norway (Serrane & Seguret 1987). Alpine thrust tectonics imposed a strong tectonic fabric sub-parallel to bedding on the Liassic shales of the Dauphinois zone. There is evidence of high pore-fluid pressures from the presence of calcite filled veins parallel to bedding or the Alpine cleavage and in thrust-related conjugate vein arrays (e.g. Beach 1981). Some of the zones of Alpine schistosity were subsequently reworked by later Alpine extensional movements, so that Alpine cleavages were folded by crenulations and compressional veins arrays were cut by tension gashes, whose sense indicates that the hangingwall moved down to the southeast.

Zones of intense Alpine fabric form the floor faults for small-scale extensional fault-arrays, and on the Plateau d'Emparis they form the roof structure for a large extensional duplex (Fig. 5) north of La Grave. Within this duplex the Alpine faults bound rotated fault blocks, within which the top of the basement is tilted towards the northeast and the faults offset Alpine age shear zones in the Lower Liassic shales. The faults curve upwards to become asymptotic to an intense Alpine fabric in the schistose Lias. Small-scale structures, such as secondary shear bands and sheath folds indicate that this zone has been reactivated as an extensional shear zone, whose hangingwall has moved down to the SE. The base of this fault zone is unknown, but presumably lies at several kilometres depth in the La Meije basement.

The regional Mesozoic fault geometry and extension direction

Figure 12 shows a simplified map of the distribution of normal faults across the Pelvoux region, based on regional mapping and an attempt at restoration of Alpine structures. There are two orthogonal trends: the main extensional faults trend NNE−SSW, while the tear faults trend WNW−ESE. These two trends also influence much of the Mesozoic extension across eastern France and are partially inherited from earlier Variscan structures. Coward & Dietrich (1989) suggest that the Liassic extension direction was controlled by variscan tear faults and that the Tethyan Ocean can be considered as a large-scale pull-apart basin on these large, reactivated Variscan structures.

Large strike-slip fault-systems seem to have acted as basement-bounding tear faults throughout several episodes of extension and inversion in NW Europe (Beach 1987, Coward & Trudgill 1989). This control on extension direction is probably related to middle and lower crustal fabrics, rather than the trend of brittle faults in the upper crust. Major tear faults offset zones of different crustal fabric and strength, so that zones of stronger crust may abut against zones of weaker crust, to produce irregular corrugations in the brittle−ductile transition. These corrugations might produce an easy-slip direction parallel to the tear faults and a difficult-slip direction perpendicular to the faults, hence tramlining subsequent fault movement.

The effect of variations in trend of Variscan structures on subsequent extension direction can be seen in the northern part of the Pelvoux Massif. The movement direction during extensional faulting can be obtained from (i) small-scale kinematic indicators on the fault surfaces and (ii) (more reliably) the trends of lateral ramps or from the curved shapes of faults in plan (e.g. Coward & Gibbs 1988a). The extension directions vary across the Plateau

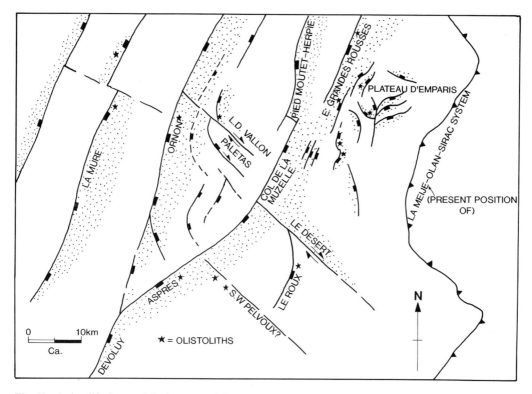

Fig. 12. A simplified map of the interpreted distribution of normal faults across the Pelvoux region during the Jurassic.

d'Emparis, as shown in Fig. 6. In the west, the extension direction was towards the WNW, perpendicular to the principal bounding faults of the Les Deux Alpes and Bourg d'Oisans half-graben. In the east, however, above La Grave, the extension direction was towards the NW or NNW. Both regions underwent Alpine extension; the variation does not reflect a change in the extension direction from the Mesozoic to Tertiary. However, the variation in extension direction may reflect the difference in basement structure, as in the La Grave region, the Variscan basement carries steep, NNW-trending shear zones, which locally could have controlled the extension direction.

On the top of the Plateau d'Emparis there are also listric faults which show NE−SW extension. Their age is unknown as their outcrop is confined to the basement and Triassic cover, where Alpine fabrics are missing and there is no possibility of observing Liassic syn-rift fill. Thus during either the Mesozoic or the Alpine phase of extension, the bulk stress ellipsoid was perhaps oblate, allowing both NW−SE and NE−SW extension.

The amount of extension

An estimate of the late-Alpine extension can be obtained from the dip of the beds and associated faults on the Plateau d'Emparis, using the equation for rotated fault blocks (Le Pichon & Sibuet 1981). This suggests a stretching factor of about 1.3 for the duplex zone above La Grave. The Mesozoic extension is more difficult to measure, because of the effects of Alpine tectonic inversion. The faults have been almost certainly back-rotated during Alpine compression, possibly to their initial Liassic dips. The beds have been shortened by ductile strain as well as folding and thrusting and hence line length balancing techniques cannot be used. A rough estimate of the Mesozoic stretch can be obtained from the thickness of the post-rift sediments. Using the subsidence equations derived for an average crust and lithosphere thickness (e.g. McKenzie 1978), the 2 km of Middle Jurassic and Cretaceous sediments observed west of Pelvoux, suggest a stretching factor of approximately 1.3. This figure assumes relatively little erosion of the sedimentary column during Middle Cretaceous uplift. Thus the crust was perhaps thinned to about 2/3 of its previous thickness during Mesozoic stretching.

If the large graben-bounding normal faults had initial dips of $c.$ 60, then after stretching by $c.$ 1.3, the faults would have had dips of $c.$ 40° and the beds would have been tilted to $c.$ 20° in the half-graben. The spacing between the large, first-order normal faults bounding the Belledonne and Grand Rousses Massif was $c.$ 15 km; though in the west, close to La Mure, the blocks are closer spaced. In the large half-graben this would correspond to a throw of $c.$ 5 km. In the Dauphinois zone as well as the Briançonnais zone, the Triassic limestones show syn-sedimentary brecciation, suggesting that they were locally eroded and redeposited under shallow-water conditions. Assuming the subsidence equations of McKenzie (1978) can be applied to the syn-rift phase of stretching and that the sediments had average densities, then the tectonic subsidence might have been $c.$ 1.8−1.9 km, that is there should have been $c.$ 3.6−3.8 km of syn-rift sediment fill in the half-graben and the amount of footwall uplift should have been $c.$ 650−750 metres (see discussion on footwall uplift by Barr 1987). This uplift would have been sufficient to cause local erosion of the Triassic sediments and underlying basement and to cause condensed, onlapping Liassic sequences to be deposited on the dip slopes of the tilted blocks. The footwalls of narrower fault blocks (e.g. at La Mure) would probably have remained below sea level throughout their stretching history (Barr 1987), in accordance with the water-depth estimates of Roux *et al.* (1988).

Discussion

The southern French Alps form an inverted basin-margin. Original Mesozoic normal faults are, in places, preserved, uplifted several kilometres above sea level. They are now partially eroded and observable in spectacular sections on the mountain sides. They show aspects of fault kinematics which may be applied to other regions of crustal extension, including the following observations.

(i) Both listric and straight faults occur in granitic basement and its sedimentary cover. No single simplistic model should be used to predict fault shapes.

(ii) Several orders of antithetic faults occur, associated with rotated fault blocks as well as irotational listric faults. These structures may possibly be ascribed to strains developed above small kinks or jogs in the fault surface or changes

in dip of the fault at the brittle−ductile transition. The presence of such fault arrays, or a roll-over geometry at the top-basement level, does not necessarily imply slip on a large-scale listric fault.

(iii) Basement fabrics appear to control local, as well as regional, extension directions.

(iv) Extension can occur on two fault orientations, apparently simultaneously; that is extension may not involve plane-strain conditions and must involve some oblique displacement. A similar situation may have occurred during Triassic extensional tectonics in parts of western Britain and the North Sea (Coward & Gibbs 1988b). Simple 2D restoration techniques should not be applied.

(v) During tectonic inversion, the top to the pre-rift basement may be back-rotated towards its initial configuration, while the half-graben infill is squeezed out in a series of upright folds and back-thrusts. An irregular, extensional fault-geometry allows the sediment-fill to be squeezed laterally. Pre-rift basement rock may also be 'squeezed' laterally, where the template of frontal and lateral ramps along one basin margin do not fit back into the sockets of frontal and lateral ramps on the opposite margin. Plane strain restoration techniques should not be applied to these thrust tectonic regimes.

Ralph Gillcrist and Bruce Trudgill acknowledge receipt of NERC grants. We are grateful for discussions with colleagues from France (Pierre-Charles Graciansky, Jean Dercourt, Arnaud Pecher), Switzerland (John Ramsay, Dorothee Dietrich, Martin Casey) and the UK (Rod Graham, Dave Roberts, Alaistair Beach, Rob Butler), together with colleagues from Imperial College (Sara Spencer, Alan Chambers, Harold Fyffe). Referee's comments caused us to omit the more interesting, yet speculative, interpretations.

References

BARR, D. 1987. Lithospheric stretching, detached normal faulting and footwall uplift. *In:* COWARD, M. P., DEWEY, J. F. & HANCOCK, P. (eds). *Continental Extensional Tectonics.* Geological Society, London, Special Publication. **28**, 75−94.

BAYER, R. *et al.* 1987. Premiers resultats de la traverse des Alpes occidentales par seismique reflexion verticale (Programme ECORS−CROP). *Comptes Rendus de l'Academie des Sciences de Paris*, **305**, 1461−1470.

BEACH, A. 1981. Some observations on the development of thrust faults in the Ultradauphinois zone, French Alps, *In:* MCCLAY, K. R. & PRICE, N. J. (eds). *Thrust and Nappe Tectonics.* Geological Society, London, Special Publication **9**, 329−334.

—— 1987. A regional tectonic model for linked tectonics in north-west Europe. *In:* BROOKS, J. & GLENNIE, K. (eds). *Petroleum Geology of North West Europe*, Graham & Trotman, London, 43–48.

BOYER, S. E. & ELLIOTT, D. 1982. Thrust systems. *Bulletin of the American Association of Petroleum Geologists*, **66**, 1196–1230.

BUTLER, R. W. H. 1983. Balanced cross-sections and their implications for the deep structure of the NW Alps. *Journal of Structural Geology*, **5**, 125–137.

—— 1986. Thrust tectonics, deep structure and crustal subduction in the alps and Himalayas. *Journal of the Geological Society, London*, **143**, 857–873.

——, MATTHEWS, S. J. & PARISH, M. 1986. The NW external Alpine thrust belt and its implications for the geometry of the western Alpine orogen. *In:* COWARD, M. P. & RIES, A. C. (eds). *Collision Tectonics*, Geological Society, London, Special Publication **19**, 245–260.

COWARD, M. P. 1986. Heterogeneous stretching and basin development. *Earth and Planetary Science Letters*, **80**, 325–336.

—— & TRUDGILL, B. D. 1989. Basin development and basin structure, West of Britain. *Bulletin of the Geological Society, France*, **8**, 483–436.

—— 1990. Shear zones at the Laxford Front, NW Scotland and their significance in the interpretation of lower crustal structure. *Journal of the Geological Society, London*, **147**, 279–286.

—— & DIETRICH, D. 1989. Alpine tectonics — an overview. *In:* COWARD, M. P., DIETRICH, D. & PARK, R. G. (eds). *Alpine Tectonics*. Geological Society, London, Special Publication **45**, 1–29.

—— & GIBBS, A. D. 1988a. *Structural interpretation with emphasis on extensional tectonics.* JAPEC Course Notes, No. 49.

—— & —— 1988b. *Tectonic development of NW Europe.* JAPEC Course Notes, No. 50.

DEBELMAS, J. & KERCHOVE, C. 1980. Les Alpes franco-italiennes. *Geologie Alpine*, **56**, 21–58.

—— & LEMOINE, M. 1970. The western Alpes: Paleogeography and structure. *Earth Science Reviews*, **6**, 221–256.

DERCOURT, J. *et al.* 1986. Geological evolution of the Tethys Belt from the Atlantic to the Pamirs since the Lias. *Tectonophysics*, **123**, 241–315.

DEWEY, J. F. 1988. Extensional collapse of orogens. *Tectonics*, **7**, 1123–1139.

——, SHACKLETON, R. M., CHANG, C. F. & SUN, Y. Y. 1988. *Philosophical Transactions of the Royal Society, London*, Series.

——, HELMAN, M. L., TURCO, E., HUTTON, D. W. & KNOTT, S. D. 1989. Kinematics of the western Mediterranean. *In:* COWARD, M. P. & DIETRICH, D. & PARK, R. G. (eds). *Alpine Tectonics*, Geological Society, London, Special Publication **45**, 265–283.

DIETRICH, D. & CASEY, M. 1989. *In:* COWARD, M. P., DIETRICH, D. & PARK, R. G. (eds). *Alpine Tectonics*, Geological Society, London, Special Publication **45**, 47–63.

—— & DURNEY, D.W. 1986. Change in direction of overthrust shear in the Helvetic nappes of western

Switzerland. *Journal of Structural Geology*, **8**, 373–381.

ENFIELD, M. & COWARD, M. P. 1987. The structure of the West Okney Basin *Journal of the Geological Society, London*, **144**, 871–884.

GIBBS, A. D. 1984. Structural evolution of extensional basin margins. *Journal of the Geological Society, London*, **141**, 609–620.

GIDON, M. 1979. Le role d'etape successives de deformation dans la tectonique Alpine du massif de Pelvoux (Alpes occidentales). Comptes Rendus de l'Academie des Sciences, Paris, **288**, 803–806.

GILLCRIST, R. 1988. *Mesozoic basin development and structural inversion in the external French Alps.* PhD. Thesis, University of London.

——, COWARD, M. P. & MUGNIER, J. L. 1987. Structural inversion and its controls: examples from the Alpine foreland and the French Alps. *Geodynamica Acta*, **1**, 5–34.

GOURLAY, P. 1986. La deformation de socle et des courverture delphino helvetiques dans la region du Mont Blanc (Alpes occidentales). Bulletin of the Geological Society, France, **8**, 159–169.

KNIPE, R. J. 1985. Footwall geometry and the rheology of thrust sheets. *Journal of Structural Geology*, **7**, 1–10.

LAUBSCHER, H. P. 1983. Detachment, shear and compression in the central Alps. *Geological Society of America Nemoir*, **158**, 19–211.

LEMOINE M., BAS, T., ARNAUD–VANNEAU, A., ARNAUD, H., DUMONT, T., GIDON, M., BOURBON, M., DE GRACIANSKY, P. C., RUDKIEWICZ, J. L. & TRIACART, P. 1986. The continental margin of Mesozoic Tethys in the western Alps. *Marine and Petroleum Geology*, **3**, 178–199.

——, GIDON, M. & BARFETY, J. C. 1981. Les massifs cristallins externes des Alpes occidentales: d'anciens blocs bascules nes au Lias lors du rifting tethysien. *Comptes Rendus de l'Academie des Sciences*, Paris, **292**, 917–920.

LE PICHON, X. & SIBUET, J. C. 1981. Passive margins: a model of formation. *Journal of Geophysical Research*, **86**, 3708–3720.

MCKENZIE, D. P. 1978. Some remarks on the development of sedimentary basins. *Earth and Planetary Science Letters*, **40**, 25–32.

MANCKTELOW, N. 1985. The Simplon line: a major displacement zone in the western Lepontine Alps. *Eclogae Geologicae Helvetiae*, **78**, 73–96.

MENARD, G. 1979. *Relations entre structures profondes et structures superficielles dans le sud-est de la France: essai d'utilisation de donnees Ieophysiques.* These 3 eme cycle, Universite de Grenoble.

MORTON, W. H. & BLACK, R. 1975. Crustal attenuation in Afar. *In:* PILGAR, A. & ROSLER, A. (eds). Afar Depression of Ethiopia. Inter-Union Commission on Geodynamics. Proceedings of International Symposium on the Afar Region and related rift problems. E. Schweizerbart'sche Verlagsbuchhandlung, Stuttgart, Germany. Scientific Report No. 14, 55–65.

RAMSAY, J. G. 1963. Stratigraphy, structure and metamorphism of the western alps. *Proceedings of the*

Geological Association, **74**, 357−391.

ROUX, M., J. P., BAS, T., DUMONT, T., GRACIANSKY, P. C., LEMOINE, M. & RUDKIEWICZ, J. L. 1988. Bathymetric evolution of the Tethyan margin of the western Alps (data from stalked crinoids): a reappraisal of eustatism problems during the Jurassic. *Bulletin of the Geological Society, France*, 8, IV, 4, 633−41.

SERRANE, M. & SEGURET, M. 1987. The Devonian basins of western Norway: tectonics and kinematics of an extending crust *In:* COWARD, M. P., DEWEY, J. F. & HANCOCK, P. L. (eds). *Continental Extensional Tectonics*, Geological Society, London Special Publication **28**, 537−548.

SIBSON, R. H. Short notes on fault reactivation. *Journal of Structural Geology*, **7**, 751−754.

SMITH, A. G. 1971. Alpine deformation and the oceanic areas of Tethys, Mediterranean and Atlantic. *Bulletin of the Geological Society of America*, **82**, 2039−2070.

SPENCER, S. 1989. *The nature of the north Pennine Front: French Alps*. PhD thesis, University of London.

STECK, A. 1987. Le massif du Simplon — reflexions sur la cinematique des nappes de gneiss. *Schweizerische Mineralogische und Petrographische Mitteilungen*, **67**, 27−45.

TAPPONIER, P. 1977. Evolution tectonique du systeme Alpin en Mediterranee: Poincinnement et ecrasement rigide-plastique. *Bulletin of the Geological Society, France*, **19**, 437−460.

TRUMPY, R. 1980. *Geology of Switzerland, a Guide Book. Part A, an Outline of the Geology of Switzerland*. Wept, Basel.

VIALON, P., ROCHETTE, P. & MENARD, G. 1989. Indentation and rotation in the Western Alpine Arc. *In:* COWARD, M. P., DIETRICH, D. & PARK, R. G. (eds). *Alpine Tectonics*, Geological Society, London, Special Publication **45**, 329−338.

WERNICKE, B. 1985. Uniform sense simple shear of the continental lithosphere. *Canadian Journal of Earth Sciences*, **22**, 108−125.

Description of brittle extensional features in chalk on the crest of a salt ridge (NW Germany)

ANDREAS G. KOESTLER[1] & WERNER U. EHRMANN[2]

[1]*Geo-Recon A.S., Bernhard Herres vei 3, 0376 Oslo, Norway*
[2]*Alfred Wegener Institute for Polar and Marine Research, P.O. Box 120161, 2850 Bremerhaven, F.R. Germany*

Abstract: At Laegerdorf, northern Germany, several large quarries provide access to study extensional deformation features in three dimensions, in the chalk overburden of a salt diapir. Numerous individual faults and the intervening blocks have been analyzed with respect to detailed fault morphology and geometry of brittle structures within the blocks. The studied fault zones, with displacements in the range of several metres, display geometries which vary within well defined limits. The fault zones are mostly very narrow (some tens of centimetres), but can widen up to a maximum of 7 m. The fractures composing a fault zone have a dominant length below 3 m. A 3D reconstruction of one quarry shows the rhombohedral shape of the fault blocks with a block width of 100 to 150 metres and the long diagonal parallel to the salt-ridge axis. The block-internal deformation is characterized by fractures which seem to be interconnected in a network. The locality of Laegerdorf is comparable with that of the Albuskjell and Ekofisk hydrocarbon reservoirs of the central North Sea in terms both of the structural setting of the deformed chalk on top of a salt diapir and the characteristics of extensional features.

Advanced techniques of modelling hydrocarbon reservoirs need an input of detailed information which includes not only sedimentological data but also a description of structural heterogeneities. The necessary structural data can only be extracted in a limited way from seismic surveys, well logs and cores. Conceptual models for the structural style of a hydrocarbon occurrence have to be combined with site-specific geological data to achieve a basis for reservoir modelling. The study of field analogues helps to bridge the gap between the site-specific data and the conceptual models. In addition, the generation of conceptual models and new ideas is stimulated by field work in analogous sedimentological and tectonic settings.

Here, we present a description of normal faults and associated fractures in Upper Cretaceous chalk overlying the crest of a salt ridge, as exposed in the quarries at Laegerdorf, NW Germany. It is thought that this locality represents a field analogue for the chalk hydrocarbon reservoirs in the Greater Ekofisk area of the central North Sea, which are also located in the crestal area of diapiric salt structures. In these reservoirs, an important characteristic is the high porosity of the chalk, but very low matrix permeability, so that production has to be from fractures. Thus, the location, frequency, orientation, interconnection, and aperture of fractures are of critical importance

for understanding the reservoir setting and for managing production and recovery enhancement. In this context, the existence of minor faults below seismic resolution is of great importance, because they can act either as seals or as pathways. Some of the pertinent questions addressed in this study are as follows. What does a minor normal fault in chalk really look like? How is the deformation accommodated along faults? In which ways are faults and fractures interconnected? How are the blocks between distinct faults deformed?

Our study was carried out in Upper Cretaceous chalk quarries near Laegerdorf, some 80 km NW of Hamburg (Fig. 1). The chalks have been pushed through Tertiary sediments to the surface by the diapiric rise of an underlying salt ridge. Today, they are exploitated by the cement industry in three large opencast mines, measuring about 1×1 km and up to 60 m deep (Fig. 1). Stratigraphically, the 420 m thick sequence of very homogeneous and carbonate-rich (>90%) chalks ranges from Middle Coniacian to Early Maastrichtian (Schulz *et al.* 1984). The tectonic position of the chalk on top of a rising salt ridge caused brittle deformation in an extensional regime. Hence, the chalk is cut by a great number of distinct faults, fracture swarms and small-scale fractures, which can be studied in great detail due to the size and the excellent conditions of the outcrops.

From ROBERTS A. M., YIELDING, G. & FREEMAN, B. (eds), 1991, *The Geometry of Normal Faults*, Geological Society Special Publication No 56, pp 113–123

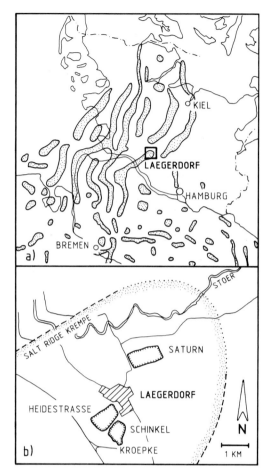

Fig. 1. Location map of the chalk quarries near Laegerdorf in NW Germany. (**a**) Salt ridge configuration (stippled) in the subsurface (from Jaritz 1973). (**b**) Detail location map of the quarries studied (this paper).

The geometrical analysis of the fault pattern, its implication for deformation in a three-dimensional strain field, and the indications for a local stress field due to diapirism overprinted by a regional stress field arising from large-scale tectonics, are presented in two earlier publications (Koestler & Ehrmann 1986, 1987). This paper focusses on the structural expression of extensional deformation in the crestal area of a salt diapir and some comparisons are drawn with deformed chalk reservoirs in the central North Sea.

Geometrical description

Systematic detailed mapping was carried out along the accessible and well exposed walls of

the Laegerdorf quarries between 1983 and 1988, and resulted in an extensive data base with several thousand measurements and geometrical observations. The three quarries are more or less rectangular in shape, the quarry walls having NW−SE and NE−SW orientations. The NE−SW direction corresponds to the long axis of the salt ridge beneath (Fig. 1). In the following, we discuss first the structural style of the distinct fault zones which compartmentalize the chalk, and then the internal deformation of the fault blocks.

Distinct fault zones (minor faults)

In the whole study area, about 15 minor faults were observed and analyzed. A minor fault in this context is defined as a fault or a fault zone with displacement exceeding 2 m. Maximum displacement on such faults measured in the quarries is about 10 m. These faults are called here 'minor' because they accommodate displacement in the range mentioned above, which would usually not be resolvable on offshore seismic surveys. So, all the description here concentrates on medium-to-small-scale features.

The most continuous and most impressive structural profile section was exposed along the NE−SW wall of Saturn quarry from 1986 onwards (Fig. 2A) (still exposed but cut back by about 5 m to the NW due to exploitation). There, six fault zones subdivide the chalk into blocks of a relatively regular size of 100 to 150 m block width. Generally, the spacing of these minor fault zones all over the exposed area seems to be very regular, 100 to 150 m measured along profiles parallel to salt ridge axis. All these minor faults in Saturn quarry strike perpendicular to the salt ridge axis and dip at about 50 to 70 degrees to the SW. There are also some structures dipping in the opposite direction (see below). Due to the doming salt ridge beneath, the chalk bedding is tilted and dips at about 10 degrees to the NE. This dip is quite constant throughout the study area (Fig. 2A). The width of the fault zones, which is defined here as the thickness of the highly fractured and brecciated zone, varies from 0.1 to about 7 m (Fig. 3a). The width of the fault zones has been analyzed by measuring the width normal to the fault surface at those places where the fault zone is bounded by two distinct slip surfaces. The histogram (Fig. 3a) displays a clear dominance of very narrow fault zone widths (<0.5 m). A second peak is at about 2.5 to 3 m, but clearly smaller than the first one. A third peak is observed at about 6 m width. In

NW-WALL OF SATURN QUARRY

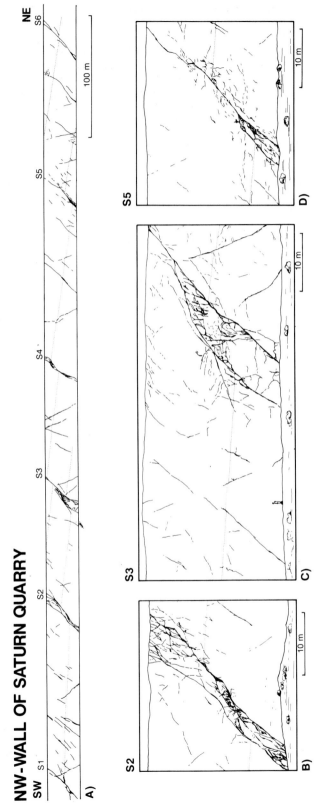

Fig. 2. Fault zones exposed at the NW wall of Saturn quarry. (**A**) Six faults with displacements of up to 10 m cut the chalk at relatively regular intervals. Note the constant dip direction and angle of the main faults and the more variable dip of the fault-block-internal structures. (**B**), (**C**), (**D**) Detail sketches of the major fault zones S2, S3 and S5. The sketches are somewhat distorted because of the 60° slope of the quarry wall. The faults are cut at an angle of about 30° to their strike direction. Note the complex fault-internal fracture pattern and the converging bordering faults which accommodate most of the total displacement.

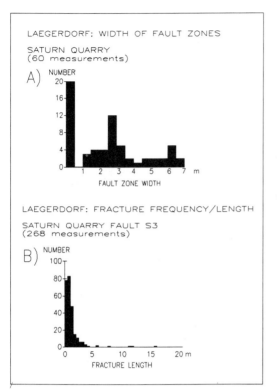

LAEGERDORF: WIDTH OF FAULT ZONES

SATURN QUARRY
(60 measurements)

A) NUMBER

FAULT ZONE WIDTH

LAEGERDORF: FRACTURE FREQUENCY/LENGTH

SATURN QUARRY FAULT S3
(268 measurements)

B) NUMBER

FRACTURE LENGTH

Fig. 3. Quantitative analysis of fault zones. (**A**) Distribution of the width of the fault zones. (**B**) Distribution of fault zone internal fracture length. For discussion see text.

Strong slickenside striations are almost ubiquitous, mainly indicating dip-slip movements (Koestler & Ehrmann 1986).

The internal features of the fault zones comprise highly strained parts, expressed as breccias (with slip on the fragment surfaces indicated by striations), less strained parts (shown by shear fractures often arranged in zones), and undeformed rock volumes, which are mostly lensoid in shape. Fractures often display a conjugate pattern with the bisector of the acute angle parallel to the border faults (Figs 2B, C), or they form a single parallel set which is conjugate to the bordering faults (Fig. 4). There are also slightly undulatory minor faults running subparallel to the discrete bounding faults, producing an anastomosing pattern enclosing both highly deformed and undeformed lenses (Fig. 2B), in addition to numerous irregular fractures of various types. In a few cases, the internal shear fractures within the fault zone accommodate part of the total displacement

addition, the zones seem to be either very narrow or wider than one metre. The upper limit of observed widths is about 7 m.

Over the whole area, the structural expression of these faults seems to be quite consistent. The fault zones consist of one or two discrete slip surfaces (Figs 2B, C, D, 4). Usually a zone of highly deformed chalk is related to a fault zone. Where two bounding slip surfaces are observed, the deformation is clearly concentrated between them in the form of a high intensity of shear fractures or breccia zones (e.g. Fig. 6). Where only one slip surface is developed, fracturing can be found on both sides of the fault, in the footwall or the hangingwall. The main displacement is accommodated on one or on both of the discrete bordering faults. These border faults often are subparallel, but can also converge and continue as one single fault (Figs 2C, D). They may be planar over several metres, but also show local curved and irregular geometries. The widths of the bordering faults vary between a few millimetres and several centimetres, and are filled with breccias or clay-enriched gouge.

Fig. 4. Fault zone sharply bordered by two subparallel single faults (Heidestrasse quarry). The displacement of *c.* 1 m is mostly concentrated on the right bordering fault. The fault-internal fractures form a parallel set, which is conjugate to the border faults. The zone has a width of about 1.2 m.

(Fig. 2C). Fracture surfaces show a large variety of characteristics ranging from shear planes with polished, clay-smeared and striated surfaces, to joints without any indication of displacement (Koestler & Ehrmann 1986). The internal fractures, both shear planes and joints, vary in length from a few decimetres to several metres. The longest ones run parallel to the bordering faults.

Fracture length distribution has been analyzed on photographs for one of the fault zones (S3). This is composed of about 260 fractures longer than 0.3 m, observed over the 40 m height of the quarry wall (Fig. 3B). Most of the fractures are 0.5 to 1 m long, with the number of longer fractures decreasing rapidly. While the decrease is approximately exponential in the range 0 to 5 m, some unsystematically distributed, relatively long fractures occur.

Breccias are taken to indicate zones of intense deformation. They occur mainly in close association with the border faults, but also as isolated highly deformed lenses within the fault zones. Fragment sizes vary from 1 millimetre to a few centimetres. While most fine-grained breccias show clay enrichment in the matrix and striated fragment surfaces indicating some relative movements, breccias with larger fragments show characteristics similar to in situ highly jointed rock without measurable displacement between the fragments. The fragment shape is defined by conjugate fracture sets related to the major fault orientation and reflecting a three-dimensional strain field (Figs 5 & 7) (Aydin & Reches 1982; Reches 1983;

Fig. 5. Close-up view of fault zone S4 (see Fig. 2A). Displacement on the fault is *c.* 8 m. The highly fractured chalk within the zone clearly defines a conjugate fracture set with four sets, which also can be found at large quarry scale (cf. Fig. 7). Note also the slickenside striations and clay enrichment in the lower part and the fine-grained breccia along the upper right border fault. Scale is in cm.

Fig. 6. Detail of a border fault at fault zone S4. The border fault is accompanied by a sharply defined fine-grained breccia. To the right, highly fractured chalk within the zone (see also Fig. 5).

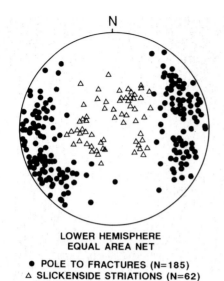

LOWER HEMISPHERE
EQUAL AREA NET

● POLE TO FRACTURES (N=185)
△ SLICKENSIDE STRIATIONS (N=62)

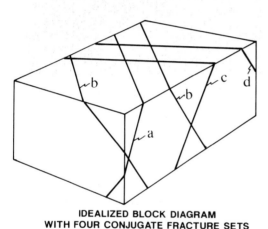

IDEALIZED BLOCK DIAGRAM
WITH FOUR CONJUGATE FRACTURE SETS

Fig. 7. Stereogram and block diagram showing the four orientation sets for fractures of Saturn quarry. This pattern is the basis for the interpretation that the chalk is deformed within a three-dimensional strain field.

Reches & Dietrich 1983; Koestler & Ehrmann 1987; Krantz 1988). Breccia zones occur as sharply bordered distinct zones (Fig. 6) or as transitional zones between fractured and highly fractured chalk.

The surfaces of the border faults always show slickenside striations and clay enrichment. Clay enrichment can result in layers of up to 1 cm thickness and extending over tens of metres along slip surfaces. Minor fractures within the fault zones show a whole spectrum from striated and clay-coated surfaces to joints without any

alteration. The same can be said of the breccia fragment surfaces at different deformation degrees. There is a correlation between displacement on fractures and breccia-fragment surfaces and their degree of clay coating and striation: the larger the displacement on shear fractures and breccia fragment surfaces, the thicker the clay coating and the more distinct the striations. Displacement in the range of some decimetres can produce up to 1 mm of argillaceous coating on the slip surfaces; displacements in the range of metres produce clay layers up to 1 cm in thickness.

Internal deformation features in the fault blocks

The deformation related to salt diapirism seems to be concentrated on the distinct minor faults and fault zones, which display a relatively regular spacing, as described above. However, the blocks in between also suffered some deformation. The deformation features in the fault blocks consist of very small faults and shear planes with displacement below 2 m and joints without any measurable displacement (Figs 2A, C & 11). Usually, fracture fequency does not substantially increase towards the faults at the block boundaries, but in some places a slight increase in fracture frequency has been observed, over a distance of 2–3 metres.

The shear fractures, with displacements less than 2 metres, and joints within the blocks show the same geometrical pattern as the minor faults. SW dips prevail, but a NE dip-direction is somewhat more accentuated (Koestler & Ehrmann 1986). Four genetically related fracture sets can be defined, if one includes the fault-block internal features into the orientation analysis (Fig. 7). The fractures occur in some places as swarms or clusters, in others as isolated features. Some subhorizontal joints, occasionally bedding parallel, are thought to be related to stress release due to unloading, not to diapirism. Stylolites have only been found at the deepest exposed levels (today flooded at the bottom of quarry Kroepke) which are stratigraphically 420 m deeper than the uppermost level exposed in quarry Saturn.

A number of interesting features and processes can be better studied on the basis of block-internal features than on the larger fault zones, because the structures are isolated and do not interfere with each other. The conclusions drawn from such observations are thought to be also applicable to fault-zone-internal processes (Gabrielsen & Koestler 1987).

The displacement transfer on conjugate fracture sets can be achieved by intensely-fractured areas between en echelon faults (Fig. 8) or by unfractured rock volumes. In the latter case displacement has to be accommodated by sediment-internal, ductile deformation at a microscopic scale. Shear fracture terminations occur with three different appearances. Firstly, a highly fractured area, mainly built up by small-scale conjugate fractures (Fig. 8). A second geometrical pattern at shear plane terminations is observed where fractures show a transition from a planar to a curved shape with numerous upwards-splaying fractures (Fig. 9). The displacement on the shear plane seems to be accommodated on these subordinate splaying fractures with a different orientation than the main slip surface. This is a typical 'horsetail' geometry as observed at terminations of large strike-slip faults (e.g. Harding *et al.* 1985) and at terminations of small-scale faults in the brittle regime (e.g. Granier 1985). Here, the horsetail

Fig. 9. Shear fracture termination accompanied by bending and accommodation of the deformation by numerous upward splaying minor fractures (Heidestrasse quarry). The marked horizontal line in the upper part is produced by quarrying. Exposure height is about 6 m.

Fig. 8. Block-internal fractures (Heidestrase quarry). The shear fracture termination in the upper central part of the figure is accompanied by intensive small-scale fracturing of the chalk. In the lower part, the deformation is transferred by en echelon fractures. Scale bar is 1 m.

geometry is documented for a normal fault, seen in vertical section. Thirdly, a shear fracture may just terminate at a distinct point. In this case, the deformation has to be absorbed by the surrounding sediment at the fault termination (ductile bead). Ductile behaviour of the sediment seems to be able to accommodate considerable strain: faults with displacement of about one metre have been observed to die out over a few decimetres.

A more dynamic aspect of faulting in this homogeneous chalk is illustrated by lensoid pockets of breccias or clay-enriched gouge which are situated along mainly-planar faults and are surrounded by concentric joints (Fig. 10). This pattern is interpreted as the result of stress concentrations at fault tips released during fault propagation. Between such lenses the fault is usually only a few millimetres wide and the surrounding rock often almost undeformed (see Fig. 10, fault to the left).

While the minor fault zones bounding the blocks are interconnected in three dimensions,

Fig. 10. Lens-shaped pockets, with enrichment of argillaceous material, which are surrounded by curved joints (Heidestrasse quarry). They probably formed at points of stress concentration during fault propagation. Scale bar is 1 m.

thus defining possible hydrocarbon reservoir units (Fig. 12), the fractures within the fault blocks do not seem to be fully linked. There is no completely interconnected network of fractures within the blocks, at least on the basis of medium-scale observations (Fig. 11). However, studying large enough outcrops, fractures are arranged in clusters which are linked together. The clustering of fractures produces a larger-scale network enclosing volumes not showing fracturing at a medium observation-scale.

The fracture frequency in the fault blocks seems to decrease towards the NE in quarry Saturn, and the displacement on the block-bounding faults decreases in the same direction (Fig. 2). A slight decrease of deformation intensity away from the crestal area of the salt ridge could be indicated by these observations. However, the profile length is not sufficient to show this clearly.

Discussion and conclusions

The geometrical variation of the pattern of fracturing along a distinct fault zone covers a wide spectrum from narrow, distinct faults to relatively-broad zones which are bordered by prominent slip surfaces and characterized by complex, internal fracture patterns (Figs 2C, D). However, comparing all the fault zones studied, the variation in structural style from one fault to another is relatively small (Fig. 2A). The geometrical pattern significantly changes in the vertical dimension, on the 40 m high quarry walls. It also changes along the horizontal extent of the fault, as can be seen by investigating the same fault on opposite quarry walls, over a distance of about 800 m (Fig. 12). The progressive exploitation of the quarry walls also gives an insight into the changes of geometrical styles over short distances. It seems that the degree of variation along the fault zones in the horizontal direction are similar to those in the vertical. Each of the faults zones accommodates displacement in about the same range (2−10 m). While the characteristics of the fault surfaces seem to mirror the displacement amount, in terms of increased clay enrichment and more distinct slickenside striations with increased displacement, the fracture density is more difficult to relate to a fault parameter. Along a single fault zone, fracture intensity is strongly varying and cannot be correlated with sedimentary heterogeneities, because the chalk at Laegerdorf is extremely homogeneous (Ehrmann 1986). Hence, the fracture pattern and fracture frequency are an expression of the stress situation during fracture propagation. This locality, therefore, provides an excellent possibility to study the spacing, fracture geometry, fracture surfaces, microtextural changes due to deformation, deformation processes, sealing potential etc., produced by a relatively simple stress field and not influenced by lithological heterogeneities.

All faults observed accommodate dip-slip movements of the adjacent blocks, as indicated by the down-dip slickenside striations. Regarding the complex fault surface geometries (Figs 2A−D) fault blocks would have had great difficulties in moving against each other. Obviously, some space problems are accommodated by intense fracturing at places of strain concentration. It seems, however, that this process cannot take up all strain. Although the geometrical patterns could also indicate strike-slip components and block rotation to allow block movements, this is not supported by outcrop-scale observations. Thus, a large

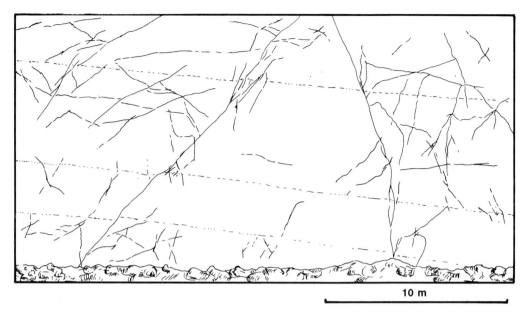

Fig. 11. Sketch of fracture network of deformed chalk situated between two distinct fault zones. The area is between fault S2 and S3 (see Fig. 2).

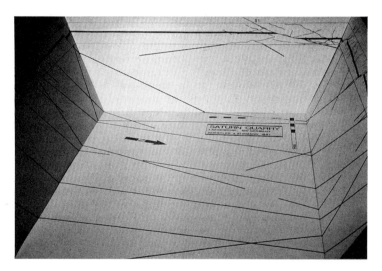

Fig. 12. Three-dimensional model of Saturn quarry indicating the fault interconnection and shape of possible hydrocarbon reservoir units. Faults and fractures have been mapped along all quarry walls, which are shown in the narrow strip at the top of the model. Displacement at the faults is illustrated by the dark line representing a sedimentary layer.

amount of strain has been accommodated within the sediment as 'ductile'-type deformation rather than brittle fracturing. The chalk does not show macroscopically any alteration in the zones where ductile deformation is expected. However, being a highly porous medium (porosity 40−50%), small changes in the sediment texture would be sufficient to absorb deformation. SEM observations (Koestler & Ehrmann 1987) indicate that such ductile deformation is expressed by a falling-apart of the coccoliths and a denser packing of the grains, resulting, of necessity, in porosity reduction. Similar processes have been observed in porous sandstones (e.g. Gabrielsen & Koestler 1987; Underhill & Woodcock 1987). This is a process which has received too little attention in petroleum geology. In faulted reservoirs, porosity reduction due to deformation implies zones of reduced permeability for hydrocarbon flow in apparently undeformed areas.

The orientation pattern of the Laegerdorf faults indicates that a three-dimensional strainfield produced the four genetically related fracture sets at all scales (Koestler & Ehrmann 1987). Four sets of related fracture or fault orientations have been observed by other authors at several localities and have been produced in experiments. They have been interpreted to be the result of three strain axis of different magnitude (e.g. Aydin & Reches 1982; Reches 1983; Reches & Dietrich 1983; Hancock 1985; Krantz 1988). To illustrate better the fault configuration in the Saturn quarry, a model has been built to illustrate the mapped quarry walls, the correlation of faults on facing quarry walls and their interconnection in three dimensions (Fig. 12). The larger faults are dominantly SW-dipping, implying a general downstepping of the fault blocks towards the crest of the salt ridge. The minor faults, as well as the structures within the fault zones and fault blocks, display the four intersecting orientation-sets. Even the orientation of the fracture surfaces bordering breccia fragments fits very well into the general pattern.

From the point of view of petroleum geology, chalk can provide a potential hydrocarbon reservoir as a result of its high porosity, particularly so in this tectonic situation, on top of a salt ridge. Hence, the size of blocks bordered by larger faults as well as the detectability and significance of the deformation features is of major interest. In Saturn quarry, the width of the fault blocks is in the range of 100 to 150 metres (Fig. 2A), while the length may exceed 500 m. The small variation in the dip angles of the larger faults implies a possible maximum height of the fault blocks equalling the thickness of the sediment on top of the diapir, which may be in the range of 450−550 m (Koestler & Ehrmann 1986).

A comprehensive fracture study of the Albuskjell Field in the Norwegian sector of the central North Sea (Watts 1983) describes two types of fractures: tension fractures, mainly connected to stylolites, and shear fractures. Albuskjell Field is located on the crest of a NW−SE striking salt ridge in an analogous structural setting to the chalk at Laegerdorf.

Watts suggested that the tension fractures are oriented mainly perpendicular to the ridge axis, as indicated by orientation data on tension fractures from one well. In our case, tension fractures of the style observed in Albuskjell have not been found. All the observed fractures are of the shear-type, occurring in four genetically related sets. However, the dynamic analysis does also indicate that the largest extension occurred parallel to the ridge, as in Albuskjell. At Ekofisk, three different types of fractures have been observed: healed, tectonic and stylolite-associated (Dangerfield & Brown 1987). The shear fractures at Laegerdorf seem to be very similar to those described as tectonic fractures from Ekofisk, which dip very steeply and show a high intensity in the crestal area, with a decreasing density towards the flanks (Fritsen & Corrigan 1990). The sediments at Laegerdorf are autochthonous chalks, in contrast to the chalk at Ekofisk, which is largely allochthonous as a result of debris flows initiated by local salt movements and faulting activity (Van den Bark & Thomas 1981; Pekot & Gersip 1987; Dangerfield & Brown 1987). How far the character of the sediment influences the fracture pattern and intensity cannot be answered with our study, because the chalk at Laegerdorf is highly homogeneous and of the same deposition type throughout the whole sequence exposed (Ehrmann 1986). We would suggest that the general fracture and fault pattern at Laegerdorf is dominantly controlled by the stress impact due to diapirism and the interaction with a regional stress overprint, and only to a minor degree by variations in the sediment character.

Evaluation of the Laegerdorf chalks as a potential analogue for a hydrocarbon reservoir brings up the question of how this type of deformation, which may have important significance for hydrocarbon exploration and production, could be mapped in the subsurface in the absence of large quarries as exposures. The displacement on the faults is too small to be detected on seismic reflection surveys. In addition, the homogeneity of the chalk gives little chance of producing any seismic reflection signal due to the lack of prominent layering. This paper describes tectonic heterogeneities in fractured chalk, lying on top of a salt ridge, from a well exposed locality, in order to present information on extensional features for the better understanding and modelling of subsurface chalk reservoirs in analogous tectonic settings.

This study was supported by GEO-RECON A.S., Oslo. The Alsen-Breitenburg Zement-und Kalkwerke GmbH and the Vereinigte Kreidewerke-Dammann

KG kindly permitted the fieldwork in their chalk quarries. The authors want to extend their gratitude to A.G. Milnes (Zurich) for helpful comments and for correction of the English text. Reviews and comments by Juan Watterson, Tim Bevan and Graham Yielding improved the paper.

References

AYDIN, A. & RECHES, Z. 1982. Number and orientation of fault sets in the field and in experiments. *Geology*, **10**, 107–112.

CORBETT, K., FRIEDMAN, M. & SPANG, J. 1987. Fracture development and mechanical stratigraphy of Austin Chalk, Texas. *American Association of Petroleum Geologists Bulletin*, **71**, 17–28.

DANGERFIELD, J. A. & BROWN, D. A. 1987. The Ekofisk Field. *In:* KLEPPE et al. (eds) *North Sea oil and gas reservoirs*. Graham & Trotman, London, 3–22.

EHRMANN, W. U. 1986. Zum Sedimenteintrag in das zentrale nordwesteuropäische Oberkreidemeer. *Geologisches Jahrbuch*, **A97**, 3–139.

FRITSEN, A. & CORRIGAN, T. 1990. Establishment of a geologic fracture model for dual porosity simulations on the Ekofisk Field. *In:* BULLER et al. (eds) *North Sea oil and gas reservoirs. Proceedings of the 2nd International Conference, Trondheim, May 8–11, 1989*. Graham & Trotman, London, 173–184.

GRABRIELSEN, R. H. & KOESTLER, A. G. 1987. Description and structural implications of fractures in late Jurassic sandstones of the Troll Field, northern North Sea. *In:* KOESTLER & OLAUSSEN (eds) *Tectonics and deposition in sedimentary basins*. Proceedings of 4th TSGS Conference, Stavanger 1986. Norsk Geologisk Tidskrift, **67**, 371–382.

GRANIER, T. 1985. Origin, damping, and pattern of development of faults in granite. *Tectonics*, **4**, 721–737.

HARDING, T. P., VIERBUCHEN, R. C. & CHRISTIE-BLICK, N. 1985. Structural styles, plate-tectonic settings, and hydrocarbon traps of divergent (transtensional) wrench faults. *In:* BIDDLE & CHRISTIE-BLICK, N. (eds), *Strike-slip deformation, basin formation, and sedimentation*. Society of Economic Palcontologists and Mineralogists, Special Publication **37**, 51–77.

JARITZ, W. 1973. Zur Entstehung der Salzstrukturen Nordwestdeutschlands. *Geologisches Jahrbuch*, **A10**, 1–77.

KOESTLER, A. G. & EHRMANN, W. U. 1986. Fault patterns in the calcareous overburden of a salt diapir: Laegerdorf, NW Germany. *Neues Jahrbuch fur Geologie und Palaeontologie*, 1986 (9): 555–569.

—— & —— 1987. Fractured chalk overburden of a salt diapir, Laegerdorf, NW Germany — Exposed example of a possible hydrocarbon reservoir. *In:* LERCHE, I. & O'BRIEN, J. J. (eds) *Dynamical geology of salt and related structures* Academic, New York 457–477.

KRANTZ, R. W. 1988. Multiple fault sets and three-dimensional strain: theory and application. *Journal of Structural Geology*, **10**, 225–237.

PEKOT, L. J. & GERSIB, G. A. 1987. Ekofisk. *In:* SPENCER et al. (eds) *Geology of the Norwegian oil and gas fields*. Graham & Trotman, London, 73–88.

RECHES, Z. 1983. Faulting of rocks in three-dimensional strain fields. II. Theoretical analysis. *Tectonophysics*, **95**, 133–156.

—— & DIETRICH, J.H. 1983. Faulting of rocks in three-dimensional strain fields. I. Failure of rocks in polyaxial, servo-control experiments. *Tectonophysics*, **95**, 111–132.

SCHULZ, M.-G., ERNST, G., ERNST, H. & SCHMID, F. 1984. Coniacian to Maastrichtian stage boundaries in the Standard Section for the Upper Cretaceous white chalk of NW Germany (Laegerdorf-Kronsmoor-Hemmoor): Definitions and proposals. *Bulletin of the Geological Society of Denmark*, **33**, 203–215.

UNDERHILL, J. R. & WOODCOCK, N. H. 1987. Faulting mechanisms in high porosity sandstones: New Red Sandstone, Arran, Scotland. *In:* JONES, M. E. & PRESTON, R. M. F. (eds) *Deformation of Sediments and Sedimentary Rocks*. Geological Society, London, Special Publication **29**, 91–105.

VAN DEN BARK, E. & THOMAS, O. D. 1981. Ekofisk: First of the giant oil fields in Western Europe. *American Association of Petroleum Geologists Bulletin*, **65**, 2341–2363.

WATTS, N. L. 1983. Microfractures in chalks of Albuskjell Field, Norwegian sector, North Sea: Possible origin and distribution. *American Association of Petroleum Geologists Bulletin*, **67**, 201–234.

Active normal faulting in central Greece: an overview

STEVEN ROBERTS & JAMES JACKSON

Bullard Laboratories, Madingley Road, Cambridge CB3 0EZ, UK

Abstract: Rapid extension in central Greece is accommodated by large active normal faults that largely control the geomorphology. The faults bound graben whose asymmetry is evident in the topography, bathymetry, vertical movements of the coastline and tilting of Neogene sediments adjacent to them. Graben up to 20 km in width appear to be simple half-graben, whereas the hangingwalls in wider graben are generally broken by faults antithetic to the major bounding faults. The graben form basins up to 100 km long, but the faults bounding these basins are segmented, with individual segments no longer than about 20 km. The fault segments step en echelon or change polarity along strike of the large basins, but are not linked by simple strike-slip ('transfer') faults: the regions between the main fault segments appear to be pervasively deformed by numerous small faults. Drainage in central Greece is controlled by fault segmentation and footwall lithology. Where footwalls consist of Mesozoic limestone the drainage is often axial, breaking through the fault system into the main basin by flowing round the ends of fault segments or through gaps where the fault segments step. In such places, drainage directly off the fault scarps is relatively minor, and the fault segmentation controls the spacing of major fans along the basin margin. Where footwalls consist of Neogene sediments, drainage may flow directly across the fault scarp, though in such cases the catchment areas are relatively small and linear. The origin of the fault segmentation is unclear, but may be related to rotations of the fault-bounded blocks about horizontal and vertical axes.

The Aegean Sea, and its surrounding regions of Greece, Albania, western Turkey, southern Yugoslavia and Bulgaria, is one of the most rapidly extending areas on the continents today. Its present day activity is manifest by its high seismicity and by the dramatic influence of large active normal faults on the topography, geomorphology and movement of the coastline relative to sea level. The region has attracted much interest, both in order to examine active extension in general, and to use the Aegean as a modern analogue to help interpret the geological record of older, now inactive, stretched sedimentary basins. Much of the published work in the Aegean has been either very general (covering the whole region) or specifically concerned with individual faults, earthquakes or basins. This paper is concerned with generalizations that can be made about the geometry of the normal faulting, and the way in which it influences geomorphology and drainage, in a sub-region of the Aegean extensional province in central Greece, from the northern Peloponnese to the island of Evvia (Fig. 1). This is one of the most active regions within the extensional province, and one of the most accessible: many of the largest active faults crop out near the coast, and are easier to study than those under the Aegean Sea itself, where greater extension has led to total submergence. For comparison, the across-strike width of the re-

gion in Fig. 1 (130 km) is very similar to that of the East Shetland Terrace in the northern North Sea.

Background

Regional considerations suggest that the N–S rate of extension across the whole province (i.e. between Crete and Bulgaria) is 40–60 mm a^{-1} (McKenzie 1978; Le Pichon & Angelier 1979; Jackson & McKenzie 1988b). An examination of this century's seismicity reveals that most of this extension is likely to be achieved by the motion of large faults during earthquakes of magnitude 6.0 and larger, and that the contribution of smaller faults (and earthquakes) and aseismic creep to the regional deformation of the upper crust is probably not significant (Jackson & McKenzie 1988a, b). This is an important deduction, affecting the perspective with which this paper discusses normal faulting. In an earthquake of magnitude 6.0, slip occurs on a fault with a length of about 10–15 km, similar in dimension to the thickness of the upper seismogenic layer of the continental crust, which in Greece is in the region of 10–15 km, based on accurate microearthquake surveys (Soufleris *et al.* 1982; King *et al.* 1985; Hatzfield *et al.* 1987; Lyon-Caen *et al.* 1988). Throughout this paper we will distinguish such faults, which we may refer to as 'large' faults, from those with lengths significantly smaller than the thickness of the seismogenic layer, and which slip in earthquakes smaller than about magnitude 5.0. (For example, an earthquake of magnitude 4.0 involves movement on a fault of only about 100 m length.) Since it is known that large faults take up most of the deformation, a knowledge of the geometry and kinematics of the large faults is a prerequisite for an understanding of how the extension is achieved: in other words, any model of the active deformation that is inconsistent with the motion on the large faults cannot be correct. This is not to say that small faults are unimportant, but simply that they do not account for much of the overall strain. In Greece, as elsewhere, most small earthquakes occur away from the large faults and represent internal deformation of the blocks bounded by major faults. They may also provide information

on the transfer of deformation from one large fault to another, which we discuss later.

The region of Fig. 1 is one of the most seismically active in the Aegean extensional province. The present rate of N–S extension across this part of central Greece is likely to be in the range 10–20 mm a^{-1} (Jackson & McKenzie 1988, 1989): a rate in agreement with a comparison of two geodetic surveys carried out in 1890–1900 and 1988 (Billiris et al. 1989). However, the overall motion across the region of Fig. 1 is NE–SW (see inset to Fig. 1b), with roughly equal amounts of N–S extension and E–W right-lateral shear, the shear component being caused by the motion of Turkey relative to Eurasia (McKenzie 1972, 1978; McKenzie & Jackson 1983, 1986).

Geological studies of the Neogene basins in central Greece, summarized by Mercier et al.

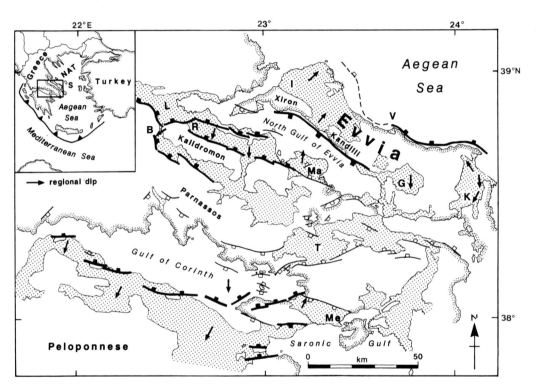

Fig. 1.(a) General fault map of central Greece, showing the principal areas (stippled) where Miocene–Recent sediments are preserved. The region is identified in the inset map, where NAT is the North Aegean Trough and S is the island of Skyros. Major range-bounding faults are shown in heavy lines with filled blocks on their downthrown side. Other 'large' faults, capable of generating earthquakes of magnitude 6.0 or greater, but with apparently less displacement or topographic expression, are shown in thinner lines with open blocks. The distinction between these two fault types is, to some extent, subjective. Some faults, such as those on the NE flanks of Kalidromon and Parnassos and on the NE side of the Megara (Me) basin; may no longer be active. Basins identified by letters are: Lamia (L), Bralos (B), Renginion (R), Istea (I), Vlachia (V), Gides (Kymi (K), Malessina (Ma), Thiva (T), Megara (Me). Arrows show approximate regional directions of dip within the Neogene basins, from Roberts (1988) and Brooks & Ferentinos (1984).

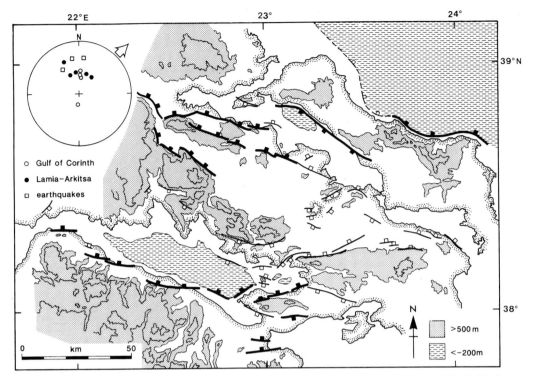

Fig. 1.(b) Topography (500 m and 1000 m contours, stippled above 500 m) and bathymetry (shaded below 200 m) in central Greece. Faults are as in Fig. 1(a). The inset shows the a stereographic projection of the slip vectors on major faults, measured at the surface in the Lamia-Arkitsa and Gulf of Corinth systems, or from fault plane solutions for earthquakes larger than magnitude 6.0. The open arrow is the direction of motion in the North Aegean Trough, and is the expected motion between the top of the figure and the bottom (see McKenzie 1978; McKenzie & Jackson 1983, 1986).

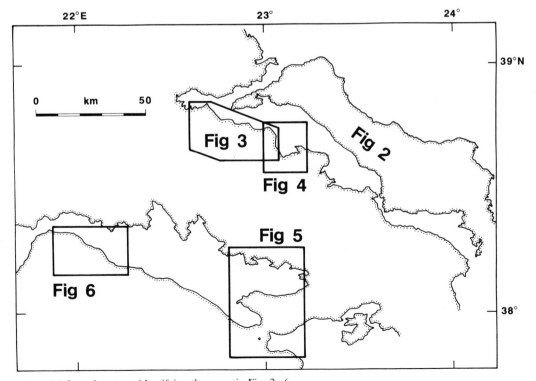

Fig. 1.(c) Location map, identifying the areas in Figs 2–6.

(1979, 1987, 1989), indicate that extension has dominated the deformation of the region since at least the early Pliocene (c. 5 Ma BP), though it may not always have been constant in orientation or rate. Within the Aegean region there is evidence that, in places, extension began during the Middle Miocene (Mercier et al. 1976; Sengor et al. 1985); though most of it is likely to have occurred in the last 5 Ma (Kissel & Laj 1988; Mercier et al. 1989). Many authors regard the extension in the Aegean province as being linked dynamically with the subduction of the Mediterranean Sea floor in the Hellenic Trench (e.g. McKenzie 1978; Le Pichon 1982; Mercier et al. 1987).

Normal faulting

General structure

The structure of central Greece is dominated by a series of large normal faults with an E–W to NW–SE strike (Fig. 1). These faults are very clearly associated with the topography, and are responsible for the development of large basins, such as the Gulfs of Corinth and northern Evvia, and the basins NE of Mt Parnassos and Evvia. All the major, range-bounding normal faults are thought to have been active in the Pleistocene, but the relative timing of their activity is less certain: some, such as that bounding the NE flank of Kalidromon (Figs 1a & 3), may no longer be active (e.g. Philip 1974; Lemeille 1977; Mercier et al. 1979). In spite of the high historical seismicity, surface faulting accompanying specific earthquakes has been reported only from the Gulf of Corinth and northern Gulf of Evvia basins.

All the basins are asymmetric, most of them with the dominant faulting on the SW side. This asymmetry is often clear from the topography, but is also seen in the tilting of young sediments and vertical movements of the coastline (discussed later). However, only the smaller basins, up to 15–20 km in width, such as those of Renginion (Fig. 3) and NE of Parnassos (Fig. 1a), look like simple 'domino-style' rotated half-graben. The larger basins, such as the Gulfs of Corinth and northern Evvia, though obviously asymmetric, are bounded by faults that are antithetic to the dominant ones. Thus on the north side of the Gulf of Corinth are a number of recent normal fault scarps that dip south. Several of these are 'large' in the seismological sense of being long enough to generate earthquakes of magnitude 6.0, but individually appear to have much less total displacement

than the large north-dipping faults on the south side of the Gulf. The fault responsible for the earthquake of 3 March 1981 near Kaparelli (Fig. 5) is an example (Jackson et al. 1982a).

Previous impressions that all the dominant faulting dips NE (e.g. Jackson & McKenzie 1983) are incorrect. A major SW-dipping normal fault system occurs along the SW side of northern Evvia, dominating the tilting, drainage and topography of the central part of the northern Gulf of Evvia and its borders (Figs 1 & 2). The structure of the northern Gulf of Evvia and of the island of Evvia itself varies dramatically along strike. At the western end of the Gulf the structure is clearly dominated by a fault system on the south side, dipping north. Farther east, at about the longitude of Arkitsa (Figs 1 & 3), the polarity of the half-graben changes, and is controlled by the fault on the north side of the Gulf, dipping south. This fault appears to die out east of Mt. Kandilli (Figs 1a & 2), where the morphology of central Evvia is dominated by a fault along the north coast of the island, dipping north and bounding a basin offshore. Thus northern Evvia resembles a twisted horst block, that cannot be realistically assessed in two-dimensions (see also Stiros 1985).

It is unclear how structures in the central part of the N Gulf of Evvia accommodate the change in polarity part of the half graben, but there is no evidence for significant strike-slip faulting in the N to NE direction. Antithetic faults are seen both east and west of the transition in polarity, on the western tip of Evvia and in the Martinon region (Fig. 4). The Atalanti–Martinon fault system (Figs 3 & 4), part of which moved in two earthquakes of magnitude 6.5 and 6.7 in 1984, is sited in the region of the transition, and changes in nature along strike. Its eastern part, from Tragana to the coastline, is opposite the large south-dipping fault flanking Mt. Kandilli on Evvia and resembles the antithetic faults on the north side of the Gulf of Corinth, in that, though 'large' in the seismological sense, it has relatively minor displacement, indicated by both the topography (a few tens of metres) and the occurrence of Miocene–Pliocene marls on both sides of the fault (Fig. 4). Its western part, from Tragana to Atalanti (Figs 3 & 4), is closer to the north-dipping fault system running west from Arkitsa, and is associated with greater topography (a few hundred metres) and a substantial basin in its hangingwall. Changes in half graben polarity have attracted attention elsewhere, notably in the Gulf of Suez (e.g. Garfunkel & Bartov 1977), the Basin and Range (Stewart 1980) and East Africa (Rosendahl et al. 1986). In the absence of off-

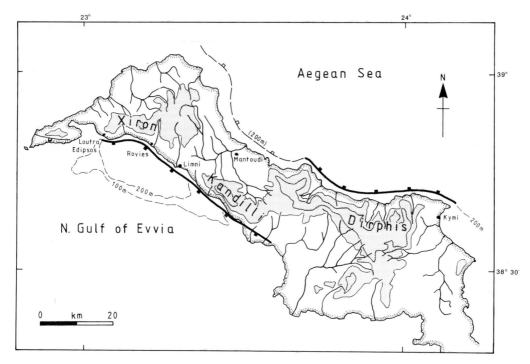

Fig. 2. Topographic map of north and central Evvia, showing the principal drainage pattern. Contours are at 400 m and 800 m, stippled above 400 m. The fault along the NE side of Dirphis is drawn to follow the 200 m bathymetric contour: the coastal morphology suggests that it is most active, or has largest displacement, in its eastern part (heavy line).

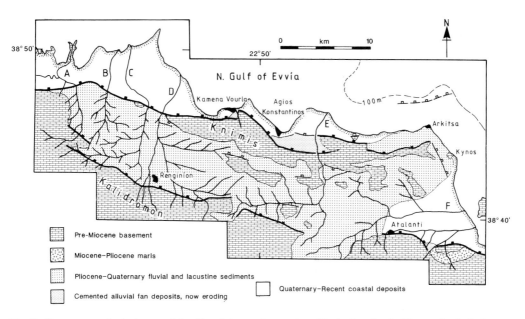

Fig. 3. Summary geological map of the Renginion graben region, illustrating the faulting and principal drainage. The geology is modified from Philip (1974). Major range-bounding faults are shown in thick lines with filled blocks on their downthrown side. Thinner lines with open blocks are smaller faults.

shore data from the N Gulf of Evvia, it is premature to compare this region with other areas.

Two possible explanations have been suggested for the presence of antithetic faulting in the half-graben of central Greece. The first attributes the antithetic faults to an abrupt decrease in the dip of the dominant faulting at depth, probably below the seismic-aseismic transition (e.g. King *et al*. 1985; Eyidogan & Jackson 1985; Jackson 1987). In this scheme, antithetic faulting would migrate in time towards the centre of the basin as the hanging wall block moves away from the point of intersection of the dominant fault with the flatter, deeper portion of the fault. This would lead to a staircase morphology of antithetic faults (see Fig. 25a of Eyidogan & Jackson 1985), each with relatively minor displacement. This resembles the situation in the Gulf of Corinth to some extent, particularly at the eastern end (Jackson *et al*. 1982a). A second explanation, advanced by Jackson & White (1989), is that the spacing of the dominant faults across strike (50 km from the southern Gulf of Corinth to the NE flank of Parnassos) is too great for the intervening block to rotate coherently about a horizontal axis, as the stresses required for it to do so would be

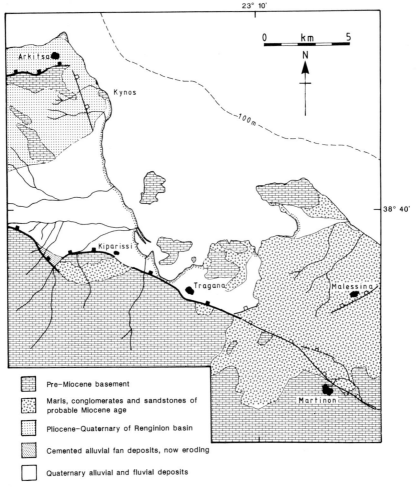

Fig. 4. Summary geological map of the Kiparissi-Martinon region, based on Philip (1974) and Rondoyanni (1984). The earthquakes of 1894 are known to have ruptured the fault from Martinon to Kiparissi, and also the segment west of Kiparissi through Atalanti (see Fig. 3). In its eastern part this fault has very subdued morphology (thin line with open blocks). Its central and western parts (heavy lines with filled blocks) follow topographic escarpments 500–1000 m high.

large (several hundred bars). Instead it breaks up by antithetic faulting.

The major fault systems that bound large topographic depressions are easy to identify. However, central Greece contains many 'large' faults with relatively small displacement, particularly around the north side of the Gulf of Corinth and the Thiva basin (Fig. 1a). We are sure that many such faults are omitted from Fig. 1, particularly because there are historical records of large earthquakes in regions where no faulting is marked (e.g. Sieberg 1932; Galanopoulos 1955; Bousquet & Pechoux 1977; Ambraseys & Jackson 1990). For this reason Fig. 1 is not a reliable guide to seismic risk.

Fault morphology, dips and slip vectors

Much of the most dramatic fault morphology in central Greece occurs where the footwall blocks are composed of Mesozoic limestone. Polished surfaces cutting through cemented limestone breccia are occasionally exposed, and sometimes revealed by earthquake movement or quarrying of scree resting against the scarp. The details of such surfaces are discussed by Hancock & Barka (1987) and Stewart & Hancock (1989). They often contain corrugations with wavelengths of cm to tens of metres and with axes aligned parallel to the slip vector. Some of the surfaces contain smaller and less continuous grooves and slickensides indicating different directions of movement on the same fault plane (e.g. Pechoux *et al.* 1973; Mercier 1976). The dips of these polished surfaces are generally steep (40–70°) and the axes of the major corrugations, when projected upwards from their exposure, generally do not intersect the hillside. In many places the slope of the preserved limestone hillside appears to be a reasonable approximation to the dip of the fault. The slip vector azimuths, based on the major corrugations or grooves, are generally N–S (± 20°), similar to those from earthquake focal mechanisms and conspicuously different from the NE–SW motion across the region as a whole (Fig. 1b, inset); an observation that led McKenzie & Jackson (1983, 1986) to suggest that the fault blocks rotate clockwise about a vertical axis. The dips seen in earthquake focal mechanisms are also steep (30–70°), and are consistent with the large faults having approximately planar cross sections from the surface to the base of the seismogenic upper crust (Jackson & McKenzie 1983; Eyidogan & Jackson 1985; Jackson 1987; Jackson & White 1989), though the available data cannot rule out changes of dip of up to about 15°.

Continuity along strike

Although basins such as the Gulf of Corinth and northern Gulf of Evvia are more than 100 km long, the faulting that flanks them is discontinuous, even when the polarity of the half-graben is unchanged (Fig. 1). Where faults crop out on land they occur in segments no longer than about 20 km. Even where the faulting is confined entirely offshore, like that flanking northern Evvia, changes in the strike, morphology, and vertical movements along the coastline suggest that the fault segments are not continuous for more than about 20 km. This segmentation of the faulting has a profound influence on the drainage and sedimentation, which is discussed later. The maximum observed segment length of 20 km potentially limits the maximum size of earthquakes in central Greece to about magnitude (M_s) 6.7, though larger earthquakes involving movement of more than one segment are possible, as in the 1970 Gediz earthquake in western Turkey (Eyidogan & Jackson 1985). Of interest here is how the fault segments are linked to each other along the basin margins.

It is clear that the segments are not linked by single strike-slip ('transfer') faults in the simple manner sometimes envisaged elsewhere (e.g. Bott 1976; Gibbs 1984; Etheridge 1986). Instead, the region between the fault segments appears to be intensively deformed by widespread minor faulting, probably accompanied by some folding. The evidence for this is both morphological and seismological.

The morphological evidence is illustrated by the example in Fig. 5, which is a map of the eastern part of the Gulf of Corinth. The Perakora peninsula occupies the region between two major normal faults dipping north: one following the NW flank of Mt Gerania, through Pisia (and which moved in the earthquake of 25 February 1981), and the other lying offshore along the NW coast of the peninsula and continuing to the west (the western part of this second fault may have moved in the earthquake of 24 February 1981). Both faults are marked by major topographic (or bathymetric) escarpments about 1000 m high. The high ridge in the footwall of the Pisia fault dies out sharply at its western end, precisely where the fault displacement itself died out in the 1981 earthquake. At its eastern end, the higher of the two faults bounding the NE flank of Gerania also loses its clear topographic expression, terminating in a canyon that allows drainage to enter the Gulf of Corinth round the end of the fault segment, and which also marked the eastern limit of surface ruptures in 1981. The topographic change associated with the eastern termination of this fault is partly influenced by footwall lithology, which changes from limestone (near Pisia) to more easily eroded igneous rocks farther east: but the 1981 surface ruptures continued at least 2 km east of the change in lithology to reach the canyon draining north. The western part of the Perakora peninsula, between the Gerania fault and the fault offshore, is severely deformed by many smaller normal faults, up to a few km in length, some of which were reactivated in 1981. The topography associated with these smaller normal faults is generally less than 100–200 m, giving a hummocky appearance to the peninsula. It is clear that no strike-slip fault crosses the peninsula to link the major faults.

A similar geometry on a smaller scale is seen on the north side of the eastern Gulf of Corinth (Fig. 5) in the Kaparelli fault system, which also moved in 1981 (Jackson et al. 1982a). Here two fault segments, each about 6 km long, were offset by 3 km. The region between the two segments was deformed by many discontinuous cracks and fissures consistent with the warping expected when passing along strike from a footwall to a hanging-wall block (see Fig. 12 of Jackson et al. 1982a). In both these examples the gradual decrease in seismic displacement along strike as the ends of the segments are reached, mirrored also in the topography, makes it inconceivable that the fault motion is transferred elsewhere by a single strike-slip fault, in the way transform faults are believed to link ridge segments in the oceans.

The seismological evidence for the nature of

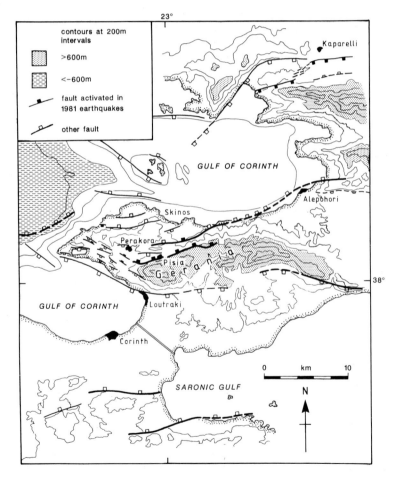

Fig. 5. Faulting, bathymetry and topography in the eastern Gulf of Corinth, after Jackson et al. (1982a), Perissoratis et al. (1986) and Collier (1988). Major range-bounding faults are shown in thick lines. Faults active at the surface in the 1981 earthquakes have filled blocks in their hanging-walls.

the linkage between fault segments comes from detailed aftershock studies of large normal faulting earthquakes. Here the data are not just from Greece (Soufleris *et al.* 1982; King *et al.* 1985; Lyon-Caen *et al.* 1988), but also from elsewhere (e.g. Idaho, USA.: Richens *et al.* 1987; Italy: Deschamps & King 1984 and Westaway & Jackson 1987). The regions where normal fault segments end or are offset are usually the sites of intense aftershock activity dispersed over a volume, with a great variety of focal mechanisms that may even include thrusting. These observations suggest a widespread fracturing by small faults and not linkage by a single fault.

Jackson & White (1989) suggest that the maximum fault segment length of about 20 km is a worldwide characteristic of active normal faults on the continents. There is no doubt that normal faults are also discontinuous on a scale smaller than this. However, it is this maximum segment length that imposes a scale on the structure, morphology and drainage in regions of active extension, particularly in central Greece. The pervasive fracturing and minor faulting between offset fault segments may contribute to the erosion and establishment of drainage systems in these locations (discussed later; see also Leeder & Gawthorpe 1987).

Uplift and subsidence

Vertical movements in central Greece are evidently related to three factors: (1) a general subsidence caused by stretching (2) a general uplift of the Peloponnese; (3) block motions caused by normal faulting that are superimposed on the first two. Most vertical movements are estimated relative to sea level. Over the last 2 Ma the movement of sea level is reasonably well known, but is best determined over the last 20000 years, during which time sea level has not been higher than present (van Andel & Shackleton 1982). Earlier in the Pleistocene sea levels were probably also never more than 10 m above the present level (Inman 1983). A reliable indicator of uplift relative to sea level is the occurrence above the highest tide mark of borings, usually in crystalline limestone, containing the bivalve *Lithophaga lithophaga (sp)* (see e.g. Lyell 1867). Bored sea cliffs erode more quickly (probably over several thousand years: Inamura 1926; Schneider 1976; Matsuda *et al.* 1978; Pirazzoli & Kawana 1986) than the intact limestone, to produce a characteristic 'notched' profile.

Subsidence in central Greece is greatest in the Aegean Sea, NE and E of Evvia, where the crustal thickness deduced from gravity data constrained by seismic refraction is less than on the mainland (Makris & Vees 1977; Makris & Stobbe 1984), indicating greater stretching offshore. Fifty km east of central Evvia, the island of Skyros (marked S on the inset to Fig. 1a) is the crest of a tilted block bounded by a normal fault with a deep basin on its NE side (see Jackson *et al.* 1982b, Jackson & McKenzie 1983). This structure is clear in the morphology of Skyros, which has a steep, rugged and uplifting NE coast and gently sloping and embayed west side (Guernet 1971; Melentis 1973; Lemeille 1977; Roberts 1988).

Several authors have remarked on the uplift of the Peloponnese, particularly along its northern edge, adjacent to the Gulf of Corinth (e.g. Dufaure *et al.* 1975; Sebrier 1977; Keraudren & Sorel 1987; Mariolakos & Stiros 1987; Collier 1988, 1990; Ori 1989). The magnitude of this uplift is uncertain, but clearly large, with Gilbert fan delta deposits now preserved more than 1000 m above sea level (Ori 1989). The timing of the uplift is also uncertain, because the uplifted sediments have proved difficult to date. Much of the uplift may be Pleistocene in age, as most of the outer part of the Hellenic Arc was subsiding through the Pliocene (Mercier *et al.* 1987). The cause of the uplift may well not be solely footwall uplift associated with the normal fault system along the southern edge of the Gulf of Corinth.

Two lines of evidence suggest that some of the uplift is causd by underplating the Peloponnese with sediments overthrust in the Hellenic Trench system further west, in the manner described by Angelier *et al.* (1982) to explain the uplift of Crete. Firstly, the thick sediments in the Ionian basin west of Greece do not appear to influence the isotopic composition of volcanic rocks above the subducting slab (Barton *et al.* 1983; Briqueu *et al.* 1986). Secondly, the seismicity indicates that the subducting slab is almost flat under the Peloponnese, steepening to about 45° only in the far NE of the Peloponnese (Hatzfeld *et al.* 1989), where the first volcanic rocks are found. The highest elevations are in the northern Peloponnese, and it may be that the general uplift caused by underplating is accentuated here by uplift in the footwall of the Gulf of Corinth normal fault system. The southern side of the Gulf of Corinth itself contains a complicated record of the interaction between uplift and sea-level change, preserved in both the exposed sediments and in terrace morphology (Freyberg 1973; Keraudren & Sorel 1987; Collier 1988, 1990). However, the hangingwalls of the active faults along the southern coast of the Gulf, and the whole of the northern coast, are subsiding, indicating that fault movement is more than able to keep pace with any regional uplift.

Rugged coastal morphology and exposed 'notches' containing recent *L. lithophaga* borings 1–2 m above sea level indicate uplift in the footwalls of the normal faults bounding the NE and SW coasts of Evvia. The footwall of the north-dipping Kamena Vourla–Arkitsa fault system contains exposed *L. lithophaga* borings at its eastern end near Kynos (Fig. 3) and river terraces in its central part, again indicating uplift relative to sea level.

Where the hangingwall blocks of the large faults are exposed on land, it is not always straightforward to distinguish tectonic vertical motions from sedimentation in rapidly prograding alluvial fan systems or from subsidence caused by settling of the foundations of archaeological sites built on unconsolidated alluvium (which is accentuated by the frequent vibrations associated with earthquakes: e.g. Ambraseys & Sarma 1969; Blackman 1971; Owen 1987). One case of hangingwall subsidence is clear: movement of about one metre on the Kiparissi–Martinon fault (Fig. 4) in the earthquakes of 1894 caused flooding of the hangingwall between Kiparissi and Tragana, making islands of Mesozoic limestone outcrops that were previously attached to land (Skuphos 1894).

Tilting

The clearest indication of relative vertical movements associated with faulting is seen in the regional dips of sediments in the Neogene basins (Fig. 1a). Sections of these sediments are fine-grained lacustrine deposits that are likely to have been deposited close to the horizontal. Most are Miocene to Pleistocene in age (Lemeille 1977; Steininger & Rogl 1984; Mettos *et al.* 1986), and were deposited in basins that were not necessarily bounded by the currently active faults. Nevertheless, in nearly all the basins the regional dip directions are those expected from the motions of the nearby major active fault systems (and are reflected in the geomorphology and drainage, discussed later). Note particularly the change in dip between northern and central Evvia (Fig. 1a), reflecting the change in polarity of the fault system along the coast.

However, there are some basins exceptional to this generalization. In the Kymi basin (Fig. 1a) dip directions are very variable and much steeper (locally up to 85°) than elsewhere

(generally up to 15–25°). Sediments in the Kymi basin are early Miocene in age (Lemeille 1977) and have probably been deformed by more than one episode of faulting (e.g. Guernet 1971; Lemeille 1977; Katsikatsos *et al* 1981). The present drainage and morphology of the Kymi basin is controlled by the large normal fault offshore, with uplift, deep erosion and incision occurring along the eastern coastal margin of the basin and decreasing southwestwards. The main rivers draining the basin flow towards the NE, with deeply incised valleys close to the coast.

In the Megara basin (Fig. 1) the regional dip is to the NE, towards a degraded normal fault scarp with a WNW–ESE strike that bounds the basin. However, the present-day geomorphology of the basin is clearly not controlled by this fault, but by a probably more recently-active fault offshore along its NW end, which has caused uplift and incision of the drainage in the NW part of the basin (Jackson *et al.* 1982a).

The sediments exposed on land in the Malessina basin (Figs 1 & 4) dip N or NE in the northern part, towards the major fault bounding Mt. Kandilli along the SW coast of Evvia, and only dip S in the southernmost part of the basin adjacent to the Martinon fault. The structure of this basin does not appear to be greatly influenced by the Martinon fault, which has a relatively small topographic expression in its eastern part.

Relations between drainage and faulting

Relationships between drainage and faulting in central Greece are illustrated using three examples.

The Renginion–Atalanti region

The Renginion basin (Fig. 3) contains fluvial and lacustrine sediments of Pliocene–Pleistocene age (Philip 1974; Ioakim & Rondoyanni 1988), with an average dip of about 10–20° towards the south, and bounded on the south side by a fault system along the limestone mountain of Kalidromon. Sediments on the north side of the basin are mostly resting unconformably on the limestone mountain of Knimis, which is the footwall of the Kamena Vourla–Arkitsa fault system. The average elevation of the Renginion basin is 300–400 m above sea level and it is currently being eroded rapidly. The segmentation of the Kamena Vourla–Arkitsa fault system is clearly expressed in the topography by the resistant Mesozoic limestone of Knimis, and exposures of fault planes strongly suggest it is still active. The morphology of the Kalidromon fault is less well developed, and it may no longer be active, though there is evidence for movement in the Pleistocene (Philip 1974; Mercier 1976). In the SE part of the basin is the western end of the Atalanti−Martinon fault, which last moved in earthquakes in 1894 (Skuphos 1984).

Only in the western part of the Renginion basin is the main drainage perpendicular to the strike of the faults (streams A, B and C on Fig. 3). These streams have relatively narrow drainage basins and cut through the Kamena Vourla fault system west of Knimis where the footwall is no longer the resistant Mesozoic basement.

In the eastern part of the basin, south of the Knimis massif, the main drainage is axial, eventually reaching the northern Gulf of Evvia either by flowing round the end of Mt. Knimis (streams D and F on Fig. 3), or by cutting through Mt. Knimis at an obvious step in the Kamena Vourla−Arkitsa fault system (stream E on Fig. 3). The drainage basins for streams D−F are far greater than those of A−C, though the combined sediment output of streams A−C is able to create a large fan system in the Gulf. The sediment output and drainage into the Gulf directly off the limestone footwall of the Kamena Vourla−Arkitsa fault system is relatively insignificant: though even this is greatest at a step in the faulting by Kamena Vourla itself.

Evvia

The topography and position of the drainage divide in north and central Evvia (Fig. 2) closely follow the two major fault systems: along the SW coast in the north and along the NE coast in the central part of the island. The deepest water in the N Gulf of Evvia is in the hangingwall of the fault system running from near Loutra Edipsos to Mt Kandilli. The saddle in the footwall escarpment of this system is located in relatively soft Neogene sediments (Figs 1a & 1b), whereas the high mountains to either side are of basement limestones and serpentinites. Much deeper water exists off the NE coast of Evvia, with the highest and most rugged topography associated with the basement limestones of Mt Dirphis.

The largest drainage basins are established in Neogene sediments and flow away from the large coastal fault systems down the dip slopes of the footwall blocks. Only small linear basins drain directly off the fault scarps into the hangingwalls, even where the Neogene sedi-

ments in the saddle of the Loutra Edipsos−Kandilli escarpment extend to the coast (Figs 1a & 2).

The western Gulf of Corinth: Egion region

The NW−SE trend of the western Gulf of Corinth is controlled by a set of almost E−W fault segments stepping to the right along the coast (Fig. 1) and offshore (Higgs 1988). Between the coastal set of faults and other, probably older or less active, normal faults to the south are Neogene sediments with regional dips of up to 30° towards the south. The sediments between the stepping coastal faults are mostly alluvial conglomerates, well exposed near Egion (Fig. 6). Older, more consolidated marls, sandstones and conglomerates are exposed in the southern part of the basin (Ori 1989). Two basement ridges, Mts Bura and Panahaiko, occur in the footwalls of the coastal faults, the fault bounding Mt Bura having probably moved in the earthquake of 1861 (Montessus de Ballore 1924; Bousquet et al. 1983).

Drainage enters the Gulf of Corinth either directly, in relatively straight channels cutting through Neogene footwall blocks, or by axial channels that reach the Gulf through steps in the fault segments. The drainage south of Mt Panahaiko flows almost E−W, and so does the River Selinous as it enters the Gulf between the Egion and Mt Bura faults, where the land surface is tilted about 3° to the south. The drainage breaks through the Mt Bura fault at both ends of the resistant basement ridge, using a step in the faulting at the eastern end. The streams entering the Gulf of Corinth in this region form large submarine fans, which are prone to slumping, and are described by Ferentinos et al. (1988). A discussion of the sedimentary facies likely to be associated with such a drainage pattern is given by Leeder & Gawthorpe (1987).

General principles

It is clear from these examples that the pattern of drainage entering large depressions such as the Gulfs of Corinth and Evvia is related to both the faulting and the footwall lithology. The resistance of footwall ridges in basement, especially basement carbonate, leads to much axial drainage, but the size of the drainage basins depends on the continuity of the footwall ridges, which in turn is mostly determined by the continuity of the faulting itself. Much sediment is derived from basins in the dip slopes of footwall blocks and reaches the sea by rivers

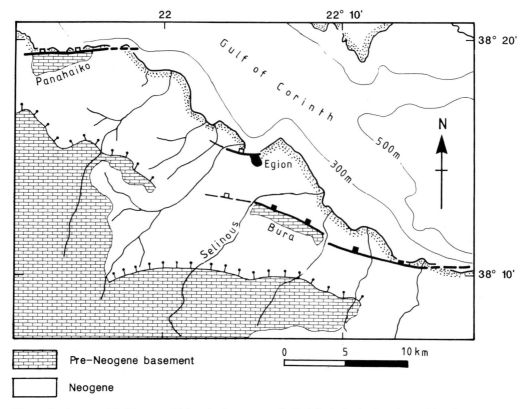

Pre-Neogene basement

Neogene

Fig. 6. Drainage and faulting near Egion, in the western Gulf of Corinth. Geology is modified from Dufaure (1978). The fault thought to be responsible for the 1861 earthquake is identified by filled blocks in its hanging-wall. The barbed basement-Neogene contacts are faults that are probably less active than the coastal fault system farther north (see also Ori 1989).

that break through gaps caused by steps between fault segments. Such basins often have larger catchment areas than the relatively narrow drainage systems that flow roughly perpendicular to strike, cutting through footwalls made of soft sediment. The smallest fans and drainage systems of all are those flowing directly off the fault controlled escarpments into the sea (see also Sabot & Maroukian 1982).

Perhaps the most important general principle is that the drainage in central Greece only starts to make sense when viewed on a scale comparable with the length of the fault segmentation, which may be up to 20 km. This may be a useful lesson when examining palaeocurrent data in tectonically older regions.

Perched basins

The segmentation of fault scarps may also affect the preservation of sediments along the escarpment systems bounding the major graben in central Greece. Near Kiparissi (Fig. 4) is a left step separating the Martinon and Atalanti (Fig. 3) segments of a fault system known to have moved in earthquakes in 1894. Southwest of Kiparissi is an area about 4×2 km^2 containing sediments with the same lithology (marls) and fossil fauna and flora as those in the Malessinna basin farther east (Fig. 4), which are thought to be Miocene in age (Rondoyanni–Tsiambaou 1984; J. Mercier, *pers. comm.*). The Kiparissi sediments are about 100 m above the level of the coastal plain to the north, and dip south by up to 16°. It appears that the Kiparissi sediments are part of a much larger basin, probably pre-dating the Atalanti–Martinon faulting, that is exposed in the step between major fault segments, but probably buried beneath the coastal plain either side of the step. (It was pointed out earlier that the 600 m high topography across the fault south of Tragana dies out progressively eastwards: near Martinon the elevation across the fault is only tens of metres, with sediments of the Malessina basin exposed on both sides: see Fig. 4.)

A second example is seen in the left step in the fault system near Agios Konstantinos, where the stream marked E in Fig. 3 breaks through Mt Knimis. Here, alluvial fan sediments dipping south up to 15° are found with an elevation up to 300 m above sea level. These are lithologically similar to those of the Renginion basin (Philip 1974), but are unfossiliferous. They occupy an area similar in size to those near Kiparissi.

It is unclear why the 'perched basins' of Kiparissi and Agios Konstantinos are exposed, though their location is clearly related to the fault segmentation. One possibility is that they are preserved at a relatively high elevation because the displacement on both fault segments dies out in the region where they meet or overlap. Another is that one fault segment is growing along strike at the expense of the other, which is dying out (in the manner of propagating rifts in the oceans), thus uplifting in its footwall sediments previously lowered in the hanging-wall of the 'dying' fault. There are few constraints on the dating and magnitude of displacement on these faults, and further speculation is not justified. Other possible examples of 'perched basins' have been described by Johnson (1930) in the Basin and Range Province of the western USA. A lesson to be learned from the occurrence of perched basins is the way in which local fault control can influence the extent and distribution of erosional unconformities or sediment preservation within extended basins. When working with sub-surface data such control must be understood first, before any discussion of regional sea-level variations becomes relevant.

Discussion

Two obvious questions arise from the observations summarized above. (1) What is the overall extension across the region of Fig. 1? (2) What is the origin of the fault segmentation, that so dramatically influences the geomorphology and sedimentation in central Greece?

No seismic refraction line exists across central Greece, though the limited data from offshore are sufficient to show that the crustal thickness is less in the Aegean than on the mainland (Makris & Vees 1977; Makris & Stobbe 1984). Recent studies in the northern North Sea (White 1990) and South China Sea (Su et al. 1990) have found that, in regions of block tilting, the overall extension estimated from the simple domino

model (i.e. $\beta = \sin\phi_0/\sin\phi_1$, where ϕ_0 and ϕ_1 are the initial and final dips of the faults) was, within error, compatible with extension estimated from both the change in crustal thickness and the observed syn- and post-rifting subsidence. These studies give us confidence that the same approach to estimating extension from the faulting in central Greece is not unreasonable. Seismogenic normal faults in central Greece typically dip 40–45° (Jackson & White 1989) and associated tilting of Miocene–Pleistocene sediments is typically up to 15–20° (Roberts 1988), suggesting that the initial fault dips were about 60°. These observations are consistent with β values of about 1.2–1.3, or extensions across the region in Fig. 1 of 20–30 km. We expect these to be minimum values: they assume that the blocks rotate coherently, which, as mentioned above, they probably do not, since they are observed to break up by antithetic faulting. Nonetheless, we believe that this estimate of extension is the right order of magnitude, though it is probably uncertain by 50%. It would require fault offsets of 5–7 km on blocks 20–25 km wide, which, in view of the topography and bathymetry associated with some of the larger faults, we do not consider to be impossible. If this extension occurred in the last 5 Ma, the average rate of stretching across central Greece would be 4–6 mm/yr, which is rather lower than the probable rate averaged over the last 100 years, thought to be in the region of 10–20 mm/yr (Jackson & McKenzie 1988a, b; Billiris et al. 1989).

The segmentation of the major normal faults is a fundamental structural characteristic of central Greece, and of other extensional provinces (e.g. Moore 1960, Garfunkel & Bartov 1977, Armijo et al. 1986). Various authors have considered possible origins of such discontinuous faulting, including: the elastic interaction of en echelon shear cracks (Segall & Pollard 1980); rotation of the stress field with depth (Mandl 1987); and the tendency of growing faults to develop arcuate strike lines, commonly concave towards the downthrown side (Mandl 1988). In the case of central Greece, there is a kinematic consideration that, in our opinion, makes it almost inevitable that the faulting should be discontinuous. We mentioned earlier that the slip vectors on the major faults were approximately N–S, whereas the overall direction of motion across the region of Fig. 1 is NE–SW (see inset to Fig. 1b). McKenzie & Jackson (1983 & 1986) pointed out that faulting with N–S slip vectors could take up the overall deformation if the faults rotate clockwise about a vertical axis as they move, which we now know occurs, from paleomagnetic studies on Evvia and Skyros (Kissel *et al.* 1986).

A component of right-lateral shear is thus distributed across central Greece by the normal faulting (even though movement on the normal faults has a left-lateral component) and leads to a clockwise sense of rotation. However, it is most unlikely that the shear gradient is uniform across the deforming zone (cf. New Zealand: Walcott 1984), and the rate of clockwise rotation is therefore likely to vary. This would inevitably break up any continuous linear marker (or fault) that spanned the zone. We are aware of no theoretical argument that is able to predict the maximum length of the fault segments that form; though, following Jackson & White (1989), we note that the observed maximum length of about 15–20 km is similar to the thickness of the seismogenic upper crust, and that it seems intuitively reasonable that the thickness of the deforming layer should influence the length and continuity of the structures that form within it.

Conclusions

Central Greece is one of the most actively extending regions on the continents, with a present-day motion of 10–20 mm a^{-1} across an area 150 km wide, and a minimum overall extension in the region of 20–30 km, most of which probably occurred during the last 5 Ma. The region consists of a number of fault-bounded half-graben, with most (but not all) the major faults dipping N to NE. Only the smaller graben, with widths up to about 20 km, appear to be simple half-graben that are bounded by significant faults on only one side and rotate coherently about a horizontal axis. The wider graben, such as the Gulf of Corinth and Northern Gulf of Evvia, while clearly asymmetric, are bounded by antithetic faults, with apparently relatively minor displacement, facing the major faults. The asymmetry of the graben is apparent in the topography, bathymetry, vertical movements of the coastline and in the regional tilting of exposed Neogene sediments adjacent to the major faults, though some dips in the Neogene sediments may be related to movement on faults that are no longer active.

The graben systems form basins up to 100 km long, such as the Gulf of Corinth and the Northern Gulf of Evvia, but the faulting bounding such basins is discontinuous, with fault segments reaching a maximum of about 20 km in length. In the Northern Gulf of Evvia the polarity of the half graben changes along strike. The island of Evvia itself is a twisted horst, with large bounding faults en echelon, rather than back-to-back. There is no seismological, geomorphological or structural evidence for fault segments being linked by simple strike-slip ('transfer') faults: instead, zones between steps or overlaps in major fault segments appear to be severely deformed by minor faulting. Zones where fault segments overlap or step are sometimes locations where sediments that would normally have been dropped to considerable depth in the hanging walls are exposed at the surface as 'perched basins'.

The segmentation of the normal fault systems is perhaps the most dramatic structural characteristic of central Greece and along with the lithology of the footwalls, profoundly influences the geomorphology and drainage. Where the footwalls consist of Mesozoic limestone, the drainage systems are mostly axial, flowing into the basins round the ends of fault segments or where fault segments step. Drainage directly off the fault scarps into the basins is relatively minor. In such regions the fault segmentation imposes a scale on the drainage, controlling the spacing of major fans along the margin of the basin. Where the footwalls consist of Neogene sediment, drainage directly across the fault scarps into the basins is more important, though the catchment areas of these streams are often relatively small and linear, compared with those in the limestone footwall terrains.

Thus the two main controls on the morphology and drainage of central Greece are the fault segmentation and the lithology of the footwalls. The origin of the segmentation is unclear, though it is a common feature of other extensional terranes, where, as in Greece, the maximum segment length is in the region of 15–20 km; similar to the thickness of the seismogenic upper crust. In central Greece the segmentation may be related to the rotation of blocks about a vertical, as well as a horizontal, axis.

We are grateful to Professor J.-L. Mercier and his colleagues for many discussions and for their work in central Greece, which has constantly guided us. We thank I.G.M.E. for permission to work in Greece, and Stathis Stiros for much logistical help. J.-L. Mercier, M. Leeder, C. Stark and A. Roberts provided thoughtful reviews that improved the original manuscript. This work was funded by N.E.R.C. We thank North Sea Sun Oil for general support of our work on active normal faulting. Cambridge Earth Sciences contribution No. 1529.

References

AMBRASEYS, N. N. & JACKSON, J. A. 1990. Seismicity and strain in central Greece between 1890 and 1988. *Geophysical Journal International*, **101**, 663–708

—— & SARMA, S. 1969. Liquefaction of soils by earthquakes. *Bulletin of the Seismological Society of America*. **59**, 61–64.

ANGELIER, J., LYBERIS, N. LE PICHON, X., BARRIER, E. & HUCHON, P. 1982. The neotectonic development of the Hellenic Arc and the Sea of Crete: a synthesis. *Tectonophysics*, **86**, 159–196.

ARMIJO, R., TAPPONNIER, P., MERCIER, J. L. & HAN TONG-LIN. 1986. Quaternary extension in southern Tibet: field observations and tectonic implications. *Journal of Geophysical Research*, **91**, 13, 803–13, 872.

BARTON, M., SALTERS, V. & HUIJSMANS, J. 1983. Sr-isotope and trace element evidence for the role of continental crust in calc-alkaline volcanism on Santorini and Milos, Aegean Sea, Greece, *Earth & Planetary Science Letters*, **63**, 272–291.

BILLIRIS, H. PARADISSIS, D., VEIS, G. ENGLAND, P., PARSONS, B., CROSS, P., RANDS, P., RAYSON, M., SELLERS, P., ASHKENAZI, V., DAVISON, M. & JACKSON, J. 1989. Geodetic determination of the strain in Greece in the interval 1900–1988. (Abstr.) *EOS: Transactions of the American Geophysical Union*, **70**, 719.

BLACKMAN, D. J. 1971. Evidence of sea level change in ancient harbours and coastal instalations. *In*: BLACKMAN, D. J. (ed.) *Marine Archaeology*, Butterworths, London, 115–137.

BOUSQUET, N., DUFAURE, J. J. & PECHOUX, P.Y. 1983. Temps historique et évolution des paysages égéens. *Mediterranée*. **2**, 3–10.

—— & PECHOUX, P.Y. 1977. La Seismicité du Basin Egéen pendant L'Antiquité. Méthodologie et premiers resultats. *Bulletin de la Sociéte Géologique de France*, **19**, 679–684.

BOTT, M.H.P. 1976. Formation of sedimentary basins of graben type by extension of the continental crust. *Tectonophysics*, **36**, 77–86.

BRIQUEU, L., JAVOY, M., LANCELOT, J. R. & TASUMOTO, M. 1986. Isotope geochemistry of recent magmatism in the Aegean arc: Sr, Nd, Hf and O isotopic ratios in the lavas of Milos and Santorini — geodynamic implications. *Earth & Planetary Science Letters*, **80**, 41–54.

BROOKS, M. & FERENTINOS, G. 1984. Tectonics and sedimentation in the Gulf of Corinth and the Zakynthos and Kefallania channels, Western Greece. *Tectonophysics*, **101**, 25–54.

COLLIER, R. 1988. *Sedimentary facies evolution in continental fault-bounded basins formed by crustal extension: the Corinth basin, Greece*. Ph.D. Thesis, University of Leeds.

COLLIER, R. E. 1990. Eustatic and tectonic controls upon Quaternary coastal sedimentation in the Corinth basin, Greece. *Journal of the Geological Society, London*, **147**, 301–314.

DESCHAMPS, A. & KING, G. C. P. 1984. Aftershocks of the Campania-Lucania (Italy) earthquake of 23 November 1980. *Bulletin of the Seismological Society of America*, **74**, 2483–2517.

DUFAURE, J.J. 1978. Le Peloponnese, Carte Géomorphologique. Institute Géographie, Paris.

——, KERAUDREN, B. & SEBRIER, M. 1975. Les terrasses de Corinthe (Grèce): Chronologie et déformations. *Comptes Rendues, Academie de Science, Paris*, **281**, 1943–1945.

ETHERIDGE, M. A. 1986. On the reactivation of extensional fault systems. *Philosophical Transactions of the Royal Society, London*, **317A**, 179–194.

EYIDOGAN, H. & JACKSON, J. A. 1985. A seismological study of normal faulting in the Demirci, Alasehir and Gediz earthquakes of 1969–70 in W. Turkey: implications of the nature and geometry of deformation in the continental crust. *Geophysical Journal of the Royal Astronomical Society*, **81**, 569–607.

FERENTINOS, G., PAPATHEODOROU, G. & COLLINS, M. B. 1988. Sediment transport processes on an active submarine fault escarpment: gulf of Corinth, Greece. *Marine Geology*, **83**, 43–61.

FREYBURG, B. von 1973. Geologie des Isthmus von Korinth. *Erlanger Geologische Abhandlungen*, **95**, 12–154.

GALANOPOULOS, A. 1955. 'Seismiki geographia tis Hellados'. *Annales Géologique de Pays Helleniques*. **6**, 83–121.

GARFUNKEL, Z. & BARTOV, Y. 1977. The tectonics of the Suez rift. *Bulletin of the Geological Survey of Israel*. **71**.

GIBBS, A. D. 1984. Structural evolution of extensional basin margins. *Journal of the Geological Society, London* **141**, 609–620.

GUERNET, C. 1971. *Contribution a l'étude géologique de l' Eubée et des régions voisines*. Thesis, Université de Paris.

HANCOCK, P. L. & BARKA, A. A. 1987. Kinematic indicators on active normal faults in W. Turkey. *Journal of Structural Geology* **9**, 573–584.

HATZFELD, D., CHRISTODOULOU, A., SCORDILIS, E. PANAGIOTOPOULOS, D. & HATZIDMITRIOU, P. 1987. A microearthquake study of the Mygdonian graben (N. Greece). *Earth & Planetary Science Letters*, **81**, 379–396.

HATZFIELD, D., PEDOTTI, G., HATZIDIMITRIOU, P., PANAGIOTOPOULOS, D., SCORDILIS, M., DRAKOPOULOS, J., MAKROPOULOS, K., DELIBASSIS, Hellenic subduction beneath the Peloponnese: first results of a microearthquake study. *Earth & Planetary Science Letters*.

HIGGS, B. 1988. Syn-sedimentary structural controls on basin formation in the Gulf of Corinth, Greece. *Basin Research*, **1**, 155–165.

INAMURA, I. 1926. On the recurrence of destructive earthquakes. *Proceedings of the Imperial Academy, Tokyo* **12**, 264–267.

INMAN, D. L. 1983. Application of coastal dynamics to the reconstruction of paleocoastlines in the vicinity of La Jolla California. *In*: MASTERS, P. M. & FLEMMING, N. C. (eds): *Quaternary coastlines and Marine Archeology*. Academic, New York.

IOAKIM, C. & RONDOYANNI, T. 1988. Contribution to the geological study of Zeli region, Locris (central Greece). *Revue de Micropaléontologie*, **31**, 129–136.

JACKSON, J. A. 1987. Active normal faulting and continental extension. *In*: COWARD, M. P., DEWEY, J. F. & HANCOCK, P. L. (eds) *Continental Extensional Tectonics*, Geological Society, London, Special Publication **28**, 3–17.

——, GAGNEPAIN, J., HOUSEMAN, G., KING, G. C. P., PAPADIMITRIOU, P., SOUFLERIS, C. & VIREUX, J. 1982a. Seismicity, normal faulting, and the geomorphological development of the Gulf of Corinth (Greece): the Corinth earthquakes of February & March 1981. *Earth & Planetary Science Letters*, **57**, 377–397.

——, KING, G. & VITA-FINZI, C. 1982b. The neotectonics of the Aegean: an alternative view. *Earth & Planetary Science Letters*, **61**, 303–318.

—— & McKENZIE, D. P. 1983. The geometrical evolution of normal fault systems. *Journal of Structural Geology*, **5**, 471–482.

—— & —— 1984. Active tectonics of the Alpine-Himalayan Belt between W. Turkey and Pakistan. *Geophysical Journal of the Royal Astronomical Society*, **77**, 185–264.

—— & —— 1988a. The relationship between plate motions and seismic moment tensors, and the rates of active deformation in the Mediterranean and Middle East. *Geophysical Journal*, **93**, 45–73.

—— & —— 1988b. Rates of active deformation in the Aegean Sea and surrounding regions. *Basin Research*, **1**, 121–128.

—— & WHITE, N. J. 1989. Normal faulting in the upper continental crust: observations from regions of active extension. *Journal of Structural Geology*, **11**, 15–36.

JOHNSON, D. 1930. Geomorphological aspects of Rift Valleys. *Proceedings of the 15th International Geological Congress*, **2**, 354–373.

KATSIKATSOS, G., BRUIJN, De H., VAN DER MEULEN, A. J. 1981. The Neogene of the Island of Euboea (Evia): A Review. *Geologie en Mijnbouw*, **16**, 509–516.

KERAUDREN, B, & SOREL, D. 1987. The terraces of Corinth (Greece): a detailed record of eustatic variations of the sea level during the last 500,000 years. *Marine Geology*, **77**, 99–107.

KING, G. C. P., OUYANG, Z. X., PAPADIMITRIOU, P., DESCHAMPS, A., GAGNEPAIN, J., HOUSEMAN, G., JACKSON, J. A., SOUFLERIS, C. & VIRIEUX, J. 1985. The evolution of the Gulf of Corinth (Greece): an aftershock study of the 1981 earthquakes. *Geophysical Journal of the Royal Astronomical Society*, **80**, 677–693.

KISSEL, C. & LAJ, C. 1988. The Tertiary geodynamical evolution of the Aegean arc: a paleomagnetic reconstruction. *Tectonophysics*, **146**, 183–201.

——, —— & MAZAUD, A. 1986. First paleomagnetic results from Neogene formations in Evia, Skyros, and the Volos region, and the deformation of Central Aegea. *Geophysical Research Letters*, **13**, 1446–1449.

LEEDER, M. R. & GAWTHORPE, R. L. 1987. Sedimentary models for extensional tilt-block/half-graben basins. *In*: COWARD, M. P., DEWEY, J. F. & HANCOCK, P. L. (eds.): *Continental Extensional tectonics*. Geological Society, London, Special Publication, **28**, 139–152.

LEMILLE, F. 1977. *Etudes néotectoniques en Grèce centrale nordorientale: Eubée centrale, Attique, Béotie, Locride et dans les Sporades du Nord, (Skiros)*. Thesis, Université de Paris-Sud, Orsay.

LE PICHON, X. 1982. Land-locked oceanic basins and continental collision: the eastern Mediterranean as a case example. *In*: HSU K. (ed.) *Mountain Building Processes*, Academic, New York 201–211.

—— & ANGELIER, J. 1979. The Hellenic arc and trench system: a key to the neotectonic evolution of the eastern Mediterranean area. *Tectonophysics*, **60**, 1–42.

LYELL, C. 1867. *Principles of Geology*. 10th Edn., Murray, London.

LYON-CAEN, M., ARMIJO, R., DRAKOPOULOS, J., BASKOUTAS, J., DELIBASSIS, N., GAULON, R., KOUSKOUNA, V., LATOUSSAKIS, J., MAKROPOULOS, K., PAPADIMITRIOU, P., PAPANASTASSIOU, D. & PEDOTTI, G. 1988. The 1986 Kalamata (S. Peloponessos) earthquake: Detailed study of a normal fault and tectonic implications. *Journal of Geophysical Research* **93**, 14,967–15,000.

MAKRIS, J. & STOBBE, C. 1984. Physical properties and state of the crust and upper mantle of the easten Mediterranean Sea deduced from geophysical data. *Marine Geology*, **55**, 347–363.

—— & VEES, R. 1977. Crustal structure of the Central Aegean sea and the islands of Evvia and Crete, Greece, obtained by refraction seismic experiments. *Journal of Geophysics*, **42**, 329–341.

MANDL, G. 1987. Discontinuous fault zones. *Journal of Structural Geology*, **9**, 105–110.

—— 1989. *Mechanics of Tectonic Faulting*. Elsevier, Amsterdam.

MARIOLAKOS, R. & STIROS, S. 1987. Quaternary deformation of Isthmus and gulf of Corinthos (Greece), *Geology*, **15**, 225–228.

MATSUDA, T. OTA, Y., ANDO, M. & YONEKURA, N. 1978. Fault mechanism and recurrance time of major earthquakes in S. Kanto district, Japan, as deduced from coastal terrace data. *Bulletin of the Geological Society of America*, **89**, 1610–1618.

McKENZIE, D. P. 1972. Active tectonics of the Mediterranean region. *Geophysical Journal of the Royal Astronomical Society*, **30**, 109–185.

—— 1978. Active tectonics of the Alpine-Himalayan belt: the Aegean Sea and surrounding regions. *Geophysical Journal of the Royal astronomical Society*, **55**, 217–254.

—— & JACKSON, J. A. 1983. The relationship between strain rates, crustal thickening, paleomagnetism, finite strain and fault movements within a deforming zone. *Earth & Planetary Science Letters*, **65**, 182–202, erratum 1984, **70**, 444.

—— & —— 1986. A block model of distributed deformation by faulting. *Journal of the Geological Society, London*, **143**, 249–253.

MELENTIS, J. 1973. La géologie de l'ile de Skiros. *Bulletin de la Sociéte Géologique de Grèce* **5**,

108−114.

MERCIER, J. L. 1976. La néotectonique, ses méthods et ses buts. Un example: l'arc égéen (Mediterranée orientale). *Revue de Géologie Dynamique et de Géographie Physique*, **18**, 323−346.

MERCIER, J. L., CAREY, E., PHILIP, H. R. & SOREL, D. 1976. La neotectonique plio-quaternaire de l'arc égéen externe et de la Mer égéen et ses relations avec séismicité. *Bulletin de la Sociéte Géologique de France*, **18**, 159−176.

——, DELIBASSIS, N., GAUTIER, A., JARRIGE, J. J., LEMILLE, F., PHILIP, H., SEBRIER, M. & SOREL, D. 1979. La néotectonique de l'Arc Egéen. *Revue de Géologie Dynamique et de Géographie Physique*, **21**, 67−92.

——, SOREL, D. & SIMEAKIS, K. 1987. Changes of the state of stress in the overiding plate of a subduction zone: The Aegean Arc from the Pliocene to the Present. *Annales Tectonicae*, **1**, 20−39.

——, ——, VERGELY, P. & SIMEAKIS, K. 1989. Extensional tectonic regimes in the Aegean basins during the Cenozoic. *Basin Research*, **2**, 49−71.

METTOS, A., IOAKIM, C. & RONDOYANNI, T. 1986. Les formations neogenes lacustres de l'Attique bu Nord-Béotie: stratigraphie palynologie et tectonique. *Geologie Mediterranéenne*, **12−13**, 167−174.

MONTESSUS de BALLORE, F.: La Geologie sismologique. Armand Colin Paris 1924.

MOORE, J. G. 1960. Curvature of normal faults in the Basin and Range province of the western United States. *Professional Papers of the U.S. Geological Survey*, **400**, 409−411.

ORI, G. G. 1989. Geologic history of the extensional basin of the Gulf of Corinth (?Miocene-Pleistocene), Greece. *Geology*, **17**, 918−921.

OWEN, G. 1987. Deformation processes in unconsolidated sands. 11−24. in: JONES, M. E. & PRESTON, R. M. F. (eds) *Deformation of Sediments and Sedimentary Rocks*. Geological Society, London, Special Publication, **29**, 11−24.

PECHOUX, P., PEGORARO, P., PHILIP, H. & MERCIER, J. 1973. Déformations Mio-Pliocene et Quaternaires en extension et en compression sur les rivages du golfe Malaique et du canal d'Atalanti (Egée, Grèce). *Comptes Rendues, Academie de Science, Paris*, **276**, 1813−1816.

PERISSORATIS, C. MITROPOULOS, D. ANGELOPOULOS, I. 1986. Marine geological research at the E. Korinthiakos Gulf. *I.G.M.E. Special issue of Geology and Geophysical Research*, Institute of Geology and Mineral exploration, Athens. 381−401.

PHILIP, H. 1974. *Etude néotectonique des rivages Egéens en Locride et Eubée nord-occidentale (Gréce)*. Thesis, Université des Sciences et Techniques du Languedoc, Montpellier.

PIRAZZOLI, P. A. & KAWANA, R. 1986. Determination de movements crustaux quaternaires d'apres la deformation des anciens rivages dans les iles Ryukyu, Japan. *Revue de Geologie Dynamique et de Geographie Physique*, **27**, 269−278.

RICHENS, W. D., PECHMANN, J. C., SMITH, R. B.,

LANGER, C.J., GOTER, S. K., ZOLLWEG, J. E. & KING, J. J. 1987. The Borah Peak, Idaho, earthquake and its aftershocks. *Bulletin of the Seismological Society of America*, **77**, 694.

ROBERTS, S. C. 1988. *Active normal faulting in central Greece and western Turkey*. PhD. Thesis, University of Cambridge.

RONDOYANNI-TSIAMBAOU, T. 1984. *Etude néotectonique des rivages occidentaux du Canal D'Atalanti, (Gréce-Central)*. Thesis, Université de Paris-Sud, Orsay.

ROSENDAHL, B. R., REYNOLDS, D. J., LORBER, P. M., BURGESS, C. F., McGILL, J., SCOTT, D., LAMBIASE, J. J. & DERKEN, S. J. 1986. Structural expressions of rifting: lessons from Lake Tanganika, Africa, *In*: FROSTICK, L. E., RENAUT, R.W., REID, I. & TIERCELIN, J. J. (eds.) *Sedimentation in the African Rifts*. Geological Society, London, Special Publication, **25**, 29−43.

SABOT, V. & MAROUKIAN, H. 1982. Geomorphology and tectonics in and around the Gulf of Corinth, Greece, *Proceedings of the Hellenic Arc and Trench System*, Athens, 174−182.

SCHNEIDER, J. 1976. Biological and inorganic factors in the destruction of limestone coasts. *Contributions to Sedimentology*, **6**.

SEBRIER, M. 1977. *Tectonique récente d'une transversale a l'arc egéen: le Golfe de Corinthe et ses régions périphériques*. Thesis, Université de Paris-Sud, Orsay.

SEGALL, P. & POLLARD, D. D. 1980. Mechanics of discontinuous faults. *Journal of Geophysical Research*, **85**, 4337−4350.

SENGOR, A. M. C., GORUR, N. & SAROGLU, F. 1985. Strike slip faulting and related basin formation in zones of tectonic escape: Turkey as a case study. *In*: Strike slip deformation, basin formation, and sedimentation. *Society of Economic Palaeontologists and Mineralogists, Tulsa*, **37**, 227−264.

SIEBERG, A. 1932. *Untersuchungen uber Erdbeben*. Aachen.

SKUPHOS, T. G. 1894. Die zwei grossen Erdbeben in Lokris. *Zeitschrift der Gesellschaft für Erdkunde. XXIX*. Berlin.

SOUFLERIS, C., JACKSON, J. A. KING, G., SPENCER, C. & SCHOLZ, C. 1982. The 1978 earthquake sequence near Thessaloniki (N. Greece). *Geophysical Journal of the Royal Astronomical Society* **68**, 429−458.

STEININGER, F. F. & ROGL, F. 1984. Paleogeography and palinspastic reconstruction of the Neogene of the Mediterranean and Paratethys. *In*: DIXON, J. E. & ROBERTSON, A. H. F. (eds): *The Geological Evolution of the Eastern Mediterranean*. Geological Society, London, Special Publication, **17**, 659−668.

STEWART, I. S. & HANCOCK, P. L. 1989. Normal fault zone evolution and fault scarp degradation in the Aegean region *Basin Research*, **1**, 139−153.

STEWART, J. H. 1980. Regional tilt patterns of the late Cenozoic basin-range fault blocks, western United States. *Bulletin of the Geological Society of America*, **91**, 46−464.

STIROS, S. C. 1985. *Archeological and geomorphic*

evidence of late Holocene vertical motions in the N. Euboean Gulf (Greece) and its Tectonic implications. Institute of Geology and Mineral exploration, Athens, internal report.

SU DAQUAN, WHITE, N., & McKENZIE, D. 1990. Extension and subsidence of the Pearl River Mouth basin, northern South China Sea. *Basin Research*, in press.

VAN-ANDEL, T. H. & SHACKLETON, J. C. 1982. Late Paleolithic and Mesolithic coastlines of Greece and the Aegean. *Journal of Field Archeology*, **9**, 445.

WALCOTT, R. I. 1984. The kinematics of the plate boundary zone through New Zealand: a comparison of short- and long-term deformations. *Geophysical Journal of the Royal Astronomical Society*, **79**, 613–633.

WESTAWAY, R. & JACKSON, J. A. 1987. The earthquake of 1980 November 23 in Campania-Basilicata (southern Italy). *Geophysical Journal of the Royal Astronomical Society*, **90**, 375–443.

WHITE, N. 1990. Resolving the extension discrepancy in the North Sea. *In*: BLUNDELL, D. J. & GIBBS, A. (eds) *Tectonic Evolution of the North Sea Rifts*, Oxford University Press.

Continental extension on sets of parallel faults: observational evidence and theoretical models

ROB WESTAWAY

Department of Geological Sciences, University of Durham, South Road, Durham DH1 3LE, UK

Abstract: Extension of the upper-crustal brittle layer is taken up in many regions on sets of sub-parallel normal faults that have sub-parallel slip vectors and are approximately planar between the earth's surface and *c.* 10 km depth. This style of faulting accommodates different deformation senses in the underlying upper mantle lithosphere in different deforming regions.

In the western North Anatolian fault zone, southernmost Italy, Tunisia and Libya, simple shear and extensional pure shear are distributed over zones up to *c.* 200 km wide and are taken up by oblique slip on faults that strike parallel to the simple shear direction. The strain rate tensor in such zones is biaxial, and although vertical vorticity is non-zero, blocks in the brittle layer do not rotate around vertical axes relative to the zone boundaries. In central Italy extension involving uniaxial extensional pure shear is taken up by normal slip on parallel faults.

In the northeastern Basin and Range province, central Greece and western Turkey, single sets of parallel faults take up extension in the interiors of deforming regions with dimensions > *c.* 500 km and appear to rotate around vertical axes relative to the boundaries of the regions. Distributed simple shear, oblique to fault strike, combined with extensional pure shear may *a priori* account for this deformation sense. However, it requires faults to strike in a unique direction that depends on the ratio of rates of pure and simple shear, and to have slip vector azimuth perpendicular to the simple shear direction. With this geometry, left-lateral slip takes up clockwise rotation and right-lateral slip anticlockwise rotation around vertical axes. To take up finite extension and rotation this unique geometry must persist over time. It is unlikely that this process explains deformation of any region considered. In contrast, uniaxial extension, whether occurring on its own or combined with rotation around a vertical axis at a non-zero rate, does not require any strong geometrical constraints: fault slip vector azimuths follow the direction of extensional pure shear and the sense of any strike-slip depends on the orientation of this direction relative to fault strike. Blocks in the brittle layer generally rotate around vertical axes at the same rate as elements in the underlying plastic deformation, which may equal half the vertical vorticity in the upper mantle lithosphere. This deformation sense, which accounts for the observed deformation in these regions, minimizes local differences in horizontal velocity between the brittle layer and the underlying upper mantle lithosphere.

In many actively-extending continental regions, the upper-crustal brittle layer contains sets of parallel active normal faults. These may be approximately planar between the earth's surface and mid-crustal depths, and separated en echelon by typically a few tens of km, with the same slip vector on all faults in a set. Although normal faults are usually segmented every few tens of km (e.g. Schwartz & Coppersmith 1984; Jackson & White 1989), a major normal fault may have along-strike extent up to several hundred km. Areas between major faults may be relatively undeformed, suggesting that deformation of the brittle layer is predominantly through slip on these faults. This style of extension is occurring in the northeast Basin and Range province of the western USA (e.g. Westaway & Smith 1989; Westaway 1989a,b);

Tibet (e.g. Armijo *et al.* 1986); central Italy (Westaway *et al.* 1989), offshore of Tunisia and Libya (e.g. Westaway 1990a,b), the Aegean Sea region, including central Greece (e.g. McKenzie & Jackson 1986) and western Turkey (Westaway 1990c). The same style is observed in many regions that extended in the geological past, including the North Sea (e.g. Barton & Wood 1984).

This article examines the kinematics of individual fault sets in the interiors of such regions. It investigates slip sense on sets of parallel oblique normal faults in the brittle layer in actively extending regions that range widely in size and deformation rate, and addresses the relationship between their slip sense and the sense of plastic deformation beneath the brittle layer.

From ROBERTS A. M., YIELDING, G. & FREEMAN, B. (eds), 1991, *The Geometry of Normal Faults*,
Geological Society Special Publication No 56, pp 143–169

143

Extension on sets of parallel faults: theory

Introduction

Many studies indicate that the uppermost c. 10–15 km of the crust is brittle and deforms by faulting, but the hotter lower crust and upper mantle lithosphere deform plastically. The composition of the upper mantle lithosphere makes it stronger than the lower crust at the temperatures usually encountered in these layers. In contrast, the frictional resistance to slip of faults that take up deformation of the brittle upper crust layer makes this layer stronger than the underlying lower crust. The question whether blocks in the brittle layer are coupled to or detached from the plastic deformation in the underlying lower crust and upper mantle lithosphere has attracted much attention. Although the lower crust is weaker than both the underlying upper mantle and the overlying brittle layer, viscous coupling between the upper mantle and the brittle layer will rapidly eliminate velocity differences between them unless they are maintained by external forces (Westaway 1990e). However, in some regions that extended in the geological past and are now uplifted and eroded, features can be mapped that are interpreted as 'detachments' that decoupled the base of the brittle layer and the underlying plastic deformation when the region was actively extending (e.g. Gans et al. 1985). It is not clear a priori how widespread or typical these features are, but in localities where the brittle layer and the underlying plastic deformation are detached, strain rate and rotation rate in the brittle layer reveal nothing about the sense of plastic deformation in underlying layers. In contrast, some people (e.g. Wernicke 1985) have suggested that active normal faults may persist as discrete planar features that take up extensional simple shear between the earth's surface and the base of the lithosphere, implying that deformation sense in any locality is the same in the lower crust and deforming upper mantle lithosphere as in the brittle layer, but velocity is not a continuous function of position in the lower crust or upper mantle lithosphere. An alternative starting assumption, the consequences of which I investigate here, is that active normal faults in the brittle layer die out in the plastic lower crust, and distributed plastic deformation occurs in the underlying upper mantle lithosphere. If one makes the additional assumption that velocities and deformation senses in the brittle layer and the upper mantle lithosphere are as similar as is possible given their different deformation mechanisms, one may derive useful relationships between them. If one does not make this assumption, but instead allows arbitrary velocity differences between the brittle layer and the underlying upper mantle lithosphere, one needs to specify some external driving mechanism to account for these velocity differences.

Brittle layer deformation in many continental regions can be readily explained as driven by large-scale plastic deformation of the underlying material that can be treated as a deforming 'fluid' on long timescales (e.g. McKenzie & Jackson 1983, 1986). Plastic deformation beneath the brittle layer can be expressed using a velocity gradient tensor, which can be decomposed into an antisymmetric rotation tensor, which describes rotation around orthogonal axes, and a symmetric strain rate tensor. Rotation around *horizontal* axes, or tilting, can be identified in actively extending regions from dips of sediments deposited in hanging-walls of active normal faults (e.g. Roberts 1988). However, evidence that the moho is flat in some such regions, for example central Greece (e.g. Makris & Vees 1977) where substantial tilting is observed in the brittle layer (e.g. Roberts 1988), indicates that the horizontal vorticity associated with brittle layer tilting dies out in the lower crust and does not persist into the upper mantle lithosphere. This evidence eliminates extensional simple shear throughout the lithosphere as a likely deformation mechanism. In contrast, rotation around *vertical* axes is only revealed directly in localities where geodetic surveys have been carried out across deforming zones and their stable surroundings that provide a reference frame, or where palaeomagnetic declination differs from north or south. Rotation around vertical axes has been identified using palaeomagnetism in some regions of active extension, including central Greece (Kissel et al. 1986). Vertical vorticity in the deforming upper mantle lithosphere probably causes such rotation, and must thus be considered along with extensional strain when investigating evolution of such regions. This article thus concerns sets of parallel oblique normal faults in the brittle layer that take up extensional strain and may rotate around vertical axes.

Theory developed by McKenzie & Jackson (1983, 1986), which can explain rotation around vertical axes of 'floating' blocks in the brittle layer as the response of the brittle layer to the vertical vorticity χ_z in the underlying plastic deformation, predicts their rotation rate ω is half χ_z. Vertical vorticity χ_z can be expressed as:

$$\chi_z = (\nabla \times \nu)_z. \qquad (1)$$

However, this theory assumes that the brittle layer comprises independent circular blocks, not sets of elongated blocks bounded by parallel planar faults. Westaway (1989a, 1990e) has shown that ω may equal $\chi_z/2$ for a floating block of any shape, provided its shape and the nature and geometry of its surroundings allow it to rotate around vertical axes, provided it is small enough for χ_z to be roughly constant beneath it, and provided extension (or shortening) in the plastic deformation beneath it is uniaxial. The brittle layer beneath any region may break up into blocks during deformation on a scale for χ_z not to vary substantially beneath any block, enabling ω to equal $\chi_z/2$ in different deforming regions with different sizes of blocks. However, the existence of one set of active oblique normal faults in a region does not necessarily indicate that the region is extending uniaxially. An obvious counterexample is provided by a set of parallel faults that takes up distributed simple shear parallel to fault strike and extensional pure shear in the perpendicular direction. The strain rate tensor for this configuration is biaxial (e.g. Westaway 1990e) but only one set of faults is active. McKenzie & Jackson (1983) showed in addition that a unique set of circumstances may exist where a single set of parallel faults in the interior of a deforming zone may take up extensional pure shear together with distributed simple shear oblique to fault strike. If a zone of width W is extending at rate dW and taking up transcurrent motion at rate bW, then faults striking at angle ϕ to the zone trend may take up this deformation, provided

$$\tan\phi = b/2d \qquad (2)$$

and provided their slip vector azimuth is perpendicular to the zone trend. McKenzie & Jackson (1983) suggested that blocks in such a configuration would rotate such that ω equals $\chi_z/2$, and the component of strike-slip on faults at their margins would have the opposite sense to the distributed simple shear across the zone as a whole. Vertical vorticity beneath such a zone will equal b and the gradient of extension velocity in the extension direction will equal d, assuming the blocks do not disturb the plastic deformation beneath the brittle layer (Westaway 1990e). In these circumstances d can be regarded as the extensional strain rate E_p for pure shear beneath the brittle layer. McKenzie & Jackson (1983) suggested that this process accounts for slip sense on parallel, oblique normal faults in central Greece. They suggested that other zones may also exist where the

unique conditions are satisfied that enable a single set of faults to take up oblique distributed simple shear and extensional pure shear. The present study was partly motivated to test whether other zones of similar sets of active normal faults satisfy these conditions. To anticipate my conclusions, not only did no other zones investigated satisfy these conditions, but also the zone in central Greece probably does not satisfy them either.

Equation (2) can be rearranged, given that $E_P=d$, $\chi_z=b$ and $\cot\gamma=\tan\phi$, to give:

$$\cot\gamma = \chi_z/2E_P = H_z \qquad (3),$$

where γ is related to fault dip δ and rake λ by:

$$\tan\gamma = \tan\lambda \cos\delta. \qquad (4).$$

Fault strike and rake are expressed using the right-handed coordinate system of Aki & Richards (1980, p. 115). The same convention is adopted for γ.

A subsequent investigation by Lamb (1987) suggests that McKenzie & Jackson's (1983) theory needs modification to take account of the fact that in general during deformation with a biaxial strain rate tensor, ω of elongated floating blocks will not necessarily equal $\chi_z/2$. Lamb (1987) also pointed out that the presence of any block in the brittle layer may disturb the underlying velocity field, and that vertical vorticity beneath the brittle layer in the part of a deforming zone taking up distributed simple shear and situated beneath a set of parallel faults, will not necessarily equal the gradient of transcurrent velocity across the zone. These points are valid even though Lamb's (1987) theory for a single, isolated, elongated, elliptical, floating block does not necessarily validly describe the kinematics of sets of blocks bounded by parallel faults. In particular, Lamb (1987) assumed velocity is continuous between the block and its surroundings, whereas active faults at block boundaries will cause discontinuities in velocity between any block and its surroundings.

Given Lamb's (1987) analogy between blocks in the brittle layer and rigid floating inclusions in a deforming fluid, one may estimate the effect block elongation has on its rotation rate. Where velocity gradients along the x axis, parallel to the deforming zone trend are zero, Lamb's (1987) equation (5) simplifies to:

$$\omega = \frac{\chi_z}{2} - \frac{(1-k^2)}{2(1+k^2)}(d\sin2\psi + b\cos2\psi) \qquad (5)$$

where $k \leq 1$ is the ratio of length to width of a block and ψ is the angle in the anticlockwise sense between its long axis and the x axis. With

$k=0.25$, $\psi=-35°$ and $b=0.7d$, values shown later to be reasonable for central Greece, assuming that distributed simple shear across the deforming zone, identified by McKenzie & Jackson (1983), is causing local deformation, ω is estimated as c. $0.75\chi_z$. It thus has the same sense as, and is not dramatically different from, the value $\chi_z/2$ obtained for floating blocks by neglecting this effect of elongation. Alternatively, it is possible a priori that blocks in the brittle layer are not analogous to floats, but instead move with the underlying upper mantle lithosphere and thus rotate at rate $\chi_z/2$ if elements in the upper mantle lithosphere rotate at this rate.

Finite deformation

On geological timescales, finite deformation of regions that are extending uniaxially with non-zero vertical vorticity will involve rotation of blocks and sets of parallel faults at their margins, through finite angles around vertical axes. Blocks will tilt, and faults will acquire progressively less-steep dips as the region extends, as described by Jackson & McKenzie (1983) and others. This rigid domino model predicts that:

$$D(t)\ \sin\delta(t) = D_0\ \sin\delta_0 \qquad (6)$$

where D is the width of a fault-bounded block, δ is fault dip, and subscript 0 denotes values when extension began. Displacement T on each fault is:

$$T(t) = D\ \cos\delta - D_0\ \cos\delta_0. \qquad (7)$$

Jackson (1987) has suggested that normal faults typically form with dip c. $60°$. Dip decreases during extension to c. $30°$, when friction on faults is likely to prevent further slip. For extension to continue further a new generation of faults will form with initial dip c. $60°$.

Dip on any fault in a set bounding rigid domino blocks is thus a function only of initial dip and local extensional strain; it does not depend on the number of faults in a set or the displacement on each fault. Assuming initial dip c. $60°$, or any other reasonable value, present-day dip thus gives extension factor directly. Assuming all blocks in a zone behave as rigid dominoes, this geometrical property allows extensional strain to be estimated without the need to resolve displacement on each of the possibly numerous individual faults that take up this extension. However, rather than behaving like rigid dominoes, blocks with width a few tens of km or more, greater than the thickness of the brittle layer, will flex, in order to maintain overall isostatic compensation, following slip on

any fault at their margins and the accompanying unloading of its footwall and relaxation of the lower crust (e.g. King et al. 1988; Jackson & White 1989). Flexing of wide blocks may occur either elastically or by slip on minor faults, and is observed in blocks that are $> c.$ 40 km wide in the northeast Basin and Range province and in the Aegean region to be discussed.

If the profile of the earth's surface across such a flexed block is approximated as a circular arc, its radius of curvature can be estimated. The smallest radii of curvature in these examples are c. 100 km, which appears to indicate the sharpest curvature around a horizontal axis that can be taken up by internal deformation of blocks. The possibility of internal deformation of blocks has important implications for use of fault dips to estimate extensional strain. Consider the schematic example in Fig. 1. A fault with initial dip $60°$ cuts the brittle layer, separating it into two blocks that have flexed. Suppose fault dip decreased during extension from 60 to $45°$. From equation (6), $\sin(\delta_0)/\sin(\delta_1)=1.22$, predicting extensional strain 0.22. In contrast, allowing for flexing of blocks in circular arcs, the width D_1 after extension of the zone that has flexed is (Fig. 1):

$$\begin{aligned} D_1 &= X_1 + X_2 + X_3 \\ &= (R_1 + h)\ \sin\theta_1 + (R_2 - h)\ \sin\theta_2 \\ &\quad + T\ \cos\delta_1. \end{aligned} \qquad (8)$$

The distance between these two points before extension is:

$$D_0 = R_1\ \theta_1 + R_2\ \theta_2. \qquad (9)$$

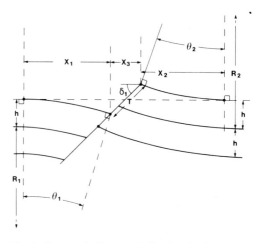

Fig. 1. Schematic diagram indicating dip δ and displacement T for a normal fault that cuts the brittle layer and has rotated to less steep dip as a result of flexing of the blocks on either side of it. See text for discussion.

Displacement T is:

$$T = [(R_1 + h)(1 - \cos\theta_1) + (R_2 - h)(1 - \cos\theta_2)]/\sin\delta_1. \quad (10)$$

If fault dip decreased during extension from 60° to 45° then $\theta_1 = \theta_2 = 15°$. With radius of curvature $R_1 = R_2 = 100$ km, similar to those observed in the northeast Basin and Range province and Aegean, and similar also to radii modelled by Stein *et al.* (1988) as consistent with an effective 'elastic thickness' of the upper-crustal brittle layer of *c.* 2–4 km, and with $2h$, the brittle layer thickness, 10 km, then T is 9.6 km, D_0 52.4 km and D_1 58.6 km. Average extensional strain across this zone is 6.2/52.4 or 0.12, less than the alternative estimate. Any other curved profile that is concave downward in fault hangingwalls and concave upward in footwalls will also predict less extension than the rigid domino model for a given change in fault dip, although the geometrical construction needed to show this is more difficult.

Provided extensional strain rate and vertical vorticity are constant throughout finite deformation, rotation angle ζ around vertical axes is:

$$\zeta = \omega t \quad (11)$$

for a block rotating at rate ω and:

$$\varepsilon = \beta - 1 = (D/D_0) - 1. \quad (12)$$

Extensional strain rate E equals E_1, the extensional eigenvalue of the strain rate tensor during uniaxial extension, and equals E_p during extension involving pure shear and distributed simple shear. In this latter case no eigenvalue of the strain rate tensor gives the correct extensional strain rate, and neither eigenvector azimuth gives the correct extension direction (Westaway 1990e). In both cases, if E is uniform over time then

$$\varepsilon = Et \quad (13),$$

and thus

$$\frac{\zeta}{\varepsilon} = \frac{\zeta}{(\beta-1)} = \frac{\omega}{E} \cong H_z. \quad (14)$$

This approximate equality is exact where $\chi_z = 2\omega$. Comparison of present-day H_z with the ratio of extensional strain to rotation angle thus provides information on the earlier kinematics of sets of parallel faults that satisfy McKenzie & Jackson's (1983) floating block model and have taken up finite deformation.

Finite rotation around vertical axes and finite extensional strain can be taken up on a set of parallel faults evolving at constant H_z only if the extension direction rotates around a vertical axis at the same rate as the faults. Conversely, if a set of parallel faults takes up extension with $|H_z|$ decreasing with time, then the local extension direction rotates around a vertical axis at a greater rate than the faults and blocks in the brittle layer. Furthermore, if field studies suggest that slip sense γ has been roughly uniform during deformation of a region then, provided equation (3) is satisfied, the ratio of E_p to ω must have remained constant over time. Together with the geometrical property that slip vector azimuth must be perpendicular to strike of the zone boundaries at all times, this provides a strong constraint on the evolution of any region containing fault-bounded blocks that rotate around vertical axes in a deforming zone that takes up distributed simple shear. Furthermore, for faults to rotate around vertical axes keeping constant slip sense γ and simultaneously keeping the correct orientation relative to the zone boundaries, these boundaries must rotate around vertical axes at the same rate as faults within the zone.

In contrast, where a set of parallel normal faults takes up uniaxial extension, ω will equal $\chi_z/2$ in the underlying upper mantle lithosphere either if blocks are floating or if they rotate with the upper mantle lithosphere (Westaway 1990e). In both cases, local extension direction during uniaxial extension is the azimuth of the extensional eigenvector of the strain rate tensor in this plastic deformation (Westaway 1990e). Faults may have any strike relative to this direction: whether a fault shows pure normal slip or a component of right- or left-lateral slip depends only on the angle between its strike and the extension direction. Such faults can take up finite extension with uniform slip sense, provided the extension direction beneath the brittle layer rotates around vertical axes relative to an external reference frame at the same rate as both elements in the plastic deformation in the upper mantle lithosphere and blocks in the brittle layer. In these circumstances no constraint exists between slip sense on faults and the ratio of extensional-strain-rate to rotation-rate around vertical axes. If γ varies with time, extension direction will change relative to both fault strike and the external reference frame. There is thus no fixed extension direction, in either the reference frame of the faults or the external reference frame, and hence no fixed direction in which extension can be restored.

Regardless of deformation sense beneath the brittle layer in any region, to quantify rotation around vertical axes information is needed to tie the reference frame provided by any fault or fault-bounded block to an external frame. The

Table 1. *Block dimensions and observed and predicted slip senses in actively extending regions*

	L_F	L_S	D	γ	E	χ_z	2ω	X	Sense
(1) Intermountain SB (N Utah-S Idaho)	200	20	25	-105	1.0	(+4.0)	(+4.0)	500	UPS
(2) Central Idaho SZ (central Idaho)	200	20	40	-055	1.0	(-4.0)	(-4.0)	500	UPS
(3) Central Italy (Abruzzo)	50	20	20	-087	1.7	~0.0	±0.0	40	UPS-N
(4) Southern Italy (Calabria)	100	20	20	-045	2.2	+10.0	(0.0)	40	SS-S
(5) Central Greece (Corinth-Evvia)	200	20	80	-055	5.0	-12.0	-12.0	500	UPS
(6) Western Turkey (Simav-Menderes)	150	20	100	-70	5.0	+12.0	+12.0	500	UPS
(7) Western NAFZ (Çanakkale)	200	30	50	-145	3.0	-20.0	0.0	100	SS-D
(8) Tunisia-Libya SZ (Tunisia-Sicily)	200		>20	-135	0.4	+1.4	(0.0)	200	SS-D

Column headers denote: X, zone boundary separation (km); L_F, typical along-strike extent of active normal faults; L_S, typical along-strike extent of active normal fault segments; D, typical separation of major fault zones; γ defined in the text; E extensional strain rate (E_1 in zones taking up uniaxial extension, F_p in zones taking up distributed simple shear); χ_z vertical vorticity (clockwise is negative); 2ω double the estimated rotation rate around vertical axes assuming rotation rate equals half the vertical vorticity in regions where rotation rate is non-zero. Sense, deformation sense: UPS, uniaxial extension, SS, distributed simple shear combined with extensional pure shear; -D, dextral, -S, sinistral, -N, normal. χ_z is estimated in zones of distributed simple shear as the ratio of transcurrent velocity to zone width, and in other zones as double the ratio of palaeomagnetic rotation angle to duration of deformation. Values in brackets are inferred from numerical models. Rows (1) and (2): all information is from Westaway (1989a). Row (3): information is from Westaway *et al.* (1989), viewing the region in the reference frame of the northern Tyrrhenian Sea region to the west of the actively extending zone. Rows (4): observed extension rate across Calabria is c. 3 mm a^{-1} over a zone c. 30 km wide (Westaway 1990b). Predicted χ_z is an upper limit estimated by Westaway *et al.* (1989). Row (7): All information is discussed in the text. Row (8): Predicted χ_z is from this article. Given NW strike of faults and eastward slip vector azimuth, observed γ is c. -135°. Westaway's (1990a) focal mechanism for the 1974 Tripoli earthquake (ϕ 297°, δ 37°; λ -141°) gives the same value.

tie may be provided in active regions using geodetic or palaeomagnetic information. In regions that extended in the past, palaeomagnetism may also constrain rotation around vertical axes relative to undeformed surroundings. However, in many cases one may neither know where the stable surroundings of ancient deformed zones were, nor have any suitable palaeomagnetic information. In these circumstances, one may only work in the reference frame provided by whatever fragment of the ancient deformed zone is available for study, and one thus loses constraint on vertical vorticity in the geographical reference frame or any other external frame. Assuming blocks in the brittle layer move with the underlying upper mantle lithosphere, and rotate at rate equal to $\chi_z/2$ when measured in the external reference frame, vertical vorticity will be zero in the reference frame that is rotating with fault-bounded blocks within a deforming zone. Thus in this reference frame one may attribute oblique slip on major faults to oblique extension only, without interpreting the deformation pattern in other reference frames. This may well explain why fieldwork has failed to provide evidence of rotation around vertical axes, both in actively-deforming regions and ancient examples. With extension direction and fault strike both rotating around vertical axes relative to the geographical reference frame, displacement and dip on normal faults (equations (6) and (7)) are the same as they would be for extensional pure shear with extension direction at all times oriented perpendicular to fault strike, and with no vertical vorticity. Thus, whether fault strike and extension directions maintain constant or variable angular separation γ during finite extensional strain, the normal component of slip on any fault rotating around a vertical axis can be validly restored in the reference frame of the fault as if only normal slip were occurring, with no rotation around vertical axes.

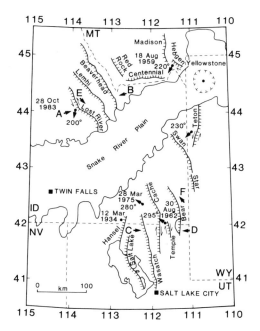

Fig. 2. Major tectonic features in the northeast Basin and Range province. Neogene and Quaternary volcanic outcrops around Yellowstone and along the Snake River plain are outlined. Northeastward movement of the Yellowstone upwelling mantle plume relative to the North American plate at 35 to 40 mm a^{-1} indicated by ages of Snake River plain volcanic rocks (Armstrong *et al.* 1975) implies that 10 Ma ago the active volcanic field was near Twin Falls, Idaho, 400 km southwest of Yellowstone. The principal normal faults on both sides of the Snake River Plain, inferred as active from evidence of earthquakes or local geomorphology, are identified with tick marks on the hanging wall. Slip vector azimuths, where known or inferred, are indicated by short single arrows, and senses of strike-slip by small double arrows. Information is from: Smith & Sbar (1974); Smith *et al.* (1985); Bache *et al.* (1980); Crone & Machette (1984); Doser (1985); Eddington *et al.* (1987); Stickney & Bartholomew (1987); Pechmann *et al.* (1987); Susong *et al.* (1987); Westaway & Smith (1989).

Extension on sets of parallel faults: observation

This section describes present-day active extension in the NE Basin and Range province, Italy, the central Mediterranean, and the Aegean Sea, which are used as examples to illustrate patterns of extension observed and to test the applicability of the theory discussed in the previous section. Parameters that describe deformation sense are summarized in Table 1.

The northeast Basin and Range province

The NE Basin and Range province comprises two sets of sub-parallel normal faults that take up active extension: the east-trending central Idaho seismic zone and the north-trending Intermountain seismic belt, which converge at Yellowstone (Fig. 2). Holocene scarp heights of up to *c.* 10 m indicate slip rates up to *c.* 1 mm a^{-1}, and given typical *c.* 30 km fault spacings, extensional strain rate is up to *c.* 10^{-15} s^{-1}

(Westaway 1989a,b). Other regions north and south of these two zones are also actively extending, but at lower rates (e.g. Eddington *et al.* 1987; Stickney & Bartholomew 1987). Beyond *c.* 150 km from Yellowstone, slip vector azimuths in both zones are oriented at *c.* 30 to 60° to the zone trend: faults in the Central Idaho seismic zone show left-lateral slip, and faults in the Intermountain seismic belt show right-lateral slip (Westaway 1989a,b). Given that slip vector azimuth is not perpendicular to zone trend, the conditions identified by McKenzie & Jackson (1983) whereby a single set of parallel faults may take up biaxial extension are not satisfied. Furthermore, neither zone is taking up distributed simple shear parallel to fault strike (Westaway 1990e). The existence of a single set of active faults in each zone thus indicates extension is uniaxial, and ω will equal $\chi_z/2$ in the uppermost mantle if blocks are floating, or $\varkappa_z$ if they move with the upper mantle lithosphere.

Both actively-deforming zones persist to *c.* 500 km distance from Yellowstone; the width of both zones parallel to fault strike is *c.* 200 km, and the overall width of the deforming region is

(a)

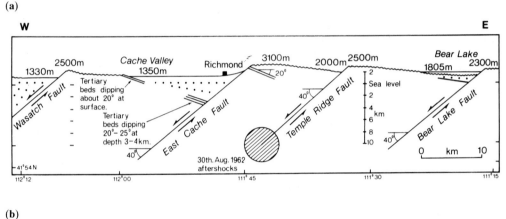

(b)

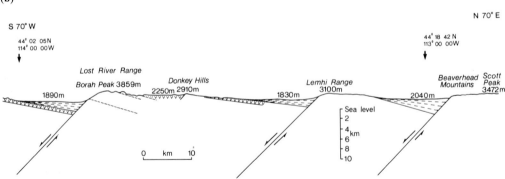

Fig. 3. (a) Cross section in a vertical plane through the Central Idaho seismic zone, showing major normal faults that bound the SW sides of the Lot River, Lemhi and Beaverhead ranges. Position of this section line, which trends N70°E approximately perpendicular to the ranges, is shown as A–B in Fig. 2. V pattern denotes Tertiary volcanic rocks; dashed line pattern denotes Neogene and Quaternary sediments; older basement rocks are unshaded. Construction of this section is described by Westaway (1989a). It uses results of a study by Stein & Barrientos (1985) of the Borah Peak earthquake of 28 October 1983 that occurred on this part of the Lost River fault that dips WSW at 45°. The same dip is assumed for other faults in the same parallel set. (b) West–East cross section in a vertical plane along 41°54'N between the Wasatch Fault and Bear Lake, from C to D in Fig. 2, showing schematically the pattern of normal faults in the upper crust. Construction of this section, described in detail by Westaway & Smith (1989), uses results of a study of the Cache Valley earthquake of 30 August 1962 that indicate a fault plane dipping west at 43°. As in (a), the same orientation is assumed for other faults that have not moved in recent earthquakes. Neogene sediments are dotted; older basement is unshaded. Information is from Bond (1978), Davis (1985), Dixon (1978), Mabey (1985) and Smith & Bruhn (1984).

c. 500 km. Viewed in section, each zone comprises domino-style blocks bounded by faults that are approximately planar between the earth's surface and the base of the brittle layer, and on which Neogene displacements of up to *c*. 10 km have developed (e.g. Stein & Barrientos 1985; Westaway & Smith 1989; Westaway 1989a,b) (Fig. 3). This planar geometry can be confirmed on faults that have slipped in recent earthquakes: seismological studies constrain one nodal plane of the focal mechanism to have the same dip as the fault at the earth's surface, and constrain the hypocentre to be near a downdip projection of the surface trace of this fault (e.g. Stein & Barrientos 1985; Westaway & Smith 1989).

Slip sense on faults within these two zones varies considerably from place to place (Fig. 2) and bears no obvious relationship to any lateral boundary conditions. Westaway (1989a,b) has suggested instead that brittle layer deformation is driven by velocity gradients within the upper mantle lithosphere. He suggested that these velocity gradients are related to return flow from the upwelling Yellowstone mantle plume, which is sheared SW by motion of the North American plate across it. Westaway (1989a,b) showed that the scale at which the region is broken into fault-bounded blocks is similar to that over which vertical vorticity varies laterally, and slip vector azimuth on faults is consistent with the likely direction of uniaxial extension in the upper mantle lithosphere beneath these zones. He predicted that χ_z is clockwise beneath the Central Idaho seismic zone and anticlockwise beneath the Intermountain seismic belt. Both sets of parallel faults thus appear to take up deformation of the brittle layer in a sense consistent with this plastic deformation inferred to be occurring in the underlying upper mantle lithosphere.

Italy

Italy contains an elongated zone of active extension (Fig. 4) with length *c*. 1000 km and width seldom as much as 100 km. The present-day northern limit of active extension is in Tuscany near lat 44° 30′ N, lon 9° 30′ E, and can be regarded as an Euler pole around which the margins of the actively extending zone, the stable northern Tyrrhenian Sea to the southwest and the northern Adriatic Sea to the northeast, are separating at angular velocity *c*. 0.3° Ma^{-1} (Westaway *et al.* 1989). The northernmost *c*. 600 km of this zone, north of lat 41° N, has a uniform southeastward trend and appears to be extending with negligible transcurrent re-

lative motion of its boundaries. Viewed in the Tyrrhenian Sea reference frame, the anticlockwise rotation of the Adriatic causes a small anticlockwise vertical vorticity beneath the actively-extending zone. Abruzzo in central Italy experienced a moderate (M_s 5.8) earthquake on 7 May 1984 following a larger event on 13 January 1915 (M_s *c*. 7) (Westaway *et al.* 1989) (Fig. 5). Co-seismic slip vector azimuth in 1984 was within *c*. 2° of the N45°E direction perpendicular to strike of the actively extending zone. Seismological studies suggest 48° SW dip of the seismogenic fault plane at *c*. 10 km depth. The same fault has *c*. 60° dip at the earth's surface, indicating minor listric curvature.

In contrast, the southernmost *c*. 400 km of the actively extending zone in southern Italy is strongly curved, changing strike from N45°W to N30°E. This curvature has been caused by extension of the southern Tyrrhenian Sea to the west, which has displaced Calabria (southernmost mainland Italy) several hundred km ESE in the past *c*. 10 Ma (e.g. Malinverno & Ryan 1987; Westaway *et al.* 1989). Active normal faults in southern Calabria strike between N20°E and N30°E and have slip vector azimuth *c*. N75°E, indicating substantial left-lateral slip with γ *c*. −60°. Examples include the Calabrian earthquake of 5 February 1793 (Tapponnier *et al.* 1987) and the Messina event of 28 December 1908 (Schick 1977; Mulargia & Boschi 1983), both of which had magnitude *c*. 7 (e.g. Westaway *et al.* 1989). Macroseismic studies of the Catania event of 11 January 1693 (Barbano & Cosentino 1981) suggest fault strike N20°E and indicate magnitude *c*. 7 also. The eastern coast of Sicily is bounded by normal faults with NNE trend (e.g. Funiciello *et al.* 1981), one of which presumably slipped in this earthquake. This zone of oblique normal faulting continues south to merge with the Tunisia−Libya seismic zone discussed later.

Palaeomagnetic studies (Aïfa *et al.* 1988) show that lower Pliocene rocks in southernmost Calabria have rotated 36° clockwise, suggesting that local clockwise vertical vorticity, averaged over the past 4 Ma, is *c*. 18° Ma^{-1}. However, Westaway *et al.* (1989) suggested that most clockwise rotation probably occurred between 4 and *c*. 2 Ma ago, when the Tyrrhenian Sea was rapidly extending, and both Tyrrhenian Sea extension and the associated rotation may have now ceased. The present-day kinematics of this region are not fully understood, but a case can be made (Westaway *et al.* 1989; Westaway 1990b) that Tyrrhenian Sea extension is now no faster than *c*. 1 mm a^{-1}, and the region is at

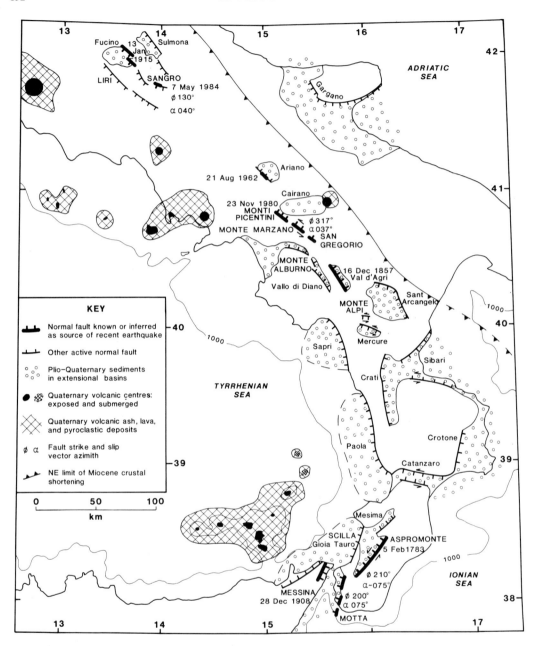

Fig. 4. Map summarizing Quaternary tectonic and volcanic activity in central and southern Italy. Quaternary volcanic centres are from Funiciello *et al.* (1981). North of Lat. 40°N they are mostly ultrapotassic alkali basalt that may be caused by local extension. Those further south, mostly calc-alkaline, are related to subduction of the Tyrrhenian Sea Benioff zone. Upper case letters denote active faults with dates of some significant normal-faulting earthquakes. Lower case letters denote Plio-Quaternary extensional sedimentary basins in hanging walls of active normal faults. Other Plio-Quaternary outcrop is omitted. Information is from Schick (1977), Funiciello *et al.* (1981), Mulargia & Boschi (1983), Westaway & Jackson (1984, 1987), Westaway (1987), Tapponnier *et al.* (1987) and Westaway *et al.* (1989). Additional major active normal faults probably exist but have not yet been identified between some faults shown on this map.

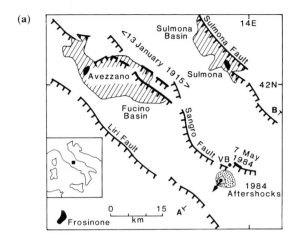

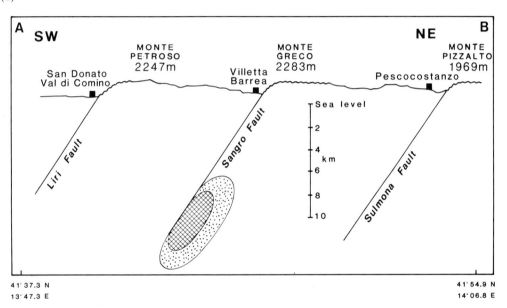

Fig. 5. (a) Map of major active normal faults that dominate the topography of central Italy, with hanging wall tick marks. Quaternary extensional sedimentary basins are shaded. Thicker lines indicate surface faulting in the Fucino earthquake (M_s 6.8) of 13 January 1915 and a surface projection of the fault segment that slipped in the Lazio-Abruzzo earthquake (M_s 5.8) of 7 May 1984. VB denotes Villeta Barrea, the village nearest the 1984 epicentre. (b) Cross section trending SW–NE across the epicentral area of the 1984 earthquake, between A and B in (a). Faults are shown assuming constant 55° dip to 12 km depth. Areas affected by aftershock activity in 1984 are indicated in both parts. Simplified from Figs 2 and 11 of Westaway *et al.* (1989).

present dominated by northeastward relative motion of the Ionian Sea to the east relative to the now stable Tyrrhenian Sea and the rest of the European plate, causing *c.* 2 mm a^{-1} extension and *c.* 5 mm a^{-1} left-lateral slip across Calabria. This relative motion is indirectly related to northward convergence between Africa and Europe (Westaway 1990a,b). Under this interpretation of the region, faults in Calabria and northeast Sicily now take up distributed left-lateral simple shear and extensional pure shear caused by relative motion of the zone boundaries.

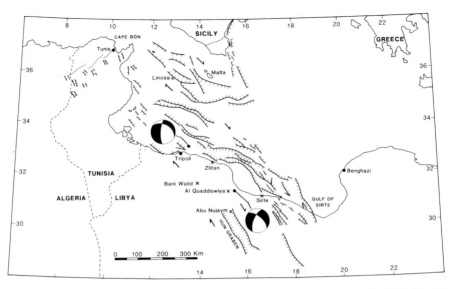

Fig. 6. Map of the central Mediterranean, showing epicentres and focal mechanisms of the Tripoli earthquake of 4 September 1974, the Sirte mainshock of 19 April 1935, and normal faults in the Tunisia−Libya seismic zone. Localities most severely damaged by the 1935 earthquake are indicated by crosses. Information from Ambraseys (1984), Boccaletti *et al.* (1984), Jongsma *et al.* (1985), and Snoke *et al.* (1988). Fig. 1 of Westaway (1990a).

The Tunisia−Libya seismic zone

Sparse earthquake activity indicates that a *c.* 1000 km long part of the central Mediterranean Sea is actively extending (Fig. 6), although extensional strain rate, *c.* 0.4×10^{-15} s^{-1}, and slip rate on individual faults *c.* 0.2 mm a^{-1} are both low (Westaway 1990a). Earthquakes that occurred locally near Tripoli on 4 September 1974 (M_s 5.6) and near Sirte on 19 April 1935 (M_s *c.* 7.0) indicate that this region is extending obliquely, extension being taken up on numerous normal faults that strike northwest,

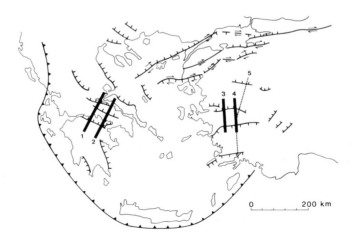

Fig. 7. Summary map of deformation occurring in Greece, western Turkey, and the Aegean Sea region, showing some of the principal normal, oblique and strike-slip faults in the region. Information from Barka & Kadinsky-Cade (1988), Jackson & McKenzie (1984), McKenzie (1978), McKenzie & Jackson (1986) and Sengör (1987). Cross section lines in Figs 10a, 10b, 11a, 11b and 11c are denoted by lines 1 to 5. Adapted from Fig. 1 of Westaway (1990c).

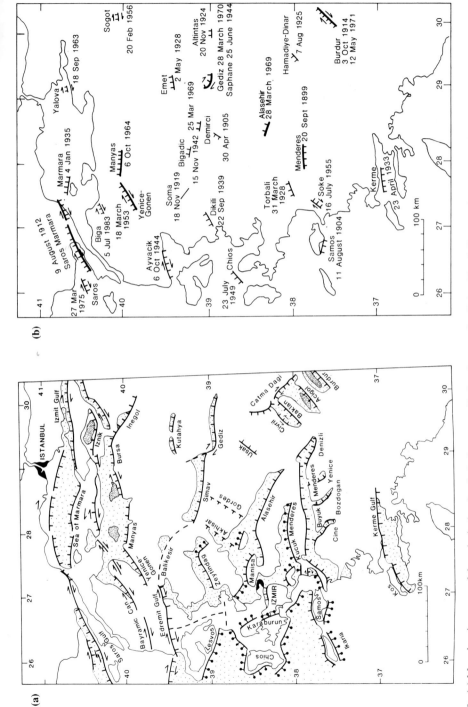

Fig. 8. (a) Map showing some of the principal active faults in western Turkey in more detail than Fig. 7. Some major topographic and bathymetric escarpments in the region that have not previously been conclusively identified as major active normal faults, although their morphology strongly suggests this, are shown as inferred faults using balls instead of tick marks in the hangingwall. Areas of low elevation relative to their surroundings are shaded, including localities on land where Quaternary sediments crop out. In some localities where one margin of such an outcrop is bounded by an active normal fault, the other margin is bounded by an antithetic normal fault that may show comparable morphology. To avoid clutter, only one fault is shown in each case. Relatively minor structural discontinuities that typically trend N–S or NE–SW, roughly perpendicular to the trend of the major active faults, are shown with dashed lines. These are also simplified from the same sources. (b) Suggested fault plane orientations for significant ($M_s > c.$ 6) earthquakes in western Turkey since 1899, with observed surface faulting identified by thick lines and source orientations inferred indirectly from local mechanisms or field evidence discussed by Westaway (1990c) by thinner lines. Information from Ambraseys (1988), Ambraseys & Finkel (1987a,b), Ambraseys & Tchalenko (1972), Eyidogan & Jackson (1985), McKenzie (1978), Jackson & McKenzie (1984), Hereçe (1985) and Barka & Kadinsky-Cade (1988).

parallel to the zone boundaries, and take up right-lateral slip with eastward slip vector azimuth. Between Tunisia and Sicily overall extension rate is c. 3 mm a^{-1} and right-lateral strike-slip rate c. 5 mm a^{-1}; both rates decrease southeastward (Westaway 1990a,b). Individual faults take up extensional pure shear and distributed right-lateral simple shear caused by the relative motion of boundaries of the deforming zone. This zone, which can be regarded as internal deformation of the African plate, deflects its motion direction relative to Europe from N20°W (e.g. Minster & Jordan 1978) to c. N50°E in the Ionian Sea between Libya, Sicily, southern Italy and Greece (Westaway 1990a,b).

The Aegean Sea region

Extension is occurring in a region with dimensions c. 700 × 700 km, covering most of Greece, the Aegean Sea, and western Turkey (Figs 7–11). The North Anatolian fault zone (NAFZ), which forms the boundary between central Turkey and the Black Sea, both aseismic

and rigid regions, enters the Aegean in its NE corner. The NAFZ takes up right-lateral strike-slip at the rate c. 30 mm a^{-1}, displacing central Turkey westward away from the convergent zone between Arabia and Eurasia further east. The southern Aegean is moving between south and SW relative to stable Europe at c. 30 to 60 mm a^{-1} (e.g. Jackson & McKenzie 1988), consistent with a present-day extensional strain rate, averaged over the whole Aegean, of c. $2–4 \times 10^{-15}$ s^{-1}. The African plate is locally moving northward or northeastward relative to stable Europe at c. 10 mm a^{-1} (e.g. Westaway 1990b), and is being subducted beneath the Aegean. Southward extension of the Aegean thus appears to result from southward collapse of the surface trace of this subduction zone, rather than being a consequence of any boundary condition related to slip on the NAFZ or across any other boundary of the region.

The principal active normal faults in western Turkey strike east–west, have a spacing of up to c. 100 km (e.g. Figs 8–9, 11), and take up extension towards S20°W, with extension rate

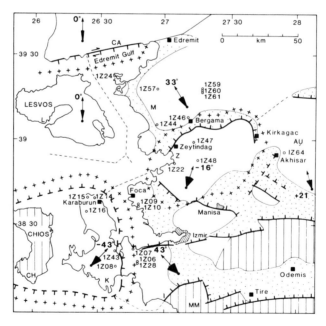

Fig. 9. Map of part of western Turkey and the northeastern Aegean Sea indicating palaeomagnetic sampling sites of Kissel *et al.* (1987) in relation to major active normal faults and block boundaries inferred from variations in Neogene palaeomagnetic rotation. Rotation angle for each block, based on palaeomagnetic observations by Kissel *et al.* (1987), is indicated with large arrow, with 95% confidence limit shown by a shaded sector. Sampling site numbers in Turkey are from Kissel (1986). Major oblique normal faults that form segments of suggested boundaries between blocks that have rotated at different rates or in different senses are shown as solid lines where clear and as dashed lines where inferred. Dashed lines indicate approximate positions of these faults at the base of the brittle layer at 10 km depth, assuming 45° fault dip. Vertical shading indicates areas where no palaeomagnetic observations are available. Adapted from Fig. 3 of Westaway (1990c).

and total extensional strain increasing westward (Westaway 1990c). Much of western Turkey has rotated anticlockwise by up to c. 40° in Neogene time (Kissel et al. 1987), as expected from the sense of vertical vorticity associated with the westward increase in southward extension rate (Westaway 1990c). Other faults have a roughly perpendicular strike (e.g. Sengör 1987; Westaway 1990c), some of which interconnect to subdivide the region into blocks that appear roughly circular in plan view (Fig. 9). The distribution of earthquakes in the past 90 a indicates that both fault sets are active (Fig. 8b). This suggests that both horizontal eigenvalues of the strain rate tensor are nonzero and hence extension is biaxial, although the eigenvalue for extension towards S20°W is much larger than that which is oriented orthogonally (Westaway 1990c). Some roughly circular blocks have rotated clockwise, in the opposite sense to the regional vertical vorticity. This anomalous rotation may be driven by frictional torques acting on their rims and not by interactions with the plastic deformation beneath them (Westaway 1990d). These blocks thus appear to be decoupled or detached from the plastic deformation in the underlying mantle lithosphere.

Extension direction differs in other parts of the Aegean. The observed, roughly westward, extension in the southern Pelopponnese and western Crete (Lyon-Caen et al. 1988) probably results from lateral variations in subduction direction, which changes from southward beneath Crete to southwestward beneath the western Pelopponnese. Provided the African plate south of the subduction zone is rigid, westward extension of the SW Aegean is required to match these variations in subduction direction. In contrast, slip vector azimuths of earthquake focal mechanisms and striations on fault planes in central Greece (Figs 7 & 10) indicate extension towards c. S10°E (e.g. Roberts 1988). Given a typical fault strike of 295°, γ is thus −55°. Geodetic reinvestigation of the position of benchmarks that were first measured c. 90 yr ago (Billiris et al. 1989) suggests extension in central Greece is occurring between due south and S20°E, at a rate up to c. 7×10^{-15} s^{-1}.

Clockwise Neogene rotation of central Greece is up to 48° (Kissel et al. 1986). However, smaller angles are observed at other localities, and typical clockwise rotation central Greece may be no greater than the 26° deduced by Laj et al. (1982) in the Ionian Islands, west of the area that has extended, and in the southern Pelopponnese. Laj et al. (1982) suggested that

clockwise rotation at these localities began no more than 6 Ma ago, although others suggest extension began elsewhere in the Aegean as much as 13 ± 5 Ma (Le Pichon et al. 1982) or 15 Ma (Mercier et al. 1989) ago.

McKenzie & Jackson (1983) suggested that central Greece takes up extension and distributed right-lateral simple shear oblique to fault strike, caused by a westward continuation of slip on the NAFZ. For a single set of faults to take up this deformation, slip vector azimuth must be perpendicular to the simple shear, requiring simple shear to be towards c. S80°W, and slip sense γ must satisfy equation (3). The observed γc. −55° implies $H_z c$. −0.7. Assuming blocks are floating, estimates for local clockwise vertical vorticity range from c. 4° Ma^{-1} (Jackson & McKenzie 1988) ($2 \times 26°/13$ Ma) to c. 14° Ma^{-1} ($2 \times 42°/6$ Ma). Local extensional strain rate of 6×10^{-15} s^{-1} and a vertical vorticity of −14° Ma^{-1} give H_z −0.7, as would, for example, 2.5×10^{-15} s^{-1} and −6° Ma^{-1}. Given that the two independent estimates for H_z can be reconciled, equation (3) appears to describe instantaneous present-day deformation of central Greece well. Moreover, faults in this geometry will rotate clockwise, in agreement with paleomagnetic observations. However, the eastward increase in Aegean extension rate will cause substantial clockwise vertical vorticity beneath central Greece (e.g. Westaway 1990c). McKenzie & Jackson's (1983) explanation of local clockwise rotation is thus not necessarily correct.

Angelier et al. (1982) suggested that the Neogene extension factor in central Greece is uniformly c. 1.2 to 1.3. Makris & Vees (1977) determined crustal thickness to be c. 32 km using seismic refraction, consistent with extension factor 1.25 assuming 40 km initial thickness. Field and seismological studies suggest major active normal faults dip at c. 45° and are approximately planar throughout the brittle upper crust (e.g. Jackson et al. 1982; Roberts 1988). Assuming rigid domino extension with 60° initial fault dip, extension factor 1.22, or extensional strain 0.22, would be predicted using equation (6). However, the brittle layer in central Greece has not extended uniformly (Fig. 10). Instead, areas with width up to 50 km have extended little, whereas other areas (comprising the major active fault zones along the Gulfs of Corinth and Atalanti) have extended substantially.

Extension across the eastern Gulf of Corinth, in the lower cross section in Fig. 10, is shown as taken up on four major NNE-dipping normal faults, labelled A to D. Each fault has a heave of c. 3 km, giving an overall observable heave

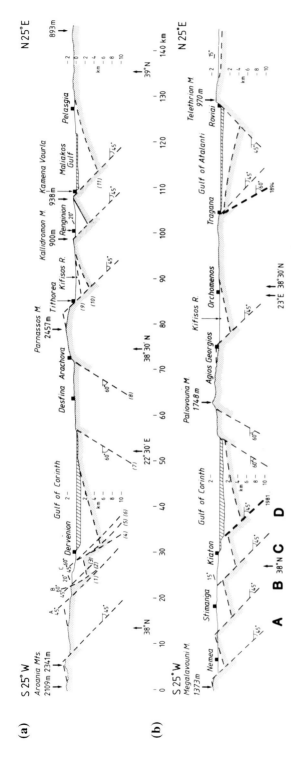

Fig. 10. Cross sections through the upper-crustal brittle layer across a 150 km wide part of central Greece, showing a representation of the present-day pattern of normal faults. See Fig. 7 for locations. **(a)** section trending N25°E between the western Gulf of Corinth and the westernmost Gulf of Atalanti (Maliakos Gulf). About 8 km local extension is deduced across the faults that bound the Gulf of Corinth, along with c. 12 km across the faults between Parnassos and the Maliakos Gulf. **(b)** Section trending N25°E between the eastern Gulf of Corinth and the eastern Gulf of Atalanti, along with c. 8 km across the faults between Agios Georgios and Telethrion. Note the substantial lateral variation in fault geometry compared with (a), particularly in the northern part of the section where the major SSW-dipping Telethrion fault has no counterpart. The c. 1 km high Telethrion escarpment is an obvious landscape feature that resembles footwalls of other active normal faults. Roberts (1988) documented NNE tilting of Neogene beds near it that demonstrates that it is indeed an active normal fault.

Fig. 11. Sections through the upper-crustal brittle layer across a 150 km wide part of western Turkey. See Fig. 7 for locations. **(a)** section trending due north along Lon. 27°43′E. About 8 km local extension is deduced across the faults that bound the Büyük Menderes graben, including the uplifted Neogene Bozköy or Azular basin (Roberts 1988). About 8 km extension also appears to have occurred across the north-dipping Alasehir fault zone north of the Boz Daglar (Boz Mountains). Allowing for a few km extension on the Kücuk menderes fault and minor north-dipping faults at the northern end of the section, total extension across the section is c. 20 km, and average extensional strain c. 20/140 or c. 0.14. **(b)** Section trending due north along Lon. 28°11′E, 40 km east of (a). About 6 km local extension appears to have occurred locally across each of the Büyük Menderes and Alasehir faults, and total extension across this section is c. 15 km. The eastward decrease in extension factor is consistent with the overall pattern observed across the eastern half of the Aegean region. Note other lateral variations in fault geometry compared with (a), particularly in the northern part of the section where no other north-dipping faults exist within c. 50 km north of the Alasehir fault zone, in contrast with further west. Instead, the hangingwall of the Alasehir fault appears to be tilted gently southward, possibly offset by an antithetic fault with < c. 1 km throw. **(c)** section sub-parallel to (b) covering a larger region at smaller scale.

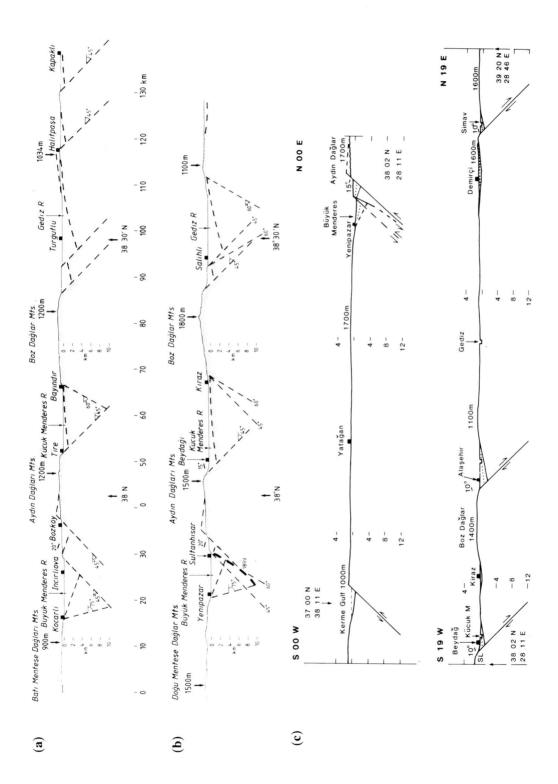

of *c*. 12 km. The northernmost fault of the parallel set, fault D, lies offshore of Kiaton and has a dip of *c*. 45°; it slipped most recently in the Corinth earthquake of 24 February 1981 (M_s 6.7) (Jackson *et al.* 1982). Displacement on this fault can be estimated from a seismic reflection record section by Myrianthis (1984), which shows that it drops top basement to *c*. 4 km below sea level. Measuring from the southern end of the cross section to the centre of the Gulf of Corinth, *c*. 12 km of extension (or heave) has occurred across a zone now *c*. 40 km wide (Fig. 10b). Local extensional strain is therefore *c*. 12/28, or *c*. 0.4. This extension can be considered to be made up of two components. First, the 15° rigid domino tilting of the narrow blocks between faults A and D takes up *c*. 6 km of extension, or about half the total. Application of the rigid domino equations ((6) and (7)) to these blocks would indicate extensional strain 0.22. The remaining *c*. 6 km extension includes a contribution from the gentle flexing of the floor of the Gulf of Corinth (hangingwall of fault D) and the Megalavouni block (footwall of fault A). These blocks do not appear to have rotated rigidly; for example, top basement beneath the Gulf of Corinth shows a progressive reduction in dip going northward. It is, however, broken up by SSW-dipping faults with *c*. 1 km throw, and may not strictly have evolved by elastic flexing. Had these two blocks been separated by a single normal fault, rather than by a set of domino-type blocks, then application of equations (8) and (9) would predict an extensional strain of *c*. 0.2 (assuming 12 km heave, 15° of flexing, and *c*. 100 km radii of curvature, as in Fig. 1). Thus the overall *c*. 0.4 Neogene extensional strain across the Gulf of Corinth region appears to be taken up partly by rigid domino tilting (within the major fault zone south of the Gulf) and partly by flexing of the wider blocks surrounding this zone.

The northern Gulf of Corinth margin, as far north as Agios Georgios, appears to have undergone no significant extension. However, the following 55 km between Agios Georgios and the Telethrion range on Evvia (Fig. 10b) has a number of major faults. Their cumulative heave is *c*. 8 km, implying extensional strain *c*. 8/47 or *c*. 0.2. Overall, the *c*. 130 km long section across the eastern Gulfs of Corinth and Atalanti (Fig. 10b) has thus extended by *c*. 20 km, giving an average extensional strain of almost 0.2. As shown above, this is made up of regions where the brittle layer has extensional strain *c*. 0.4 (southern margin of the Gulf of Corinth), *c*. 0 (Gulf of Corinth to Agios Georgios), and *c*. 0.2 (Agios Georgios to Telethrion). Given that the

moho appears flat beneath this section (Makris & Vees 1977), plastic deformation beneath the brittle layer during extension is likely to have been complex, involving net flow from beneath regions where the brittle layer has relatively low extensional strain to beneath regions where the brittle layer has relatively high extensional strain. Flow in this manner is predicted in theoretical models of extension (e.g. King *et al.* 1988) that also predict flexing of the brittle layer into curved profiles that resemble those observed. The section 30 km further WNW (Fig. 9a) shows extension *c*. 8 km across the southern Gulf of Corinth margin and *c*. 12 km across the set of parallel faults between Parnassos and Pelasgia. These regions that have both extended substantially with extensional strain *c*. 0.4 are also separated by a zone *c*. 50 km wide that has extended little. This section has also extended overall by *c*. 20 km, giving extensional strain *c*. 0.2. Average extensional strain in central Greece is thus roughly as predicted assuming rigid domino extension with a present-day fault dip of 45° and an initial dip of 60°. However, this agreement arises only because the widths of parts of central Greece that have extended by *c*. 0.4 and those that have extended little are roughly equal.

Although both sections in Fig. 10 show

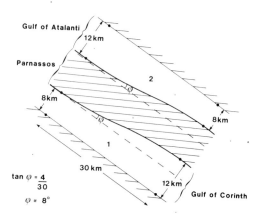

Fig. 12. Schematic diagram, not to scale, indicating how uniform overall extension across central Greece that is non-uniformly partitioned as a result of lateral variations in heave between the Gulf of Corinth and Gulf of Atalanti fault zones rotates the intervening block around vertical axes relative to the outer margins of both fault zones. The resulting *c*. 8° anticlockwise rotation partially cancels the *c*. 45° clockwise rotation caused by the clockwise vertical vorticity beneath the western half of the Aegean region.

roughly the same overall extension, the different partitioning of extension between them causes the central part of each to flex anticlockwise by c. 8° around a vertical axis relative to the ends (Fig. 12). This local anticlockwise rotation cancels some of the regional clockwise rotation caused by the regional clockwise vertical vorticity. Lateral variations in heave on a set of faults may thus cause substantial rotation around vertical axes that is unrelated to the vertical vorticity in the underlying upper mantle lithosphere. In contrast, other active fault zones in western Turkey have developed lateral variations in heave and curvature around vertical axes (Fig. 8a), as a result of lateral variations in extensional strain and rotation. Radius of curvature of the Alasehir and Buyuk Menderes fault zones in western Turkey (Fig. 8a) is c. 200 km. The c. 40° change in strike of these fault zones between the Aegean coastal region and the eastern edge of the actively-extending zone is consistent with the angle through which palaeomagnetic studies indicate that the Aegean coast has rotated anticlockwise in response to regional vertical vorticity.

Fault spacing in central Greece thus varies between < 10 km within major fault zones, where blocks behave as rigid dominoes and most extension has taken place, and c. 80 km between fault zones where blocks appear flexed and little extension has occurred (Fig. 10). To avoid the need to model these two scales of faulting, a simplified model can be developed where extensional strain 0.2 is taken up on a single set of notional faults that bound blocks which behave as rigid dominoes. Given the property of the rigid domino model that exten-

sional strain is independent of the throw on any individual fault, the spacing of the notional faults in the model is immaterial. A spacing of c.40 km can be adopted, that is intermediate between the two true scales of blocks in central Greece. This does not imply that any real block c.40 km can be adopted that is intermediate this scale would flex as in Fig. 3. This approach thus cannot address the rate of development of dip or displacement for any real fault in central Greece. Nonetheless, it is useful in investigating the development of extensional strain given the present-day strain rate.

One can now attempt to investigate whether McKenzie & Jackson's (1983) floating block model can account for the finite Neogene extensional strain and clockwise rotation in central Greece. One may try to restore a strain of c. 0.2 and a clockwise rotation of c. 45° c. 0.8 radian assuming H_z has either remained constant at -0.7 or has varied. If H_z has remained constant, with constant E_p 6×10^{-15} s^{-1}, χ_z-14° Ma^{-1}, and $\omega = \chi_z/2$, then extensional stain of 0.2 is restored in c. 1.3 Ma, along with only 10° of clockwise rotation (Table 2). A previous earlier fault generation taking up the same E_p and H_z could restore 30° more clockwise rotation in c. 4.7 Ma. However, although some evidence exists for an earlier Neogene fault generation in central Greece (e.g. Jackson et al. 1982b), this evolution history predicts total extensional strain c. 1 and is thus unlikely. Likewise, even if the prediction using Lamb's (1987) theory is correct, that ω is c. $0.75\chi_z$, the present generation of faults can still only take up c. 15° clockwise rotation, much less than is observed.

Assuming alternatively that extensional

Table 2. *Evolution of active normal faults in central Greece: (1)*

t (Ma)	D (km)	δ (deg)	φ (deg)	λ (deg)	γ (deg)	T (km)	H_z	E_p (10^{-15} s^{-1})	χ_z (deg Ma^{-1})
−1.33	32.83	59.49	285.37	−70.44	−55.01	0.38	−0.70	6.0	−14.45
−1.00	34.49	55.09	287.78	−68.17	−55.01	3.45	−0.70	6.0	−14.45
−0.67	36.24	51.31	290.19	−66.37	−55.01	6.37	−0.70	6.0	−14.45
−0.33	38.07	47.98	292.59	−64.89	−55.01	9.20	−0.70	6.0	−14.45
0.00	40.0	45.0	295.0	−63.67	−55.01	12.0	−0.70	6.0	−14.45
0.33	42.01	42.33	297.41	−62.64	−55.01	14.77	−0.70	6.0	−14.45
0.67	44.11	39.88	299.81	−61.76	−55.01	17.56	−0.70	6.0	−14.45
1.00	46.32	37.63	302.22	−61.00	−55.01	20.40	−0.70	6.0	−14.45
1.33	48.64	35.55	304.62	−60.34	−55.01	23.29	−0.70	6.0	−14.45
1.67	51.08	33.62	307.03	−59.76	−55.01	26.25	−0.70	6.0	−14.45
2.00	53.64	31.82	309.44	−59.26	−55.01	29.30	−0.70	6.0	−14.45
2.33	56.33	30.14	311.84	−58.81	−55.01	32.43	−0.70	6.0	−14.45

t is time relative to the present: negative values denote the past. D and T are notional fault spacing and displacement, δ fault dip, φ strike, λ rake, γ slip sense, E_p, extensional strain rate for pure shear and χ_z vertical vorticity. H_z was defined in equation (3). Values assumed *a priori* are highlighted. Other values are derived from them using equations (6), (7), and (11)−(14).

Table 3. *Evolution of active normal faults in central Greece: (2)*

t (Ma)	D (km)	δ (deg)	ϕ (deg)	λ (deg)	γ (deg)	T (km)	H_z	E_p (10^{-15} s^{-1})	χ_z (deg Ma^{-1})
−6.5	32.74	59.75	249.50	−1.83	−0.92	0.16	62.15	0.07	−14.00
−6.0	32.77	59.68	253.00	−2.54	−1.28	0.23	44.69	0.09	−14.00
−5.5	32.82	59.52	256.50	−3.51	−1.78	0.32	32.12	0.13	−14.00
−5.0	32.88	59.33	260.00	−4.86	−2.48	0.44	23.08	0.18	−14.00
−4.5	32.97	59.08	263.50	−6.70	−3.45	0.61	16.56	0.25	−14.00
−4.0	33.09	58.73	267.00	−9.21	−4.81	0.85	11.88	0.34	−14.00
−3.5	33.26	58.24	270.50	−12.60	−6.71	1.18	8.50	0.48	−14.00
−3.0	33.51	57.58	274.00	−17.07	−9.35	1.63	6.07	0.67	−14.00
−2.5	33.85	56.68	277.50	−22.82	−13.01	2.26	4.33	0.94	−14.00
−2.0	34.34	55.46	281.00	−29.90	−18.05	3.14	3.07	1.33	−14.00
−1.5	35.04	53.83	284.50	−38.09	−24.83	4.35	2.16	1.88	−14.00
−1.0	36.07	51.65	288.00	−46.89	−33.54	6.05	1.51	2.70	−14.00
−0.5	37.61	48.77	291.50	−55.60	−43.91	8.46	1.04	3.92	−14.00
0.0	40.00	45.00	295.00	−63.66	−55.00	11.95	0.70	5.82	−14.00

See Table 2 for notation.

strain rate has increased linearly over time with χ_z constant, an alternative evolution history can be proposed (Table 3), which restores roughly the correct extensional strain and clockwise rotation. Assuming this restoration, the Aegean would have appeared 6 Ma ago as in Fig. 13. The faults in central Greece would have initiated as almost pure left-lateral strike-slip faults with strike *c.* 250° and eastward slip vector azimuth. However, Mercier *et al.* (1989) have shown that γ was probably *c.* −75° in Pliocene time, shortly after extension began in central Greece, indicating little left-lateral slip occurred then. In contrast, McKenzie & Jackson's (1983) floating block model requires the ratio of $|\chi_z|$ to $|E_p|$ to have been larger then than now, and hence the proportion of left-lateral strike-slip to be larger then than now. It thus cannot restore local extension and rotation in a manner that is consistent with field observations in the region.

The alternative possibility, that clockwise rotation of central Greece has been caused by the eastward increase in extension rate, and that extension of central Greece is caused by local uniaxial extension in the direction oblique to fault strike (Westaway 1990c), remains feasible. Under this interpretation, the observed left-lateral strike slip on active normal faults in central Greece arises simply because extension direction and strike direction are *c.* 55° different. The observed symmetry of rotation rates on opposite sides of the Aegean (Westaway 1990c), clockwise in central Greece and anticlockwise in western Turkey, is also consistent with rotation on both the west and the east sides of the region being caused by extension rate increasing towards its centre.

The western end of the North Anatolian fault zone

As the NAFZ enters the northeastern Aegean region it splits into several sub-parallel branches, each of which develops a component of normal slip as well as the predominant right-lateral slip. At the longitude of Çanakkale (Figs 7 & 8), 200 km west of the eastern limit of active extension, the zone taking up this normal slip is *c.* 100 km wide. With a normal slip rate across it of *c.* 10 mm a^{-1} (Westaway 1990c,d), local extensional strain rate is *c.* 3×10^{-15} s^{-1}. Given the 30 mm a^{-1} slip rate on the NAFZ, local χ_z or $\nabla\times\mathbf{v}$ is $(30/100 - 10/200)$ Ma^{-1} or $14°$ Ma^{-1} (equation (1)) clockwise. H_z predicted from vertical vorticity and extensional strain rate is thus *c.* −1.4. However, despite this large, clockwise, expected, local, vertical vorticity, palaeomagnetic studies (Kissel *et al.* 1987) show no local Neogene rotation. The Saros earthquake of 27 March 1975 (M_s 6.7) that occurred on the northern main local strand of the NAFZ had ϕ 041°, δ 60° and λ −125° (Jackson & McKenzie 1988), giving γ −144°. The Yeniçe−Gönen earthquake of 18 March 1953 (M_s 6.9), which occurred further east, where the proportion of extension is less, had ϕ 240°, δ 70° and λ −155° (Westaway 1990c), giving γ −171°. On the pure right-lateral part of the NAFZ further east, γ is *c.* −180°. Slip sense on branches of the western NAFZ is thus consistent with each taking up a proportion of the relative motion of the boundaries of this zone, and is not as required for McKenzie & Jackson's (1983) floating block model. The absence of Neogene rotation around vertical axes is as expected for oblique normal faults that take up

(a)

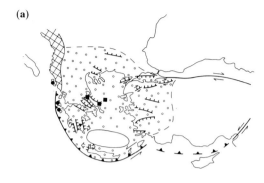

(b)

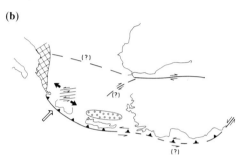

Fig. 13. Schematic diagrams indicating suggested pattern for tectonic evolution of the Aegean region over the past c. 6 Ma. Zones of significant instantaneous active extension at times depicted are dotted, and some significant active faults are shown: normal faults with hangingwall ticks; and strike-slip faults with double arrows indicating slip sense. (a) Present-day. Some major active normal faults are marked, along with paleomagnetic sampling sites used by Laj *et al.* (1982) (triangle in the southern Peloponnese, circles in the zone of active shortening in and around the Ionian islands further west) and Kissel *et al.* (1986) (squares). (b) c. 6 Ma ago. (b) has been constructed using the following reasoning: (1) the aseismic Black Sea and Balkan regions are held fixed forming a reference frame; (2) c. 30 mm $^{-1}$ right-lateral slip on the North Anatolian fault is restored, translating this region c. 200 km further east. The west coast of Turkey and other coastlines are shown only to indicate their relative positions. It is most unlikely that the same coastlines existed c. 6 Ma ago; (3) Crete has been displaced 200 km northward restoring the c. 200 km extension of the central Aegean, and 100 km eastward movement to preserve its position roughly equidistant between SW Greece and SW Turkey. This is equivalent to restoring it by c. 220 km in direction N27°E, implying average extensional strain rate in this direction in the region NNE of Crete over the past 6 Ma was c. 4×10^{-15} s^{-1}; (4) 40° clockwise rotation of the Peloponnese has been restored; (5) the c. 250° strike and instantaneous almost pure left-lateral slip sense required c. 6 Ma ago if the faults now active in central Greece have taken up local extensional strain and rotation around vertical axes are shown.

distributed simple shear and strike parallel to the direction of simple shear (Westaway 1990e).

Discussion

Zones that take up extensional pure shear and distributed simple shear parallel to fault strike

The actively extending zones described in the previous section comprise two types. In the first, which includes Italy, the Tunisia–Libya seismic zone, and the western end of the North Anatolian fault zone, active faults are sub-parallel to zone boundaries, zone width between rigid boundaries is < c. 200 km, but length parallel to strike may be much greater. Faults take up extensional pure shear in the direction perpendicular to zone boundaries, and in some cases also take up distributed simple shear in the direction parallel to fault strike; each fault within the zone takes up a fraction of the relative motion between the zone boundaries. Where distributed simple shear is occurring, vertical vorticity beneath the brittle layer is non-zero and yet faults and blocks between them do not rotate around vertical axes relative to the zone boundaries during deformation, regardless of the width of individual blocks in relation to the width of the deforming zone. During distributed simple shear the strain rate tensor in the underlying upper mantle lithosphere will be biaxial (Westaway 1990e). However, this symmetric strain rate tensor on its own will describe biaxial pure shear; distributed simple shear can only be fully described using an asymmetric velocity gradient tensor (Westaway 1990e). Relative motion of zone boundaries may either be purely extensional as in northern or central Italy, right-lateral as in the Tunisia–Libya seismic zone and the western North Anatolian fault zone, or left-lateral as in southernmost Italy. Other active examples of relatively narrow actively-extending zones that may also take up some distributed simple shear include the Rio Grande rift and the Red Sea, and many ancient examples have been identified.

Sets of parallel faults that may take up uniaxial extension and may rotate round vertical axes

The second type of actively-extending zone is larger, with lateral extent > c. 500 km. Fault orientations show no particular angular relationship to zone boundaries. Individual fault-bounded blocks may have a width of up to c. 100 km and a length of up to c. 200 km, but each is small compared with the overall dimensions of the deforming zone. Sets of faults of this type in the northeast Basin and Range province, central Greece and western Turkey have been discussed. One suggestion to account for the kinematics of the set in central Greece (McKenzie & Jackson 1983) requires that the strain rate tensor beneath the brittle layer is biaxial, that vertical vorticity is non-zero, and that the faults are arranged at any time with a unique orientation that allows a single set to take up the biaxial extension and to respond to the vertical vorticity in the underlying plastic deformation by rotation around vertical axes. This suggestion requires the slip vector azimuth on faults to be perpendicular to zone boundaries. It predicts that clockwise rotation will require a component of left-lateral strike-slip and anticlockwise rotation a component of right-lateral strike-slip. In neither zone in the northeast Basin and Range province, nor in western Turkey, do slip vector azimuths show the correct orientation for this to be a feasible explanation. Slip vector azimuth in central Greece does have the required orientation and faults do have the required sense of strike-slip to take up the observed clockwise rotation. However, if this suggestion is followed it is impossible to restore simultaneously the Neogene extensional strain and rotation in central Greece. Furthermore, even during instantaneous deformation, McKenzie & Jackson's (1983) floating block model requires substantial mismatch between velocity at many localities in the brittle layer and in the underlying upper mantle lithosphere (Westaway 1990e). During biaxial extension the overlying brittle layer would most likely subdivide into blocks bounded by two sets of faults that can take up the biaxial extension of the underlying uppers mantle lithosphere without such mismatch (Westaway 1990e). This would be so unless one is dealing with the special case where the biaxial deformation comprises distributed simple shear with faults parallel to the direction of shearing (Westaway 1990e), where no rotation occurs around a vertical axis.

It is thus likely instead that extension in the upper mantle lithosphere beneath these zones in the Aegean and NE basin and Range province is uniaxial. It may well be that the strength of sets of blocks in the brittle layer, combined with the viscous coupling that exists across the lower crust between the brittle layer and the plastically deforming upper mantle lithosphere, imposes this constraint of uniaxial extension on the form of plastic deformation in the underlying upper mantle lithosphere. If one accepts that extension beneath such zones is uniaxial, then, if blocks in the brittle layer are floating, rotation rate around vertical axes will equal half the vertical vorticity in the underlying plastic deformation and slip vector azimuth on faults in the brittle layer will indicate extension direction in this underlying deformation (Westaway 1990e). If one assumes that velocity in the upper mantle lithosphere is a continuous function of position with no discontinuities beneath fault zones in the brittle layer, then the sense of any component of strike slip on faults at block margins need bear no relationship to the rotation sense of blocks around vertical axes; it simply depends on the angular difference between fault strike and slip vector azimuth (Westaway 1990e). In these circumstances slip on faults does not take up rotation of blocks in the brittle layer relative to their stable surroundings. Instead, sets of blocks simply rotate around vertical axes at the same rate in response to the regional vertical vorticity χ_z. Apart from results of palaeomagnetic and geodetic investigations, nothing that is observable in any such fault zone can constrain rotation sense and rate. However, even within such zones, frictional interactions between individual blocks and their surroundings may effectively decouple some blocks from the underlying plastic deformation allowing relative rotation of blocks, as suggested in parts of western Turkey. Lateral variations in heave on faults may cause some blocks to flex around vertical axes, also contributing to lateral variations in rotation around vertical axes. The sharpest radii of curvature observed along block margins in these regions are c. 100 km around horizontal axes and c. 200 km around vertical axes. Although theoretical models (e.g. King et al. 1988) can explain such curvature around horizontal axes as a result of elastic flexing of fault-bounded blocks, some such blocks are broken up by minor internal faults (e.g. Fig. 10) and are unlikely to have evolved entirely by elastic flexing. Whether such blocks are analogous to floats, and hence rotate at rate $\chi_z/2$, or move with the plastic deformation in the underlying uppermost mantle lithosphere, and hence may rotate at rate $\chi_z/2$, cannot in general be resolved at present. However, in the latter case, velocity mismatch between each block and the underlying plastic deformation is minimized (Westaway 1990e); it may thus perhaps be expected.

In both the Aegean and the NE Basin and Range province, the large-scale plastic deformation beneath the brittle layer that is driving brittle layer deformation is caused by flow that exists in the upper mantle for other reasons: in the Aegean, because the Hellenic Benioff zone to the south is collapsing southward; and in the NE Basin and Range province because the region appears to be interacting with an up-welling mantle plume that is being sheared sideways. Both flow patterns cause divergent velocity fields in the uppermost mantle, which drive brittle layer extension, as well as vertical vorticity that drives rotation around vertical axes. Several other examples are known of continental regions that appear to have extended due mainly to collapse of underlying Benioff zones. These include the Mio—Pliocene extension of the Tyrrhenian Sea (Fig. 4) and the middle Miocene extension of the Pannonian basin in Hungary (e.g. Malinverno & Ryan 1987).

Other regions

In some regions, which may have dimensions of hundreds of km or more, extension is driven by buoyancy forces caused by earlier thickening. Buoyancy forces appear important in controlling the present-day extension of the Tibetan plateau (e.g. England & McKenzie 1982) and the South American Altiplano. They appear likely to have also been important in controlling the evolution of the central Basin and Range province during early Tertiary east—west extension following Laramide crustal thickening (e.g. Wernicke et al. 1987), the northwest—southeast Devonian extension of much of northwestern Europe following Caledonide thickening (e.g. McClay et al. 1986; Séguret et al. 1989), and the mainly Permian north—south extension of much of central Europe following Hercynian thickening (e.g. Ménard & Molnar 1988). The name 'collapse basin' has been suggested for any region where extension follows earlier thickening (Séguret et al. 1989), in which extension is driven mainly by buoyancy forces.

Of the two active examples, Tibet is extending in the east-west direction, perpendicular to the direction of north—south shortening at its margins (e.g. Armijo et al. 1986), and the Altiplano is extending northeast—southwest, subparallel to the direction of shortening at the margins of the Andes (Suárez et al. 1983). In the ancient examples, most extension appears to have occurred in the direction of earlier shortening, by reactivation of older reverse faults as normal faults after shortening ended; this process has been studied in detail (Sonder et al. 1987). Overthickened regions will attempt

to evolve to reduce gradients in crustal thickness by extending towards adjacent areas of lower crustal thickness. Extension direction throughout any such region is thus likely to be roughly perpendicular to the region's boundaries and, assuming these are roughly straight, will not vary much laterally. Assuming that the region has become uniformly thickened, lateral variations in extension velocity are likely to be relatively small. Given these two assumptions, vertical vorticity will be small. Extension in such regions would thus be expected to approximate uniaxial pure shear perpendicular to the zone boundaries with no rotation around vertical axes, and would not be expected to show the relatively rapid lateral variations in extension direction, extensional strain rate and vertical vorticity observed in, for example, the Aegean and the NE Basin and Range province. Observed extension of the brittle layer in Tibet and the Altiplano appears to approximate uniaxial pure shear as expected.

Given the widespread interest in the evolution of the North Sea, one may ask into which category its Triassic to Jurassic extension falls. Unlike its earlier Devonian extension, this Mesozoic extension was unrelated to collapse following crustal thickening immediately beforehand, although some faults that took up Mesozoic extension appear reactivated from earlier Devonian extension (McClay et al. 1986). The part of the North Sea that extended substantially in the Mesozoic is up to c. 200 km wide and c. 1000 km long (e.g. Barton & Wood 1984), of similar dimensions to active zones in the central Mediterranean, Italy, the Rio Grande rift, and the Red Sea. The relatively narrow width of the zone that extended and the observation that the strike of most faults is subparallel to its boundaries suggest that deformation involved either extensional pure shear, in which case slip vector azimuth would be expected perpendicular to zone boundaries, or extensional pure shear combined with distributed simple shear parallel to zone boundaries, in which case expected slip vector azimuth would be oblique to fault strike. Either way, it is unlikely that substantial rotation around vertical axes of any block within the North Sea occurred relative to the zone boundaries during extension.

Conclusions

The actively extending regions discussed contain sets of sub-parallel faults that are approximately planar between the earth's surface and the base of the brittle layer. Active faults dip typically at

c. $40°-60°$, and are separated by distances of c. $20-100$ km. Some larger fault zones contain individual faults up to c. 10 km apart. Fault-bounded blocks with width $> c$. 30 km do not evolve as rigid dominoes. In these blocks top basement typically develops curvature that is concave upward in fault footwalls and convex upward in hangingwalls.

The role of individual faults in taking up regional deformation in the brittle layer depends on the scale and deformation sense of the region where they are situated. In zones with horizontal dimensions $> c$. 500 km, the plastic deformation of the uppermost mantle, to which fault-bounded blocks in the upper-crustal brittle layer appear coupled, seems to involve uniaxial extension. The angular velocity of blocks around vertical axes may equal half the local vertical vorticity in the underlying upper mantle lithosphere. In these circumstances, slip sense on faults at block margins indicates the extension direction in the underlying plastic deformation, but provides no information to constrain the sense of vertical vorticity in the underlying plastic deformation. However, locally, rotation around vertical axes may also occur for other reasons, as demonstrated by the examples in Figs 8 & 12.

In contrast, zones of active extension with width $<c$. 200 km take up extensional pure shear and may also take up distributed simple shear parallel to faults and zone boundaries. In cases where the boundaries of such a zone are separating with no transcurrent motion, such that no distributed simple shear is present, the strain rate tensor beneath the brittle layer comprises uniaxial extension, and blocks within such a zone will also not rotate relative to the surroundings of the zone. Where distributed simple shear is present, vertical vorticity beneath the brittle layer will be non-zero, but provided faults strike parallel to the simple shear direction they will not rotate around vertical axes. The narrow width of the zone that extended in the North Sea in Mesozoic time suggests that faults within it took up extensional pure shear and possibly also distributed simple shear. Although the sense of any distributed simple shear across the North Sea at this time is unclear, no rotation around vertical axes would be expected of blocks within the North Sea relative to its surroundings during this phase of extension.

I thank Rob Gawthorpe, James Jackson, Nick Kusznir, Paul Sellers, Leslie Sonder and Nicky White for discussions, and Steve Roberts for a copy of his PhD thesis. Helpful comments by Graham Yielding and two anonymous reviewers were appreciated. Financial support was provided by U.K. Natural Environment Research Council grants GR3/6966, 6967 and 7345.

References

AÏFA, T., FEINBERG, H. & POZZI, J.-P. 1988. Pliocene-Pleistocene evolution of the Tyrrhenian arc: paleomagnetic determination of uplift and rotational deformation. *Earth and Planetary Science Letters*, **87**, 438–452.

AKI, K. & RICHARDS, P. G. 1980. *Quantitative seismology, theory and methods*. Freeman, San Francisco.

AMBRASEYS, N. N. 1984. Material for investigation of the seismicity of Tripolitania (Libya). *In:* BRAMBATI, A. & SLEJKO, D. (eds) *Osservatorio di Geofisica Sperimentale silver anniversary volume*. Osservatorio di Geofisica Sperimentale, Trieste, Italy, 143–153.

—— 1988. Engineering seismology. *Earthquake Engineering and Structural Dynamics*, **17**, 1–105.

—— & FINKEL, C. 1987a. The Saros-Marmara earthquake of 9 August 1912. *Earthquake Engineering and Structural Dynamics*, **15**, 189–211.

—— & —— 1987b. Seismicity of Turkey and neighbouring regions, 1899–1915. *Annales Geophysicae*, **5b**, 701–726.

—— & TCHALENKO, J.S. 1972. Seismotectonic aspects of the Gediz, Turkey, earthquake of March 1970. *Geophysical Journal of the Royal Astronomical Society*, **30**, 229–252.

ANGELIER, J., LYBERIS, N., LE PICHON, X. & HUCHON, P. 1982. The tectonic development of the Hellenic arc and the sea of Crete: a synthesis. *Tectonophysics*, **86**, 159–196.

ARMIJO, R., TAPPONNIER, P., MERCIER, J. & HAN, T.-L. 1986. Quaternary extension in southern Tibet: field observations and tectonic implications. *Journal of Geophysical Research*, **91**, 13803–13872.

ARMSTRONG, R. L., LEEMAN, W. P. & MALDE, H. E. 1975. K-Ar dating, Neogene volcanic rocks of the Snake River Plain, Idaho. *American Journal of Science*, **275**, 225–251.

BACHE, T. C., LAMBERT, D. G. & BARKER, T. G. 1980. A source model for the March 28, 1975, Pocatello Valley earthquake from time-domain modeling of teleseismic P-waves. *Bulletin of the Seismological Society of America*, **70**, 405–418.

BARBANO, M. S. & COSENTINO, M. 1981. Il terremoto dell'11 Gennaio 1693. *Rendiconti della Societa Geologica d'Italia*, **4**, 517–522.

BARKA, A. A. & KADINSKY-CADE, C. 1988. Strike-slip fault geometry in Turkey and its influence on earthquake activity *Tectonics*, **7**, 663–684.

BARTON, P. & WOOD, R. 1984. Tectonic evolution of the North Sea basin: crustal stretching and subsidence. *Geophysical Journal of the Royal Astronomical Society*, **79**, 987–1022.

BILLIRIS, H., PARADISSIS, D., VEIS, G., ENGLAND, P., PARSONS, B., CROSS, P., RANDS, P., RAYSON,

M., SELLERS, P., ASHKENAZI, V., DAVISON, M. & JACKSON, J. 1989. Geodetic determination of the strain of Greece in the interval 1900 to 1988. *EOS, Transactions of the American Geophysical Union*, **70**, 719 (abstr.).

BOCCALETTI, M., NICHOLICH, R. & TORTORICI, L. 1984. the Calabrian Arc and the Ionian Sea in the dynamic evolution of the central Mediterranean, *Marine Geology*, **55**, 219–245.

BOND, J. G. 1978. *Geologic map of Idaho*. Idaho Bureau of Mines and Geology, Moscow, ID.

CRONE, A. J. & MACHETTE, M. N. 1984. Surface faulting accompanying the Borah Peak earthquake, central Idaho. *Geology*, **12**, 664–667.

DAVIS, F. D. 1985. *Geologic map of the northern Wasatch Front, Utah*. Utah Geological and Mining Survey map 53. Utah Geological and Mining Survey, Salt Lake City, UT.

DIXON, J. S. 1978. Regional structural synthesis, Wyoming salient of western overthrust belt. *American Association of Petroleum Geologists Bulletin*, **66**, 1560–1580.

DOSER, D. I. 1985. Source parameters and faulting processes of the 1959 Hebgen Lake, Montana earthquake sequence. *Journal of Geophysical Research*, **90**, 4537–4556.

—— & SMITH, R. B. 1985. Source parameters of the 28 October 1983 Borah Peak, Idaho, earthquake from body wave analysis. *Bulletin of the Seismological Society of America*, **75**, 1041–1051.

EDDINGTON, P. K., SMITH, R. B. & RENGGLI, C. 1987. Kinematics of Basin and Range intraplate extension. *In:* COWARD, M. P., DEWEY, J. F. & HANCOCK, P. L. (eds) *Continental Extensional Tectonics*, Geological Society, London, Special Publication, **28**, 371–392.

ENGLAND, P. C. & MCKENZIE, D. P. 1982. A thin viscous sheet model for continental deformation. *Geophysical Journal of the Royal Astronomical Society*, **70**, 295–321 (with 1983 correction: **73**, 523–532).

EYIDOGAN, H. & JACKSON, J. A. 1985. A seismological study of normal faulting in the Demirci, Alasehir and Gediz earthquakes of 1969–1970 in western Turkey: implications for the nature and geometry of deformation in the continental crust. *Geophysical Journal of the Royal Astronomical Society*, **81**, 569–607.

FUNICIELLO, R., MONTONE, P., SALVINI, F. & TOZZI, M. 1988. Caratteri strutturali del promontorio del Gargano, *In: Atti del 740 Congresso della Societa Geologica d'Italia, Napoli, October 1988*. Societa Geologica d'Italia, Roma

——, PAROTTO, M. & PRATURLON, A. 1981. *Carta tettonica d'Italia, scala 1:500 000*, Consiglio Nazionale delle Ricerche Geodynamics Project Publication 269. Consiglio Nazionale delle Ricerche, Roma

GANS, P. B., MILLER, E. L., MCCARTHY, J. & OULDCOTT, M. L. 1985. Tertiary extensional faulting and evolving ductile-brittle transition zones in the northern Snake Range and vicinity: new insights from sesimic data. *Geology*, **13**, 189–193.

HEREÇE, E.I. 1985. *The Yeniçe-Gönen earthquake of 1953 and some examples of recent tectonic events in the Biga peninsula of northwest Turkey*. MSc thesis, Pennsylvania State University.

JACKSON, J. A. 1987. Active normal faulting and crustal extension. *In:* COWARD, M. P., DEWEY, J. F. & HANCOCK, P. L. (eds) *Continental Extensional Tectonics*, Geological Society, London, Special Publication, **28**, 3–17.

——, GAGNEPAIN, J., HOUSEMAN, G., KING, G. C. P., PAPADIMITRIOU, P., SOUFLERIS, C. & VIRIEUX, J. 1982a. Seismicity, normal faulting and the geomorphological development of the Gulf of Corinth (Greece): the Corinth earthquakes of February and March 1981. *Earth and Planetary Science Letters*, **57**, 277–397.

——, KING, G. C. P, & VITA-FINZI, C. 1982b. The neotectonics of the Aegean: an alternative view. *Earth and Planetary Science Letters*, **61**, 303–318.

—— & MCKENZIE, D. P. 1983. The geometrical evolution of normal fault systems. *Journal of Structural Geology*, **5**, 471–482.

—— & —— 1984. Active tectonics of the Alpine-Himalayan belt between western Turkey and Pakistan. *Geophysical Journal of the Royal Astronomical Society*, **77**, 185–265.

—— & —— 1988. The relationship between plate motions and seismic moment tensors, and the rates of active deformation in the Mediterranean and Middle East. *Geophysical Journal*, **93**, 45–73.

—— & WHITE, N. J. 1989. Normal faulting in the upper continental crust: observations from regions of active extension. *Journal of Structural Geology*, **11**, 15–36.

JONGSMA, D., VAN HINTE, J. E. & WOODSIDE, J. M. 1985. Geological structure and neotectonics of the north African continental margin south of Sicily. *Marine and Petroleum Geology*, **2**, 156–179.

KING, G. C. P., STEIN, R. S. & RUNDLE, J. B. 1988. The growth of geological structures by repeated earth-quakes: 1. conceptual framework. *Journal of Geophysical Research*, **93**, 13307–13318.

KISSEL, C. 1986. *Apport du paléomagnétisme à la compréhension de l'evolution géodynamique Tertiaire du domaine Égéen de l'Epire à l'Anatolie occidentale*. PhD thesis, Université de Paris-sud centre d'Orsay

——, LAJ, C. & MAZAUD, A. 1986. First paleomagnetic results from Neogene formations in Evia, Skyros and the Volos region, and the deformation of central Aegea. *Geophysical Research Letters*, **13**, 1446–1449.

——, ——, SENGÖR, A. M. C. & POISSON, A. 1987. Paleomagnetic evidence for rotation in opposite senses of adjacent blocks in northeastern Aegea and western Anatolia. *Geophysical Research Letters*, **14**, 907–910.

LAJ, C., JAMET, M., SOREL, D. & VALENTE, J. P. 1982. First paleomagnetic results from Mio-Pliocene series of the Hellenic sedimentary arc. *Tectonophysics*, **86**, 45–67.

LAMB, S.H. 1987. A model for tectonic rotations

about a vertical axis. *Earth and Planetary Science Letters*, **84**, 75–86.

LYON-CAEN, H., ARMIJO, R., DRAKOPOULOS, J., BASKOUTASS, J., DELIBASSIS, N., GAULON, R., KOUSKOUNA, V., LATOUSSAKIS, J., MAKROPOULOS, K., PAPADIMITRIOU, P., PAPANASTASSIOU, D. & PEDOTTI, G. 1988. The 1986 Kalamata (south Peloponnesus) earth-quake: detailed study of a normal fault, evidences for east-west extension in the Hellenic arc. *Journal of Geophysical Research*, **93**, 14967–15000.

MABEY, D. R. 1985. Regional gravity and magnetic anomalies in the Borah Peak region of Idaho. *In: Proceedings of Workshop 28 on the Borah Peak, Idaho, earthquake*. United States Geological Survey Open-file Report 85–290, 680–686.

MCCLAY, K. R., NORTON, M. G., CONEY, P. & DAVIS, G. H. 1986. Collapse of the Caledonian orogen and the Old Red Sandstone. *Nature*, **323**, 147–149.

MCKENZIE, D. P. 1978. Active tectonics of the Alpine-Himalayan belt: the Aegean Sea and surrounding regions. *Geophysical Journal of the Royal Astronomical Society*, **55**, 217–254.

—— & JACKSON, J. A. 1983. The relationship between strain rates, crustal thickening, paleomagnetism, finite strain and fault movements within a deforming zone. *Earth and Planetary Science Letters*, **65**, 182–202 (with 1984 correction: **70**, 444).

—— & JACKSON, J.A. 1986. A block model of distributed deformation by faulting. *Journal of the Geological Society of London*, **143**, 349–353.

MAKRIS, J. & VEES, R. 1977. Crustal structure of the central Aegean Sea and the islands of Evia and Crete, Greece, obtained by refractional seismic experiments. *Journal of Geophysics*, **42**, 329–341.

MALINVERNO, A. & RYAN, W. B. F. 1986. Extension in the Tyrrhenian Sea and shortening in the Appennines as result of arc migration driven by sinking of the lithosphere. *Tectonics*, **5**, 227–245.

MÉNARD, G. & MOLNAR, P. 1988. Collapse of a Hercynian Tibetan Plateau into a late Palaeozoic European Basin and Range province. *Nature*, **334**, 235–237.

MERCIER, J. L., SOREL, D., VERGELY, P. & SIMEAKIS K. 1989. Extensional tectonic regimes in the Aegean basins during the Cenozoic. *Basin Research*, **2**, 49–71.

MINSTER, J. B. & JORDAN, T. H. 1978. Present-day plate motions. *Journal of Geophysical Research*, **83**, 5331–5354.

MULARGIA, F. & BOSCHI, E. 1983. The 1908 Messina earthquake and related seismicity. *In:* KANAMORI, H. & BOSCHI, E. (eds) *Earthquakes: Observation, Theory and Interpretation*, 85th course. Societa Italian di Fisica, Bologna, Italy, 493–518.

MYRIANTHIS, M. 1984. Graben formation and associated seismicity in the Gulf of Corinth (central Greece). *In:* DIXON, J. E. & ROBERTSON, A. H. F. (eds) *The Geological Evolution of the Eastern Mediterranean*, Geological Society, London, Special Publication, **19**, 709–725.

PECHMANN, J. C., NASH, W. P., VIVEIROS, J. J. & SMITH, R. B. 1987. Slip rate and earthquake potential of the East Great Salt Lake Fault, Utah. EOS, *Transactions of the American Geophysical Union*, **68**, 1369 (abstr.).

ROBERTS, S. C. 1988. *Active normal faulting in central Greece and western Turkey*. PhD. Thesis, University of Cambridge.

SCHICK, R. 1977. Eine seismotektonische Bearbeitung des Erdbebens von Messina im Jahre 1908. *Geologisches Jahrbuch*, E11, 3–74 (in German).

SCHWARTZ, D. P. & COPPERSMITH, K. J. 1984. Fault behavior and characteristic earthquakes: examples from the Wasatch and San Andreas fault zones. *Journal of Geophysical Research*, **89**, 5681–5698.

SÉGURET, M., SÉRANNE, M., CHAUVET, A. & BRUNEL, M. 1989. Collapse basin: a new type of sedimentary basin from the Devonian of Norway. *Geology*, **17**, 127–130.

SENGÖR, A. M. C. 1987. Cross-faults and differential stretching of hanging walls in regions of low-angle normal faulting: examples from western Turkey. *In:* COWARD, M. P., DEWEY, J. F. & HANCOCK, P. L. (eds) *Continental Extensional Tectonics* Geological Society, London, Special Publication, **28**, 575–589.

SMITH, R. B. & BRUHN, R. L. 1984. Intraplate extensional tectonics of the eastern Basin-Range: inferences on structural style from seismic reflection data, regional tectonics, and thermal-mechanical models of brittle-ductile deformation. *Journal of Geophysical Research*, **89**, 5733–5762.

——, RICHINS, W. D. & DOSER, D. I. 1985. The 1983 Borah Peak, Idaho, earthquake: regional seismicity, kinematics of faulting and tectonic mechanism. *In:* Proceedings of workshop 28 on the Borah Peak, Idaho, earthquake. United States Geological Survey Open-file Report 85–290, 236–263.

—— & SBAR, M. L. 1974. Contemporary tectonics and seismicity of the western United States with emphasis on the Intermountain Seismic Belt. *Bulletin of the Geological Society of America*, **85**, 1205–1218.

SONDER, L. J., ENGLAND, P. C., WERNICKE, B. P. & CHRISTIANSEN, R. L. 1987. A physical model for Cenozoic extension of western North America. *In:* COWARD, M. P., DEWEY, J. F. & HANCOCK, P.L. (eds) *Continental Extensional Tectonics* Geological Society, London, Special Publication, **28**, 187–201.

STEIN, R. S. & BARRIENTOS, S. E. 1985. High-angle faulting in the inter-mountain seismic bekt: geodetic investigation of the 1983 Borah Peak, Idaho, earthquake. *Journal of Geophysical Research*, **90**, 11355–11366.

——, KING, G. C. P. & RUNDLE, J. B. 1988. The growth of geological structures by repeated earthquakes: 2. field examples of continental dip-slip faults. *Journal of Geophysical Research*, **93**, 13319–13332.

STICKNEY, M. C. & BARTHOLOMEW, M. J. 1987. Seismicity and late Quaternary faulting of the northern

Basin and Range province, Montana and Idaho. *Bulletin of the Seismological Society of America*, **77**, 1602−1625.

SUÁREZ, G., MOLNAR, P. & BURCHFIEL, B. C. 1983. Seismicity, fault plane solutions, depth of faulting, and active tectonics of the Andes of Peru, Ecuador, and southern Colombia. *Journal of Geophysical Research*, **88**, 10403−10428.

SUSONG, D. D., SMITH, R. B. & BRUHN, R. L. 1987. Quaternary faulting and sementation of the Teton fault zone, Grand Teton National Park, Wyoming. EOS, *Transactions of the American Geophysical Union*, **68**, 1244 (abstr.).

TAPPONNIER, P., TORTORICI, L. & WINTER, T. 1987. Faulting during the 1783 Calabria earthquakes and tectonics of the Messina Strait. *Terra cognita*, **7**, 305 (abstr.).

WERNICKE, B. P. 1985. Uniform-sense normal simple shear of the continental lithosphere. *Canadian Journal of Earth Sciences*, **22**, 108−125.

——, CHRISTIANSEN, R. L., ENGLAND, P. C. & SONDER, L. J. 1987. Tectonomagmatic evolution of Cenozoic extension in the North American cordillera. *In*: COWARD, M. P., DEWEY, J. F. & HANCOCK, P. L. (eds) *Continental Extensional Tectonics*, Geological Society, London, Special Publication, **28**, 203−221.

WESTAWAY, R. 1987. The Campania, southern Italy, earthquakes of 1962 August 21. Geophysical *Journal of the Royal Astronomical Society*, **88**, 1−24.

—— 1989a. Deformation of the NE Basin and Range Province: the response of the lithosphere to the Yellowstone plume? *Geophysical Journal International*, **99**, 33−62 (with 1990 correction: in press).

—— 1989b. Northeast Basin and Range province active tectonics: an alternative view. *Geology*, **17**, 779−783.

—— 1990a. The Tripoli, Libya, earthquake of 4 September 1974: implications for the active tectonics of the central Mediterranean. *Tectonics*, **9**, 231−248.

—— 1990b. Present-day kinematics of the plate boundary zone between Africa and Europe, from the Azores to the Aegean. *Earth and Planetary Science Letters*, **96**, 393−406.

—— 1990c. Block rotation in western Turkey: 1. Observational evidence. *Journal of Geophysical Research*, in press.

—— 1990d. Block rotation in western Turkey and elsewhere: 2. Theoretical models. *Journal of Geophysical Research*, in press.

—— 1990e. Discussion of and correction to: Deformation of the NE Basin and Range Province: the response of the lithosphere to the Yellowstone plume? *Geophysical Journal International*, submitted.

——, GAWTHORPE, R. & TOZZI, M. 1989. Seismological and field observations of the 1984 Lazio-Abruzzo earthquakes: implications for the active tectonics of Italy. *Geophysical Journal*, **98**, 489−514.

—— & JACKSON, J. A. 1984. Surface faulting in the southern Italian Campania-Basilicata earthquake of 23 November 1980. *Nature*, **312**, 436−438.

—— & —— 1987. The earthquake of 1980 November 23 in Campania-Basilicata (southern Italy). *Geophysical Journal of the Royal Astronomical Society*, **90**, 375−443.

—— & SMITH, R. B. 1989. Source parameters of the Cache Valley (Logan), Utah, earthquake of 30 August 1962. *Bulletin of the Seismological Society of America*, **79**, 1410−1425.

Fault-displacement studies

The geometry of normal faults in a sector of the offshore Nile Delta, Egypt

A. BEACH[1] & P. TRAYNER[2]

[1]Alastair Beach Associates, 11 Royal Exchange Square, Glasgow G1
3AJ, UK
[2]GECO Exploration Services, Merlin House, Boundary Road,
Woking, Surrey, GU21 5BX, UK

Abstract: This paper presents an interpretation of the geometry of normal faults in part of the offshore Nile Delta. The structure is dominated by north-dipping faults that are clearly imaged on seismic reflection profiles, and affect sediments of Pliocene−Pleistocene age, together with the underlying Miocene sequences that contain potential hydrocarbon reservoir rocks. The geometrical analysis is carried out in several stages. Firstly, time slice maps of the fault pattern are produced in order to establish the overall fault geometry of the area. Secondly, for each individual fault identified, structure contours on the fault surface itself are mapped. This procedure serves to highlight any complexities in the geometry of the faults, and allows potential inconsistencies in the interpretation to be identified. Thirdly, horizon interpretations and correlations are made across the faults, and these are checked for consistency by constructing maps of the magnitude of the dip slip component of displacement within the fault surface. The complete geometric analysis makes it possible to extend the results from the good data areas in the upper parts of seismic sections to the poorer quality areas lower down. In this way it is possible to derive an interpretation of the structural geometry of the Miocene reservoir sequences. The seismic reflections from the Miocene are poor and irregular, and structural interpretation and modelling reduces the uncertainty associated with the reservoir geometry. The structural interpretation is presented as a model of tilted and fault bounded blocks, with considerable horizontal separation. This provides a much clearer and more consistent picture of the reservoir geometry, and contrasts with previous interpretations that have shown a more or less continuous reservoir sequence with little structure. The geometrical interpretation should form the basis for a new hydrocarbon play in the area because it predicts the locations of footwall crests, as well as areas where reservoir is missing because of separation across faults.

The Nile Delta is a lobate build-up, dating back to the Miocene. In the northern onshore area, and in the offshore area, the basement is deep and the thickness of Tertiary sequences large. The Messinian sea-level drop initiated the development of the present delta cone, which is composed of up to 10 000 feet of Plio−Pleistocene clastics. The geometry of normal faults affecting these sequences and the potential hydrocarbon reservoirs in the Miocene, are clearly illustrated in a seismic data-set in the eastern part of the offshore delta. An understanding of the geometry of the faults is important in delineating the structure of potential hydrocarbon traps in the Miocene, and several techniques have been used. The results presented here are derived from an interpretation of a grid of 2D seismic lines, with dip lines running N−S and having a spacing of 4 km, and strike lines running E−W with a variable spacing of 4−12 km. The data were acquired by Mobil in 1977−1978, and reprocessed by Merlin Geophysical in 1987. The data are time migrated sections to 5.7 secs TWT (two-way time). In general, the data quality is good within the Plio−Pleistocene sequences, but poor below the Miocene. A structural analysis is initially carried out in the upper parts of the section, where the uncertainties associated with the interpretation are least, and this interpretation is then extrapolated down section. Figure 1 shows the location of the study area, and shows that the two El Temsah wells are located in the SE of this area, providing stratigraphic ties to seismic lines.

Figure 2 shows a generalized N−S geoseismic section through the area to illustrate the structural style that has been compiled from panels of several different adjacent seismic lines. The faults are north-dipping and curved in profile on the time sections, with rotation of hangingwall sequences, and increasing horizontal separation

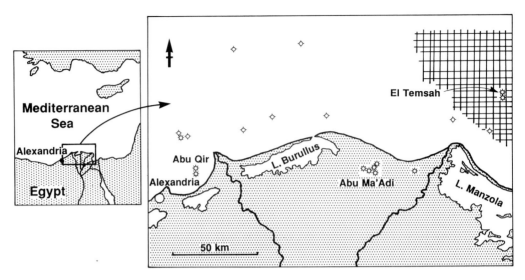

Fig. 1. Location map. The grid of seismic data used in this study is shown in the offshore NE sector of the Nile Delta, adjacent to the El Temsah wells.

of beds down sequence. The interpretation shown on Fig. 2 shows that successively younger sequences become thicker further north, and there is thus an overall south to north migration of fault activity with time through the Plio–Pleistocene. Sequences down to the late Miocene are shown on Fig. 2. Below this level, it is difficult to make an interpretation from the seismic data, and therefore structural modelling techniques are required in order to establish the most acceptable geometric interpretation at these levels.

Time-slice mapping

One of the main problems in the interpretation of seismic data from thick deltaic sequences is the difficulty in correlating horizons across faults. It is therefore more appropriate to approach the interpretation by establishing the geometry of the faults, which in general are clearly imaged on the data, and carry out systematic horizon correlation as a consistent fault interpretation is built up. The first stage in this procedure is to interpret the overall fault geometry in plan view, and this is most conveniently achieved by mapping faults at a constant time, rather than the more conventional mapping at one horizon. Figure 3 shows such a time slice map at 3 secs TWT. A set of E–W-trending and north-dipping faults are bounded along the SW side by a NW–SE-trending fault zone. If extension has occurred more or less normal to the E–W extensional faults (ie these

are dip-slip faults), then the NW–SE bounding fault has undergone a component of oblique slip movement. One fault has been picked out for more detailed analysis, and is indicated in Fig. 3 as SF.

Structure-contour mapping

Figure 4a shows an uninterpreted seismic panel through fault SF, and Fig. 4b shows an interpreted seismic panel from an adjacent line. The location of these lines is shown in Fig. 3. Figure 4a shows the degree of certainty with which the trace of the fault surface may be interpreted on the seismic data. At the sea floor, there is a small break, but immediately below this the data are poor and do not clearly show the fault surface. From 1.5 to 2.4 secs TWT, the fault can be interpreted from horizon cut-offs, but below this a fault surface reflection is present, though the quality of this reflection deteriorates down section. The second stage of the structural analysis is to map the fault surface itself and to draw structure contours in TWT on this surface, as shown in Fig. 5. This procedure serves to identify geometric anomalies in the fault surface, which may result either from misinterpretation of the data or from structural complexities in the geometry of the fault. Single faults have been interpreted to show a simple and smooth surface geometry (Barnett et al. 1987; Walsh & Watterson 1988a), and this would appear to be the case at the scale of observation here (Fig. 5). The third stage of the structural

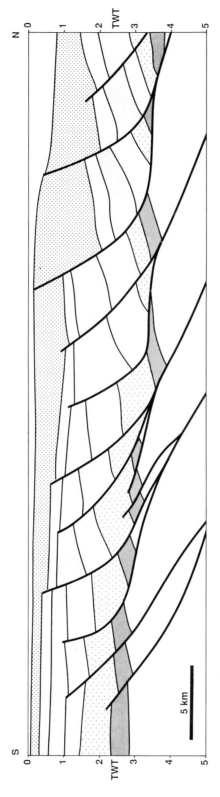

Fig. 2. North–south geoseismic section through the study area, showing the structural style of north-dipping curved faults and rotated fault blocks. The dark-coloured layer is the Upper Miocene, the stippled and white layers above this are the Plio–Pleistocene sequences.

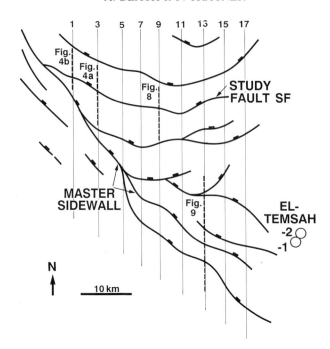

Fig. 3. A time-slice map of the fault geometry at 3 secs TWT, showing a master sidewall fault zone trending NW–SE and E–W-trending extensional faults. The location of fault SF, studied in more detail, and the dip-direction seismic lines, are shown.

analysis is to establish an interpretation of correlated horizons in the footwall and hanging-wall. Several approaches to this can be adopted to ensure a consistency in interpretation where horizon correlations are difficult to make.

Fault displacement analysis

The most practical approach to this problem is to make an initial interpretation and construct structure-contour maps on horizons, and then

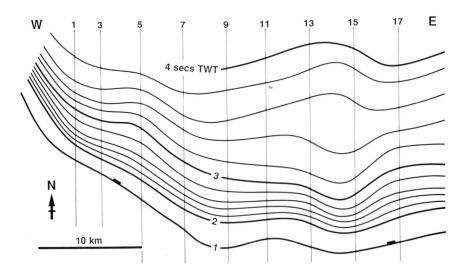

Fig. 5. Structure contour map in secs TWT for the fault surface identified in Fig. 3. The traces of the dip direction seismic lines are shown.

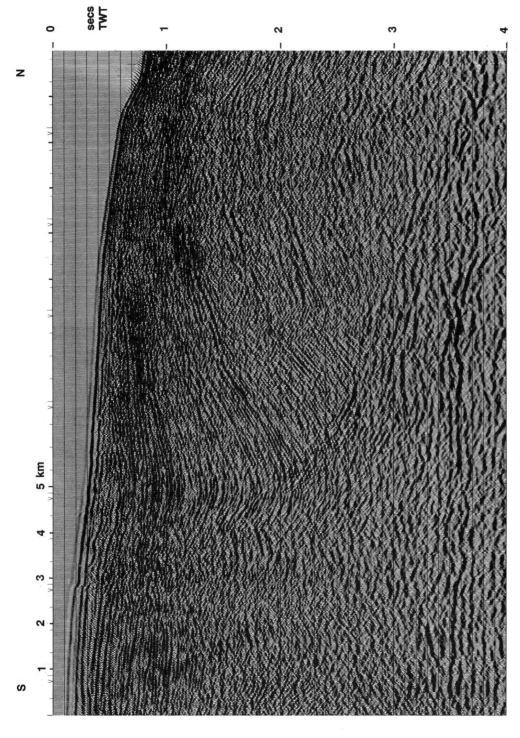

Fig. 4. (a) Uninterpreted seismic line 3 showing the geometry of fault SF, and the rotated sequences in its hangingwall (see Fig. 3 for location).

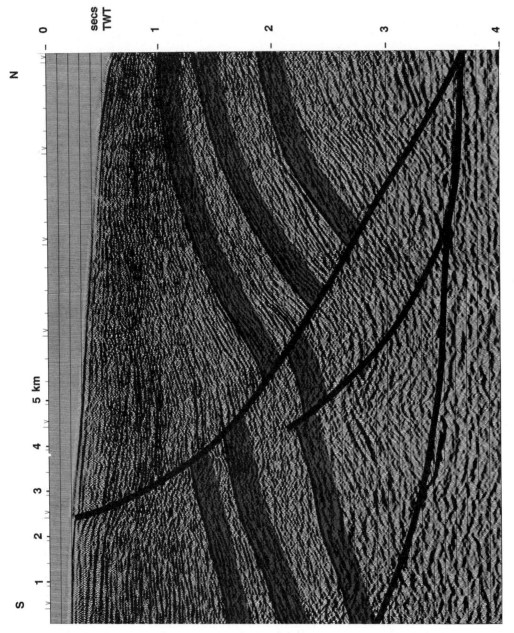

Fig. 4. (b) Interpreted seismic line 1 across fault SF (see Fig. 3 for location).

to map contours of fault displacement within the fault surface from each horizon. It has been established that the consistency of fault displacements acts as a useful check on the validity of the interpretation (Walsh & Watterson 1989) and provides a basis for modifying this interpretation. Figure 6 shows two-way-time contours on the uppermost horizon shown in Fig. 4b, and Fig. 7 plots contours of displacement (in metres) within the fault surface.

Figure 6 shows that there are systematic changes in structure along the fault. These are illustrated by comparing the hangingwall geometries in the seismic panels shown in Figs 4a & 8. In Fig. 4a the hangingwall shows simple rollover into the fault, while in Fig. 8 the uppermost horizon shows a syncline with a dip up towards the fault, and the lower layers show little curvature. The cause of this systematic change in geometry is not known.

Implications of the structural analysis

When a consistent geometrical interpretation of

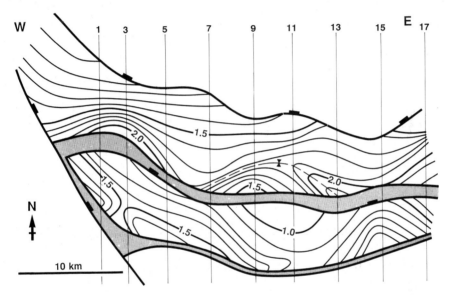

Fig. 6. Structure contours for the uppermost horizon interpreted on the seismic sections in Figs 4b & 8. Contours in secs TWT. Positions of dip direction seismic lines are shown.

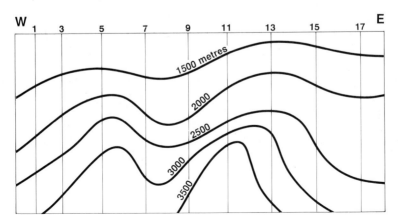

Fig. 7. Contours of dip slip displacement in metres within the fault surface mapped in Fig. 5. The traces of dip direction seismic lines are shown.

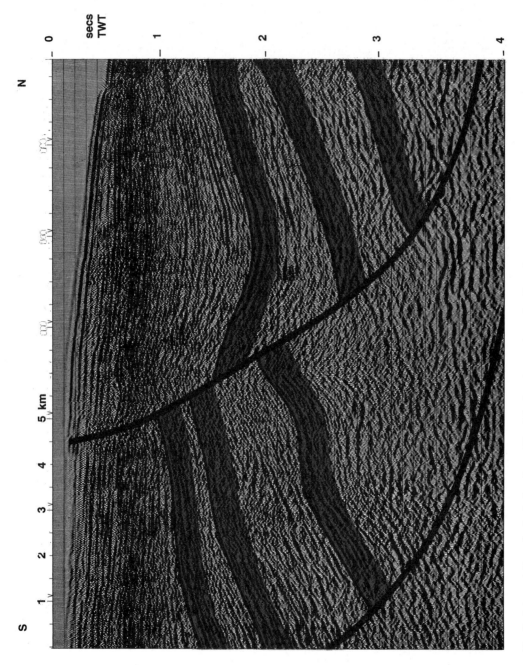

Fig. 8. Interpretation of seismic line 9, see Fig. 6 for location, and text for discussion.

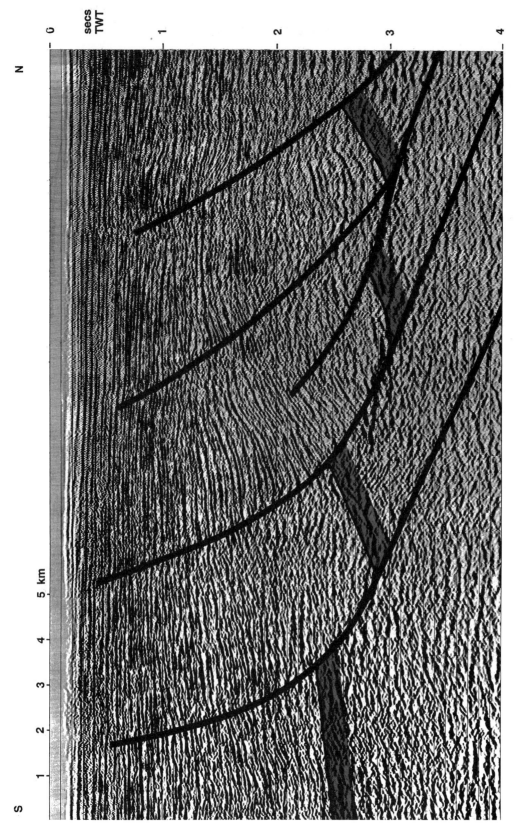

Fig. 9. Interpretation of seismic line 13, see Fig. 3 for location and text for discussion.

the fault and its footwall and hangingwall has been made by following the above procedures, it is possible to consider extrapolating the interpretation to deeper levels where the seismic data are of poorer quality and more difficult to interpret. In particular, the seismic reflections from the Messinian sequences, that contain potential hydrocarbon reservoirs, are complex, discontinuous and irregular. The reflectors are identified firstly from the El Temsah well ties and then on adjacent seismic lines. Figure 9 shows an interpretation of the geometry of the Messinian sequence. In this figure, the data on the geometry of the fault surface and on the displacement pattern within the fault surface have been extrapolated downwards to give a consistent structural interpretation (Barnett et al. 1987; Walsh & Watterson 1988b). The Messinian is thus interpreted to be present in tilted and fault-bounded blocks, with considerable horizontal separation between them. The poor quality of seismic reflections from such structures is a combined result of the structural dip of the Messinian and the curved ray paths through the progressively tilted Plio-Pleistocene sequences overlying the Miocene.

The development of a systematic interpret-ation in areas of structural complexity is an important procedure in deducing the geometry of potential reservoir targets because it avoids as much as possible the use of models, and relies instead on the application of principles and techniques derived from the analysis of data. The interpretation presented here provides the basis for a new concept for hydrocarbon exploration in the area.

References

BARNETT, J. A. M., MORTIMER, J., RIPPON, J. H., WALSH, J. J. & WATTERSON, J. 1987. Displacement geometry in the volume containing a single normal fault. *American Association Petroleum Geologists Bulletin*, **71**, 925–937.

WALSH, J. J. & WATTERSON, J. 1988a. Dips of normal faults in British Coal Measures and other sedimentary sequences. *Journal of the Geological Society, London*, **145**, 859–874.

—— & —— 1988b. Analysis of the relationship between displacements and dimensions of faults. *Journal of Structural Geology*, **10**, 239–247.

—— & —— 1989. Diplacement gradients on fault surfaces. *Journal of Structural Geology*, **11**, 307–316.

The displacement patterns associated with a reverse-reactivated, normal growth fault

T. J. CHAPMAN[1] & A. W. MENEILLY[2]

GECO Exploration Services, Boundary Road, Woking, Surrey, GU21 5BX, UK

Abstract: The displacement geometry of a seismically imaged reverse fault is investigated with the aid of displacement contour and horizon separation diagrams. The present downward decreasing reverse displacement resulted from the reverse reactivation of an originally normal growth fault.

The purpose of this paper is to analyse the displacement variations of a reverse fault, imaged on a three-dimensional (3D) seismic survey. The displacements will be described using displacement-contour diagrams (Rippon 1985; Barnett *et al.* 1987; Walsh & Watterson 1989) and stratigraphic separation diagrams (Chapman *et al.* 1978; Elliott & Johnson 1980; Jenyon 1988; Gibson *et al.* 1989).

The fault is situated in the Southern North Sea area within a largely Mesozoic sequence. We show that the reverse fault was originally a normal growth fault that subsequently became inverted. The 3D survey was analysed on GECO's Charisma seismic workstation. A full account of the methods used is given by Chapman & Meneilly (1990).

The studied fault segment is approximately 3 km long, north to south (Fig. 1). It occurs beneath a major unconformity, from a depth of approximately 500 metres down to a maximum of approximately 2.5 km, corresponding to two-way reflection travel-times of 500 ms (milliseconds) and 1800 ms respectively (the upper part of the fault is shown in Fig. 2a).

The horizontal time-slices (horizontal displays of the 3D-defined reflection surfaces) (Fig. 1) and two east–west seismic sections (Fig. 2) across part of the 3D survey illustrate the structure of the reverse fault zone. In the higher part of the fault an anticlinal fold is developed in the hangingwall (Fig . 2), and this can be traced along a large portion of the fault (Fig. 1). The geometry of this fold varies from rounded in the north (Fig. 2a) to angular in the south where it takes the form of a true kink bank

(Fig. 2b). This fold is related to the reverse displacement on the fault, and accommodates part of it, that is the near-field displacements adjacent to the fault, (Barnett *et al.* 1987). Small areas of reverse drag also occur close to the fault, e.g. between 1000 ms and 1200 ms on Row 95 (Fig. 2a).

The reverse displacement on the fault is defined by the distance between hangingwall and footwall horizon cut-offs plus a component accommodated by the folds, (which are mainly in the hanging wall in the volume containing the fault). The vertical component of each of these, in two-way time, was measured on the seismic workstation. In the case of the main hangingwall anticline, the total reverse displacement is the sum of that accommodated by the fold and that by discrete slip on the fault surface (see Fig. 3).

Displacement variations

The vertical components of displacement on E−W profiles (termed rows) were measured and plotted on a N−S orthographic projection of the fault plane. In most simple faults the concentric displacements contours are ellipses elongated normal to the slip direction (Barnett *et al.* 1987; Walsh & Watterson 1989). Since the displacement contours on the fault analysed in this paper are generally horizontal (Fig. 4) it is assumed that the fault has mainly dip-slip displacement. The actual slip-direction history cannot be determined because it is the apparent dip-slip component that is recorded. If there was a large element of strike-slip displacement, inferences about the fault movement history would be less certain.

Three contoured diagrams for the vertical components of reverse displacement are shown in Fig. 4. These are each based on more than 300 sample points. Figure 4a shows the displacement measured between hangingwall and

[1]Current address: UNOCAL UK Ltd, 32 Cadbury Road, Sunbury-on-Thames, Middlesex, TW16 7LU, UK

[2]Current address: 2 Prinkham Cottages, Marsh Green, Edenbridge, TN8 5QT, UK

From ROBERTS A. M., YIELDING, G. & FREEMAN, B. (eds), 1991, *The Geometry of Normal Faults*, Geological Society Special Publication No 56, pp 183–191

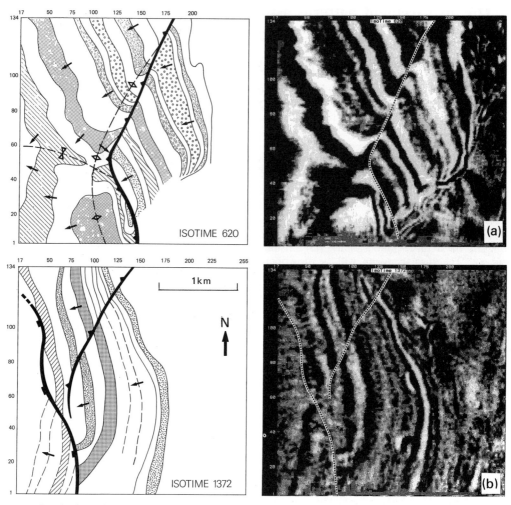

Fig. 1. Two isotime slices and structural interpretations of the reverse fault. Note the hangingwall anticline and greater displacement at the shallower level (isotime 620 ms, Fig. 1a) and absence of folds close to the fault at depth (isotime 1372 ms, Fig. 1b).

footwall horizon cut-offs. This varies from zero in the lower part and increases upwards to over 40 ms with two highs of over 70 ms. Figure 4b shows the amount of reverse displacement accommodated by folds, most of which is by the hanging-wall anticline. The 0 ms contour marks the intersection of the fold's axial trace with the fault as seen in Fig. 2. The displacement increases upwards towards local highs where the hangingwall folds are well developed. The prominent high with over 60 ms of displacement in the south corresponds to the well developed kink band shown on Row 21 (Fig. 2b) The fold amplitude decreases in the middle of the fault between rows 41 and 61, but then increases

northwards giving a vertical displacement of over 30 ms. The total vertical displacement measured directly from the seismic profiles is shown in Fig. 4c. It is the sum of the displacements on the other two contour diagrams and provides a check on the individual determinations.

Compared with the fault displacement measured at the fault (Fig. 4a) the contours of total reverse displacement (Fig. 4c) vary in a more regular and smooth manner, only interrupted where the areas of local reverse drag (Fig. 4b) are developed. The amount of total, vertical, stratigraphic separation across the fault is very large in the south, reaching over 90 ms

W   E

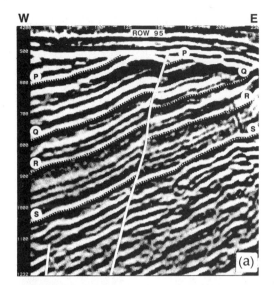

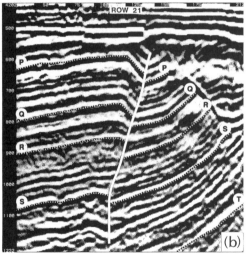

Fig. 2. Two representative E−W seismic sections across the reverse fault. Row 95 (Fig. 2a) in the north shows a rounded profile for the hanging wall anticline whereas Row 21 (Fig. 2b) in the south is angular, taking the form of a kink band. The vertical scale is in two-way time (milliseconds) and extends from approximately 400 metres to almost 2 km in the equivalent depth. Horizontal scale − 100 rows = 2.5 km.

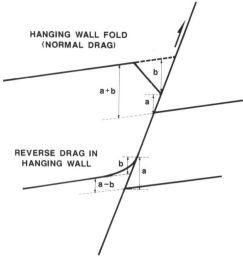

Fig. 3. The total vertical displacement (or horizon separation across a reverse fault zone, accommodated by slip on the fault and fold accommodated displacement.

(this is approximately equivalent to an actual displacement of 100 metres). All three contour diagrams display predominantly horizontal contours with a largely vertical variation in the amount of displacement.

It is of interest that the area of maximum displacement accommodated by slip on the fault in the south does not coincide with that accommodated by folding. This situation is possibly analagous to that where a synthetic splay fault shares the total displacement with the main fault. The displacement on the splay pads out a displacement deficit on the master fault. The synthetic splay in this case takes the form of a fold or kink. The inflexion point between regional dip and the fold defines the wall of a distributed shear zone, which is, in effect, the synthetic splay. The two 'bull's eyes' on the total displacement contour diagram (Fig. 4a) and stronger displacement gradient in the south may have resulted from the coalescence of two faults or may be related to the abrupt change in fault orientation (Fig. 1).

The total reverse vertical displacement across the fault shown in Fig. 4c, is clearly the result of reverse movement on the fault. However, we will now show that it is the result of a complex fault history involving earlier syn-sedimentary normal faulting followed by reverse reactivation of the same fault.

To unravel the fault history, we have produced a series of restorations across the fault zone, which show the relationships prior to the reverse movement. These were produced by using the horizon-flattening function on the workstation (Fig. 5). This selectively flattens a single horizon and adjusts all the others by a vertical component. By flattening horizon P, and projecting the bedding reflectors up to the

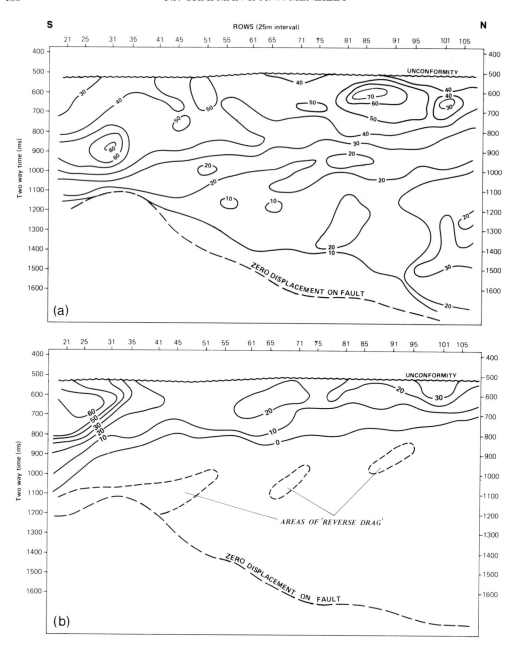

fault we produce a restoration corresponding to the end of deposition of the preceeding sedimentary sequence (Fig. 5b). Figure 6 shows a series of restorations derived by sequentially flattening each horizon. These restorations are only approximate since the fault restoration is not carried out rigourously and the effects of compaction are not taken into account. The change in thickness of some units across the fault is evidence of syn-sedimentary faulting and proves that this fault must have originally been normal. Furthermore, because some units thicken across the fault and some do not, it is evident that there was a complex history of alternating periods of growth faulting and periods of sedimentation without active faulting.

We conclude that the pattern of displacement, although increasing steadily downwards, would

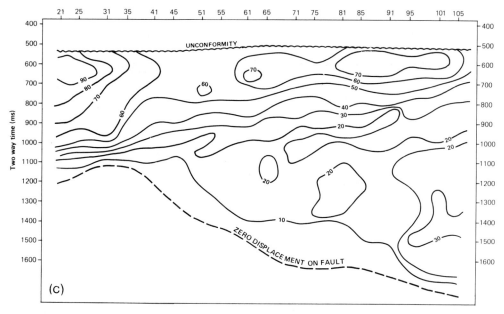

Fig. 4. N−S vertical displacement contour diagrams (in ms) of the reverse fault: (a) displacement measured as the vertical separation between footwall and hangingwall cut-offs; (b) fold-accommodated reverse vertical displacement; (c) total reverse vertical displacement across fault zone.

have been more complicated than for a single fault completely enclosed in lithified sediments. The apparent maximum displacement would have been at least 1200 ms on present datum. This is in complete contrast to what we observe today where the displacement high is close to the top of the fault.

The restoration in Fig. 6 shows the variation in displacement with time for one section across the fault. We can extend this approach to the whole fault surface with the aid of horizon separation diagrams.

Horizon separations

The vertical separation of specific horizons between hangingwall and footwall can be plotted on a vertical projection of the fault (Fig. 7). Again one could plot the components of slip on the fault plane and folding separately from the total displacement. However, it is the latter that is relevant to sedimentation-related movements on the fault and allows a direct comparison of sequence thicknesses across the fault without the complicating effects of near-field displacement structures. It should be noted that the contoured displacement plots (Fig. 4) are based on many more horizons than those shown on the separation diagram (Fig. 7).

This type of diagram is referred to variously as a stratigraphic or horizon separation diagram, fault-plane profile or fault slice (see Chapman *et al.* 1978; Elliot & Johnson 1980; Brown *et al.* 1987; Jenyon 1988; Allan 1989; Harding & Tumanis 1989 and Bouvier *et al.* 1989).

From the horizon-separation diagram (Fig. 7a) the decrease in displacement downwards can be appreciated by comparing the hangingwall and footwall positions of each horizon. The hangingwall horizon cut-offs are above the footwall cut-offs so the sense of movement is reverse. This shows the same variation in displacement, as indicated by the separation of individual horizons, as that contoured in Fig. 4c.

Fig. 7b shows a restored horizon separation diagram of the fault at the time of deposition of horizon P and is directly comparable with the restoration shown in Fig. 6. In contrast to the present stratigraphic separation diagram (Fig. 7a) the hangingwall cut-offs are now below the footwall cut-offs, giving the fault a normal sense of displacement. Furthermore, the displacements increase downwards. It should be noted that for horizon T the separate more westerly normal fault (see Figs 1 and 5) accommodates some of the displacement and a

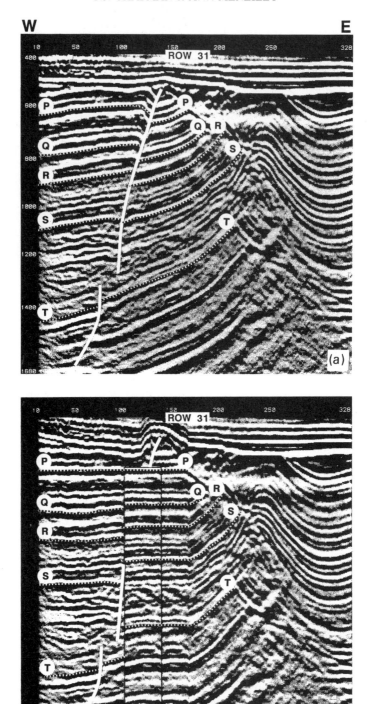

Fig. 5. Row 31 (Fig. 5a) with flattening of horizon P and lateral shift of seismic panel for direct comparison of hangingwall and footwall stratigraphies (Fig. 5b). Note marked thickness increase in hangingwall indicating syn-sedimentary normal faulting. Horizontal scale — 100 rows = 2.5 km.

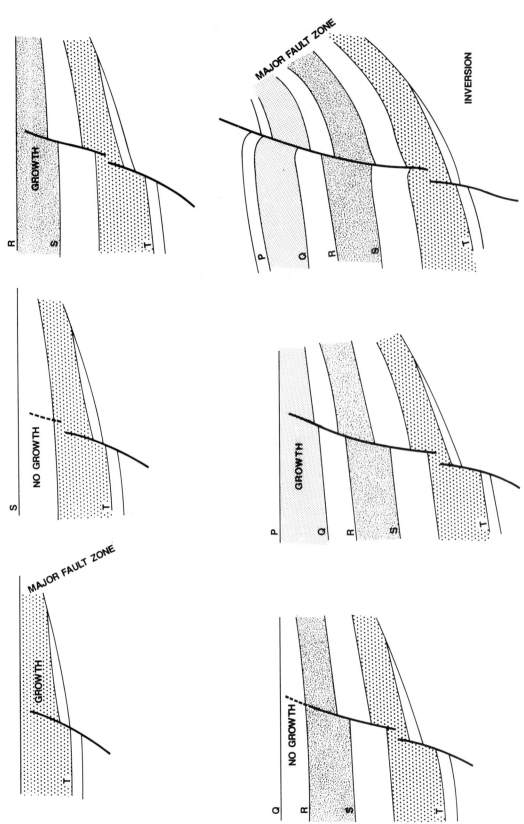

Fig. 6. Sequential restorations of Row 31 produced by successively flattening older horizons. Note alternating episodes of syn-sedimentary fault activity and sedimentation without faulting.

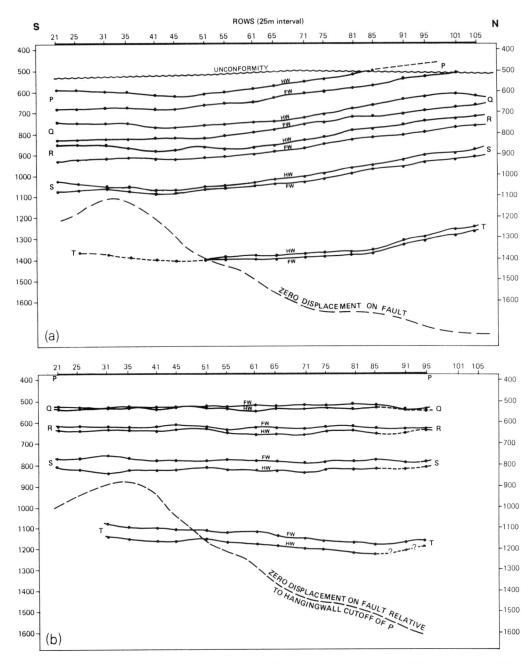

Fig. 7. (a) Horizon separation diagram for reverse fault. This shows the hangingwall (HW) and footwall (FW) positions of horizons without the effects of fold structures near the fault; i.e. the total stratigraphic separation across the fault analogous to Fig. 4c. The reverse displacement decreases downwards. (b) Restored horizon separation diagram at the time of deposition of horizon P. Compare with (a), in particular the switch of hangingwall and footwall horizon positions giving normal displacement increasing downwards.

small complex overlap zone occurs between the two faults (see Fig. 6). It is possible to construct restored horizon separation diagrams for each restoration stage as for the sections (Fig. 6).

It is apparent from the restored horizon-separation diagram (Fig. 7b) that the whole of the fault was originally normal at least along the segment studied, with little lateral variation in displacement. The approximate values of vertical displacements variation shown are 50 ms for horizon T decreasing upwards to 0 ms for P. Due to erosion of beds above horizon P we cannot determine the final displacement configuration of the fault prior to inversion (reverse reactivation of the fault) or know the maximum normal displacement on it. After the maximum amount of normal displacement, reverse movements were superimposed, resulting in the final displacement pattern of Fig. 4c. This diagram therefore shows displacement values which are less than the actual reverse displacements. It also shows a greater variation from bottom to top than the total reverse displacement on the fault. The final displacement configuration displayed in Figs 4c and 7a has resulted from a complex history of reverse dip-slip movements superimposed on earlier syn-sedimentary normal movements.

Conclusions

1. Displacement-contour and horizon separation diagrams derived from seismic data in two-way-time offer a new approach to analysing fault displacement geometry and history of fault movement.

2. Restorations of cross sections and of horizon separation diagrams show that the fault analysed in this paper had a complex history of normal growth followed by reverse reactivation (inversion).

3. The normal-fault, displacement history comprised alternating periods of growth faulting and periods of sedimentation without active faulting.

4. Reverse reactivation of the normal growth-fault took place both by movement on the fault plane and by folding in the hangingwall. The combined horizon separation due to both components produces a more regular displacement contour pattern than if the components are plotted separately.

Nederlandse Aardolie Maatschappij B.V. are thanked for access to a proprietary 3D survey. The Charisma Department GECO UK is thanked for technical assistance.

References

ALLAN, U. S. 1989. Model for hydrocarbon migration and entrapment within faulted structures. *The American Association of Petroleum Geologists Bulletin*, **73**, 803–811.

BARNETT, J. A. M., MORTIMER, J., RIPPON, J. H., WALSH, J. J. & WATTERSON, J. 1987. Displacement geometry in the volume containing a single normal fault. *The American Association of Petroleum Geologists Bulletin*, **71**, 925–937.

BOYER, S. E. & ELLIOTT, D. 1982. Thrust systems. *The American Association of Petroleum Geologists Bulletin*, **66**, 1196–1230.

BOUVIER, J. D., KAARS-SIJPESTEIJN, C. H., KLUSENER, D. F., ONYEJEKWE, C. C. and VANDER PAL, R. C., 1989. Three dimensional seismic interpretation and fault sealing investigations, Nun River field, Nigeria, *The American Association of Petroleum Geologists Bulletin*, **73**, 1397–1414.

BROWN, A. R., EDWARDS, G. S. & HOWARD, R. E. 1987. Fault slicing-A new approach to the interpretation of fault detail. *Geophysics*, **52**, 1319–1327.

CHAPMAN, G. R., LIPPARD, S. J. & MARTYN, J. E. 1978. The stratigraphy and structure of the Kamasia Range, Kenya rift Valley. *Journal of the Geological Society, London*, **135**, 265–281.

CHAPMAN, T. J. & MENEILLY, A. W. 1990. Fault displacement analysis in seismic exploration. *First Break*, **8**, 11–22.

ELLIOTT, D. & JOHNSON, M. R. W. 1980. Structural evolution in the northern part of the Moine trust belt, NW Scotland. *Transactions of the Royal Society of Edinburgh* **71**, 69–96.

GIBSON, J. R., WALSH, J. J. & WATTERSON, J. 1989. Modelling of bed contours adjacent to planar normal faults. *Journal of Structural Geology*, **11**, 317–328.

HARDING, T. P. & TUMANIS, A. C. 1989. Structural interpretation of hydrocarbon traps sealed by basement normal block faults at stable flank of foredeep basins and at rift basins. *The American Association of Petroleum Geologists Bulletin*, **73**, 812–840.

JENYON, M. K. 1988. Fault-salt wall relationships, southern N Sea. *Oil and Gas Journal*, **76**–81.

RIPPON, J. H. 1985. Contoured patterns of the throw and hade of normal faults in the Coal Measures (Westphalian) north-east Derbyshire. *Proceedings of the Yorkshire Geological Society*, **45**, 147–161.

WATTERSON, J. 1986. Fault dimensions, displacements and growth. *Pure and Applied Geophysics*, **124**, 365–373.

WALSH, J. J. & WATTERSON, J. 1989. Displacement gradients on fault surfaces. *Journal of Structural Geology*, **11**, 307–316.

Geometric and kinematic coherence and scale effects in normal fault systems

JOHN J. WALSH & JUAN WATTERSON

Department of Earth Sciences, University of Liverpool, P.O. Box 147, Liverpool L69 3BX, UK

Abstract: Fault displacements derived from a seismic reflection survey of an offshore oilfield are projected onto a vertical plane parallel to the fault strike and the displacement values contoured. In addition to those for single faults, displacement diagrams are also constructed for fault arrays by aggregating the displacement values on selected faults. Displacement contours form regular and systematic patterns, even when there is no continuity between the fault surfaces in the array. A system in which linkage between the elements of a fault array is achieved by ductile strain of the intervening rock is referred to as soft-linked and is regarded as the general case. Geometrical coherence, with regular and systematic displacement patterns, exists at all stages in the growth of a fault array, implying a kinematic coherence requiring a high degree of synchronous movement, as opposed to sequential development, on individual elements in the array.

Conventional maps and diagrams allow representation of only two orders of magnitude of fault displacement rather than the five or more which may occur. A soft-domino model is presented in which the role of ductile strains is acknowledged both in accommodating varying displacements on fault surfaces and in extension on structures too small to be represented individually, and in which the rotation of rigid fault blocks is of reduced importance when compared with rigid-domino models.

To the extent that any seismic interpretation is based on incomplete data it incorporates, either explicitly or implicitly, some elements of a preferred conceptual model. The manner in which faults are linked with neighbouring faults, if linked at all, is one such element and determines, for example, the way in which a fault map is drawn from a series of interpreted seismic sections. Although the concept of geometric coherence in arrays of faults is not a novel one, the consequences of such coherence are not always acknowledged in interpretation of fault geometry and timing. The degree and types of fault linkage represent a basic difference between fault models and have an important bearing on the hydraulic connectivity of a faulted reservoir formation.

Examination of the geometric coherence in fault systems requires consideration of scale effects and of the range of fault sizes which should be taken account of in a conceptual fault model. A model should give due recognition to the existence and effect of faults on a wide range of scales even though only a restricted range of fault sizes can be represented on maps, cross sections and block diagrams. Soft-domino models (Barnett *et al.* 1987; Gibson *et al.* 1989) are characterized by non-rigid behaviour of the rock volume between faults and allow for incorporation of the effects of ductile strain.

A ductile strain is a systematic change in shape due to structures too small to be individually represented on the scale of a particular map, cross section or diagram; it is therefore characterized by an absence of geometrical discontinuities. The scale range of structures contributing to ductile strain therefore varies with the scale of the map or diagram and extends upwards from that of structures due to grain scale processes to that of faults with maximum displacements of 100 m or greater in the case of regional cross sections and maps.

Analysis of the geometry of fault arrays

Strike-projections

In most of the figures in this article the geometries of individual faults and fault arrays are represented by strike-projections (Fig. 1). No single graphical projection allows the full three-dimensional geometry of a fault to be represented but a strike-projection illustrates some aspects of the geometry not apparent on conventional map and cross section projections. Strike-projections are constructed by projecting displacement values at points on a fault surface onto a surface parallel to the fault strike (Rippon 1985a,b, Barnett *et al.* 1987, Childs *et al.* 1990);

From ROBERTS A. M., YIELDING, G. & FREEMAN, B. (eds), 1991, *The Geometry of Normal Faults*, Geological Society Special Publication No 56, pp 193–203

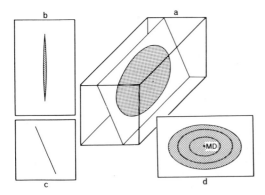

Fig. 1. (a) Rock volume with elliptical fault surface. (b) Map projection of fault. (c) Cross section projection. (d) Strike-projection on vertical plane parallel to the fault strike with contours of equal displacement centred on maximum displacement (MD).

plane-vertical projection surfaces are used for all the projections illustrated here. The displacement values are contoured to allow a visual appreciation of the pattern of displacement variation over the fault surface. Some degree of regularity of form and spacing of the contours would be expected *a priori* in a natural system and this regularity has been demonstrated on small-scale faults (Roux 1979; Rippon 1985a,b; Barnett *et al.* 1987). Abrupt changes in displacement, shown as very close spacing of displacement contours, are not normally to be expected because of the compatibility problems to which they give rise, but they can of course occur at boundaries of salt or other incompetent materials and at unconformities and free surfaces. On an ideal single blind fault the displacement is a maximum at the centre of the elliptical fault surface and reduces systematically to the zero displacement contour, or tip-line, of the fault (Roux 1979; Barnett *et al.* 1987; Walsh & Watterson 1987). Examination of the displacement variation on fault surfaces is useful when considering the relationship between two or more adjacent faults (Pfiffner 1985) and for quality control of seismic interpretations (Barnett *et al.* 1987, Childs *et al.* 1988). The strike-projections illustrated have been constructed using Fault Analysis Projection System (FAPS) software developed by the Liverpool Fault Analysis Group.

Data

The fault projections illustrated are derived from 151 seismic reflection lines at 100 m spacing

from a single oilfield. The lines are each 6.125 km long and the total area covered is *c.* 92 km^2. The seismic lines are sub-perpendicular to fault strike and fault displacements, expressed as the two-way time (TWT) difference between the hanging-wall and footwall cut-offs, are derived from six mapped reflectors. For reasons of confidentiality, maps and complete cross sections of the field are not available for publication. The interpretation used is that made by company staff with some reinterpretation based on the results of FAPS-generated projections. Seismic velocity variations are sufficiently small as not to be significant for the purposes of this article. Fault displacement values are throw values unless stated otherwise; strike-projection displacement diagrams can be plotted for throw, heave or total dip-slip displacement but those illustrated are plotted using throw values.

Fault linkage

Two end member types of linkage are distinguished. *Hard-linked* faults are those in which the fault surfaces are linked on the scale of the map or cross section in use. Interpretations assuming hard linkage have become usual in thrust complexes (Boyer & Elliott 1982) and similar interpretations have subsequently been advocated for normal fault arrays (Gibbs 1984). *Soft-linked* faults are those between which a mechanical and geometric continuity is achieved by ductile strain of the rock volume between them, rather than by continuity of their fault surfaces. Solf-linked faults will appear to be isolated from one another, on the scale of the map or cross section in use.

Where the geometries of adjacent faults are interdependent, as shown for example by complementary variations in displacement, the faults are considered to be geometrically linked. As seen on a map or cross-section faults may be strike-linked i.e. one is essentially a lateral continuation of the other, dip-linked i.e. one fault surface is essentially an upwards or downwards continuation of the other, or occluding i.e. the fault surfaces overlap on a strike-projection. In most cases strike-linked and dip-linked faults also have some degree of overlap producing relay zones (Ramsay & Huber 1987, Larsen 1988, Walsh & Watterson 1990). The heaves of occluding faults are additive when the local or regional extension is measured. This article considers mainly the linkage of occluding and strike-linked faults.

Geometric coherence

Single fault strike-projections

Figure 2 shows a strike-projection of what is represented on a 1:12 500 scale map as a single isolated fault. The ordinate of the projection is represented in two-way time and displacement contours in (msec × 10); assuming a seismic velocity of 3 km s^{-1}, the maximum displacement is *c.* 60 m and the vertical exaggeration *c.* 1.5. The zero displacement contour represents the limit of detectable displacement on the seismic lines which is estimated to be no more than 10 m. The contours are derived from 62 displacement measurements on four mapped reflectors and show the displacement variation to be systematic with the fault dying out upwards, downwards and laterally. The fault, when mapped on this scale, closely approaches the idealized single fault (Fig. 1). The contour spacing below the centre of the fault is less than that above the centre; this may be due to a real difference in rates of change of displacement above and below the fault centre but could also be due to increase in seismic velocity with depth. A velocity change will make the TWT ordinate scale non-linear with respect to depth and will also represent similar displacements by shorter travel times below the fault centre.

The maximum dimension of the fault as mapped is 1800 m, corresponding to a 16 cm trace on a 1:12 500 map. However, to represent the fault by a single 80 cm trace on a 1:2500 map would almost certainly be misleading. Had this

fault been mapped by methods which allowed realistic representation on a scale of 1:2500 (i.e. the scale of standard mine plans for UK coalfields which are constructed from direct observations of faults), it would very likely be shown to consist of a discontinuous array of fault traces and splays. On a scale of 1:1, as in outcrop, a single fault trace 1800 m long would not be expected. That a multiplicity of fault traces observed on one scale is routinely represented as a single fault on another scale reflects a belief that a multiplicity of small faults comprises a geometrically coherent system in which each individual element is necessary. The systematic displacement variation seen when this array is mapped as a single fault shows that a high degree of order must exist in the array of smaller elements. In this case, representation as a single fault is inevitable because the seismic method does not permit resolution of the, probably numerous, individual elements within the array.

The routine assumption of geometric coherence referred to above can be tested by quantitative construction of a small-scale projection from data on a larger-scale projection, as is done below.

Aggregate strike-projections

Aggregate strike-projections are constructed, on each seismic line, by summing the displacements on selected faults along each horizon and plotting as for a single fault. The method is illustrated on a diagrammatic seismic section in

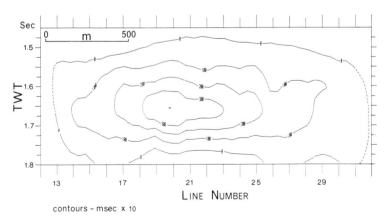

contours - msec × 10

Fig. 2. Strike-projection showing contours of displacement for a single isolated fault. Displacement values (*n*=62) are derived from measurements on four mapped reflectors. Assuming a velocity of 3 km s^{-1}, the maximum displacement is *c.* 60 m and the vertical exaggeration is 1.53. The absence of computer-derived lateral tip-lines is an artifact of the contouring routine used, but as the fault is not seen on lines 12 and 32, manually-drawn lateral tip-lines are shown (broken lines).

Fig. 3. The aggregate displacement on horizon X for the closely spaced array of faults, A, B & C, is a + b + c. Other combinations of faults can be selected at will and an aggregate displacement strike-projection plotted for each combination. An aggregate displacement plot for an array of closely spaced faults, spanning *c.* 200 m across the strike of the faults, is shown in Fig. 4. The displacement contours show a regularity similar to that on the single fault (Fig. 2) but with the important difference that the contour spacing is *c.* 15 m for the single fault and is *c.* 75 m for the aggregate plot. The aggregate plot is constructed from 1280 individual displacement values on 153 faults and fault splays, which all lie within 200 m of the single major fault. Only the upper part of the fault array is imaged on the seismic sections. The systematic pattern and spacing of the contours are similar to those of a 'single' fault and, as the spaces between the faults are small relative to the lengths of their traces, demonstrate that representation of the array, shown in Fig. 4, by a single 6 cm fault trace on a 1:250 000 map would be realistic even though several smaller faults are represented on the original 1:12 500 map. The importance of individual small faults and

splays to the geometric coherence of the array is illustrated in Fig. 5 which shows a small area of the strike-projection of Fig. 4. Figure 5a shows the aggregate displacement plot with all elements included and the cross section (Fig. 5c) shows the elements present on one seismic line. Fig. 5b shows the same aggregate plot but with a single splay excluded (Fig. 5c). Removal of this splay results in a markedly increased irregularity of the displacement contours demonstrating that this splay is necessary for geometrical coherence of the system. The splay is close to the upper tip-line of the array and, as shown in Fig. 5c, is hard-linked to other elements of the system.

The significance of aggregating displacements on faults which are not hard-linked is shown in Fig. 6. Figure 6b shows an aggregate displacement plot of a major fault and associated hard-linked splays one of which is shown in the cross section (Fig. 6a). Between lines 3 & 17 the displacement contours of 100 ms and greater show a prominent irregularity. A small fault (Y) is isolated from the main fault both on the cross section illustrated and on all other seismic lines on which it has been identified. When displacements on this isolated fault are included

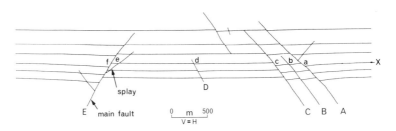

Fig. 3. Schematic cross section showing method of aggregating displacements on fault arrays (see text for details). The aggregate displacement on horizon X for all faults on the cross section is a + b + c + d + e + f. Two fault segments of fault E are identified i.e. the main fault and a fault splay.

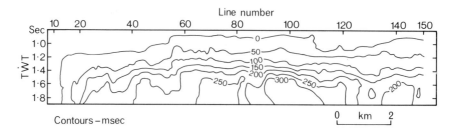

Fig. 4. Strike-projection showing contours of aggregate displacement for a fault system comprising a main fault and 153 dominantly hard-linked splays. Displacements are derived from six mapped reflectors. 736 aggregate displacement values are contoured and these were obtained from a total of 1280 individual displacements. Assuming a velocity of 3 km s^{-1} the maximum displacement is *c.* 450 m and the vertical exaggeration is 1.38.

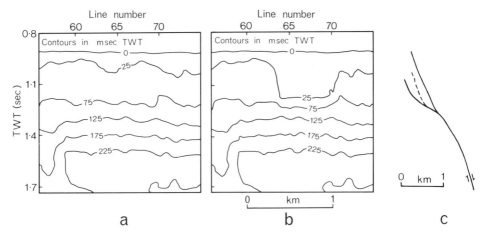

Fig. 5. (a) Enlargement of a small area of the strike-projection shown in Fig. 4 incorporating 120 aggregate displacement values, including displacements ($n=219$) from all splays, as in Fig. 4. For a velocity of 3 km s^{-1} the maximum displacement is c. 415 m and the vertical exaggeration is 1.38. (b) As (a) but with displacement data from one splay subtracted ($n=211$). (c) Cross section on line 65 with the splay subtracted in (b) shown as dashed line.

in the aggregate plot (Fig. 6c) the contour irregularity is greatly reduced, although not eliminated. Although isolated, the fault is clearly necessary to the geometrical coherence of the array of which it must be regarded as a part. The residual irregularity of the displacement contours is thought to be due to some of the displacement at this point being accommodated by plastic shear deformation in the relatively thin slice of rock between the isolated fault and the main fault.

Figure 7a shows the aggregate displacement plot for all the faults in the field which have the dominant dip direction. The maximum displacement is c. 600 m and 4082 individual displacement readings are incorporated in the plot. The faults included in the aggregate plot are distributed over 6 km in the direction normal to the fault strike and the main faults are clearly

isolated from one another, at least within the imaged depth range and in respect of the minimum imaged fault size. The numbers of main faults and of fault segments (main faults plus splays) included in the aggregate plot at differ-

Fig. 6. (a) Cross section showing the faults (heavy lines) plotted in (b) and (c). (b) Strike-projection showing contours of aggregate displacement for a fault system comprising a main fault and 19 hard-linked splays. (c) Strike-projection of main fault and splays as in (b) but with addition of the isolated fault (y) in the hangingwall of the main fault system shown in (a). Displacements are derived from six mapped reflectors. 240 aggregate displacement values are contoured in each strike-projection and these values were obtained from a total of 292 (b) and 312 (c) individual displacements. Assuming a velocity of 3 km s^{-1} the maximum displacement is c. 270 m and the vertical exaggeration is 0.73.

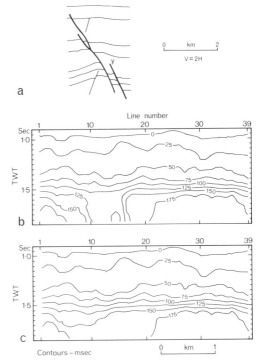

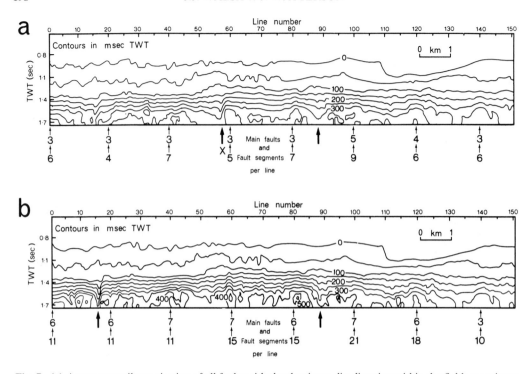

Fig. 7. (**a**) Aggregate strike-projection of all faults with the dominant dip-direction within the field: prominent contour irregularities are shown (heavy arrows). (**b**) Strike-projection of all faults in the field: residual sharp contour irregularities are shown (heavy arrows). Displacements are derived from six mapped reflectors. 872 aggregate displacement values are contoured in each strike-projection and these values were obtained from a total of 4082 (a) and 4949 (b) individual displacements. Assuming a velocity of 3 km s^{-1} the vertical exaggeration is 1.55 and the maximum displacements are 675 m (a) and 750 m (b). The numbers of main faults and the numbers of fault segments aggregated are shown for selected lines.

ent points on the strike-length of 15 km are shown on Fig. 7. The overall contour pattern is again similar to that of a single fault but with some prominent irregularities (arrowed) the system, in respect of the main faults at least, is demonstrably soft-linked. The prominent irregularity at X is greatly reduced in Fig. 7b which includes all the faults in the field, i.e. both the dominant set and a set with an opposed dip; there are no cross faults in this field. Aggregating throws on faults with opposing dips produces values of no obvious geological significance but a similar pattern would be expected for aggregate fault heaves, representing aggregate extension. Residual sharp contour irregularities (Fig. 7b, arrowed) occur at positions corresponding to lateral tips of main faults in the array. It is not yet known whether these irreularities represent interpretational artefacts or places where an unusually high proportion of displacement is accommodated by ductile shear, i.e. a continuous displacement, with a corresponding reduction in the

discontinuous displacement accommodated along fault surfaces. Figure 8a shows a small part of the aggregate displacement plot of Fig. 7 and the same area is shown in Fig. 8b but with the displacements on a single fault within the array subtracted. The reduction in the regularity of the displacement contours caused by the removal of this single fault demonstrates a reduced geometric coherence of the system and it is concluded that this single fault is an essential part of the system rather than an arbitrary or unrelated structure.

The principal conclusion drawn is that the pattern of aggregate displacement on an array of faults, the traces of which are up to 6 km apart and which have no direct physical continuity with the main rupture surfaces, is both systematic and similar to that which would be expected on a small part of the surface of a very large single fault surface. Each fault in the field is therefore an integral and essential part of a single, geometrically coherent fault system which, for some purposes and on some scales,

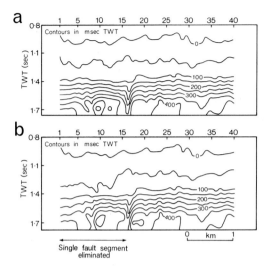

Fig. 8. (a) Enlargement of part of the strike-projection shown in Fig. 7b (b) As (a) but with a single fault subtracted. Displacements are derived from six mapped reflectors. 234 aggregate displacement values are contoured in each strike-projection and these values were obtained from a total of 1417 (a) and 1344 (b) displacements. Assuming a velocity of 3 km s^{-1} the maximum displacement is 630 m and the vertical exaggeration is 1.41.

can properly be regarded as a single fault. The system is largely soft-linked and such linkage demands a significant degree of ductile deformation in the rock volume containing the array of faults. Further evidence for significant ductile strain is provided by the displacement variation on fault surfaces which is evident on all scales (Watterson 1986, Barnett *et al.* 1987, Gibson *et al.* 1989). On no fault surface for which a displacement plot has been constructed, in any of the several data sets which we have examined, has displacement been shown to be constant. The variable displacements on all the individual fault segments in a fault array, on all the scales illustrated, are thus dependent on the precise positions, sizes and displacement distribution patterns of all other fault elements within the array. To this extent, the omission of a fault segment from a seismic interpretation potentially can be detected. Faults formed at different times and with unrelated displacements could also be distinguished by this method.

Kinematic coherence

In the cases illustrated, a geometric coherence

can be demonstrated to exist in an array of faults on which movement has ceased. It can then be inferred that a comparable degree of coherence characterised the array throughout all stages of its development. If so, then the timing and rates of displacement at each point on the surfaces of all faults and splays in the array are related to the timing and rates of displacement at all other points in the array i.e. the array is kinematically coherent. Not all points on all fault surfaces will be active throughout the life of the array but the time at which each fault surface is initiated, the rate at which it grows and the time at which it ceases to grow are fixed in relation to the overall growth history of the array. A considerable degree of synchronous growth is necessary in such a system.

Interpretations of the sequential growth of individual fault segments and splays based on their geometrical relationships as seen in 2D sections are inconsistent with the evidence for a high degree of synchronous growth of the individual surfaces and the progressive increase in displacement on each surface. Sequential forward propagation of either normal fault or thrust arrays (Butler 1982; Gibbs 1984) is unlikely. For any individual fault elements, forward, rearward (Eisenstadt & De Paor 1987; Price 1988) and lateral propagations are of equal significance for any individual fault element even though the overall dimensions of a regional scale array may be fixed at the time of initiation. Four separate surfaces, linked on three branch-lines, are shown diagramatically in Fig. 9. The variable displacement on each is not shown. In the cross section represented by the plane ABCD, three of the individual elements are represented and, given this single cross section, it might be tempting to deduce a sequence of formation. However, when lateral propagation of each surface is taken into account the order in which each element first appears in any one cross section is not necessarily related to the order in which each new displacement surface is first generated. It is also possible that displacement on all four surfaces took place synchronously. Given that the lateral boundaries of only one of the surfaces are shown in the block diagram (Fig. 9b) it is not possible to say which of the other three surfaces has the greatest extent and displacement. Given the degree of interdependence of displacements on all individual elements in the array and the three-dimensional nature of the geometric coherence which has been demonstrated, it is unrealistic to make a simple sequential kinematic interpretation of any single cross section.

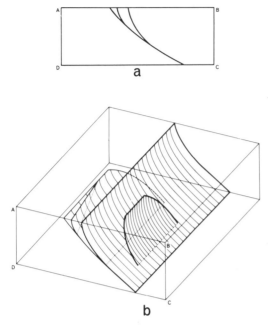

Fig. 9. (a) Cross section of hypothetical fault with two hard-linked splays. (b) Block diagram showing the geometry of part of the fault array of which (a) is a cross section on the front of the block (ABCD).

Effects of scaling

The range of scales on which fault arrays are geometrically coherent is not known. We believe that coherence is likely to persist on the basin scale but have not yet been able to assemble sufficient data to test this assertion which assumes that faults with displacements up to at least 5 km form part of coherent arrays. The smallest scale of fault which contributes to coherent arrays has, likewise, not been demonstrated but fault population studies (Childs *et al.* 1990) suggest that displacements down to 10 cm or less are systematic elements in a coherent, larger-scale geometry. We believe it likely that faults with maximum displacements ranging over at least five orders of magnitude may form elements of a single coherent array whereas even a good map can represent faults with displacements ranging over only *c.* two orders of magnitude. This raises the question of what is actually represented on a map.

On a map on scale 1:250 000 the minimum length of fault trace represented may be 5 cm, corresponding to 12.5 km; a fault of this length would have a maximum displacement of *c.* 1 km (Walsh & Watterson 1988a) and faults with smaller maximum displacements would not be represented. If the 1:250 000 map is derived from a larger-scale map on which smaller faults have been identified, then the faults represented on the smaller-scale map may be aggregated so that what is represented as a 1 km maximum displacement fault may be an array of smaller faults with aggregate maximum displacement of 1 km; most maps do incorporate some degree of aggregation as a convenient simplification which overcomes some of the scale limitations of graphical representaton. Whether a smaller fault is included in an aggregated array will depend to some extent on its position relative to a larger fault — if distant from a larger fault then a smaller fault is unlikely to be included in an aggregated array. These considerations are relevant to fault maps on all scales and even in fully aggregated maps there will be no record of faults which are below the limit of resolution of the method used to acquire the data from which the map is constructed. All maps and diagrams therefore under-represent the strain accommodated by faulting although for some purposes such under-representation may be of little significance. Faulting on a scale below that which is represented on a map or diagram constitutes a ductile strain.

Although fault sizes represented on maps of different scale have been referred to in terms of their trace lengths, the limits can also be referred to in terms of the minimum fault displacements which are represented. In general, the smallest fault displacement represented on a structural contour map is determined by the smallest displacement which can be detected as a contour offset, which in turn depends on the spacing of the structural contours. This limitation means that, as the displacement on a fault varies along the length of the fault trace, the fault trace on the map shows only that part of the apparent fault on which displacement is greater than the limit imposed by the contour spacing; the dimensions of a fault will therefore vary with the scale of map or section on which it is represented.

The fault model

A conceptual soft-domino fault model is shown in Fig. 10 which illustrates the principal conclusions derived from analysis of geometrical and kinematic coherence in several datasets and incorporates features previously described (Barnett *et al.* 1987; Gibson *et al.* 1989). The principal features shown in the block diagram are as follows. Each fault shows a systematic non-linear variation in displacement (Walsh & Watterson 1987). The sum of the displacements

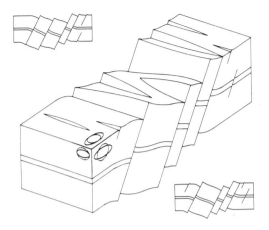

Fig. 10. Conceptual block diagram showing the principal features of the soft-domino fault model (see text for details). Insets show cross sections on sides of the block. Strain ellipses on the sides of the block show the ductile strain, for the block as a whole, accommodated by structures which are too small to be represented on the diagram (unstrained circles shown with broken lines): the amount of strain shown is arbitrary.

on all faults encountered on any line through the block and parallel to its length, is the same for all lines, i.e. the whole array shown can be considered as a small part of a single much larger fault. The block as a whole has not rotated relative to the horizontal and the marker horizon is at the same elevation at both ends of the block. The unchanged relative elevations of the marker horizon at both ends is achieved by reverse drag of horizons on both sides of each fault and, unlike the rigid-domino model, is not dependent on fault block rotation. The variable displacement on individual faults is accommodated by heterogeneous ductile strains. The ductile strain accommodated by structures too small to be individually represented on the diagram is shown by the strain ellipses. Plane strain is assumed in which there is no change of dimension in the direction parallel to the fault strike; the amounts of ductile strain shown by the strain ellipses is arbitrary. If the volume represented by the block diagram were to be illustrated on a much smaller scale than in Fig. 10, all of the fault-related deformation would be represented as a ductile extension by necking. For simplicity, faults dipping in only one direction are shown and the number of smaller faults shown relative to the number of larger faults is less than would be expected (Childs *et al.* 1990). The maximum displace-

ments of faults illustrated range over *c.* two orders of magnitude. All material lines and planes within the block, other than lines parallel to the length of the block, have been rotated and faults have shallower dips than when initiated. Only the final geometry is shown but similarly constrained geometries existed at all stages in the evolution of the fault system and the faults are more nearly synchronous than sequential. Although blocks between individual pairs of faults have been rotated they have not been rotated as rigid blocks. No scale is shown because similar geometries will exist whatever the block length — except for features due to isostatic effects and thermal subsidence, which are not incorporated in the diagram. The displacement/dimension ratios of the largest faults shown are, however, typical for faults with maximum displacements of several kilometres rather than the much smaller ratios typical for faults with maximum displacements of several metres (Walsh & Watterson 1988a). Also not illustrated is the likely shallowing of fault dips to 45° (Walsh & Watterson 1988b), and the downward change from the discontinuous geometry of brittle faults to the continuous geometries of ductile shear zones (Bak *et al.* 1975; Grocott 1977; Sibson 1977; Ramsay & Huber 1987), both of which would be apparent on the larger scale. The soft-domino model is similar in many respects to that which has long been applied to ductile straining of single crystals (Taylor 1938) in which glide planes are bounded by dislocations along their tip-lines. In the crystal model, individual glide planes do not extend across the crystal, but, in common with soft-domino faults, rotate throughout the deformation. The rigid-domino model requires propagation of faults across the whole of the faulted layer before either regional strain or fault rotation can begin. When soft-domino faults have grown sufficiently to span the faulted layer, further deformation is characterized by elements of both the soft and rigid-domino models i.e. rigid block rotation and rotation by internal deformation of major fault blocks.

It is apparent from Fig. 10 that the question of whether the strain illustrated is a simple shear or a pure shear strain is scale-dependent. On the scale of an individual fault or shear zone the strain is a simple shear but on the scale of a block incorporating many faults the strain is a pure shear. The concept of simple shear in the upper crust contrasting with pure shear in the lower crust (Kusznir & Egan 1990) simply reflects an unstated assumption that upper crustal strains are accommodated on fewer and larger structures than equivalent strains in the lower crust. The evidence from mid-crustal rocks (Bak *et al.* 1975; Escher & Watterson 1974; Coward 1976) is that individual ductile shear zones accommodate displacements of similar scale to those of the largest upper crustal faults.

Conclusions

(1) Displacement contours on strike-projections of both single faults and fault arrays have simple and systematic patterns and spacing.

(2) An array of faults on one scale can be, and often is, represented by a single fault on a smaller-scale representation.

(3) Each individual fault or splay is necessary to the geometrical coherence of an array.

(4) A significant degree of soft linkage is usual in fault arrays but the type of linkage is strongly scale-dependent.

(5) Fault arrays are kinematically coherent during growth and this implies a high degree of synchronous fault movement within an array.

(6) Sequential fault propagation interpretations are of doubtful validity.

(7) Deformation by faulting may involve faults with sizes spanning five orders of magnitude. Because graphical representations can show only two orders of magnitude of fault size, normal fault models must incorporate the effects of ductile extension.

(8) Variable displacement on fault surfaces is accommodated by heterogeneous ductile strain.

(9) Soft-domino models are characterised by ductile rotation of faults and beds at all stages of deformation and by the reduced significance of rigid block rotation compared with rigid domino models.

(10) The distinction between simple and pure shear deformation when applied to regional stretching is scale-dependent.

We thank Conrad Childs, John Gibson, Chris Lavers and other members of the Liverpool Fault Analysis Group for their considerable efforts in developing FAPS software, data handling and preparation of diagrams and for much useful discussion. Thanks are due to Britoil plc for access to data. Funding by the European Coal and Steel Commission and British Coal (contract 7220 AF825), by Britoil (contract 6050) and the University of Liverpool Research Development Fund is gratefuly acknowledged. Publication is with the permission of Britoil and British Coal but the views expressed are those of the authors and do not necessarily correspond with those of either British Coal or Britoil.

References

BAK, J., SØRENSEN, K., KORSTGÅRD, J., NASH, D. & WATTERSON, J. 1975. Tectonic implications of Precambrian shear belts in western Greenland. *Nature*, **254**, 556–559.

BARNETT, J. A. M., MORTIMER, J., RIPPON, J. H., WALSH, J. J. & WATTERSON, J. 1987. Displacement geometry in the volume containing a single normal fault. *The American Association of Petroleum Geologists Bulletin*, **71**, 925–937.

BOYER, S. E. & ELLIOTT, D. 1982. Thrust systems. *The American Association of Petroleum Geologists Bulletin*, **66**, 1196–1230.

BUTLER, R. W. H., 1982. The terminology of structures in thrust belts. *Journal of Structural Geology*, **4**, 239–245.

CHILDS, C., LAVERS, C., WALSH, J. J. & WATTERSON, J. 1988. A new system for quantitative fault analysis from seismic reflection data (Abs). *Interne Skrifter Institutt for Geologi*, Universitet i Oslo.

——, WALSH, J. J. & WATTERSON, J. 1990. A method for estimation of the density of fault displacements below the limit of seismic resolution in reservoir formations. *In: North Sea Oil and Gas Reservoirs II*. Norwegian Institute of Technology, Trondheim. Graham & Trotman, London, 309–318.

COWARD, M. P. 1976. Strain within ductile shear zones. *Tectonophysics*, **34**, 181–197.

EISENSTADT, G. & DEPAOR, D. G. 1987. Alternative model of thrust-fault propagation. *Geology*, **15**, 630–633.

ESCHER, A. & WATTERSON, J. 1974. Stretching fabrics, folds and crustal shortening. *Tectonophysics*, **22**, 223–231.

GIBBS, A. D. 1984. Structural evolution of extensional basin margins. *Journal of the Geological Society, London*, **141**, 609–620.

GIBSON, J. R., WALSH, J. J. & WATTERSON, J. 1989. Modelling of bed contours and cross-sections adjacent to planar normal faults. *Journal of Structural Geology*, **11**, 317–328.

GROCOTT, J. 1977. The relationship between Precambrian shear belts and modern fault systems. *Journal of the Geological Society, London*, **133**, 257–262.

KUSZNIR, N. J. & EGAN, S. S. 1990. Simple shear and pure shear models of extensional sedimentary basin formation: application to the Jeanne D'Arc Basin, Grand Banks of Newfoundland. *The American Association of Petroleum Geologists Memoirs*.

LARSEN, P-H. 1988. Relay structures in a Lower Permian basement-involved extension system, East Greenland. *Journal of Structural Geology*, **10**, 3–8.

PFIFFNER, A. P. 1985. Displacements along thrust faults. *Eclogae Geologicae Helvetiae*, **78**, 313–333.

PRICE, R. A. 1988. The mechanical paradox of large overthrusts. *Geological Society of America*

Bulletin, **100**, 1898–1908.

RAMSAY, J. G. & HUBER, M. I. 1987. *The techniques of modern structural geology. Vol. 2, Folds and fractures*. Academic, London.

RIPPON, J. H. 1985a, Contoured patterns of the throw and hade of normal faults in the Coal Measures (Westphalian) of north-east Derbyshire. *Proceedings of the Yorkshire Geological Society*, **45**, 147–161.

—— 1985b, New methods of forecasting the throw and hade of faults in some North Derbyshire Collieries. *Transactions of the Institute of Mining Engineers*, 198–204.

ROUX, W. F. 1979. *The development of growth fault structures*. American Association of Petroleum Geologists, Structural Geology School Course Notes.

SIBSON, R. H. 1977. Fault rocks and fault mechanisms. *Journal of the Geological Society, London*, **133**, 191–213.

TAYLOR, G. I. 1938. Plastic strain in metals. *Journal of the Institute of Metals*, **62**, 307–324.

WALSH, J. J. & WATTERSON, J. 1987. Distributions of cumulative displacement and seismic slip on a single normal fault surface. *Journal of Structural Geology*, **9**, 1039–1046.

—— & —— 1988a. Analysis of the relationship between displacements and dimensions of faults. *Journal of Structural Geology* **10**, 239–247.

—— & —— 1988b. Dips of normal faults in British Coal Measures and other sedimentary sequences. *Journal of the Geological Society, London*, **145**, 859–873.

—— & —— 1989. Displacement gradients on fault surfaces. *Journal of Structural Geology*, **11**, 307–316.

—— & —— 1990. New methods of fault projection for coalmine planning. *Proceedings of the Yorkshire Geological Society*, **48**.

WATTERSON, J. 1986. Fault dimensions, displacements and growth. *Pure and Applied Geophysics*, **124**, 365–373.

Analogue-modelling and
section balancing

Numerical and analogue modelling of normal fault geometry

G. DRESEN[1], U. GWILDIS[2] & TH. KLUEGEL[2]

[1]*Department of Earth, Atmospheric and Planetary Sciences, Massachussets Institute of Technology, Cambridge, MA 02139, USA*
[2]*Geologisches Institut der TH Darmstadt, Schnittspahnstr, 9, 6100 Darmstadt, Germany*

Abstract: In an attempt to constrain the influence of boundary conditions on fault nucleation and propagation processes, basement-controlled normal faulting has been simulated using analogue clay models and plane-strain finite element models. Two opposing basement configurations were investigated and the results of the analogue and numerical models were compared.

In the first series of clay models subsidence of a basement block along an inclined normal fault and along a vertical fault was simulated. An upwards-propagating fault initiated at the base of the clay model. The final fault geometry was consistent with the geometry of the stress distribution calculated in the finite element model. No listric fault developed.

In the second experiment horizontal basement extension was simulated and, as expected from the numerical calculations, these boundary conditions resulted in the formation of listric faults. The results of the analogue and numerical experiments show that initial fault geometry can be predicted successfully from the stress distribution at the elastic limit.

Although the existence of gravity-driven listric normal faults is frequently reported (Yielding *et al*. this volume; Shelton 1984) there is increasing evidence that planar normal faults may control basin development (Yielding *et al*. this volume). Despite extensive regional studies and detailed kinematic analyses no successful approach yet exists that allows us to describe fully the boundary conditions and driving forces that determine normal fault geometry in a defined structural setting. Factors controlling fault orientation are numerous and among others include material anisotropies and pore pressure variations. Large extensional strain and compaction may affect the final fault geometry, such passive fault rotation is important in both consolidated and soft-sediment deformation (Mandl 1988). The principal aim of this paper is to discuss the effect of the stress distributions resulting from various plane strain boundary conditions on the geometry of faulting. Stress distribution significantly controls the complex processes of fault nucleation and propagation. These in turn will determine the initial fault geometry and its subsequent development.

Numerical modelling

Finite element models were established using the STATAN-package, Version 1980, and the ADINA-package, Version 1983, to investigate the elastic-plastic response of a continuum under plane strain conditions. The STATAN and ADINA generated meshes comprised 565 four-node isoparametric elements (Fig. 1) and 225 eight-node isoparametric elements (Fig. 2) respectively. Dimensions and material parameters of a clay cake were introduced in both models (see Table 1). Two different sets of plane strain boundary conditions were imposed: vertical displacement of a basement block, and extension above a planar detachment.

The subsidence of a basement block was simulated numerically by the incremental vertical displacement of basal nodes 1−7 on the left-hand part of the STATAN-generated finite element model in Fig. 1. The left-hand boundary of the mesh was regarded as a plane of symmetry. Horizontal displacement of the boundary-nodes was not allowed.

Two different finite element models were used to simulate extension above a planar detachment. In the first model (STATAN) the boundary of the detachment was placed between node 21 and node 22 in the fine part of the mesh (Fig. 1). In a second model (ADINA) a different mesh lay-out was used (Fig. 2). Here the left boundary was regarded as a symmetry plane and the basal nodes were progressively displaced towards the right.

In the calculations carried out with STATAN a nonlinear-elastic constitutive law was assumed. The elastic limit was defined by the Mohr-Coulomb criterion $\tau = c + \sigma_N \tan\varphi$. The

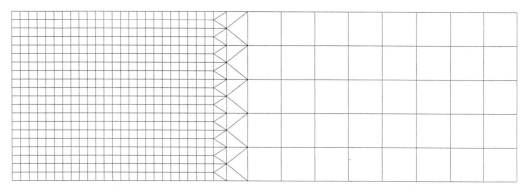

Fig. 1. Finite element mesh used for the calculations carried out with STATAN, Version 1980. The mesh comprises 565 isoparametric elements, either triangular or four-node quadrilateral. Dimensions and material properties used in the calculations are given in Table 1.

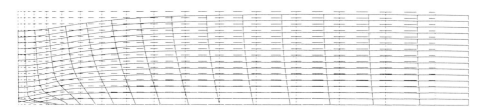

Fig. 2. Finite element mesh generated by the ADINA package, Version 1983. The mesh comprises 225 eight-node isoparametric elements. The dashed lines show the undeformed mesh. Subsidence above an extending basement is shown by the solid lines. Magnification of the displacement is ×2600.

parameter τ is the shear stress, c is the cohesive shear strength, σ_N is the normal stress and φ is the angle of internal friction. The actual values of c and φ are given in Table 1. Model sizes and material parameters introduced in both models are comparable to those used in the analogue experiments.

In the model created with ADINA, a linear-elastic/perfectly-plastic constitutive law was assumed and the elastic limit was defined by the Drucker–Prager yield condition $F = \alpha I_1 + J_2^{1/2} - K = 0$ (Drucker & Prager 1952) with an associated plastic flow rule to model initial shear zone development. (Walters & Thomas 1982). The parameter I_1 is the first invariant of

the stress tensor and J_2 is the second invariant of the stress deviator. α and K are material parameters related to φ and c by the following expressions: $\alpha = \tan\varphi/(9 + 12\tan^2)^{1/2}$, $K = 3c/(9 + 12\tan^2\varphi)^{1/2}$. The calculation was usually stopped when the elastic limit was first reached in one element of the respective structure. The stress distribution at the onset of plastic failure was assumed to determine the geometry of the incipient fault.

Analogue modelling

A clay cake (90 cm × 40 cm × 10 cm) was deformed using three different experimental

Table 1. *Actual values of the defining material properties used in the calculations with ADINA and STATAN*

	E KN/m$_2$	v	φ (deg)	C (KN/m^2)	ρ (g/cm^3)	H (cm)	L (cm)
ADINA	5000	0.4	24	20	20	15	67.5
STATAN	22500	0.47	20	20	18.5	20	60

E = Young's modulus, v = Poisson ratio, φ = friction angle, c = cohesive shear strength, ρ = density, H and L = height and length of the structure respectively.

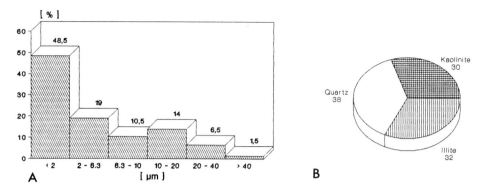

Fig. 3. Material composition of the clay used in the experiments. (**a**) Grain size distribution(%). (**b**) Mineralogical composition(%). The clay is commercially available from Erbsloeh GmbH (Geisenheim, FRG). Data kindly provided by Erbsloeh GmbH.

configurations. The clay is commercially available and had the grain size distribution and the mineralogical composition given in Fig. 3. The water content was 29% by weight. The angle of internal friction and the cohesive strength were both determined in an undrained and unconsolidated test to be 15° and 9 kN m^{-2} respectively. The first analogue experiment was carried out using a divided metal table with the clay cake placed on it (Fig. 4a). One half of the table was moved downwards simulating subsidence of a basement block along a vertical fault. In the second experiment the fault inclination was modified to dip at 60°. The prescribed displacement velocity was 1.25×10^{-3} cm s^{-1} in both cases. In the third experiment the clay cake was placed half on a metal table and half on a rubber transport band (Fig. 4b). Extension of the basement and the clay cake was achieved by moving the rubber band at a velocity of 5×10^{-3} cm s^{-1}. Grinding paper attached to the transport band provided a good frictional contact between the extending basement and the clay.

Results

Subsidence of a basement block

Numerical models. The displacement field resulting from subsidence of a basement block is shown in Fig. 5a. In Fig. 5b the stress distribution at the elastic limit is given and the direction of the principle stresses is indicated. The angle β between the greatest principal stress σ_1 and the normals to the conjugate shear planes is $\beta = \mp 45 \pm \frac{1}{2}\varphi$. According to the stress distribution on Fig. 5b, the formation of convex-upward listric faults (McClay & Ellis

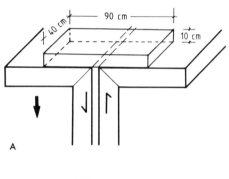

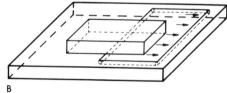

Fig. 4. Configuration of the clay cake experiments. (**a**) Divided metal table simulating a basement fault. It was used with a fault inclination of 90° and 60° respectively. (**b**) Table with a rubber transport band for horizontal extension tests.

1987) is expected. Fault nucleation is indicated by the contours of the ratio $G = \tan\varphi_{act}/\tan\varphi$ as shown in Fig. 5c. A contoured value of $G = 1.00$ defines the elastic limit of the material. $\tan\varphi_{act}$ corresponds to the actual differential stress (Fig. 6).

Analogue models. Fault formation under these boundary conditions in the analogue experiments is shown in Figs 7a & 7b. The propagation and orientation qualitatively agrees with the numerical results. First, a steeply inclined, linear

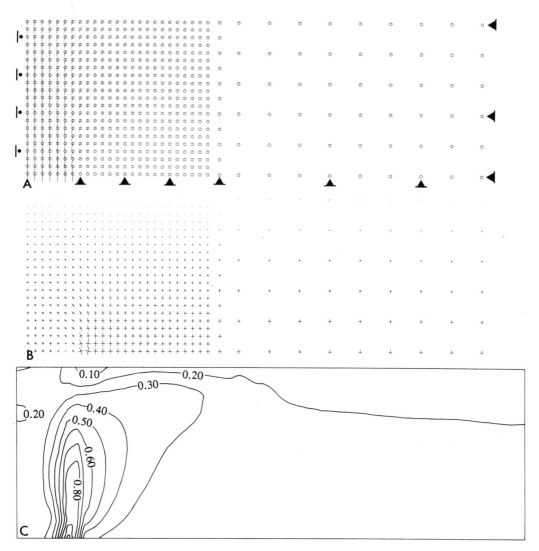

Fig. 5. Finite element model of a subsiding basement block. All plots refer to the stress state at the elastic limit. **(a)** Boundary conditions: triangles = fixed nodes, vertical bar/dot = vertical slip but zero lateral displacement. The displacement of the internal nodes is indicated by arrows. Stepwise increase of vertical subsidence of the basement block was driven by the lithostatic load. Maximum displacement at the bottom of the structure is 0.1 cm. Note the displacement discontinuity between node 7 and 8 on the bottom row. **(b)** Distribution of the principal stresses at the elastic limit. The length of the bars refers to the respective magnitude of the compressive stresses. As faults and shear fractures are inclined with 45 +/−φ/2 to the maximum compressive stress this stress distribution suggests the formation of a convex-upward fault. **(c)** Contours of the yield parameter G defined in the text indicate failure location at the bottom of the structure.

fault formed at the edge of the subsiding basement block (Fig. 7a). A curved shear fracture is visible to the lower left of the open tension crack. The uppermost tension cracks are connected by a shear fracture (arrow), suggesting, that fault propagation upwards was accomplished by the complex interplay of steeply inclined en echelon tension cracks which are linked in part by short shear fractures. The decrease in the inclination of the tension fractures (Fig. 7a) and also the orientation of the final fault (Fig. 7b) is consistent with the orientation of the principal stresses determined numerically (Fig. 5b). Similar fault geometries

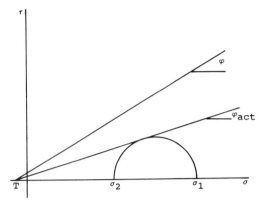

Fig. 6. The tangent to the Mohr circle representing the actual differential stress and going through T on the abscissa gives φ_{act}. The elastic limit is reached if this attains the value of the friction angle φ of the material. The yield parameter G is defined as: $G = \tan\varphi_{act}/\tan\varphi$.

were observed at the margin of downward-moving blocks in the sandbox experiments by Koopman *et al.* (1987).

Analogue experiments above a basement fault with an inclination of 60° were also performed (Fig. 8a). Faulting was again initiated at the bottom of the clay cake and the final fault (Fig. 8b) is only very gently curved. It is slightly steeper than the basement fault.

Horizontal extension of the basement

Numerical models. Two different finite element meshes were used to simulate extension above a planar detachment. In the STATAN-generated model the detachment boundary was within the fine part of the mesh (Fig. 1). Although the displacement field developed during progressive deformation is asymmetric (Fig. 9a), the dis-

Fig. 7. Clay model of a vertically subsiding basement block. The height of the clay cake is 10 cm. (**a**) Vertical displacement is 1.25 cm down to the left. At the base of the model the formation of open tension cracks and towards the left of it almost horizontal shear fractures can be observed. Note that different tension cracks are connected by shear segments (triangle). Moving upwards the tension cracks show a decrease in inclination. Deformed air bubbles on the clay surface indicate the strain in the surrounding of the fault. (**b**) Vertical displacement is 2 cm down to the left. The lower part of the fault has already experienced enough slip to smooth the surface whereas in the upper part the fault is still propagating through the material.

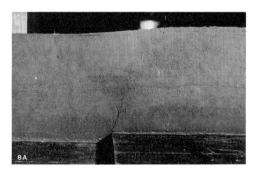
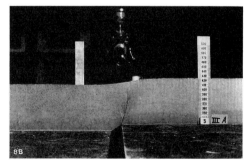

Fig. 8. Clay model with basement subsidence along a 60° inclined fault plane. (**a**) Displacement along the fault is 1.05 cm. Fault propagation is accomplished by the formation of tension cracks that are linked by curved fault segments (triangle). Small secondary fractures open in the hanging-wall which may be due to local irregularities in the developing surface. (**b**) Displacement along the fault is 1.65 cm. The fault plane is moderately curved in this cross section. The upper part fails dominantly in tension.

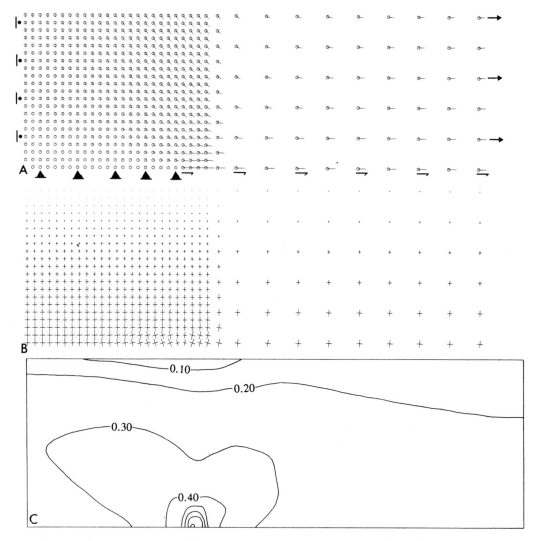

Fig. 9. Finite element model (STATAN) to simulate horizontal extension. All plots refer to a stress state at the elastic limit. (**a**) Boundary conditions triangles = fixed nodes, arrows = applied horizontal displacement (0.02 cm), vertical bars/dots = zero horizontal displacement but free vertical slip. Internal displacements are indicated by the vector centred on each node. The displacement field is asymmetric with respect to the boundary between the zero-slip and free-slip nodes at the base. This is in contrast to the stress distribution shown in (**b**) where the distribution of principal stresses suggests the formation of a steepening-upward listrict fault. (**c**) Contours of the failure parameter G indicate failure nucleation at the bottom of the structure.

tribution of principal stresses at failure is symmetric (Fig. 9b). Contours of the ratio G suggest that fault nucleation is likely to occur at the base of the structure (Fig. 9c).

In the second model (ADINA) a different mesh lay-out was used (Fig. 2). The left boundary was regarded as a plane of symmetry and the basal nodes were progressively displaced to the right. The deformed structure is magnified

and opposed to the original mesh in Fig. 2. The directions of the principal stresses at the elastic limit are shown in Fig. 10.

The stress distribution of Figs 9b & 10 are consistent with upwards steepening, listric faults. The asymmetric displacement field of Fig. 9a suggests the development of an asymmetric graben structure.

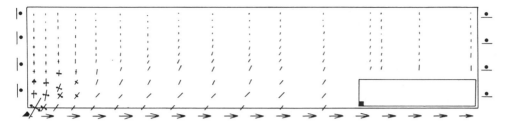

Fig. 10. Stress distribution due to extension above a detachment. Boundary conditions: triangle = fixed node, arrows = applied displacement, bars/dots = displacement is restricted to be parallel with the bar. The left boundary is fixed horizontally and taken as a plane of symmetry. Arrows indicate tensional stresses and bars compressive stresses. Curvature of the principal stresses is consistent with the formation of listric faults. The inserted diagram (bottom right) is taken from the bottom left corner of the model and shows the location of plastic failure at the point.

Analogue models. In the analogue models (Figs 11a, 11b & 12), the initial extension due to the sideward movement of the transport band was widely distributed at the bottom of the clay cake. An interfingering system of conjugate shear fractures and some tension gashes developed rapidly and almost contemporaneously at the bottom of the clay cake. Further development was asymmetric; a listric fault zone developed in the right-hand side, whereas as a broad zone of antithetic faulting developed on the left-hand side of the half-graben (Fig. 11a). The left flank of this half-graben can be regarded as a rollover, with extension accommodated by a closely-spaced array of linear shear fractures. These show an antithetic sense of shear with respect to the rotation of the hanging-wall. A similar set of small faults developed on the opposite side of the clay cake (Fig. 12). In this case, however, the broad antithetic zone developed on the other flank of the half-graben, demonstrating clearly that the transport direction of the rubber band does not predetermine the position and type of the different fault zones. Upward development of this zone was comprised by the nucleation of new faults, the broadening of the fault zone due to the propagation of individual antithetic faults, and the progressive rotation of the relatively older fault segments. The formation of the listric fault again included nucleation of en echelon cracks which coalesced to form a single fault plane. Fault displacement was distributed in a broad listric fault zone bounded by two master faults. Differing inclinations of the two master faults demonstrates clearly the varied options for fault propagation under these boundary conditions (Figs 9b & 10).

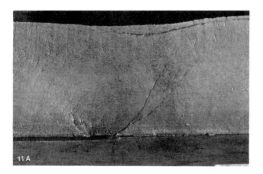

Fig. 11. Clay model of horizontal extension above a detachment. The height of the clay cake is 10 cm. The boundary between the table and the rubber transport band is indicated. (a) Horizontal displacement towards the left is 2.60 cm (7% extension). The initial extension is distributed in a system of conjugate fractures at the bottom of the clay cake. The formation of a listric fault zone is opposed to a broad zone of faults antithetic to the rotation of the rollover. Both fault zones propagate upwards, (b) Horizontal displacement towards the left is 3.60 cm (11% extension). The antithetic faults at the left flank of the structure fail in tension in the upper part.

Fig. 12. Opposite view of the clay cake. Horizontal displacement towards the right is 3.60 cm (11% extension). Instead of a listric fault zone a system of closely spaced antithetic faults developed and clearly dominates the propagating fault zone towards the top of the clay cake. This demonstrates that the position of the listric fault zone shown in Fig. 11 is not determined by the rubber band.

The different stages of fault development show that, although the whole fault is clearly curved, the master faults consist of linear segments of a definite length. Once the fault cuts the surface, subsequent slip contributes to form a smooth curvature (Fig. 13).

Along strike, a single fault consisted of different segments, as was also observed in the cross section. The listric fault zone shows strain localization on a few dominant surfaces, where-

Fig. 13. The upper surface of the clay cake shows, that the halfgraben is bounded by a listric fault zone with slip localized on a few fault planes. The dominating faults developed in the hanging-wall. Along strike the fault segments are linked by tilted and extended fault bounded blocks. This extension led to the formation of relatively younger faults orientated at high angles to the main faults. Corresponding with the broad fault zone on the opposite flank slip is widely distributed here in the hanging wall.

as in the downthrown flank of the half-graben strain is more evenly distributed over the broad zone of antithetic faults (Fig. 13).

Discussion

To investigate the influence of stress distribution on fault geometry, the boundary conditions that were imposed in the numerical and analogue models were chosen to be as general and simple as possible. The faults that formed in the clay cake experiments agreed qualitatively with the stress distributions calculated numerically. The agreement between the stress distribution in plastic deformation with that of an elastic solution has also been reported by Mandl (1988). Thus our analysis supports the idea, that the dominant stress reorientation is achieved before the elastic limit is reached.

For the formation of curved faults, it is critical that an appropriate stress field exists prior to failure. The material must therefore be able to sustain substantial shear strain before failing. This can be demonstrated with the Mohr circle (Fig. 14). Starting from an initial lithostatic stress state the supposition of a progressively increasing shear stress induces a reorientation of the principal stresses, and also an increase in the differential stress; ultimately the elastic limit of the material is reached. The amount of stress reorientation possible within the elastic range is thus limited by the angle of internal friction, the cohesive shear strength of the material, and the pore pressure. For example reduction of the cohesive shear strength influences strongly fault geometry under these boundary conditions. This is especially true for the low mean stresses that exist in analogue experiments (Fig. 14). Regarding this it is clear that in extension tests performed with sand, having a low cohesive shear strength fault curvature is usually very small (McClay et al. 1987) as opposed to the curvatures observed in clay cake experiments.

The existence of an appropriate stress field represents only one aspect of the formation of curved faults. Other factors controlling normal fault geometry not discussed here range from drastic rheological changes with depth to passive fault rotation induced by compaction and extension. However processes like gravity sliding (Crans et al. 1980; Vendeville, this volume) demonstrate the importance of the stress boundary conditions for the final fault geometry. Fault curvature is also enhanced because the propagation of normal faults near the surface is dominated by tensional failure (Fig. 8b); this has been observed in nature (Jackson & McKenzie 1983).

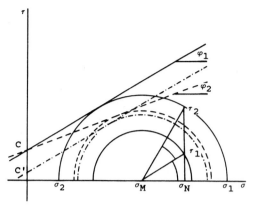

Fig. 14. The effect of superposing a shear stress on a pre-existing state of loading is clearly shown in a Mohr circle construction. Increasing the shear stress from τ_1 to τ_2 at a given normal stress σ_N results (a) in an increase in differential stress $(\sigma_1 - \sigma_2)/2$ and (b) a progressive reorientation of the principal stresses about an angle β. This process is limited by the strength of the material, by means of the Coulomb failure criterion. The dashed line and circle indicate a decrease of the friction angle and the corresponding stress limit. The dash-dotted line corresponds to a decrease in cohesive shear strength. It is clearly seen from this that under experimental conditions of generally low mean stresses σ_M a variation of the cohesion has a greater effect on the stress distribution at the elastic limit than a variation of the friction angle.

The numerical, and also the analogue experiments show that fault nucleation is located at the bottom; this was to be expected because of the displacement singularity developed at this point. As it was demonstrated in the clay cake experiments, the faults propagated towards the top of the structure. The propagation process included the complex interplay of numerous cracks that finally linked up to form a single fault plane. The critical zone in front of the fault, where these cracks were formed, enlarged with increasing fault length and the cracks were aligned in an en echelon manner. No consistent predominance of a specific crack mode could be observed. Instead, an almost contemporaneous development of shear and tension cracks reminiscent of the sliding crack first studied by Brace & Bombolakis (1963) could be recognized.

Conclusions

(1) Comparison of numerical and analogue models shows clearly that the stress distribution at the beginning of plastic deformation determines the fault geometry up to a considerable finite extension.

(2) The displacement boundary conditions determine the stress distribution, the location where failure first occurs and the fault orientation and geometry.

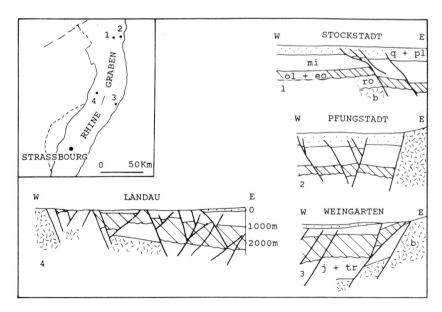

Fig. 15. Basement-involved faulting in the Rhine graben. The sections show examples of the border fault zones with a clear predominance of planar faults that affect the sedimentary cover and in part the basement. From BEB (1985).

(3) The amount of stress reorientation depends on the strength of the material and the pore pressure.

(4) The boundary conditions chosen for our models can be compared to natural examples which is of course not possible for the deformation mechanisms involved. Figure 15 shows an example of basement involved faulting from the Rhine graben. Here the faults that limit subsiding basement blocks show a predominantly planar development. This seems also to be true for the western and eastern border faults of the graben, although it is not clear what these faults are like at greater depth. However, extension of the sedimentary cover was probably accomplished by planar faulting. This structural setting can be compared to the first set of numerical and analogue models in which the effect of a subsiding basement block was simulated.

Examples of gravity-driven and salt-detached faults are shown in Figs 16 & 17, respectively.

The slightly inclined, nearly horizontal detachments may cause a reorientation of the stress field that can result in the formation of listric faults, as was shown in the second set of our models above. However if an appropriate stress distribution does not exist a priori, it is critical for the formation of curved faults that the affected material can sustain a significant amount of shear strain prior to failure, in order to allow for stress reorientation.

Considerable damage is done to the rock prior to faulting, and therefore the final fault geometry will vary to some extent. Thus, constraining fault geometry is not only limit by the amount of data actually available but also by the width of the area affected by deformation. Isolating and investigating the different factors controlling fault curvature of which we mentioned but an important few may gain us more insight into fault development, rather than relying on geometric−kinematic considerations.

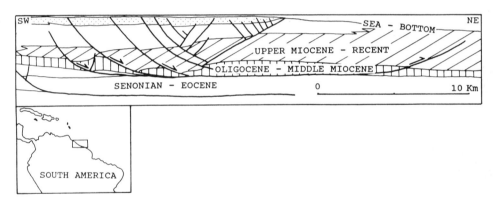

Fig. 16. Gravity sliding in the Guyana Basin offshore NE S. America. Synsedimentary listric faults developed in the younger sediments at the slope above a basal detachment. From Veeken (1983).

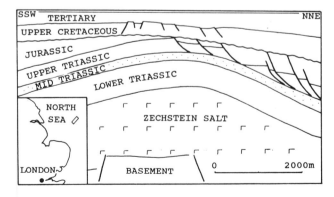

Fig. 17. Listric faulting on the side of a salt pillow. The cross section shows a Zechstein pillow in the southern North Sea (from Owen & Naylor 1983). Late Jurassic halokinesis initiated faulting of the overlying sediments. The faults flatten in a decollement in mid-Upper Triassic halites.

We thank H. Schwarz (Ruhr-Universitaet, Bochum) for use of the laboratory and U. Arslan, A. Roberts, M. Casey and G. Lloyd for their constructive comments. J. Fredrich kindly·polished our English.

References

ADINA 1983. *Automatic dynamic incremental non-linear analysis*. Adina Engng. Inc., Watertown, Mass.

BEB 1985. *Erdoelgeologische Exkursion in den Rheingraben*. Excursion notes, 22.

BRACE, W. F. & BOMBOLAKIS, E. G. 1963. A note on brittle crack growth in compression. *Journal of Geophysical Research*, **68**, 3709–3713.

CRANS, W., MANDL, G. & HAREMBOURE, J. 1980. On the theory of growth faulting. A geomechanical delta model based on gravity sliding. *Journal of Petroleum Geology*, **2**, 265–307.

DRUCKER, D. C. & PRAGER, W. 1952. Soil mechanics and plastic analysis of limit design. *Quarterly Journal of Applied Mathematics*, **10**, 157–165.

JACKSON, J. A. & McKENZIE, D. 1983. The geometrical evolution of normal fault systems. *Journal of Structural Geology*, **5**, 471–482.

KOOPMAN, A., SPEKSNIJDER, A. & HORSFIELD, W. T. 1987. Sandbox model studies of inversion tectonics. *Tectonophysics*, **137**, 379–388.

MANDL, G. 1988. *Mechanics of tectonic faulting*. Elsevier, Amsterdam.

McCLAY, K. R. & ELLIS, P. G. 1987. Analogue models of extensional fault geometries. In: COWARD, M. P., DEWEY, J. F. & HANCOCK, P.C. (eds.) *Continental Extensional Tectonics*. Geological Society, London, Special Publication, **28**, 109–125.

OWEN, P. G. & NAYLOR, N. G. 1983. A salt pillow structure in the southern North Sea. *In*: BALLY, A.W. (ed). *Seismic Expression of Structural Styles*. American Association of Petroleum Geologists, Studies in Geology series, Vol. 2, 2.3.3.1–3.

SHELTON, J. W. 1984. Listric normal faults: An illustrated summary. *American Association of Petroleum Geologists Bulletin*, **68**, 801–815.

STATAN 15 Version Bodenmechanik 1980. TH Darmstadt.

VEEKEN, P. C. H. 1983. Guyana Basin, Offshore Northeast South America. *In*: BALLY, A. W. (ed). *Seismic Expressions of Structural Styles*. American Association of Petroleum Geologists, Studies in Geology series, Vol. 2, 2.3.2.7–10.

VENDEVILLE, B. This volume. Mechanisms generating fault curvature: a review illustrated by physical models.

WALTERS, J. V. & THOMAS, J. N. 1982. Shear zone development in granular materials. *Proceedings of the 4th International Conference on Numerical Methods in Geomechanics*, 263–273.

YIELDING, G., BADLEY, M. & FREEMAN, B. This volume. Seismic reflections from normal faults in the Northern North Sea.

Normal fault geometry and fault reactivation in tectonic inversion experiments

ROBERT W. KRANTZ *

Laboratoire de Tectonique, Universite de Rennes, 35042 Rennes, France

Abstract: Scaled physical models of extensional structures associated with fault reactivation were achieved in sand by superimposing extensional tectonics on thrust faults created during prior episodes of horizontal shortening. The extension produced three distinct responses: selective reactivation of pre-existing thrusts, favouring the steepest thrusts and those dipping more than a critical value; development of new normal faults that were linked to or developed within the zone of thrust faults; or generation of new normal faults in previously unfaulted domains. Linked normal faults showed a wide range of orientations and most dipped less steeply than the unlinked faults, which had dips clustered about the value predicted from the internal friction coefficient of sand. During extension of a distributed fault model, reactivation of existing thrusts influenced the location, dip direction, and dip magnitude of linked normal fualts. Compared to natural fault systems, the models showed many geometric similarities especially regarding linked normal faults.

Tectonic inversion occurs when regions that have undergone subsidence are transformed into uplifts (positve inversion) or when uplifted regions are subject to subsidence (negative inversion) (Gillcrist *et al.* 1987). Commonly, positive inversion is achieved when extensional tectonics are followed by compressional tectonics. Conversely, negative inversion often results when compressional tectonics give way to extensional tectonics.

Thus inversion tectonics often superimpose structures of contrasting dynamics. In the case of faults, those produced in the initial stage are present during the inversion stage, and may influence further structural development. Pre-existing faults are surfaces or zones of weakness, with mechanical properties different from surrounding intact material. Under favourable conditions faults may reactivate (Brun & Choukroune 1983; Etheridge 1986). During inversion tectonics, this reactivation may be in the sense opposite to that of the original fault development. Specifically, during negative inversion, thrust faults may be reactivated as normal faults. Even where not reactivated, older structures may control the location and geometry of new faults.

The purpose of this paper is to discuss the geometry of normal faults observed in experimental models of extension superimposed on previously shortened and thrust-faulted media.

These include both reactivated thrust faults and newly developed normal faults. Mechanical theory suggests that the probability of reactivation of a fault depends on its orientation with respect to the superimposed stresses (Bott 1959; Jaeger 1960; Sibson 1985). In order to investigate the relationship of thrust orientation to reactivation and normal fault development, an initial series of experiments included progressively steeper thrust dips prior to extension. A final experiment investigated extensional structures developed in a distributed fault system, and is probably more analogous to the real world.

Experimental procedure

The key to successful and meaningful modelling of earth processes lies in the proper scaling of model parameters with respect to the real world (Hubbert 1937). Model materials must not only mimic natural geometries but must have scaled mechanical properties.

Quartz sand is a common analogue for brittle rocks in laboratory modelling (Hubbert 1951; Koopman *et al.* 1987). Dry sand exhibits elastic-frictional plastic behaviour, and geometry of structures is independent of strain rate. When densely packed, sand has coefficients of internal and sliding friction similar to rock, which results in appropriate fault geometries. Shear testing of dense sand (Krantz 1990) has determined a small value of cohesion at the proper scale for modelling fault processes in the upper 1 to 10 km of the crust. Together, the friction and cohesion parameters can be used to

---

* Current address: ARCO Oil and Gas Company, Exploration Reseach, 2300 West Plano Parkway, Plano, Texas 75075, USA.

From ROBERTS A. M., YIELDING, G. & FREEMAN, B. (eds), 1991, *The Geometry of Normal Faults*, Geological Society Special Publication No 56, pp 219–229

construct Mohr envelopes for initiation and reactivation of faulting in sand (Fig. 1). These envelopes predict that new normal faults should dip about 67° and that extensional reactivation of reverse faults should be restricted to faults dipping 40° or more.

The model apparatus for the initial series consists of a 35 cm wide box with a moving end wall and attached basal plate (Fig. 2). The length of the box can vary from 20 to 60 cm. The basal plate creates a velocity discontinuity at the bottom of the sand pile, where most fault structures root. The glass side walls were treated with Rain-X, a commercial product designed to treat automobile windshields. This treatment successfully minimized frictional boundary effects between the glass and the sand as demonstrated by straight fault scarps and absence of blurring of markers. The moving end wall and basal plate were attached to a horizontal screw jack, driven by a motor with electronic speed control. Since the width of the box was constant, deformation was essentially plane strain.

The experimental procedure for the initial series was as follows:

(1) initial sedimentation to a uniform depth with the box horizontal to a uniform depth, including passive marker layers of dyed sand;

(2) 5 cm of shortening with the box horizontal, typically producing one or more forethrusts and a conjugate backthrust all rooted at the basal velocity discontinuity;

(3) tilting of the box towards the 'hinterland' by various degrees (0 to 20°, by 5° increments for successive experiments) to progressively increase the dip of the forethrusts;

(4) erosion of the thrust belt and central popup to the new horizontal by vacuum;

(5) additional sedimentation with horizontal marker layers;

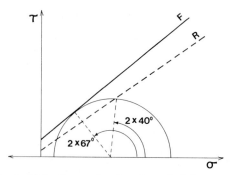

Fig. 1. Mohr diagram for densely-packed dry quartz sand based on the data from Krantz (1990). The failure and reactivation (sliding) envelopes are designated F and R, respectively. Using principal stress levels appropriate for the depths of sand used in the models (5−15 cm), the diagram predicts that the limit for reactivation of existing faults is those dipping no less than 40° and that new normal faults should dip 67°.

(6) 5 cm of extension with the box tilted, along with localized sedimentation to maintain the horizontal upper surface.

Photographs taken through the side walls and of the top surface at regular intervals recorded the development of the fault structures.

The final experiment used a similar apparatus but with a rubber base attached to the end walls, both of which are free to move in or out. With the uniformly stretching rubber base there is no velocity discontinuity. Scissor-like accordian rails on either side of the box maintain a constant width for the rubber sheet so that the deformation is again plane strain. For the final experiment, initial horizontal shortening produced a distributed system of reverse faults. Additional sedimentation without erosion

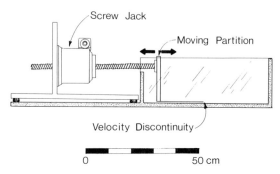

Fig. 2. Drawing of model apparatus used for the initial series. The sand model is deformed in the box on the right-hand side formed by the fixed end wall and glass side walls. The moving end wall and attached basal plate are connected to the horizontal screw jack, which in turn is driven by an electronic motor (not shown).

created a horizontal layer of unfaulted material above the faults. The model was then extended to its original length. Photographs again recorded the development of the model as seen at the top surface and through the glass side walls.

Results from the initial series

Figures 3–7 present the results of the five inversion experiments in this series. The figures include tracings of photographs of the intermediate stage (after shortening, tilting, erosion, and sedimentation but prior to extension) and the final stage for each model, all drawn to the same scale. The basal inclination is equal to the tilt of the box. Faults are shown as solid heavy lines, except for non-reactivated thrusts in the final stage shown as dashed lines. The numbers refer to the sequence of development of the fault during each stage of deformation. Reactivated faults are identified with an 'R'.

For all the experiments, the initial shortening phase produced conjugate reverse faults dipping

25 to 30° with the box horizontal. The number and precise geometry of forethrusts depended on the depth of the sand pack; thicker sand inhibited the development of multiple forethrusts producing fault splays that merged updip. Thrust dips less than 25° (as seen on some of the dip histograms) are from back thrusts rotated toward the horizontal.

All of the experiments in the series also developed normal faults during the extension phase. Where existing thrusts were reactivated, normal slip was commonly transferred to new normal faults linked to the reactivated fault. Examples of linked faults will be described below. Even where existing reverse faults where not visibly reactivated, normal faults that developed within the thrusted domains displayed unexpected geometries, especially in terms of dip. On the dip histograms, these normal faults from within the thrusted domains have been grouped with the linked faults. Finally, all experiments displayed steeply dipping normal faults that did not link to reactivated thrusts or

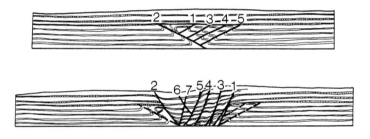

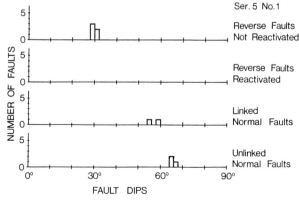

Fig. 3. Model with 0° tilt. Tracings of photos of intermediate stage (after shortening, erosion to horizontal, and addition of new sediment) and final stage (after extension). Key to fault types: solid heavy lines are faults active during that phase of deformation; dashed lines are existing faults not reactivated. Numbers refer to order of fault development. 'R' indicates reactivated fault. Final length of model is 38 cm. Histogram shows distribution of fault dips according to fault type. No reverse faults were reactivated in this model.

develop within thrust fault zones. Commonly, this last type of normal fault did develop during the late stages of extension and in previously unfaulted domains. These are listed as unlinked normal faults on the histograms.

Figure 3 shows the results from the experiment with no tilting, that is the model was horizontal for both shortening and extension. During the extension phase, none of the thrust faults were visibly reactivated. Extension produced a set of simple conjugate normal faults. The two splays of normal fault No 1, however, developed within the zone of existing thrusts, and dipped 8 to 10° less than normal faults developed in previously unfaulted terrane. The two splays of fault No 1 appear as linked normal faults on the histogram of fault dips. The unlinked faults had dips in the range of 65 to 68°, as was predicted from the friction coefficient for dense sand (see Fig. 1).

Beginning with Fig. 4, an increment of tilt was introduced before the extension phase. For the model with 5° tilt, the thrust with the steepest dip (38°, thrust No 5) showed a small amount of normal-slip reactivation early during the exten-

sion. Other thrusts with slightly shallower dips were not reactivated. True linked normal faults developed as the normal slip of the reactivated thrust was projected up up-dip into the layer of sediment added after the shortening phase. The linked splays of normal fault No 1, along with normal fault No 3, which developed in the thrust zone, had dips about 10° less than the unlinked faults (normal faults Nos 4–7).

Figure 5 shows the model with 10° tilting, which included more significant reactivation. Thrust No 1 and a portion of thrust No 3, dipping 40 to 42°, were strongly reactivated with normal slip, while thrusts dipping 38 to 40° had no visible reactivation. Linked normal faults (the various splays of normal fault No 2) dipped less than unlinked faults, including one linked segment that dipped only 37°.

Results from the model with 15° of tilt are given in Fig. 6. During the extension phase, thrust faults Nos 3 and 4, dipping 43 to 50°, were selectively reactivated while those dipping 40 to 43° were not. Linked normal faults (normal faults Nos 1 and 3) showed a range of dips, mostly less than unlinked faults. One of the

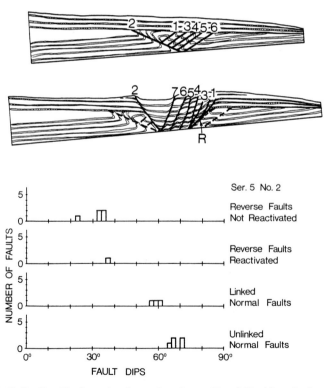

Fig. 4. Model with 5° tilt. (See Fig. 3 caption for explanation and key.) Final length of model is 38 cm. Thrust No 5 was reactivated at depth and is linked to the two splays of normal fault No 1.

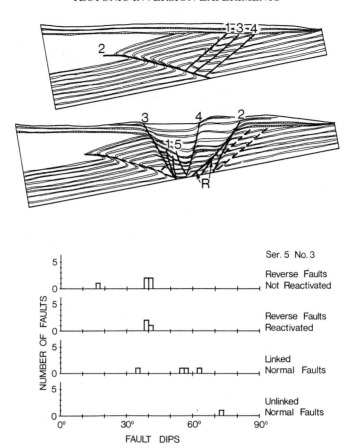

Fig. 5. Model with 10° tilt. (See Fig. 3 caption for explanation and key.) Final length of model is 38 cm. Nearly all of thrust No 1 and part of thrust No 2 were reactivated with normal slip. Normal fault No 2 developed linked to the reactivated thrusts.

linked faults (No 3) merged with a reactivated thrust to form a long-lived listric fault, with a resulting asymmetric basin with layers of syn-extension sediments thicker toward the right side. The unlinked faults (Nos 5 and 6) display steeper dips, and along with the conjugate faults dipping to the right, define a symmetry with vertical and horizontal axes. This symmetry supports the assumption that the principal stress directions are vertical and horizontal, despite the inclination of the model floor.

The final model in this series, with 20° of tilt, is shown in Fig. 7. All of the thrust faults, with dips in the range of 42 to 53°, were reactivated with normal slip. (The original backthrust, rotated to a dip of only 4°, was not of course.) The reactivation on these faults was the largest magnitude of any of the models. Linked normal faults (No 3) developed late in the extension phase, and had dips mostly less than the un-

linked faults, except for fault No 1. This one steep linked fault is a precursor fault (Koopman *et al* 1987) and is an artifact of fault processes in sand during the initial stage of extension.

Interpretation of the initial series

The response to extensional inversion observed in the experiments can be characterized by three distinct fault mechanisms: reactivation of original reverse faults with normal slip, development of new normal faults linked to reverse faults or within the zone of existing thrusts, and development of new normal faults in previously-unfaulted domains.

Reactivation occurs where original reverse faults show a decrease or reversal of sense of slip to become normal faults. Commonly, small increments of reactivation are revealed only by normal offset of the overlying sand layers added

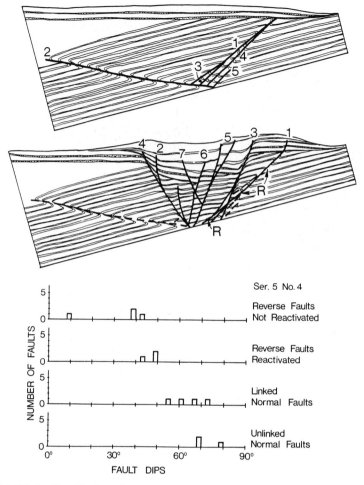

Fig. 6. Model with 15° tilt. (See Fig. 3 caption for explanation and key.) Final length of model is 37 cm. All or part of thrusts Nos 1, 3 & 4 were reactivated with normal slip. Normal faults Nos 1 and 3 were linked to the reactivated thrusts, the latter forming a listric normal fault with the thrust at depth.

before extension. Reactivation may be selective in space, ranging from a short segment of the original fault (Fig. 4, reverse fault No 5) to the entire fault (Fig. 7, reverse fault No 1). It may also be selective in time, and is generally more favoured during the early stages of inversion (Fig. 5), although it may persist for longer intervals (Fig. 7). As seen on the summary histogram of fault dips (Fig. 8), the probability of reactivation is largely a function of the dip of the pre-existing faults. For this experimental series, faults dipping less than about 40° were not likely to reactivate, while those dipping more than about 40° were very likely to re-activate. This limiting value matches the pre-dicted value obtained from the reactivation envelope for sand (Fig. 1). In the three models

with partial reactivation, only the steepest thrusts were selectively inverted.

During the extension phase all experiments developed new normal faults within the zone of existing thrusts or somehow linked to reverse faults reactivated with normal slip. Linked normal faults may be the updip extensions of reactivated reverse faults (Figs 3–6) or may connect reactivated segments of reverse faults (Fig. 6). As seen on the summary histogram of fault dips, these linked normal faults show a wide range of orientations with both mean and mode significantly less than the unlinked faults. Most linked normal faults had dips intermediate between reactivated reverse faults and new, unlinked normal faults.

The final stages of all experiments were

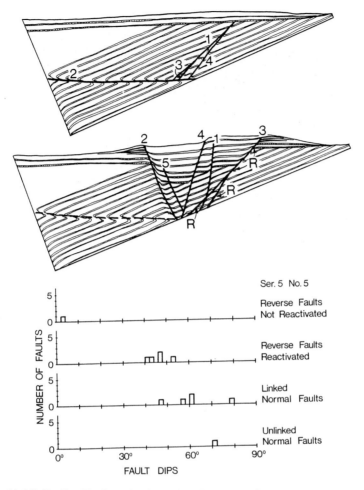

Fig. 7. Model with 20° tilt. (See Fig. 3 caption for explanation and key.) Final length of model is 45 cm. Thrusts Nos 1, 3 and 4 were completely reactivated with normal slip. The reactivated thrust faults and the linked normal fault No 3 comprised a long-lived normal slip structure that accounts for much of the extensional strain in the model.

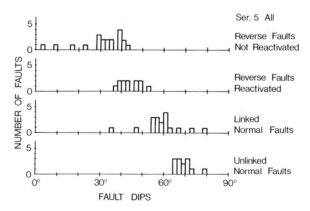

Fig. 8. Summary histogram of fault dip distribution according to fault type for all models combined. The data suggest that the limit for reactivation is about 40°. Unlinked normal faults display a mean dip of about 68°.

226   R.W. KRANTZ

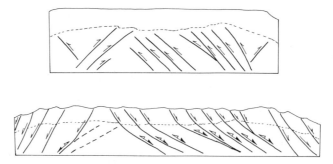

Fig. 9. The distributed fault model. Tracings of photographs of the intermediate stage (after shortening and addition of new sediment above dashed line; and final stage (after extension). Arrows show sense of slip on the faults; double-headed arrows indicate reverse faults reactivated with normal slip. Heavy dashed lines in the final stage are reverse faults not reactivated. Final length of the model is 21 cm. In the final stage, all normal faults, except those attributed to boundary effects at the model ends, are linked to reactivated thrusts.

characterized by the development of new normal faults in previously unfaulted domains. These normal faults show a narrow range of orientations with a mean dip (67°) identical to that predicted for faulting in dense sand (see Fig. 1). New normal faults conjugate to the unlinked faults showed equally steep dips; planes bisecting the conjugate pairs were near-vertical as expected.

Distributed fault system model

Figure 9 shows the results of the model using the rubber-based apparatus. During the initial shortening stage, the uniform contraction of the rubber base generated a system of reverse faults across the model. Unlike the models in the initial discussed above, individual thrusts in the distributed faulting model revealed little displacement, but underwent significant rotations with progressive shortening. Thus faults generated at original dips of 25–30° were rotated to steep dips up to about 60°. In addition, faults developed simultaneously rather than in any particular sequence.

During the extensional phase, nearly all of the existing reverse faults were reactivated with normal slip. One thrust was partially reactivated (only the deeper portion) and one thrust was not visibly reactivated. Each reactivated thrust projects updip into the post-shortening, pre-extension sediment as a linked normal fault. These linked faults dip less steeply than ideal normal faults (65–70°) and, except for faults near the ends of the model that are due to boundary effects, are the only normal faults developed during the extensional phase. Thus the location, dip direction, and probably dip magnitude of the normal faults in the overlying

sediment are functions of the reactivated reverse faults below. Although sediment was not added during the extension of this model, the location of basins in the hanging wall of each normal fault would also have been influenced by the existing thrusts.

Comparison to natural examples

Several examples of extensional systems have been intrerpreted as containing reverse faults reactivated with normal slip. Perhaps the best known is the fault system in the continental shelf north of Scotland. Figure 10 shows the interpretations of the MOIST profile (Brewer & Smythe 1984) and DRUM (Cheadle et al. 1987). Both of these interpretations show similarities to the distributed fault model including normal fault location and dip direction corresponding to partially or completely reactivated reverse faults at depth and linked normal faults which dip more steeply than the thrusts but at moderate to low angles. Brewer & Smythe (1984) suggest that faults probably underwent rotations during progressive deformation. Cheadle et al. (1987) also make the point that in western UK continental shelf, sedimentary basin location may be a function of pre-existing thrust systems that have perhaps localized extension and subsidence due to reactivation. Brewer & Smythe (1986) draw the same conclusion for some of the basins on the Hebridean shelf.

The generalized cross sections of Chapman (1989) for the Melville sub-basin of the Western Approaches basin, southwest UK (Fig. 11) show relationships of reactivation of a pre-existing thrust zone (the Variscan zone) to the development of linked normal faults. The geometry is

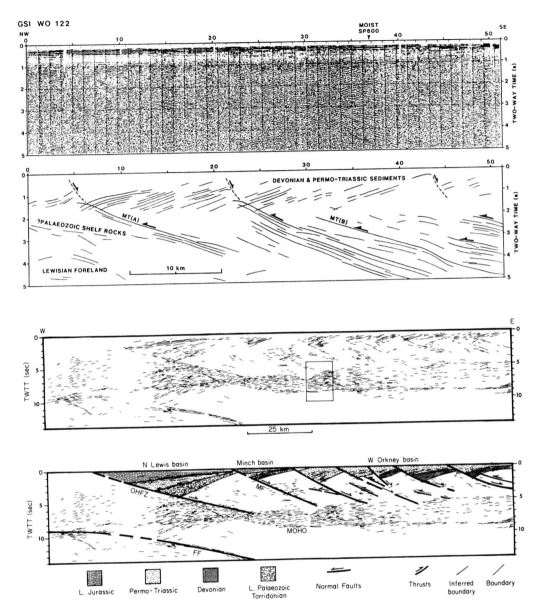

Fig. 10. Interpretations of the MOIST seismic profile from Brewer & Smythe (1984) and the DRUM seismic profile from Cheadle *et al.* (1987), both from the continental shelf north of Scotland. The interpretations show normal faults linked to reverse faults at depth suggested to be reactivated with normal slip. Compare to Fig. 9

similar to the experiment shown in Fig. 6, especially the listric nature of normal fault No 3 as it joins the reactivated thrust at depth. His developmental sequence also suggests that thrust reactivation can be both partial in space, and repeated in time, behaviour seen in several experiments. The interpretation of SWAT 6 and 7 from the Western Approaches by Cheadle *et al.* (1987) also suggests normal faults linked

to reactivated thrust structure at depth.

Finally, both the cross section and tectonic development for the southern Apennines of central Italy by Endigoux *et al.* (1989) (Fig. 12) suggest that late stage extension superimposed on thrust structures produced normal slip reactivation of selected thrusts and associated linked normal faults .

N   S

PERMIAN–LOWER TRIASSIC

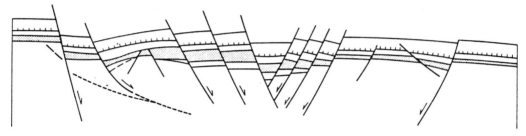

LATE JURASSIC–EARLY CRETACEOUS

Fig. 11. Generalized cross sections from the evolutionary sequence of the Melville sub-basin of the Western Approached basin, southwestern UK from Chapman (1989). Listric normal faults are shown linked to the Variscan thrust zone, interpreted to be reactivated with normal slip during different episodes of extensional deformation. Compare to Fig. 6.

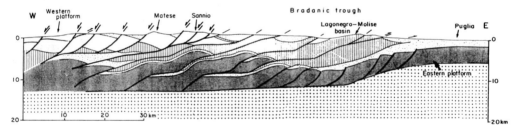

Fig. 12. Geological cross section for the southern (Apennines) of central Italy from Endignoux *et al.* (1989) showing listric normal faults linked to reactivated thrust structures.

Conclusions

Experimental models have successfully demonstrated three distinct negative inversion mechanisms. These are normal-slip reactivation of pre-existing thrust faults, generation of new normal faults linked to pre-existing thrusts, whether reactivated or not, and development of new unlinked normal faults in previously unfaulted domains. Thrust reactivation is favoured on pre-existing faults that dip steeper than a certain critical value; reactivation is also favoured on the steepest thrust in any one ex-

periment. Thus reactivation of very low-angle thrusts as normal faults should be considered unlikely, and reactivation should be expected on portions of thrusts with steeper dips (ramps). Such geometry has been suggested for the Lewis thrust of western Montana, where a listric normal fault has been generated above a ramp during extensional reactivation of the thrust. Royse (1983) reported similar features from the fold and thrust belt of Utah, Wyoming, and Idaho.

Linked normal faults show a wide range of orientations but generally dip less steeply than unlinked faults. Rotations of faults within distributed fault systems can obscure the original orientations and makes mechanical interpretations based on present-day dips difficult. Nevertheless, the location of linked normal faults and associated hanging-wall basins, and the dip directions can be strongly influenced by preexisting underlying thrusts.

This project was funded by Societe Nationale Elf Aquitaine. I would like to thank Jean-Pierre Brun and the Universite de Rennes for the opportunity to work with the physical modelling laboratory. Jean-Jaques Kermarrec helped with model construction and operation. Constructive reviews by Bill Horsfield of Shell, Alan Roberts of Badley, Ashton & Associates and an anonymous reviewer are greatfully acknowledged.

References

Bott, M. H. P. 1959. The mechanics of oblique slip faulting. *Geology Magazine*, **96**, 109–117.

Brewer, J. A. & Smythe, D. K. 1984. MOIST and the continuity of crustal reflector geometry along the Caledonian–Appalachian orogen. *Journal of the Geological Society of London*, **141**, 105–120.

—— & —— 1986. Deep structure of the foreland to the Caledonian orogen, NW Scotland: results of the BIRPS WINCH profile. *Tectonics*, **5**, 171–194.

Brun, J.-P. & Choukroune, P. 1983. Normal faulting, block tilting, and decollement in a stretched crust. *Tectonics*, **2**, 345–356.

Chapman, T. J. 1989. The Permian to Cretaceous structural evolution of the Western Approaches basin (Melville sub-basin), UK *In*: Cooper, M. A. & Williams, G. D. (eds) *Inversion Tectonics*, Geological Society, London, Special Publication **44**, 177–200.

Cheadle, M. J., McGreary, S., Warner, M. R. & Matthews, D. H. 1987. Extensional structures on the western UK continental shelf: a review of evidence from deep seismic profiling *In*: Coward, M. P., Dewey, J. F. & Hancock, P. L. (eds) *Continental Extensional Tectonics*, Geological Society, London, Special Publication **28**, 445–465.

Endigoux, L., Moretti, I. & Roure, F. 1989. Forward modeling of the southern Apennines. *Tectonics*, **8**, 1095–1104.

Etheridge, M. A. 1986. On the reactivation of extensional fault systems. *Philosophical Transactions of the Royal Society of London*, **317**, 179–194.

Gillcrist, R., Coward, M. & Mugnier, J.-L. 1987, Structural inversion and its controls: examples from the Alpine foreland and the French Alps: *Geodinamica Acta*, **1**, 5–34.

Hubbert, M. K. 1937. Theory of scale models as applied to the study of geologic structures. *Geological Society of America Bulletin*, **48**, 1459–1520.

—— 1951. Mechanical basis for certain familiar geologic structures. *Geological Society of America Bulletin*, **62**, 355–372.

Jaeger, J. C. 1960. Shear failure of anisotropic rock. *Geology Magazine*, **97**, 6–72.

Koopman, A., Speksnijder, A. & Horsfield, W. T. 1987. Sandbox models of inversion tectonics. *Tectonophysics*, **137**, 379–388.

Krantz, R. W. 1990. Measurements of friction coefficients and cohesion for faulting and fault reactivation in laboratory models using sand and sand mixtures. *Tectonophysics*, in press.

Powell, C. M., Williams, G. D. & Seago, R. D. 1988. Using pre-existing cleavage to define extensional fault geometries: an example from Glacier National Park, Montana. *Geology*, **16**, 878–880.

Royse, F. 1983. Extensional faults and folds in the foreland thrust belt, Utah, Wyoming, and Idaho (abs.). *Geological Society of America Abstracts with Programs*, **15**, 295.

Sibson, R. H. 1985. A note on fault reactivation. *Journal of Structural Geology*, **7**, 751–754.

Physical and seismic modelling of listric normal fault geometries

K. R. McCLAY, D. A. WALTHAM, A. D. SCOTT & A. ABOUSETTA

Department of Geology, Royal Holloway and Bedford New College,
University of London, Egham, Surrey TW20 0EX, UK

Abstract: Scaled analogue models of listric fault systems display a characteristic rollover anticline and crestal collapse graben features. Faults nucleate in sequence into the hangingwalls of the crestal collapse graben and towards the footwall of the master fault. Superposition of crestal collapse grabens produces complex fault arrays. When the basal detachment surface is tilted a characteristic panel of unfaulted synfault stratigraphy forms adjacent to the detachment. These experiments produce structures with close similarities to listric growth fault systems on prograding delta slopes. Synthetic seismic sections of the experimental models have been produced using Kirchhoff integral techniques. These illustrate the complexities in trying to image complex structures in listric fault systems but also show good agreement with natural seismic examples.

The nature of extensional fault systems in the brittle upper crust has been the focus of recent heated debate between those in favour of major planar fault systems (e.g. Jackson 1987; Roberts & Jackson, this volume) and those in favour of major deformation on listric fault systems (e.g. Gibbs 1983). In this paper we focus solely upon listric fault systems which are particularly characteristic of prograding delta systems (e.g. Bruce 1973; Ellenor 1984; Bally *et al.* 1981; Shelton 1984). In these environments many faults show characteristic listric shapes even after depth conversion and decompaction, and are the result of progressive growth. The listric shape is kinematically likely for these faults (Ellis & McClay 1988; Vendeville & Cobbold 1988).

Scaled analogue models have provided dramatic new insights into the geometries and progressive evolution of extensional fault systems (McClay & Ellis 1987; Ellis & McClay 1988; McClay 1990; Vendeville & Cobbold 1988). In particular, the analogue modelling technique has so far focussed upon the sequences of faulting, fault geometries, and fault block shapes in the hangingwalls of extensional faults (Ellis & McClay 1988; McClay 1990). Ellis & McClay (1988) documented in detail the fundamental fault geometries within the hangingwalls of listric extensional fault systems in sandbox models. These results and those of more advanced experiments were compared with the seismic expressions of natural extensional fault systems by McClay (1990). In this paper, however, we present the first results of seismic simulations which use geometric templates generated from two listric analogue models. The simulated sections are compared

with real data from a seismic reflection survey from the NW coast of the Gulf of Mexico, which is the best documented example of a listric growth fault regime.

Experimental method

The experimental programme of sandbox modelling was carried out in a modification of the deformation rig described by Ellis & McClay (1988) (Fig. 1a). The dimensions of the apparatus are 150 cm × 20 cm × 20 cm with listric fault models typically having initial dimensions of 35 cm × 20 cm × 10 cm. The deformation apparatus used for the experiments is shown in Fig. 1b. It consists of a rigid, listric footwall block with a movable plastic sheet draped over it and attached to the moving wall. The experimental method is described in detail in Ellis & McClay (1988) and the reader is referred to that paper for details.

Two types of footwall block were used; one in which the listric fault soles out on a horizontal detachment, and one in which the basal detachment is dipping at 10° in the direction of extension. The latter style of model fault geometry has not been described before. Each experiment was repeated several times and identical structural styles were produced.

In the experiments described in this paper, we used homogeneous, 300 μm grain size sand packs to simulate brittle deformation of the upper crust. Hubbert (1937, 1951), Horsfield (1977), Naylor *et al.* (1986) and Ellis & McClay (1988) have all discussed scaling of analogue model experiments. They conclude that cohesionless sand models simulate the deformation of brittle sedimentary sequences which

From ROBERTS A. M., YIELDING, G. & FREEMAN, B. (eds), 1991, *The Geometry of Normal Faults,*
Geological Society Special Publication No 56, pp 231–239

(a)

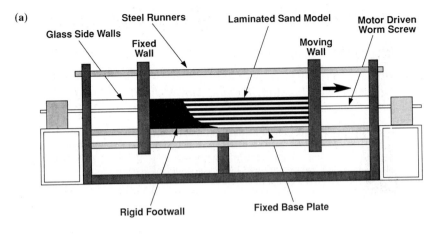

(b)

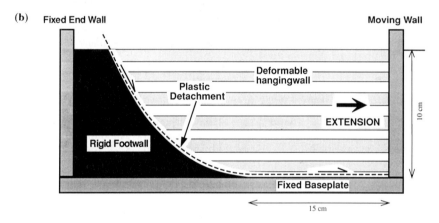

Fig. 1. (**a**) Schematic diagram of the deformation apparatus. Various basal geometries may be added to the base of the sand model. The configuration shown is for a simple listric fault with a horizontal detachment. (**b**) Detail of the experimental configuration for a simple listric fault experiment.

have a Navier−Coulomb criterion of failure. In these experiments, sand models have model to prototype ratios of 10^{-4} to 10^{-5}. This translates to a 10 cm thick model simulating the behaviour of sedimentary sequence between 1 and 10 km thick.

The models described in this paper have limitations in that the footwall is rigid and does not deform, whereas in some natural fault systems isostatic footwall uplift may be expected. In addition, the geometry of the experiment set-up forces constant displacement on the sole-fault, whereas in natural fault systems variations would be expected (Williams & Vann 1987; Wheeler 1987).

Experimental results

Simple listric fault with horizontal basal detachment

The results of experiment K1 (from McClay 1990) are shown in Fig. 2. Characteristic features of this deformation geometry are a well developed roll-over anticline with a series of crestal collapse graben structures (Fig. 2a). Each crestal collapse graben is bounded by a planar antithetic fault on the downslope (basinward) side and a negatively-listric (convex upwards) synthetic fault in the prefault sequence which becomes listric in the synfault sequence on the

(a)

(b)

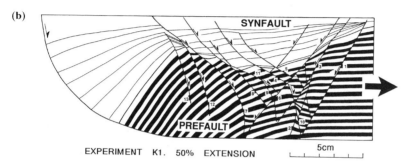

Fig. 2. (**a**) Experiment K1. Simple listric fault with alternating layers of coloured and white sand in both the synfault and prefault section. The prefault layers are the uniform black, grey and white bands, and the synfault layers are the alternating grey and white bands, with variable thickness. Extension was to the right. 50% extension of the initial model length. (**b**) Fault sequence and architecture diagram for experiment K1.

upslope (landward) side (Fig. 2a). As extension proceeds successive crestal collapse grabens are superimposed with the resultant progression of fault sequences towards the detachment (Fig. 2b). The overall geometries of this listric system at 50% extension are very similar to those described in detail in Ellis & McClay (1988).

Simple listric fault with tilted basal detachment

In experiment E44 the same basic geometry as K1 was used but the basal detachment surface was tilted at 10° to the right (Fig. 3). The total extension achieved was 100% over the initial length of the model. The final fault geometries show distinct contrasts to experiment K1 briefly described above and to other examples where the basal detachment surface was horizontal (Ellis & McClay 1988; McClay 1990).

As in K1 (Fig. 2), the deformation in the prefault layers is characterized by the successive development of crestal collapse graben (Fig. 3)

developed within the roll-over anticline. As extension proceeds, early formed faults are translated down the detachment and move out of the influence of the actively forming roll-over, therefore becoming inactive and buried by later synfault sedimentation. In the synfault sequence the synthetic crestal collapse graben faults develop into an array of listric growth faults (Fig. 3a) with their geometry mimicking that of the underlying basal detachment. A panel of unfaulted synfault sediments is found adjacent to the major basal detachment (Fig. 3a). This is a feature of this type of experiment (see also McClay (1990)) and is found in many natural listric growth fault systems. The fault sequences (Fig. 3b) show similar hanging-wall nucleation patterns as in experiment K1 and other experiments (McClay 1990).

The two experimental described above (Figs 2 & 3) are typical of the range of listric fault geometries produced where the detachment shape does not change during extension. These experiments have been repeated many times with similar resultant geometries.

(a)

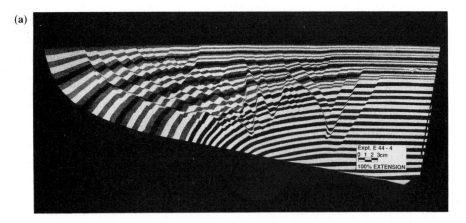

(b)

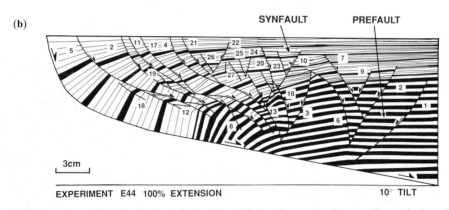

Fig. 3. (a) Experiment E44. Simple listric fault with a 10° tilted lower detachment. The prefault and synfault layers consist of alternating black, grey and white bands. The prefault layers are uniform and the synfault layers have variable thickness. Extension was to the right. 100% extension of the initial model length. (b) Fault sequence and architecture diagram for experiment E44.

Seismic modelling

The final extensional geometries of experiments K1 and E44 (Figs 2 & 3) provide structural templates for the seismic modelling. The models were scaled up to an appropriate size for basin scale structures (see Figs 4a & 5a). Arbitrary reflection coefficients between 0.05 and 0.1 were assigned to each of the boundaries as indicated on the Figs 4a & 5a. On parts of Fig. 5a closely spaced reflectors appear to merge but this is a plotting artefact.

Kirchhoff wave equation modelling (Hilterman 1970; 1975 & Trorey 1970) was used to produce zero offset synthetic seismic traces. This simulates the appearance of an unmigrated stacked section from a 2D survey over the structures.

For these simulations a linearly increasing velocity with depth has been used to calculate seismic travel times. The expression used was

$$v = 1500.0 + 1.0z \qquad (1)$$

where v is the acoustic velocity in m s^{-1} and z is the depth in metres. Hence, the velocity was 1500 m s^{-1} at surface and 4500 m s^{-1} at a depth of 3 km. It should be noted that the use of a slowly varying velocity function, such as equation (1), to generate seismic travel times is not inconsistent with the reflection coefficients being used since travel times depend largely on the broad features of the velocity whereas reflectivity is generated by high frequency changes in seismic velocity (and density) (Berkhout 1985).

The results are shown in Figs 4b & 5b (experiments K1 and E44 respectively). These show geometrical distortions which could be misleading to an unwary interpreter of a similar field section. Firstly, the increasing velocity with depth greatly exaggerates the thickness of the upper beds compared to the lower ones. This effect could be removed by time migration

(a)

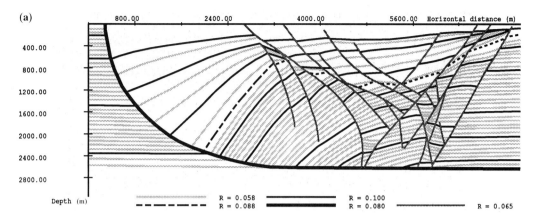

(b)

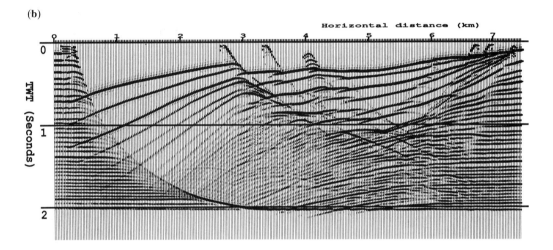

(c)

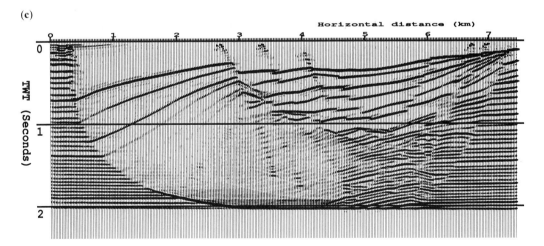

Fig. 4. (a) Line drawing of experiment K1 for input into seismic modelling programs. Key indicates reflection coefficients used. (b) Kirchhoff modelled zero offset section. (c) Migration of Fig. 4b.

(a)

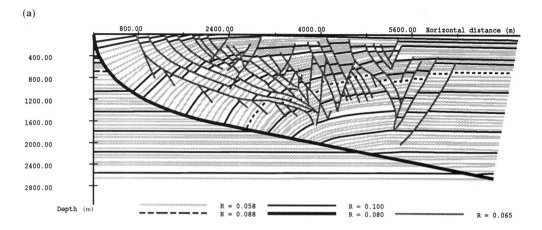

(b)

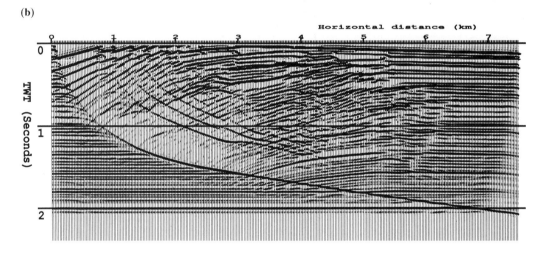

(c)

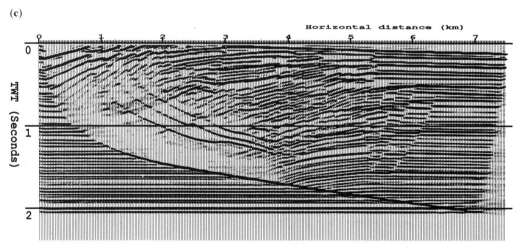

Fig. 5. (**a**) Line drawing of experiment E44 for input into seismic modelling programs. Key indicates reflection coefficients used. (**b**) Kirchhoff modelled zero offset section. (**c**) Migration of Fig. 5b.

followed by depth conversion although this requires highly accurate velocity information to produce good results. Secondly, the fault geometry undergoes some interesting distortions. The positions of these faults are indicated by two different phenomena, i.e. the fault plane reflections themselves and also the bedding plane termination positions. Unsurprisingly, these do not coincide for unmigrated data but, more interestingly, the fault generated bed terminations can be highly misleading with the hangingwall synthetic fault nearest the bounding fault in Fig. 4a appearing as an antithetic fault in Fig. 4b (this feature is at approximately x = 3 km, 0.8 s< t < 1.5 s). Another feature clearly visible on the stacked sections is the loss of steeply dipping reflectors. This is an artefact of the modelling technique but simulates accurately a genuine effect in real data. The use of source and receiver arrays attenuates seismic energy not travelling nearly vertically (see for example Newman & Mahoney 1973). Thus steep data is also lost in real surveys.

After migration the results (Figs 4c & 5c) show further problems. Steeply dipping events are spatially aliased leading to failure of migration with accompanying high noise contamination. These effects would be removed if the survey could be reshot with a smaller CMP spacing (i.e. a smaller trace spacing on the stacked section). The overall effect of the failure to image very steep dips, together with the failure to migrate more moderate dips, is an apparent gap in the data immediately above the bounding fault. Indeed, there is even a faint suggestion of horizontal layering in these areas due to migration noise. These effects could be very serious in real data if multiple contamination is present.

Comparing Figs 4c & 5c to an example of real field data (Fig. 6) several interesting observations can be made. Firstly, the bounding fault is imaged at low dips but is lost as its dip becomes higher on both the real and synthetic examples. This strongly suggests that this frequently seen phenomenon is due to failure to image steep dips rather than a loss of acoustic impedance contrast at shallow depths. Secondly, in Fig. 6, the steeply dipping beds adjacent to the bounding fault are lost at the very high dips and are replaced by nearly horizontal events (e.g. reflector A) suggesting that these are artefacts caused by spatial aliasing and/ or multiples as discussed in the previous paragraph.

Discussion and conclusions

The analogue experimental models described above (Figs 2 & 3) are realistic models of growth fault systems and show marked similarities in geometry to listric fault systems in deltaic environments (Fig. 6). In particular the major detachment maintains its shape as growth progresses (Fig. 6) and a distinct roll-over with superposed crestal collapse grabens is produced.

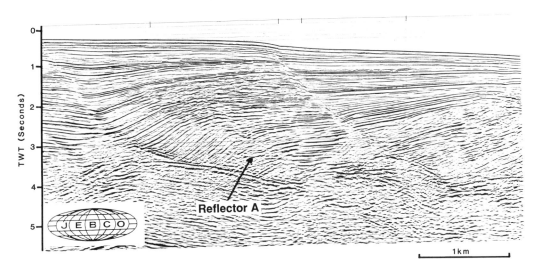

Fig. 6. Migrated seismic section of a listric fault system with a dipping basal detachment surface, Gulf of Mexico. Note the panel of unfaulted, sediments adjacent to the fault surface. Seismic section courtesy of Jebco Seismic.

With a tilted basal detachment surface (Fig. 3) a distinctive band of non-faulted synfault units is juxtaposed against the basal fault surface. This feature is commonly found in growth faults in the Gulf of Mexico (Fig. 6) and other deltaic provinces such as the Niger Delta and the Barram Delta of Brunei (Ellenor 1984). In the experiments the fault pattern and the nucleation sequence are complex, reflecting the super-position of successive crestal collapse structures. These features are also observed in growth fault structures both on seismic sections (e.g. Fig. 6) and in outcrop (Snow & White, 1989). In these environments and in the experimental models sedimentation keeps pace with or is greater than the extension such that the growth segment maintains a listric geometry (see Ellis & McClay 1988; Vendeville & Cobbold 1988). This is in contrast to behaviour in sediment-starved extensional systems such as parts of the Basin and Range where significant footwall uplift has been postulated (Wernicke & Axen 1988) and the extensional detachment surface becomes significantly deformed.

The synthetic seismic sections produced by modelling the experimental structures show similarities to natural examples of listric fault systems. The synthetic seismograms (Figs 4 & 5) demonstrate some of the problems in imaging steeply dipping reflectors in the listric system. In particular, as one would expect, the seismic models show the difficulty of imaging the complex structures that are generated adjacent and abutting onto the basal detachment surface (Figs 4 & 5). In seismic surveys across listric fault systems a lack of resolution is commonly found in this region (Fig. 6). This seismic modelling programme is at an early stage and much more detailed research needs to be carried out particularly on velocity variations at depth and within the structures.

This research was supported by a Natural Environment Research Council Grant (GR3/6658A). JEBCO Seismic Ltd is thanked for permission to publish the seismic section in Fig. 6. P. Buchanan drafted Fig. 1 and Miss S. Muir drafted Figs 3 & 4. Miss J. Brown typed the manuscript and K. D'Souza and K. Denyer are also thanked for the photographic work. B. Freeman, F. Peel and B. Vendeville provided thoughtful and interesting reviews.

References

BALLY, A. W., BERNOULLI, D., DAVIS, G. A. & MONTDERT, T. L. 1981. Listric normal faults, Oceana Acta, proceedings 26th International Geological Congress, Paris, 1980, 87–101.
BERKHOUT, A. J. 1985. 3-d seismic processing with an eye to the future. *World Oil*, October, 91–94.
BRUCE, C. H., 1973. Pressured shale and related sediment deformation: Mechanism for development of regional contemporaneous faults. *American Association of Petroleum Geology Bulletin*, **57**, 878–886.
ELLENOR, D. W. 1984. The oil and gas resources of Brunei, In: JAMES, D. M. D. (ed.) The geology and hydrocarbon resources of Negra Brunei Darussalam: Kota Batu, Muzium Brunei, 103–139.
ELLIS, P. G. & McCLAY, K. R. 1988. Listric extensional fault systems-results of analogue model experiments. *Basin Research*, **1**, 55–70.
GIBBS, A. D. 1983. Balanced cross-section construction from seismic sections in areas of extensional tectonics. *Journal of Structural Geology*, **5**, 153–160.
HILTERMAN, F. J. 1970. Three dimensional seismic modelling. *Geophysics*, **35**, 1020–1037.
—— 1975. Amplitudes of seismic waves- A quick look. *Geophysics*, **40**, 745–762.
HUBBERT, M. K. 1937. Theory of scaled models as applied to the study of geological structures. *Geological Society of America Bulletin*, **48**, 1495–1520.
—— 1951. Mechanical basis for certain familiar geological structures. *Geological Society of America Bulletin*, **62**, 355–372.
HORSFIELD, W. T. 1977. An experimental approach to basement controlled faulting. *Geologie en Mijnbouw*, **56**, 363–370.
JACKSON, J. A. 1987. Active normal faulting and crustal extension. In: COWARD, M. P., DEWEY, J. F. & HANCOCK, P. L. (eds.) Continental Extensional Tectonics. Geological Society, London, Special Publication, **28**, 3–17.
McCLAY, K. R. 1990. Physical models of structural styles during extension. In: TANKARD, A. J. & BALKWILL, H. (eds), Tectonics and stratigraphy of the North Atlantic Margins, American Association of Petroleum Geologists Memoirs **46**.
—— & ELLIS, P. G. 1987. Analogue models of extensional fault geometries. In: COWARD, M. P., DEWEY, J. F. & HANCOCK, P. L., Continental Extensional Tectonics, Geological Society, London, Special Publication, **28**, 109–125.
NAYLOR, M. A., MANDL, G. & SIJPESTEIN, C. M. K. 1986. Fault geometries in basement induced wrench faulting under different initial stress states. *Journal of Structural Geology*, **8**, 737–752.
NEWMAN, P. & MAHONEY, J. T. 1973. Patterns — with a pinch of salt. *Geophysical Prospecting*, **21**, 197–219.
ROBERTS, S. & JACKSON, J. A. (This volume). Active normal faulting in central Greece: An overview.
SHELTON, J. W. 1984. Listric normal faults: An illustrated summary, *American Association of Petroleum Geologists Bulletin*, **68**, 801–815.
SNOW, J. K. & WHITE, C. 1990. Listric normal faulting and synorogenic sedimentation, northern Cottonwood Mountains, Death Valley region, California. In: WERNICKE, B. (ed.) *Basin and Range Extensional Tectonics Near the Latitude of*

Las Vegas, Geological Society of America Memoir, in press.

TROREY, A. W. 1970. A simple theory for seismic diffractions. *Geophysics*, **35**, 762−784.

VENDEVILLE, B. & COBBOLD, P. R. 1988. How normal faulting and sedimentation interact to produce listric fault profiles and stratigraphic wedges. *Journal of Structural Geology*, **10**, 649−659.

WERNICKE, B. & AXEN, G. J. 1988. On the role of isostasy in the evolution of normal fault systems. *Geology*, **16**, 848−851.

WHEELER, J. 1987. Variable-heave models of deformation above listric normal faults: the importance of area conservation. *Journal of Structural Geology*, **9**, 1047−1049.

WILLIAMS, G. & VANN, I. 1987. The geometry of listric normal faults and deformation in their hangingwalls. *Journal of Structural Geology*, **9**, 789−795.

Mechanisms generating normal fault curvature: a review illustrated by physical models

BRUNO VENDEVILLE

Applied Geodynamics Laboratory, Bureau of Economic Geology, The University of Texas at Austin, University Station, Box X, Austin, Texas 78713, USA

Abstract: This paper briefly reviews the mechanisms generating fault curvature during extension, illustrates them using physical models, and discusses their applicability at different scales and for specific extensional styles. These mechanisms are in two groups. In the first, initially curved fault planes are essentially of mechanical origin. They commonly result from marked vertical changes in stress orientation and rheology within the faulted layer. Experiments suggest that such mechanisms are more likely to influence secondary faults that form where deformation and displacements are severely constrained. The second group includes faults that become curved after they form, either by volume loss due to compaction, by internal deformation of fault blocks, or by interacting sedimentation and faulting. Fault curvature due to compaction is mainly restricted to growth-faulted areas. Internal deformation of blocks affects fault shapes at the transition zone between continuous and discontinuous deformation. Block rotation during rapid deposition can lead to strongly curved fault profiles. Blocks or faults are distorted during block rotation to maintain geometric compatibility within and between the blocks. This review suggests that normal growth faults in deltaic areas are more likely to be listric than crustal-scale normal faults.

Recent years have shown a growing interest in the geometry of normal faults in sedimentary basins, passive continental margins, and detached sediments in deltaic areas. Determining whether fault planes are curved or planar is particularly important because of its direct implications on the estimated amount of extension and the tectonic relation between faulted rocks and their substrate. Jackson & White (1989) and Jackson *et al.* (1988) pointed out that structural analysis of normal faults must take into account fault scale. They distinguished (1) faults that affect cover rocks above a detachment layer from (2) large-scale faults due to basement-involved crustal extension. Although detached sediments provide numerous examples of gravity-controlled listric normal faults above salt or overpressured shales (Fig. 1; Edwards 1976; Balley *et al.* 1981; Bally 1983; Shelton 1984), the occurrence of crustal listric normal faults remains debated (e.g. Morton & Black 1975; De Charpal *et al.* 1978; Le Pichon & Sibuet 1981; Wernicke & Burchfield 1982; Jackson & White 1989; Yielding *et al.* this volume).

Analysis of the mechanisms that generate fault curvature can be valuable where it is not known whether faults are curved or planar. As will be described, these mechanisms are diverse, and their applicability greatly varies with scale and geological context. Where the actual fault geometries remain uncertain, one can narrow down the range of possible fault shapes by considering which mechanism, if any, could have caused curved faults at that scale and in this geological context.

Except for the review by Mandl (1988, pp 25−43), most studies treated individual mechanisms for generating fault curvature in isolation (e.g. Price 1977; Crans *et al.* 1980; Jackson & McKenzie 1983; Kligfield *et al.* 1984; Barr 1987; Vendeville & Cobbold 1988), rather than considering potential mechanisms altogether. This paper briefly reviews different mechanisms generating listric faults, illustrates them qualitatively using physical models where appropriate, and discusses their applicability at different scales and in different contexts. Although models were designed to be dynamically scaled with respect to their natural counterparts, a detailed description of model scaling is beyond the scope of this paper and is provided elsewhere (Vendeville 1987; Vendeville & Cobbold 1987; Vendeville *et al.* 1987; Jackson & Vendeville 1990).

This review distinguishes two categories of listric normal faults: (1) faults that are curved when they initially form and (2) faults that become curved after they form with or without coeval deposition.

From ROBERTS A. M., YIELDING, G. & FREEMAN, B. (eds), 1991, *The Geometry of Normal Faults,*   241
Geological Society Special Publication No 56, pp 241−249

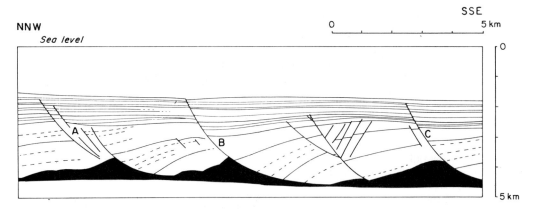

Fig. 1. Depth-converted seismic section from the Rhône delta area showing Plio-Pleistocene sediments affected by listric normal growth faults above a Messinian salt layer (black). A, B, and C are faults referred into text. From Vendeville (1987), with permission of the Institut Français du Pétrole, Total CFP and ELf-Aquitaine.

Initial fault curvature

Vertical changes in rheological properties or in the orientation of principal stresses can change fault dip, causing an initial fault curvature. Mathematical solutions suggest that a vertical change in rheology alone cannot lead to a pronounced curvature of the fault plane: for example, a large vertical decrease of the internal friction angle from 30° to 0° causes a mere 15° decrease in fault dip (Brun *et al.* 1985). A large change in fault dip may occur if the material is highly cohesive; but the influence of cohesion on the fault dip rapidly decreases with depth and cannot account for dips of less than 45°. To induce significant fault curvature, a vertical change in rheology must be accompanied by shear stress along rheological interfaces, as on delta slopes (Crans *et al.* 1980; Mandl 1988). Unfortunately, no experimental material has yet been found that would allow gravity-scaled modelling with a gradual change in rheology with depth.

By contrast, the effect of spatial changes of stress orientation with depth can be readily simulated using homogeneous, frictional-plastic models made of dry sand (e.g. Horsfield 1977; Vendeville *et al.* 1987; Mandl 1988). These changes may take place in two or three dimensions.

Stress changes in two dimensions

Curved stress trajectories cause initially curved faults. Two-dimensional analytical solutions show that a basal shear stress can induce curved stress trajectories, provided that the component

of shear stress changes vertically with respect to the normal stresses (Hubbert 1951; Sanford 1959). A shear stress may be imposed by body force (gravity) oblique to a frictional boundary (layering, basement-cover interface), such as in tilted sediments. Sand models inclined a few degrees showed fault planes with little or no curvature despite a strong basal shear stress (Vendeville *et al.* 1987). This suggests that stress trajectories remained straight across most of the model. At both small and large scale, a basal shear stress may also be caused by ductile underflow (e.g. salt or lower continental crust). However, both experiments (Brun *et al.* 1985; Vendeville *et al.* 1987) and theory (Mandl 1989, pp 26–28) suggest that the shear stress due to ductile underflow remains low unless unrealistically high stress gradients are postulated. Hence fault curvatures are low.

Vertical and lateral changes in stress orientations are more important where master faults locally constrain displacements and deformation. Curved second-order faults commonly form in the hangingwalls of master faults in experiments. Models of rollover faulting (McClay & Ellis 1987) displayed initially convex-upward normal faults. Models of basement induced faulting (Horsfield 1977; Patton 1984; Vendeville 1987) also displayed initially curved fault planes whose curvature was induced by strong vertical and lateral changes of the orientation of the principal stresses near the basement fault (Sanford 1959; Couples 1977).

Stress changes in three dimensions

Natural normal faults and experiments

commonly show curved traces in map view.
This curvature can be caused by local changes
in stress orientation at the tip of a laterally
propagating fault (Mandl 1988), or by lateral
friction. Experimental models and natural
examples are not strictly two-dimensional
(i.e. plane stress) throughout because of frictional shear stresses along lateral block boundaries. Also, lateral friction can affect fault
geometries in vertical sections: in models, side
views and sections cut near the lateral walls
commonly display different fault geometries
than sections cut away from lateral walls
(Vendeville 1987; see also McClay & Ellis 1987).
As an empirical rule, close to the lateral boundaries, fewer faults form, one set of faults dominates and fault planes are curved, whereas they
are planar away from the side walls (Mandl
1988). Strongly curved faults formed in a sand
model of rift-transform-rift where the lateral
friction was high along the transform segment
(Fig. 2, see also Faugère et al. 1986). The traces
of the normal faults curved towards and along
the transform direction in response to shear
stresses parallel to it. Transform-parallel vertical
sections cut far from the transform zone displayed planar normal faults, whereas sections
close to the transform zone displayed both
convex- and concave-upward fault planes
(Figs 2 B, C). These planes flattened or fault
displacements died out at various depths in the
sand layer, although the model rheology was
initially homogeneous. In detached sediments
in the Gulf of Mexico, such faults have been
interpreted previously as being of compactional
origin (Carver 1968), but clearly the model
shows that the same geometry can be produced
by three-dimensional changes in stress orientation. At larger scale, similar three-
dimensional stress changes can induce listric
faults in the brittle crust of transfer zones between continental rifts (e.g. Rosendahl et al.
1986).

Curvature after fault formation

Internal deformation can increase the curvature
of an initially planar or a slightly curved fault
after it forms. Faults are distorted by strain
of the fault blocks or by volume loss due to
compaction. During this distortion, both the
hangingwall and the footwall must deform.

Curvature due to strain of fault block

Fault orientation or geometry can change where
rocks containing the faults are not deformed
solely by slip along fault planes, but also by a

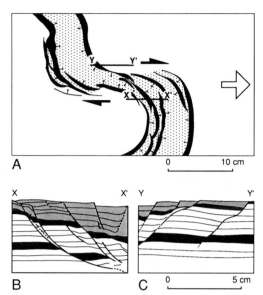

Fig. 2. Experimental model of Rift-Transform-Rift
geometry (sand only). A: Map view of the model
after deformation showing curved fault traces near
the transform zone. Marks on downthrown side.
Stippled areas mark grabens. White arrow indicates
direction of extension, black arrows indicate shear
along the transfer zones. B&C: Transform-parallel
vertical sections in the model showing concave- and
convex-upwards fault planes (see location Fig. 2a).
Grey layers are syn-rift. Also note the decrease in
fault throw with depth.

component of strain caused by the stretching
itself, by elastic isostatic effects, simple shear,
or local diapiric rise of a ductile substrate.
Jackson & McKenzie (1983) showed that vertical pure shear can reduce to some extent the
original fault dip. Initially planar faults can
become curved where extension also includes a
horizontal or oblique component of shear strain
(and a shear strain gradient), for instance where
extension of the brittle layer is induced by flow
of an underlying ductile layer. In experiments
by Brun et al. (1985), simple shear in the ductile
substrate distorted initially planar faults at the
base of the faulted layer. Sand models uniformly
stretched at the base (Fig. 3) showed initially
planar faults later distorted by horizontal simple
shear at the base of fault blocks during extension. Physical models of extensional salt diapirs
(Fig. 4) also lead to listric fault geometries in a
faulted overburden distorted by diapirism of a
ductile substrate.

How much a strain mechanism can contribute
to fault curvature depends on the scale, the
rheology, and the structural context where

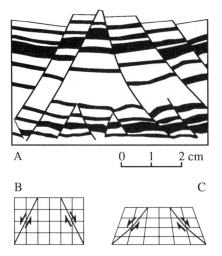

Fig. 3. Curved faults in sand model of uniform extension (after Vendeville *et al.* 1987; their Fig. 2) showing a concave-upwards fault (A). Initially planar faults (B) were later distorted by inhomogeneous strain of the horst (C).

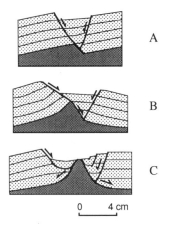

Fig. 4. Curved fault in sand model of extensional diapirism (after Jackson & Vendeville 1990). An initially near-planar fault (A) was later distorted by a viscous diapir (dark grey) piercing the hangingwall (B & C).

faulting takes place. First, such a mechanism requires that extension is not homogeneous at the scale of the fault. Hence it cannot be expected where stretching is strictly uniform. Second, fault curvature increases with finite strain. Hence this mechanism cannot lead to strongly listric faults during early stages of extension. Third, in faulted layers overlying a

ductile substrate (regardless of scale), the extent of possible fault distortion due to flow of the substrate (e.g. lower continental crust at large scale, or salt or shales at the scale of cover rocks) depends on the relative strengths of the brittle and the ductile layers. Where the strength of the ductile layer is lower than that of the brittle layer (low viscosity or low strain rate), fault blocks are little or not affected by ductile flow. Faults would remain planar. Where the strength of the ductile layer is higher than that of the brittle layer, ductile flow can cause strain of the base of overlying fault blocks and fault distortion.

At crustal scale, a lateral offset between the extension zones in brittle upper crust and a ductile lower crust induces vertical changes in horizontal stretch and horizontal component of simple shear in the brittle–ductile transition zone (Coward 1986). Although this should not affect fault shapes in the brittle upper continental crust, it is likely to distort lower fault segments in the brittle–ductile transition zone. Fault finite curvatures depend on initial fault dips, fault locations, fault orientations with respect to the sense of horizontal simple shear, the total amount of strain, and the thickness of the transition zone. If the transition zone is thin, only a short basal segment of the fault plane is deformed and sharply curved, in a detachment-like geometry. If the transition zone is thicker, the curvature is lower and involves a larger segment of the fault plane. By contrast, deformation of poorly lithified sediments involves both faulting and a significant component of block strain and is more likely to induce distortion of the initial fault planes. In areas of detached sediments, fault-block distortion is also favoured by buoyant rise of the mobile substrate (e.g. salt or shales).

Curvature due to compaction

In sedimentary basins the volume of compacting sediments decreases progressively with depth towards an asymptotic limit where the rock has a zero porosity (Sclater & Christie 1980; Xiao & Suppe 1989). The dip of an initially planar fault plane thus decreases to a critical value that depends on the initial fault dip, initial porosity, and amount of compaction (Jones & Addis 1984; Xiao & Suppe 1989). To induce curved faults, both the hangingwall and the footwall must compact. Because compaction is proportional to the depth of burial, compaction-induced fault curvatures are restricted to growth faults in regions of rapid deposition. Although compaction plays a major role in the flattening of growth faults at depth, it cannot by itself account for fault dips that become horizontal at depth or that flatten more than the predicted critical angle (e.g. 37° in the example by Xiao & Suppe 1989). Furthermore, problems of geometrical compatibility between blocks arise where the nature of the sediments, and hence their response to compaction, changes across the fault. Potential gaps or overlaps must then be accommodated by other mechanisms, such as deformation of one (see Verral 1981; White *et al.* 1986) or both fault blocks. In the latter case, a strain component is superimposed on the compaction effect and distorts the fault plane.

Curvature due to interacting sedimentation and faulting

Despite a geometric similarity, growth faults are mechanistically different from non-growth faults described in preceding sections. Growth faults that form by continual propagation into accumulating layers record mechanical and kinematic changes in the system.

This mechanistic difference is obvious when one tries to apply the concept of initially listric faults to the progressive evolution of growth faults (Fig. 5). Suppose that vertical changes in the mechanical properties in the sedimentary pack (e.g. basal shear stress, lithostatic pressure, fluid pressure) cause the potential faults to form concave upwards (Fig. 5 A, B, top row). Subsequent deposition of a new layer above both the hanging and footwall changes some mechanical properties of the system (e.g. increases lithostatic pressure). Hence the profile of the new potential fault is different from the profile of the older fault segment depth (Fig. 5 A, B, middle and bottom rows). This leads to two distinct modes of growth-fault propagation.

The first mode (Fig. 5 A) assumes that any change in the mechanical state — i.e. every step of sedimentation — forms a new fault that cuts through the entire footwall with a profile fitting the new potential fault (Fig. 5 A, middle row). Older, deeper fault segments in the hanging wall become inactive and are then passively deformed by rollover folding (Fig. 5, bottom row). Although some growth faults display similar patterns (Fig. 1, fault A), many natural examples display a single fault plane despite being several kilometres deep (Fig. 1, Faults B and C). This suggests a second mode, in which older, deeper fault segments remain active and propagate into the newly deposited sediment (Fig. 5 B). During propagation, the

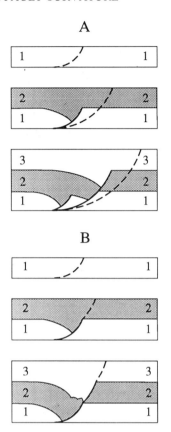

Fig. 5. Two modes of evolution of initially listric normal growth faults. Left column: A new fault plane form after each depositional stage. Right column: Lower fault segments remain active throughout extension. Dashed lines are incipient fault planes. Thick solid lines are fault traces after displacement. Rollover geometries were calculated assuming accommodation by vertical shear.

new fault segment must satisfy the new mechanical constraints. Its shape must match the profile of the new potential slip plane, whereas the shapes of older deeper fault segments remain unchanged (Fig. 5 B, second and third rows). Compiled for several steps, this procedure leads to segmented fault. Although the attitude of each fault segment reflects the mechanical state at the time of its formation, the shape of the overall fault plane cannot be directly related to the mechanics of the whole package (compare Fig. 5 A and B). Instead, the overall curvature depends mainly on the average dip of each fault segment and on the thickness of each layer (Fig. 5 B). The geometry of the overall growth fault clearly depends on the history of deformation and sedimentation.

Kinematic processes alone can generate listric

growth faulting (Dailly 1976; Barr 1987; Vendeville & Cobbold 1987, 1988). For example, an isotropic, homogeneous brittle layer subjected to a uniform stress field deforms along faults with a constant dip with respect to the orientation of the compressive stress, here vertical (Fig. 6 A). Once formed, faults are assumed to remain active and to propagate with a constant dip into new sediments deposited at the top surface while fault blocks rotate (Fig. 6 B). Combined step by step, this process generates an overall curved fault plane. Experiments of syndepositional gravity gliding provide good illustrations of the interaction between faulting, block rotation and sedimentation (Fig. 7; Vendeville 1987; Vendeville & Cobbold 1987). Faults were planar where fault blocks had not rotated (Fig. 7a, Block 1), but concave upwards (Fig. 7a, Blocks 2, 3) or, rarely, convex downwards (Fig. 7b Block 1) where fault blocks rotated during extension and deposition.

Application of a rotation-sedimentation mechanism specifically constrains fault-block deformation. Assuming rigid blocks (i.e. no distortion) precludes any differential rotation within the fault block. Hence, the vorticity must be identical for every material particle within a block, whatever its depth and the fault dip at this depth. Barr (1987) and Vendeville & Cobbold (1988) based their mechanisms on

domino-style rotation during sedimentation. Fault segments, once formed, rotate during uniform horizontal stretching. Older fault segments rotated more and have lower dips, whereas younger fault segments rotated less and have higher dips. Within each layer the fault plane and the bedding have identical angles of rotation and satisfy the equation:

$$\sin \theta_0 / \sin \theta = \beta \qquad (1)$$

(Le Pichon & Sibuet 1981) where $0 \leq \theta_0 \leq 90°$ is the initial dip of the fault segment, θ its dip after rotation, and $\beta \geq 1$ is the horizontal stretch. As a result, the rotation $R = \theta_0 - \theta$, for a given increment of stretch $\Delta\beta$ varies with the initial fault dip as follows:

$$\partial R / \partial \theta_0 = 1 - \frac{\cos \theta_0}{(\Delta\beta^2 - \sin^2 \theta_0)^{1/2}}. \qquad (2)$$

$\partial R / \partial \theta_0$ is always positive and non-zero as long as $\Delta\beta > 1$. Therefore, for a given incremental stretch, $\Delta\beta$, high fault dips cause high rotations, whereas low fault dips cause low rotations. Applied incrementally to growth faults (Fig. 8 A), domino behaviour induces potential gaps due to differential rotation between deeper, older layers, bounded by a gently dipping fault segment, and shallower, younger layers, bounded by a steeply dipping fault segment. Hence a domino-sedimentation mechanism must include a component of internal deformation of fault blocks (Fig. 8 B). In sand experiments described by Vendeville & Cobbold (1988), closely spaced listric growth faults rotated in domino style during syndepositional stretching. Fault blocks must have been distorted to accommodate differential rotation between layers. Models in Fig. 7 show that domino-style kinematics cannot account for large extensions where fault blocks lose contact with each other at depth. Block rotation was essentially caused by differential loading by the overburden and was accommodated by flow of the ductile substrate. Moreover, this latter experiment illustrated how problems of geometric compatibility also arise between rigid blocks: to maintain continuity between fault blocks, fault planes should have constant curvature with depth and share the same centre of rotation, an unlikely condition. Instead, both model and natural examples suggest that local deformation of the block edges (mainly hanging-walls, see Fig. 7a, Block 3) maintains compatibility across the faults.

To induce curved faults, a model of interacting faulting, block rotation, and sedimentation requires sediments to be deposited on

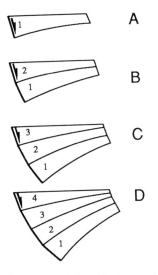

Fig. 6. Fault curvature induced by interacting sedimentation, planar faulting and block rotation. A, Initial stage. B, C, D, Further stages after several increments of deposition, rotation, and fault propagation. Modified after Dailly (1976) and Vendeville & Cobbold (1988).

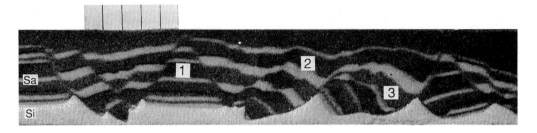

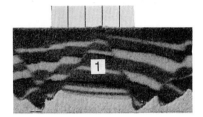

Fig. 7. Two vertical sections in a model of syndepositional gravity gliding above a 2° slope, showing curved growth faults and rotated fault blocks, 1, 2, 3 referred to in text (from Vendeville 1987 and Vendeville & Cobbold 1987). (Si)=ductile silicone putty; (Sa)=brittle sand layers. Scale bars every centimetre. Slope to the right.

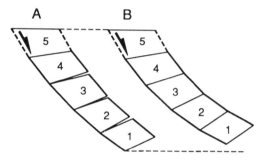

Fig. 8. Geometric compatibility within fault blocks during interacting rotation and sedimentation. Thick lines are fault planes; thick dashed lines are incipient fault planes. A: Potential gaps occur if fault segments strictly obey a domino-style rotation. B: Rotation of rigid blocks maintains continuity between the layers but leads to a more curved fault.

both the hangingwall and footwall. Therefore, its application is restricted to syntectonic sediments during rapid deposition. Fault curvature affects only layers deposited during block rotation. Where block rotation and faulting start as soon as the first layers are deposited (e.g. above salt on many delta slopes) the entire fault plane is curved, although the fault plan does not necessarily become horizontal at depth. In basement-involved extensional basins, only the upper fault segments in the synrotation sediments would be curved, whereas deeper fault segments in the pre-rotation layers and the basement would remain planar (Barr 1987).

Discussion and conclusion

This review shows that many different mechanisms can generate fault curvature during and after faulting. Some mechanisms can act alone. Some require superimposition of another mechanism: mechanisms of compaction or interacting sedimentation and faulting must include a component of internal deformation to maintain geometric compatibility within and between fault blocks. Fault curvatures in nature are probably produced by combinations of several mechanisms, and further studies are needed to elucidate how these effects combine.

Not all mechanisms can apply at any scale or in any geological context; hence, two listric faults having an identical geometry, but in two different contexts, do not necessarily reflect a similar kinematic and mechanical history. The potential mechanisms for fault curvature are especially different between small-scale growth faults and large-scale faults in the continental crust. Experimental results suggest that, at the scale of the brittle continental crust, only a few mechanisms can produce curved fault shapes. Except in transfer zones where rapid stress changes in three dimensions can occur, the applicable mechanisms (e.g. basal shear stress, rheology change, block strain) cause only moderately curved faults whose curvatures are restricted mainly to the brittle/ductile transition zone where faults are aseismic. Recent surveys of active normal faults by Jackson (1987) and Jackson & White (1989) similarly indicate that fault planes have negligible curvature in the upper, brittle continental crust. Most of the change in fault dip occurs in the transitional or lower crust.

By contrast, many mechanisms generating fault curvature apply to smaller-scale faults, especially deltaic growth faults in detached sedimentary cover. Abrupt changes in rheologies and common slope-parallel shear stress along décollement interfaces cause initially curved faults. Because deltaic growth faults commonly undergo block strain, compaction, and interacting deposition and rotation, they are more likely to be curved than crustal-scale normal faults.

I thank B. Colletta, M.P.A. Jackson, S. Laubach, J. Letouzey, S. Serra, and P.R. Cobbold for fruitful discussions, and N. White and D. Barr for reviews. This research was conducted partly at (1) the Laboratoire de Tectonophysique, University of Rennes, (2) the Center for Tectonophysics, Texas A&M University, and (3) the Applied Geodynamics Laboratory, The University of Texas at Austin. The experimental work was financed by grants from the Institut Français du Pétrole (1984–1987), Total CFP (1984–1987), and Amoco Production Co. (1987–1988). Published by permission of the Director, Bureau of Economic Geology.

References

BALLY, A. W. (ed.) 1983. *Seismic expression of structural styles*. American Association of Petroleum Geologists, Studies in Geology 15, vol. 2–3.

—, BERNOUILLI, D., DAVIS, G. A. & MONTADERT, L. 1981. Listric normal faults. *Oceanologica Acta*, NoSP, 87–101.

BARR, D. 1987. Structural/stratigraphic models for extensional basins of half-graben type. *Journal of Structural Geology*, 9, 491–500.

BRUN, J. P., CHOUKROUNE, P. & FAUGERE, E. 1985. Les discontinuités significatives de l'amincissement crustal: Application aux marges passives. *Bulletin de la Société Géologique de France*, 8, 139–144.

CARVER, R. E. 1968. Differential compaction as a cause of regional contemporaneous faults. *American Association of Petroleum Geologists Bulletin*, 52, 414–419.

COUPLES, G. 1977. Stress and shear fracture (fault) trajectories resulting from a suite of complicated boundary conditions with application to the Wind River Mountains. *Pure and Applied Geophysics*, 115, 113–133.

COWARD, M. P. 1986. Heterogeneous stretching, simple shear and basin development. *Earth and Planetary Science Letters*, 80, 325–336.

CRANS, W., MANDL, G. & HAREMBOURE, J. 1980. On the theory of growth faulting: A geomechanical delta model based on gravity sliding. *Journal of Petroleum Geology*, 2, 265–307.

DAILLY, G. C. 1976. A possible mechanism relating progradation, growth faulting, clay diapirism and overthrusting in a regressive sequence of sediments. *Bulletin of Canadian Petroleum Geology*, 24, 92–116.

DECHARPAL, O., GUENNOC, P., MONTADERT, L. & ROBERTS, D. G. 1978. Rifting, crustal attenuation and subsidence in the Bay of Biscay. *Nature*, 275, 706–711.

EDWARDS, M. B. 1976. Growth faults in Upper Triassic deltaic sediments, Svalbard. American *Association of Petroleum Geologists Bulletin*, 60, 341–355.

FAUGERE, E., BRUN, J. P. & VAN DEN DRIESSCHE, J. 1986. Asymmetric basins in pure extension and in wrenching: Experimental models. *Bulletin Centres Recherche Exploration-Production Elf-Aquitaine*, 10, 13–21.

HORSFIELD, W.T. 1977. An experimental approach to basement-controlled faulting. *Geologie en Mijnbouw*, 56, 363–370.

HUBBERT, M. K. 1951. Mechanical basis for certain familiar geological structures. *Geological Society of America Bulletin*, 62, 355–372.

JACKSON, J. & MCKENZIE, D. 1983. The geometrical evolution of normal fault systems. *Journal of Structural Geology*, 5, 471–482.

JACKSON, J.A. 1987. Active normal faulting and crustal extension. *In*: COWARD, M. P., DEWEY, J. F. & HANCOCK, P. L. (eds), *Continental Extensional Tectonics*, Geological Society, London, Special Publication 28, 3–17.

—— & WHITE, N. J. 1989. Normal faulting in the upper continental crust: observations from regions of active extension. *Journal of Structural Geology*, 11, 15–36.

——, ——, GARFUNKEL, Z. & ANDERSON, H. 1988. Relations between normal-fault geometry, tilting and vertical motions in extensional terrains: an example from the southern Gulf of Suez. *Journal of Structural Geology*, 10, 155–170.

JACKSON, M. P. A. & VENDEVILLE, B. C. 1990. The rise and fall of diapirs during thin-skinned extension. Abstract American Association of Petroleum Geologists Annual Meeting, June 3–6, 1990, San Francisco, in press.

JONES, M. E. & ADDIS, M. A. 1984. Volume change during sediment diagenesis and the development of growth faults. *Marine and Petroleum Geology*, 1, 118–122.

KLIGFIELD, R., CRESPI, J., NARUK, S. & DAVIS, G. H. 1984. Displacement and strain patterns of extensional orogens. *Tectonics*, 3, 577–609.

LE PICHON, X. & SIBUET, J. C. 1981. Passive margins: a model of formation. *Journal of Geophysical Research*, 86, 3708–3721.

MANDL, G. 1988. *Mechanisms of tectonic faulting: models and basic concepts*, Elsevier, Amsterdam.

MCCLAY, K. R. & ELLIS, P. G. 1987. Analogue models of extensional fault geometries. *In*: COWARD, M.P., DEWEY, J. F. & HANCOCK, P. L. (eds), *Continental Extensional Tectonics Geological Society, London, Special Publication* 28, 109–125.

MORTON, W. H. & BLACK, R. 1975. Crustal attenuation in Afar. *In*: PILGER, A. & ROSLER, A. (eds),

Afar Depression of Ethiopia. Inter-Union comm. Geodyn. Sci. Report **14**, 55–65. Schweizerbart'sche Verlagsbuchhandlung, Stuttgart.

PATTON, T. L. 1984. *Normal-fault and fold development in sedimentary rocks above a pre-existing basement normal fault.* PhD dissertation, Texas A&M University, College Station, Texas.

PRICE, N. J. 1977. Aspects of gravity tectonics and the development of listric faults. Journal of the Geological Society of London, **133**, 311–327.

ROSENDAHL, B. R., REYNOLDS, D. J., LORBER, P. M., BURGESS, C. F., MCGILL, J., SCOTT, D., LAMBIASE, J. J. & DERKSEN, S. 1986. Structural expression of rifting: lessons from Lake Tanganyika, Africa. *In*: FROSTICK, L. E., RENAUT, R.W., REID, I. & TIERCELIN, J. J. (eds.), *Sedimentation in the African Rifts*, Geological Society, London, Special Publication **25**, 29–43.

SANFORD, A. R. 1959. Analytical and experimental study of simple geologic structures. *Geological Society of America Bulletin*, **70**, 19–52.

SCLATER, J. G. & CHRISTIE, P. A. F. 1980. Continental stretching: an explanation of the post mid-Cretaceous subsidence of the Central North Sea basin. *Journal of Geophysical Research*, **785**, 3711–3739.

SHELTON, J. W. 1984. Listric normal faults: an illustrated summary. *American Association of Petroleum Geologists Bulletin*, **68**, 801–815.

VENDEVILLE, B. 1987. Champs de failles et tectonique en extension. Modélisation expérimentale. Mémoires du Centre Armoricain d'Etudes Structurales des Socles **15**, Rennes, France.

—— & COBBOLD, P. R. 1987. Synsedimentary gravitational sliding and listric normal growth faults: insights from scaled physical models, *Comptes Rendus de l'Académie des Sciences de Paris*, t. **305**, série II, 1313–1319.

—— & —— 1988. How normal faulting and sedimentation interact to produce listric fault profiles and stratigraphic wedges. *Journal of Structural Geology*, **10**, 649–659.

——, ——, DAVY, P., BRUN, J. P. & CHOUKROUNE, P. 1987. Physical models of extensional tectonics at various scales. *In*: COWARD, M. P., DEWEY, J. F. & HANCOCK, P. L. (eds.), *Continental Extensional Tectonics*, Geological Society of London Special Publication **28**, 95–107.

VERRAL, P. 1981. *Structural interpretation with application to North Sea problems.* Course notes No. 3, Joint Association for Petroleum Exploration course (U.K.).

WERNICKE, B. & BURCHFIELD, B. C. 1982. Modes of extensional tectonics. *Journal of Structural Geology*, **4**, 105–115.

WHITE, N. J., JACKSON, J. A. & MCKENZIE, D. P. 1986. The relationship between the geometry of normal faults and that of the sedimentary layers in their hanging walls. *Journal of Structural Geology*, **8**, 897–909.

XIAO, H. B. & SUPPE, J. 1989. Role of compaction in listric shape of growth normal faults. *American Association of Petroleum Geologists Bulletin*, **73**, 777–786.

YIELDING, G., BADLEY, M. & FREEMAN, B. (This volume). Seismic reflections from normal faults in the northern North Sea.

Calculating normal fault geometries at depth: theory and examples

NICKY WHITE[1] & GRAHAM YIELDING[2]

[1]*Bullard Laboratories, Madingley Rise, Madingley Road, University of Cambridge, Cambridge CB3 0EZ, UK*
[2]*Badley Ashton & Associates Ltd, Winceby House, Winceby, Horncastle, Lincs LN9 6PB, UK*

Abstract: In recent years, a large number of methods relating the shape of a normal fault at depth to the shape of a sedimentary horizon in its hangingwall have been described. Such methods are best used in areas where it can be assumed that the footwall remains relatively undeformed during extension. This assumption may not always be valid, especially in the case of large-scale, basement-extending normal faults. Conservation of area (or solid area when compaction occurs) must be the fundamental constraint. The advantages and disadvantages of the various methods are briefly outlined. A general model which assumes that hangingwall deforms by arbitrarily inclined simple shear and differential compaction is discussed. Fault geometry, the inclination of simple shear, and compaction parameters may all be determined from N beds using a simple inversion scheme based on this general method. The algorithm has previously been tested on synthetic data using a range of fault geometries. Such testing indicates that all unknown parameters including fault geometry can, in general, be uniquely determined provided that the geometries of two or more beds within the hangingwall are known. It is important that hangingwall and footwall stratigraphies are accurately known, though uncertainty in either could be included as a bounded variable within a formal inversion scheme. In this paper, the method is applied to laboratory-modelled normal faulting and to depth-converted seismic reflection data. Results suggest that hangingwalls deform by bulk, antithetically inclined, simple shear. Differential compaction of hangingwall sediments is often important and should be taken into account.

Over the last twenty years there has been considerable interest in determining the shape of normal faults at depth. For large-scale active faults, the best method is to use focal mechanism solutions combined with surface break information (e.g. Jackson 1987). In sedimentary basins, seismic reflection data are used while field mapping can be useful in well exposed regions (e.g. the Basin and Range Province; Wernicke & Burchfiel 1982). However, there are circumstances when none of these methods can be applied and geometric techniques must be employed to calculate the likely fault geometry.

Since Verrall (1981) first introduced the so-called 'Chevron construction' to the geological community, a large number of section-balancing schemes for normal faulting have been proposed. Most of these use the geometry of one horizon within the hangingwall to determine the fault geometry at depth. Such methods fall into three broad categories: (a) shear models, (b) flexural-slip models and (c) constant-slip models. All methods assume that deformation occurs within the plane of the section. They also assume that the footwall remains rigid and so

are applicable principally to detached fault systems within the sedimentary fill of a basin. Footwalls of major basement-penetrating normal faults can rotate and/or deform internally (see, e.g. Jackson & White 1989). In such cases, geometrical methods should be applied with great care.

Shear models assume that the hangingwall deforms by bulk simple shear which can be either vertical (Verrall 1981) or arbitrarily inclined (White *et al.* 1986). Flexural-slip models assume that well developed plane-parallel stratification within the hangingwall allows deformation to occur by flexural slip (Davison 1986). Constant-slip models assume that the amount of slip at any point along the fault plane during extension remains constant (Williams & Vann 1987). More recently, Waltham (1989) has argued in favour of a much more general approach where the particle displacement field within the hangingwall is arbitrarily defined.

The most useful models are those which can solve both the forward and inverse problems. The forward problem is where bed geometries are calculated from a given fault geometry and is mainly used to get an idea of the sort of bed geometries to be expected for a whole range of fault geometries. The more practical inverse problem is where the fault geometry is calculated from one or more bed geometries. The latter problem is of some interest to the oil industry.

The purpose of this short paper is firstly to discuss briefly these different types of model. A general modelling scheme is then proposed, based on the shear model. This scheme is applied to laboratory-modelled normal faulting and to depth-converted seismic reflection data.

Which model?

The problem with having a plethora of models for hangingwall deformation is that in order to calculate a unique fault geometry, it is first necessary to decide which model is most appropriate. Clearly, this *ad hoc* situation is rather unsatisfactory: it would be much simpler and far more useful if just one model could be used in a whole range of situations. The purpose of this short paper is to make the case for such a model. A general section-balancing scheme for normal faulting should have a relatively small number of parameters which describe the deformation in a simple but realistic way. Its suitability must be assessed by rigorous testing on models and data where the fault geometry is accurately known. Before discussing one possible method, each of the three sets of models will be examined further.

In the shear model, inhomogeneous simple shear leads to the development of shear (similar) folds in the hangingwall block. Shear folds can occur in the presence or absence of well developed stratification. Shear planes may be infinitely close and are not necessarily visible in naturally deformed rock (Ramsay 1967). The development of a shear fold in the hangingwall of a normal fault can be considered in terms of a constant horizontal component of extension and a varying vertical component of collapse (Verrall 1981).

The shear model was first proposed by Verrall (1981), who used a simple graphical technique (the 'Chevron construction') to relate fault and bed geometries (Fig. 1a). Since then, Gibbs (1983, 1984) has applied the method to large-scale normal faulting in the North Sea. The usual objection to the model in this form is that vertical simple shear is unrealistic since minor faults within hangingwalls are usually inclined. Subsequently, White *et al.* (1986) derived a general solution which does not fix the inclination of the planes along which simple shear occurs and which can be modified to include

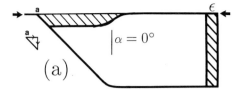

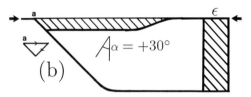

Fig. 1. Difference between vertical shear and inclined shear. Heave (apparent horizontal displacement) is identical in both cases. Depth of bed prior to extension (i.e. regional) indicated by arrows. (a) Vertical shear ($\alpha = 0°$), (b) Inclined shear ($\alpha = +30°$). Note that the area of depression in the hangingwall and the excess area due to extension, ϵ, (both shaded) are equal in each case. The vector diagrams show horizontal and vertical components of displacement for point a in each case.

differential compaction and footwall rotation. Vertical simple shear is clearly just one special case within this more general scheme.

The most important feature of shear models is that cross-sectional area is preserved. When compaction is taken into account, *solid* area is preserved. Bed-length does not remain constant and the orthogonal thickness of beds decreases with increasing dip of the strata. A simple relationship between extension and heave (apparent horizontal displacement) can be derived, where, depending on the inclination of the shear planes, the amount of extension is greater or less than the heave (Fig. 1b, White *et al.* 1986). Heave is equal to extension only when simple shear is vertical (Fig. 1a).

The flexural-slip model assumes that when the hangingwall has a well developed plane-parallel stratification, extension is accommodated by flexural-slip folding. As folding proceeds, the individual layers are flexed such that the uppermost layers slip over the lower layers towards the fold axis. Bed-length and the orthogonal thickness of layers remain constant. Suppe (1983) and Davison (1986) have proposed graphical methods for solving both the forward and inverse problems. Unfortunately, certain geometries are only possible provided arbitrary amounts of horizontal shear are applied to the hangingwall (Suppe 1983).

The flexural-slip model has several significant disadvantages (White 1987). Firstly, antithetic faulting is often observed within the hangingwall block. Since this disrupts layering it will inhibit inter-bed slip. Secondly, thickness variations such as those which occur as a result of growth-type faulting may cause problems since plane-parallel stratification is required for efficient inter-bed slip (Ramsay 1967). Thirdly, it is not clear how the problem of area changes in certain circumstances can be avoided (Wheeler 1987). Flexural-slip models will not be considered any further although it is important to note that there may be circumstances when small amounts of inter-bed slip occur as beds deform by, say, bulk simple shear.

Both the flexural-slip model and the shear model do not, in general, conserve slip along the fault. In the shear model, slip decreases if simple shear is vertical and the fault shallows out with depth. Williams & Vann (1987) argue that this is unreasonable since it implies that the fault initiated at the surface and propagated downwards. Alternative models which conserve slip are proposed instead. However, as Williams & Vann (1987) state, a consequence of conserving slip is that, in their model at least, area is no longer preserved (see also Wheeler 1987). In addition, their propagation argument does not apply to the generalized shear model of White et al. (1986) where, depending on the inclination of the shear, slip can increase or decrease down the fault.

Waltham's (1989) finite difference scheme, where the particle displacement field within the hangingwall is arbitrarily defined, has several disadvantages. Only the less important forward problem can be solved and differential compaction of hangingwall sediments has not been allowed for.

In summary, we would emphasize that conservation of mass (i.e. area or solid area in the case of compaction) must be a fundamental constraint for any model. The proposed constant-slip model fails in this regard and should therefore be rejected. While inter-bed slip may well be an important mechanism in some situations, flexural-slip models are generally difficult to justify. In contrast, the shear model conserves mass, predicts faulting within the hangingwall, and can be easily modified to allow for compaction.

A general method

Apart from conserving mass, any general method should allow the hangingwall to deform in an intuitively reasonable way that agrees with observation on the appropriate scale. Some allowance for differential compaction of hangingwall material as it is progressively buried (e.g. growth faulting) is also desirable. To be of general use, such a model must allow us to solve the inverse problem (i.e. calculate the fault geometry from the bed geometry) and not just the forward model. Here we attempt to show that the arbitrarily inclined simple shear model (White et al. 1986), which allows for compaction, adequately accounts for hangingwall deformation. As before, the method assumes that the footwall is rigid and undeformable and that deformation occurs by plane strain.

White et al. (1986) derived a generalized shear model where the inclination of planes along which simple shear occurs is not fixed (Fig. 1). A more usable version of their scheme (i.e. one which allows for large displacements) was proposed by White (1987) and is used here. In both cases, it was suggested that differential compaction should also be taken into account since sediments within the hangingwall may contain considerable amounts of water. As deformation proceeds, this water is expelled and the sediments compact, often accounting for up to 30% of the strain (Ramsay 1967).

Most workers assume that the strain caused by compaction is uniaxial, the axis of shortening being vertical (e.g. Sclater & Christie 1980; Wood 1981). This assumption is reasonable provided that lateral changes in facies and thickness of sedimentary layers can be neglected. However, it is unlikely to be an accurate description of the strain field in a region which is undergoing burial and tectonic deformation at the same time. The equations governing the behaviour of such a system are discussed by McKenzie (1984).

No attempt has been made here to solve this more general problem. Instead, an empirical expression, which relates porosity, $\phi(z)$, to depth, z (e.g. Sclater & Christie 1980), is used:

$$\phi(z) = \phi_0 \exp(-z/\lambda) \qquad (1)$$

where ϕ_0 is the initial porosity and λ is the porosity decay length.

The equation relating the deformation of the hangingwall to the geometry of the fault (White 1987) is:

$$F'(x' + h') = F'(x') - R'(x') + B'(x' + h')$$
$$+ \phi'_0 \lambda' \{ \exp(-F'(x')/\lambda') - \exp(-R'(x')/\lambda')$$
$$- \exp(-F'(x' + h')/\lambda')$$
$$+ \exp(-B'(x' + h')/\lambda') \} \qquad (2)$$

where $F'(x')$ and $B'(x')$ are y' co-ordinates of the fault and bed at the point x' respectively, all in a reference frame rotated through α (the inclination of shear); h' is the rotated heave, ϕ'_0, the rotated initial porosity, and λ' the rotated compaction decay length (White 1987, Fig. 2). $R'(x')$ is the rotated shape of the bed before extension (i.e. the 'regional'). Equation (2) may be solved by iteration, either for F when B is given, or for B when F is given. When $\phi_0 = 0\%$, equation (2) reduces to a much simpler form:

$$F'(x' + h') = F'(x') - R'(x') + B'(x' + h'). \qquad (3)$$

This equation provides the initial solution. Five iterations usually yield a solution accurate to ~ 1 cm.

Equation (2) assumes that the hangingwall deforms by simple shear alone. If the strain field is more complicated, such equations do not hold. Thus if the shear is inclined and compaction is vertical, the fault geometry cannot be calculated since removing the effect of vertical compaction would require *a priori* knowledge of the fault geometry. This difficulty is avoided by assuming that compaction occurs by uniaxial shortening parallel to the shear direction within the hangingwall. Provided α is less than 45°, this is unlikely to be any worse than assuming that compaction occurs by uniaxial shortening in a

purely vertical direction. This assumption is more fully justified in a later paper.

Equation (2) has four unknowns: the fault geometry (F), the inclination of simple shear (α), the initial porosity (ϕ_0), and the porosity decay length (λ). In certain circumstances, depending on the quality of the data, one or more of these parameters may be fixed. In the most general case, however, only broad constraints can be applied:

(a) α is unlikely to be less than 0° and is probably not greater than 60° (Anderson 1951);

(b) ϕ_0 cannot be less than 0% and is given an arbitrary upper limit of 90%;

(c) for the main categories of sediment, λ varies between 2 and 10 km (Sclater & Christie 1980).

α can be assumed to be identical for different beds within the hangingwall block. Since hangingwall sediments are generally not uniform but consist of interbedded layers of different sediment types, ϕ_0 and generally represent the bulk compaction parameters of the hangingwall as a whole.

Unfortunately, these generalizations concerning shear inclination and compaction mean that the geometry of a single bed in the hangingwall does not uniquely determine the geometry of the fault unless both the inclination of shear and the amount of compaction are known (Figs 3a & 3b). Sometimes, shear inclination may be estimated (White *et al.* 1986) but in general all three parameters are poorly determined. Not knowing α is worse than not knowing ϕ_0 while changing λ makes very little difference at all.

To calculate the geometry of the fault and the values of α, ϕ_0 and λ, the geometries of at least two beds must be known. In addition, the initial portion of the fault (down to the point where each bed meets the fault) and the appropriate heaves (h) and regionals (R) are required.

As is schematically illustrated in Fig. 4a, each bed can be used to calculate a fault geometry for any given values of α, ϕ_0 and λ. $\mathscr{A}$, which is the areal difference between the two faults, is then calculated by numerical integration. This areal difference could be weighted along the calculated fault traces in many different ways. For given bed geometries, $\mathscr{A}$ is a function of *three* parameters: α, ϕ_0, and λ (Fig. 4b). To calculate the correct fault geometry, $\mathscr{A}$ must be minimized with respect to all three. Many algorithms are now available which can perform this minimization process automatically (Scales 1985). It can be demonstrated that a unique minimum exists for the

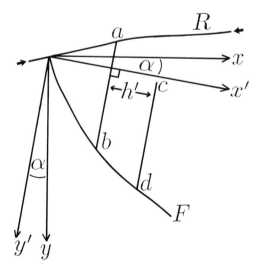

Fig. 2. Co-ordinate system and geometrical relationships used to derive Eqn. 2. Generalised shape of bed prior to extension (regional) indicated by arrows. In the rotated frame, $a = R'(x')$, $b = F'(x')$, $c = B'(x' + h')$, and $d = F'(x' + h')$. Solid lengths $|ab|$ and $|cd|$ are equal. For clarity, the deformed position of a single point (c) on the bed is shown.

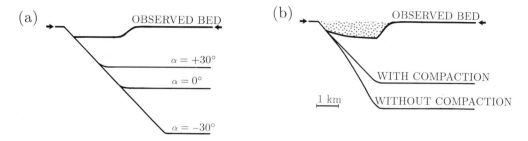

Fig. 3. (a) Three different faults are predicted for the same observed bed geometry by changing α, the inclination of simple shear. The depth to décollement increases as α increases. **(b)** Two different faults are predicted for the same observed compacted bed ($\alpha = 0°$, $\phi_0 = 60\%$, and $\lambda = 2$ km). The correct fault is found if only the correct values of ϕ_0 and λ used. Note the consequences of ignoring compaction. Arrows indicate the regionals in each case.

whole range of fault geometries from planar through to listric (White 1987).

Although only two beds are actually needed to find the correct fault geometry, the solution will be much better constrained if a larger number is used. In general, N beds can be used to calculate N faults for any given values of α, ϕ_0, and λ. The total area, $\Sigma_{i=1}^{N-1} \Sigma_{j=i+1}^{N} \mathcal{A}_{ij}$, which is the sum of the areas between each and every pair of calculated faults, must then be minimized. $N(N-1)/2$ areas are calculated altogether.

Applications

The algorithm can be tested in a variety of different ways. The most obvious way is to apply it to synthetic data (i.e. run the forward model to calculate a set of beds for a particular fault geometry and then inverse model the same

beds). It is useful for testing the self-consistency of the scheme in the early stages. More importantly, this testing has demonstrated that a unique solution can be obtained for a range of fault geometries from planar through to listric (White 1987). Thus, in general, there exists a single minimum value of $\mathcal{A}(\alpha, \phi_0, \lambda)$ within $\alpha-\phi_0-\lambda$ space (Fig. 4b).

Laboratory models

The second method of testing is to apply the algorithm to laboratory-produced normal faulting where the geometry of the fault plane is accurately known and where the hangingwall deformation can be observed in detail. Here just one example of wet clay modelling taken from Cloos (1968) is discussed although the conclusions drawn are based on applying the method to the sand-box models of McClay &

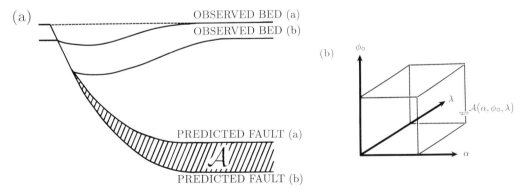

Fig. 4. The inverse problem: (a) in general, for the given values of α, ϕ_0, and λ, faults (a) and (b) can be calculated using beds (a) and (b). The dashed line indicates the regional for bed (a); the regional for bed (b) is similar. To find the correct fault geometry and the correct values of α, ϕ_0, and λ, the area $\mathcal{A}$ between two calculated faults must be minimized by varying α, ϕ_0, and λ. (b) Area $\mathcal{A}$ is a function of α, ϕ_0, and λ. A minimum value of $\mathcal{A}$ can be determined by systematically searching $\alpha-\phi_0-\lambda$ space.

Ellis (1987) and Ellis & McClay (1988) as well.

Figure 5a shows that although some antithetic faulting is visible in parts of the hangingwall, the detailed deformation is superficially more complicated. Clearly, planar inclined simple shear does not, at first glance, seem to be particularly appropriate.

Four beds were used to calculate the fault geometry. Each bed was horizontal prior to extension, at a depth given by the layering within the footwall. If vertical shear is assumed (as in the 'Chevron construction' of Verrall (1981)), the four calculated faults fail to coincide with either each other or with the actual fault plane (Fig. 5b). The best solution (i.e. when $\mathscr{A}$ is a minimum) is obtained when $\alpha = 41°$ (Fig. 5c). In this case, the fit between calculated and observed geometries is surprisingly good.

Allowing for compaction, whether the shear be inclined or not, gives poor results (Figs 5d & 5e) as would have been expected since no compaction has occurred.

Figures 5b–5e suggest that although hangingwall deformation appears, in detail, to be complex, *it can be represented by bulk inclined simple shear*. In fact, the complex small-scale rotations and synthetic faults in the lower part of the hangingwall are quite consistent with bulk simple shear: these details of the deformation are a consequence of the vorticity generated by bulk simple shear. The angular velocity of a small circular disk embedded within the hangingwall is easily calculated (Fig. 6). If v is the velocity vector at a point in the hangingwall then, since the y component of the velocity, v_y, is zero, we have:

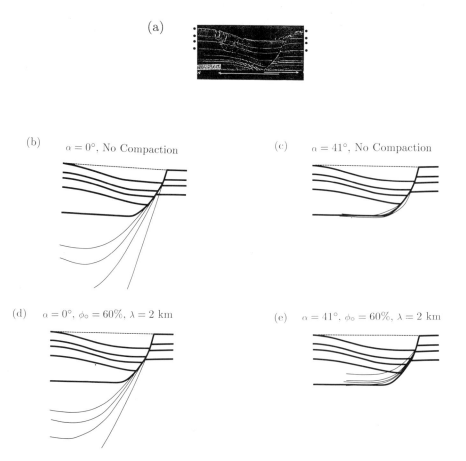

Fig. 5. (a) Wet clay model of normal fault (Cloos 1968). Note complex, small-scale deformation in the lower half of the hangingwall. Solid circles indicate regionals (pre-extension levels) of four beds used in the inverse modelling. (b)–(e) Inverse models of (a) using geometry of four hangingwall horizons to determine the fault geometry. Thick lines, observed beds and fault; thin lines, calculated faults; dashed line, regional for shallowest bed (other regionals are similar). Note best fit is example (c).

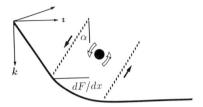

Fig. 6. Coordinate system and geometrical relationships used to determine vorticity, and hence rotation, of small circular disk inscribed in hangingwall.

$$\nabla \times \boldsymbol{v} = -\frac{\partial v_z}{\partial x}\boldsymbol{j}. \qquad (4)$$

Following White *et al.* (1986), in a frame rotated through α we get:

$$\omega = -\frac{1}{2}U_0'\frac{d^2 F'}{dx'^2} \qquad (5)$$

where ω is the angular velocity, U_0' is the horizontal velocity, and F' is the z' coordinate of a point on the fault, all measured in the rotated frame. Thus the rotation, θ, of a small disc embedded at position $x_0' + \epsilon'$ in the hangingwall is given by:

$$\theta = \frac{1}{2}\left\{\left[\frac{dF'}{dx'}\right]_{x'_0} - \left[\frac{dF'}{dx'}\right]_{x'_0+\epsilon'}\right\} \qquad (6)$$

where ϵ' is the amount of extension in the rotated frame. The sense of rotation is anti-clockwise if the dip of the fault decreases with depth in the positive x direction and vice versa.

In Fig. 5a, small fault-bounded blocks within the lower part of the hangingwall appear to have rotated coherently as extension proceeded rather than deforming internally. The deepest of these blocks has rotated by *c.* 26°. The expected rotation, calculated using Equation (6), is the same. Some of the sand-box models of McClay & Ellis (1987) and Ellis & McClay (1988) provide excellent examples of such rotations.

Seismic reflection data

The scheme described here can also be applied to depth-converted seismic reflection data. Testing can be carried out on sections where the fault plane reflection has been clearly imaged although the method will obviously be of most value when there is no knowledge of the fault plane. Here, two examples, both from areas of surficial, gravity-driven, faulting rather than

areas of basement extension, are presented. Methods used to calculate normal fault geometries can only be applied with great care to basement-extending normal faults since the assumption of a rigid footwall may not be valid.

The first example (Fig. 7a) is from the Gulf of Mexico and has previously been interpreted by Wernicke & Burchfield (1982) and White *et al.* (1986). However, in both cases only the time section was used. To depth-convert, we assume that the published section is of standard aspect ratio (no horizontal scale is given). Image-ray migration was carried out using a velocity variation given by:

$$V = 1800 + 0.22z \qquad (7)$$

where V is the velocity in m s^{-1} at a depth of z m. This velocity gradient is typical of that observed in sand-shale sequences, reflecting the increase in velocity with compaction. As it turns out the fault-calculation method works equally well on the time section so inaccuracies in the horizontal scale and depth conversion are not important in this particular example. In general, however, it is better to work with accurately depth-converted sections.

Figure 7a shows the uninterpreted time section. It is clear that a considerable amount of 'growth' has occurred within the hangingwall. Note the presence of a small-amplitude, large-wavelength hangingwall syncline, indicative of differential compaction (White *et al.* 1986). The fault plane reflection is especially clear.

The Wernicke & Burchfield (1982) interpretation is shown in Fig. 7b and shows a series of planar rotational normal faults in the hangingwall. As discussed in the previous section, the detailed deformation does not concern us here. What is important is whether or not the deformation can be adequately represented by *bulk* inclined simple shear.

Five depth-converted beds have been used to determine the fault geometry at depth (Fig. 7c–f). Since this is a growth fault structure, the regional or pre-extensional depth of each bed is the same, dipping 3° to the right. If vertical shear and no compaction are assumed, all five calculated faults overestimate the depth of the observed fault and fail to coincide with each other (i.e. the area difference, $\mathscr{A}$, is large) (Fig. 7c). Combinations such as inclined shear and no compaction (Fig. 7d) or vertical shear and compaction (Fig. 7e) also fail to predict the correct fault geometry. A systematic search through $\alpha-\phi_0-\lambda$ space yields the best solution: $\alpha = 34°$, $\phi_0 = 50\%$, and $\lambda = 2$ km (Fig. 7f). Not only do the calculated faults coincide quite well with each other but they also agree well with

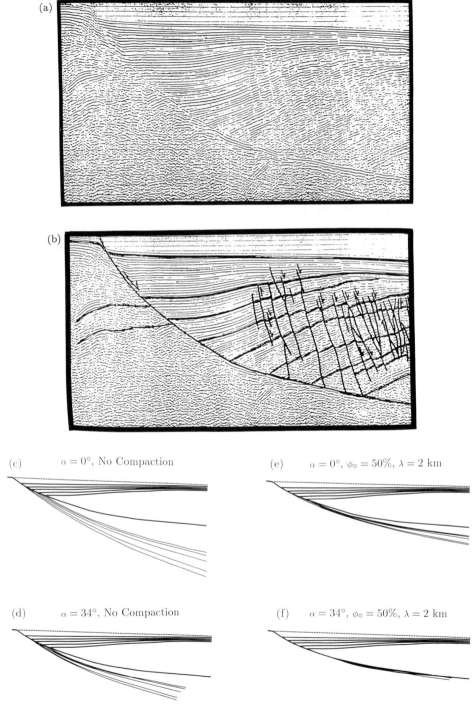

Fig. 7. (a) Uninterpreted seismic reflection section from the Gulf of Mexico (from Wernicke & Burchfiel 1982). (b) Interpretation by Wernicke & Burchfiel. (c)−(f) Inverse models of depth-converted version of (a) using the geometry of five hangingwall horizons. The regional of each bed is the same (dashed line) and dips 3° to right. Note best fit is example (f).

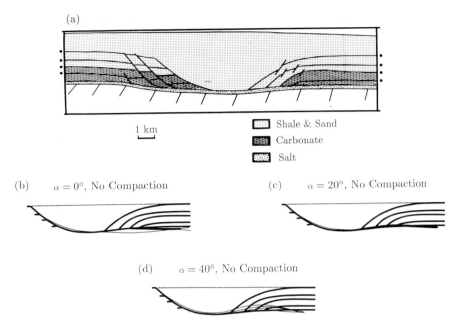

Fig. 8. (**a**) Interpreted, depth-converted seismic reflection section from a passive continental margin setting similar to Fig. 7. Solid circles indicate regionals of four beds used in inverse modelling. (**b**)–(**d**) inverse models of (a) using the geometry of four hangingwall horizons. Dashed line indicates regional of shallowest bed, other regionals being similar. Note best fit is example (c).

the observed fault geometry. If the next five beds down the fault are used, an identical solution is obtained giving confidence in the method. It is worth noting that the solution to this example presented by White *et al.* (1986) is only approximately correct since their scheme is only accurate provided the heave is small.

The second example (Fig. 8) comes from a similar passive continental margin setting to the first. The profile is depth-converted already. The fault is listric, soling out on a thin layer of salt. The example differs from both Figs 5 & 7 in that the hangingwall sediments (shales and carbonates) have been displaced a considerable distance down the fault (Fig. 8a). Therefore only a small portion of the observed fault requires to be predicted using the algorithm. All four observed beds from the hangingwall are used to calculate the actual fault geometry. The regional for each bed is assumed to be horizontal prior to extension, the depth being given by the footwall stratigraphy. Vertical shear gives a poor fit (Fig. 8b), the best fit being for $\alpha = 20°$. A larger α of, say, $40°$ gives a very poor fit. Both hangingwall and footwall strata are buried under about 3 km of sediments which means that *differential* compaction within

the hangingwall is small and its inclusion does not alter the results.

Conclusions

The most important conclusion is that, despite the fact that hangingwall deformation is often quite complex in detail, it can be represented as a combination of inclined simple shear and, where appropriate, differential compaction. We emphasise that such simple shear may not always be very clearly manifested since it represents the *bulk* deformation: in detail the vorticity caused by bulk simple shear introduces local complexity in the form of small-scale rotation and synthetic faulting.

The inclination of simple shear and the presence or absence of differential compaction (and its degree) do not have to be known in order to calculate fault geometries at depth. Simply by assuming that several beds have been deformed in a similar fashion due to extension on the same fault, all unknown parameters including the fault geometry can, in theory, be determined. Throughout we have assumed that the hangingwall and footwall stratigraphies are accurately known. In circumstances where this assumption is invalid, stratigraphic cutoffs can be included as bounded parameters within a more formal inversion scheme.

This work is supported by a Natural Environment Research Council Grant to the British Institutions Reflection Profiling Syndicate (BIRPS). NW also gratefully acknowledges a British Council Studentship and generous support from Merlin Geophysical Ltd. Depth conversion of Fig. 7a was carried out on the Sattlegger I.S.P. system installed at Badley, Ashton & Associates. Jake Hossack and John Wheeler provided helpful reviews. Department of Earth Sciences Contribution Number 1479.

References

ANDERSON, E. M. 1951. *The Dynamics of Faulting*. Oliver & Boyd, Edinburgh.

CLOOS, E. 1968. Experimental analysis of Gulf Coast fracture patterns. *American Association of Petroleum Geologists Bulletin*, **52**, 420–444.

DAVISON, I. 1986. Listric normal fault profiles: calculation using bed-length balance and fault displacement. *Journal of Structural Geology*, **8**, 209–210.

ELLIS, P. G. & McCLAY, K. R. 1988. Listric extensional fault systems — results of analogue model experiments. *Basin Research*, **1**, 55–70.

GIBBS, A. D. 1983. Balanced cross-section construction from seismic sections in areas of extensional tectonics. *Journal of Structural Geology*, **5**, 153–160.

—— 1984. Structural evolution of extensional basin margins. *Journal of the Geological Society, London*, **141**, 609–620.

JACKSON, J. A. 1987. Active normal faulting and crustal extension. *In*: COWARD, M. P., DEWEY, J. F. & HANCOCK, P. L. (eds) *Continental Extensional Tectonics*. Geological Society, London, Special Publication, **28**, 3–17.

—— & WHITE, N. J. 1989. Normal faulting in the upper continental crust: observations from regions of active extension. *Journal of the Geological Society, London*, **11**, 15–36.

McCLAY, K. R. & ELLIS, P. G. 1987. Analogue models of extensional fault geometries. *In*: COWARD,

M. P., DEWEY, J. F. & HANCOCK, P. L. (eds) *Continental Extensional Tectonics*. Geological Society, London, Special Publication, **28**, 109–125.

McKENZIE, D. 1984. The generation and compaction of partially molten rock. *Journal of Petrology*, **25**, 713–765.

RAMSAY, J. G. 1967. *Folding and Fracturing of Rocks*. McGraw-Hill, San Francisco.

SCALES, L. E. 1985. *Introduction to Non-linear Optimisation*. McMillan London.

SCLATER, J. G. & CHRISTIE, P. A. F. 1980. Continental stretching: An explanation of the post-mid-Cretaceous subsidence of the Central North Sea Basin. *Journal of Geophysical Research*, **85**, 3711–3739.

SUPPE, J. 1983. The geometry and kinematics of fault-bend folding. *American Journal of Science*, **283**, 684–721.

VERRALL, P. 1981. *Structural interpretation with applications to North Sea problems*. Course Notes No. 3, JAPEC (UK).

WALTHAM, D. 1989. Finite difference modelling of hanging wall deformation. *Journal of Structural Geology*, **11**, 433–437.

WERNICKE, B. & BURCHFIEL, B. C. 1983. Modes of extensional tectonics. *Journal of Structural Geology*, **4**, 105–115.

WHEELER, J. 1987. The geometry of listric normal faults and deformation within their hanging walls: a discussion. *Journal of Structural Geology*, **9**, 811–815.

WHITE, N. 1987. Constraints on the measurement of extension in the brittle upper crust. *Norsk Geologisk Tidsskrift*, **67**, 269–279.

——, JACKSON, J. A. & McKENZIE, D. P. 1986. The relationship between the geometry of normal faults and that of the sedimentary layers in their hanging walls. *Journal of Structural Geology*, **8**, 879–909.

WILLIAMS, G. & VANN, I. 1987. The geometry of listric normal faults and deformation in their hanging walls. *Journal of Structural Geology*, **9**, 789–795.

WOOD, R. J. 1981. The subsidence history of CONOCO well 15/30–1, central, North Sea. *Earth & Planetary Science Letters*, **54**, 306–312.

Index

Adda fault zone 30
Aegean extensional province
  drainage patterns 134-6
  extensional measurements 154-62
  fault morphology 131-3
  perched basins 136-7
  seismicity 125-8
  structure 128-31
  uplift and subsidence 133-4
Agios Konstantinos basin 137
Alasehir fault 159
Albuskjell field 122
Alpine Mountains
  compressional history 100-1
  evolution 93-4
  extension estimates 108-10
  extensional history
    early 97-100
    late 101-4
  fault geometry 106-8
  geological setting 94-6
  reworking 108
Altiplano extensional province 165
Alwyn fault 4
Alwyn field 5, 10-11
analogue modelling of fault geometry
  listric faults
    methods 231-2
    results 232-3
  planar and curved faults 219-20, 255-7
    methods 208-9, 220-1
    results 209-11, 213-14, 221-3
    results discussed 223-6
antithetic faulting 130-1
Apennines fault reactivation studies 227-8
Arkitsa fault system 129, 134
Arzular basin 159
Aspres fault 109
Atalanti fault 129
Atalanti Gulf 158

Balder Tuff 19
basement control on faulting
  analogue modelling
    methods 208-9
    results 209-11, 213-14
  numerical modelling
    methods 207-8
    results 209, 211-12
basin studies
  marginal stratigraphic studies
    erosional features 72-4
    with pre-rift sequence 68-72
    without pre-rift sequence 64-8
  modelling 42-3
    role of listric faults 43-8
    role of planar faults 48-50
Basin and Range extensional province 149-51
Bear Lake Formation 150
Belledonne massif 96, 97
bending stresses 55-6
Bourg d'Oisans half graben 98, 104

Bozköy basin 159
Brae field 6
Brent field 5, 9
Brent Group 5, 9
Briançonnais zone subsidence history 97-100
brittle versus plastic responses 144-6
Buchan Graben 18
buoyancy, role in extension of 164-5
Bura basement ridge 135, 136
Büyük Menderes graben 159

Cantagallo field 10
Carboniferous stratigraphy of the Alps 97
Celtic Sea 48
Central Graben 8
  basin margin studies 64, 67
  fault studies 29-40
    see also Coffee Soil fault
  origins 19
  subsidence studies 19-23
chalk, behaviour in extension of
  deformation features 118-20
  geological setting 113-14
  minor fault analysis 114-18
  role model for North Sea chalk field 120-2
Chalk Group 19, 21
Chevron construction 251, 252
clay cake faulting experiments
  methods 208-9
  results 209-11, 213-14
Coffee Soil fault
  geological setting 29-30, 72
  geometry 30-5
  kinematics 35-40
coherence in fault systems
  geometric 195-9
  kinematic 199
  scale factor effects 200
collapse basins defined 165
compaction and fault curvature 244-5
constant-slip modelling 253
Corinth, Gulf of
  drainage patterns 135
  extension measurements 157-60
  fault morphology 131-3
  seismicity 125-8
  structure 128-31
  uplift and subsidence 133-4
Cormorant field 5, 9
Cormorant Sandstone 4
Cretaceous stratigraphy
  Germany 113-22
  North Sea 18-19
Cromer Knoll Group 18, 19, 21
crust-mantle deformation 144-6
curvature on faults 214
  post-faulting causes 243-7
  syn-faulting causes 242-3

Dan fault zone 30
dating methods for rifting 35-6
Dauphinois zone subsidence history 97-100

Dee field 30
deformation
    modelling of 42-3
    response styles 41-2
    role of listric faults 43-8
    role of planar faults 48-50
delta studies *see* Nile
deltaic growth faults 248
depth migration 80
Deux Alpes half graben 98, 104, 106-8
Devoluy fault 109
dip effects on hydrocarbon reservoirs 11
dip-linked faults 194
displacement studies 183-7
    use of ellipses 194
distributed fault model 226
domino model
    faults 86-7, 200-1
    half graben geometry 61-2
Don field 5-6
drainage patterns and structure 134-7
Draugen field 68, 70
DRUM seismic profile 226-7
ductile deformation 121-2
ductile strain 193

earthquakes and faulting 125-6, 151, 153
East Cache fault 150
East Shetland Basin 4-5, 84-6
Egion extensional region 135
Egypt
    delta stratigraphy 173
    fault displacement studies 176-82
Ekofisk field 113, 122
Emparis, Plateau d' 99, 106, 108-9
End-of-the-World fault 4
Evvia, Gulf of
    drainage patterns 135
    fault morphology 131-3
    seismicity 125-8
    structure 128-31
    uplift and subsidence 133-4
extension and fault modelling
    analogue
        role of basement 208-9, 209-11, 213-14
        role of listric faults 231-3
        role of reactivation 219-26
    numerical 42-3, 144-6
        role of basement 207-8, 211-12
        role of buoyancy 164-5
        role of finite deformation 146-9
        role of listric faults 43-8
        role of planar faults 48-50
    seismic 233-7
extensional provinces
    Alps 109-10
        Mesozoic 97-100
        Permo-Carboniferous 97
    Altiplano 165
    Basin and Range 149-51
    Germany 113-22
    Greece 125-8, 154-62
    Italy 151-2
    Libya 153-4
    North Sea 165
    Tibet 165
    Tunisia 153-4

Fault Analysis Projection System 194
fault linkage 194
fault plane attitude 11, 146
fault zone quantification 114-20
Fladen Group 19
flexural cantilever model 48-50
    development 57-9
    summary 62-4
flexural isostatic model 62
flexural-slip model 252-3
footwall traps 9-10
footwall uplift modelling 76
Forties Approaches Basin 18
France *see* Alpine Mountains
Frøya High 64-8, 76

geometric coherence 195-9
geometry of faults
    Alpine studies 106-10
    effect on hydrocarbons 11-12
    seismic studies 64-74
Germany
    chalk behaviour in extension
        deformation features 118-20
        geological setting 113-14
        minor fault analysis 114-18
        role model for North Sea chalk field 120-2
    Rhine Graben studies 215, 216
Gorm fault zone 30
Grand Banks 46
gravity sliding 216
Great Glen fault 1
Greece
    drainage patterns 134-6
    extension measurements 154-62
    fault morphology 131-3
    perched basins 136-7
    seismicity 125-8
    structure 128-31
    uplift and subsidence 133-4
Gullfaks field 5
Guyana Basin 216

half graben behaviour modelling 61-2
    North Sea studies 23-6
halokinesis and faulting 216
Halten Terrace 68-70
Haltenbanken fault system 68
hangingwall geometry 251-2
    flexural slip modelling 252-3
    shear modelling 252
hangingwall traps 10
hard-linked faults 194
Heather Formation 18
Hild gasfield 11, 12
Horda Platform 18, 72, 76, 80-4
Hordaland Group 19, 21
horizon separation and faulting 187-91
horizontal extension and fault modelling 211-14
Hudson field 9
Humber Group 4, 18, 19
Hutton fault 84-5

image ray migration 80
inversion tectonics 219
    Alpine studies 100, 102-3

analogue modelling 219-20
  methods 220-1
  results 221-3
  results discussed 223-6
Italy, extensional province studies in 151-2

Jeanne d'Arc Basin
  listric-fault-based model 45, 46
  planar-fault-based model 50-2
Jens-Otto fault 30
Jurassic stratigraphy
  Alps 97
  North Sea 18-19

Kamena Vourla fault 129, 134-5
Kaparelli fault system 132
Kimmeridge Clay Formation 4, 18
kinematic coherence 199
Kiparissi basin 137
Kücuk Menderes fault 159
Kymi basin 134

La Grave 106-8
La Meije fault 109
La Meije massif 99
La Mure fault 109
La Paletas half graben 104
laboratory modelling *see* analogue modelling
Laegerdorf structural studies 113-22
Le Desert fault 109
Le Roux fault 109
Leman gasfield 11, 12
Lewis Basin 42, 48
Libya, extensional province studies in 153-4
Lindesnes Ridge 2-4
linked fault model 61-2
Liri fault 153
listric faults
  Alpine studies 106-8
  causes
    post-faulting 243-7
    syn-faulting 242-3
  deformation effects 79
  modelling
    analogue 213-14, 216, 231-3
    numerical 45-8
    seismic, 233-7
lithosphere deformation 144
Lulu fault zone 30

Magnus Basin 5
Malessina basin 134
Maliakos Gulf 158
Mandal fault 30
mantle-crust deformation studies 144-6
Marnock field 7-9
mechanical property effects on faults 245
Mediterranean extensional province 151-4
Megara basin 134
Melville sub-basin 226-8
Messinian sequences 173, 182
Mexico, Gulf of 237, 257, 258
Minch Basin 42, 48
modelling *see* analogue *also* numerical *also* seismic
MOIST seismic profile 226-7

Montrose Group 19, 21
Moray Firth Basin 2, 6, 10, 18
Moray Group 19, 21
More Basin 5, 64

Neogene tectonics
  Basin and Range 150
  Greece 154-62
Ness Formation 9
Nile delta
  fault displacement studies 176-82
  stratigraphy 173
normal fault defined 1, 4
  see also listric *also* planar
North Anatolian Fault Zone (NAFZ) 154-6
North Sea Basin
  controls on hydrocarbons 4-9
  exploration history 9-12
  half graben modelling 23-6
  problems of interpretation 1-4
  reverse fault studies 183-91
  subsidence studies 19-23
  tectonostratigraphy 18-19
  see also Central Graben *also* Norwegian Rift *also*
    Viking Graben
Norwegian Rift basin margin studies
  erosional features 72-4
  with pre-rift sequences 68-72
  without pre-rift sequences 64-8
numerical modelling of fault geometry
  role of basement 207-12
  role of buoyancy 164-5
  role of finite deformation 146-9
  role of listric faults 43-8
  role of planar faults 48-50

occluding faults 194
Olaf fault zone 30
Ornon fault 109
Osprey field 11
Outer Isles fault 42, 48
Øygarden fault 80-2

Paletas fault 109
Panahaiko basement ridge 135, 136
parallel fault modelling 144-6
Peloponnese uplift 133
Pelvoux massif 96, 97
Penguin field 5
Perakora peninsula 131-2
perched basins 136-7
Permo-Carboniferous stratigraphy of the Alps 97
planar faults
  Alpine studies 106-8
  deformation effects 79
  North Sea seismic evidence 86-8
  role in basin modelling 48-52
plastic versus brittle responses 144-6
Pleistocene tectonics of Greece 133
Plio-Pleistocene tectonostratigraphy
  Egypt 173
  Greece 133, 134, 173
pop-up structure 102
porosity changes and deformation 121-2
pure normal fault defined 4
pure shear 42-3, 47, 49, 162-3

quartz sand in analogue modelling 219
Quaternary tectonics
    Greece 133, 152
    Italy 152

reactivation
    analogue modelling of 219-20
        methods 220-1
        results 221-3
        results discussed 223-6
    field-based studies
        Apennines 227-8
        North Sea 183-91
Renginion basin 134-5
reverse fault studies
    displacement measurements 183-7
    horizon separation 187-91
rheology and fault curvature 242
Rhine Graben fault modelling 215, 216
rift sequence dating
    initiation 35-6
    termination 38-9
rigid-domino fault model 86-7
Ringkøbing-Fyn High 64, 67, 76
Roches d'Armentier half graben 104
Rogaland Group 19
rollover, controls on 79
rotation and fault curvature 245-7

salt diapirism structures 113-22
salt-detached faults 216
sand-box modelling 219, 231
Sangro Formation 153
Scott field 10
seals for hydrocarbons and fault types 10-11
section balancing 251
sedimentation and fault curvature 245-6
seismic studies
    field-based
        Nile delta 174-82
        North Sea 31-5, 66, 73, 80-6
        N Scotland 42, 48
    modelling 233-7, 257-9
shear fracture studies 119
shear modelling
    analogue 255-7
    numerical 253-5
    seismic 257-9
    see also pure shear also simple shear
Shetland Platform 64, 66, 76
simple shear 42-3, 47, 49
Skyros structural studies 133
Snorre field 6-7, 8
soft domino fault model 200-1
soft-linked faults 194
Southern Vestland Arch 72, 76
Statfjord fault 4
Statfjord field 5
Statfjord Formation 4, 9

Strathspey field 5
strain induced fault curvature 243-4
stress field and fault curvature 242-3
stress riser 103
strike-linked faults 194
strike projections 193-4
structure-contour mapping 174-6
subsidence studies
    field-based
        Greece 133-4
        North Sea 19-23
    modelling 209-11
Sulmona Formation 153

Tail End Graben
    rift dating
        initiation 35-6
        termination 38-9
    structural setting 29-30
    subsidence style 36-8
tectonic inversion
    Alpine studies 100, 102-3
    analogue modelling 219-20
        methods 220-1
        results 221-3
        results discussed 223-6
Temple Ridge Formation 150
Tertiary tectonostratigraphy
    Basin and Range 150
    Egypt 173
    Greece 133, 134, 154-62
    North Sea 18-19
Tethyan Ocean and Alpine development 93, 108
Thistle field 9
thrust development 100-1, 105
Tibet, extensional province studies in 165
tilting 134, 144
time-slice mapping 174
time migration 80
tip line 194
Triassic stratigraphy of the Alps 97
Troll fault blocks 73
Trondelag Platform 68-70, 76
Tunisia, extensional province studies in 153-4
Turkey, extensional province studies in 154-6, 159
Tuscany, extensional province studies in 151-2
Tyrrhenian Sea 151

uplift effects 76, 133-4

Viking Graben 4
    basin margin studies 64, 66, 72, 75
    formation model 52-5
    subsidence studies 19-23
vorticity in deformation 144-5

Wasatch Formation 150
Western Approaches Basin 226-8
Witch Ground Graben 10, 11, 19